Law and Society

Sociological Perspectives on Criminal Law

Law and Society

Sociological Perspectives on Criminal Law

JAMES M. INVERARITY

Department of Sociology
University of Minnesota

PAT LAUDERDALE

Center for the Study of Justice
Arizona State University

BARRY C. FELD

Law School
University of Minnesota

Little, Brown and Company
Boston   Toronto

Library of Congress Cataloging in Publication Data

Inverarity, James.
    Law and society.

    1. Criminal law. 2. Sociological jurisprudence.
3. Criminal law—United States. I. Lauderdale, Pat.
II. Feld, Barry. III. Title.
K5029.I58   1983   345   82-17959
ISBN 0-316-41940-0   342.5

Library of Congress Catalog Card Number 82-17959

ISBN 0-316-41940-0

9 8 7 6 5 4 3 2 1

MV

Published simultaneously in Canada
by Little, Brown and Company (Canada) Limited

Printed in the United States of America

Acknowledgments

Extracts from *The Dialectics of Legal Repression: Black Rebels Before
the American Criminal Courts* by Isaac D. Balbus, copyright © 1973 by
Russell Sage Foundation.

Extracts from Emile Durkheim, *The Rules of Sociological Method*,
translated by Sarah A. Solovay and John H. Mueller, edited by George
E. G. Catlin, copyright 1938 by George E. G. Catlin; renewed 1966 by
Sarah A. Solovay, John H. Mueller, and George E. G. Catlin. Reprinted
by permission of Macmillan Publishing Co., Inc.

To Morris Zelditch, Jr.
J.I. & P.L.

To the Good People on North Bustie Road
B.F.

Foreword

One can discern two polar themes in the history of visual art. Compare, for instance, the paintings by the Florentine Piero della Francesca, with those by the Dutch artist, Peter Bruegel the Elder. In the former the painter sets out large areas of vivid color with clear boundaries between them, and suggests, rather than precisely draws, smaller details. The Florentine School is often associated with an emphasis on overall composition—with what might be called the "deductive" approach to details. In contrast to this is the "inductive" approach. Bruegel builds up his composition from carefully drafted small figures, emphasizing the precision of his small details.

The analogy to art also informs our understanding of comparative law. The common law tends to the inductive structure whereby judicial decisions on questions concerning particular situations are used to build up general principles of law. The civil law of the European continent tends to be more deductive. Broad principles are set out in legislative codes and these are then applied to determine the results in particular situations.

Parallels between sociology and art have been drawn before in other contexts, and they can be extended to include the presence of these polar tendencies as well. As workers in this area have struggled to answer the basic questions of how a society consisting of huge numbers of people and a great variety of institutions can hang together and function, two major ways of thinking about the problem have emerged. First, there are a small number of what may be called grand theories which, like the paintings of the Florentine School, leave the details primarily to a deductive process. Second, there are an enormous number of investigations of one or another small aspect of social functioning, each one leaving to some far distant day the placement of its findings in an overall context. Of course, even more than painting, sociology requires both composition and detail. It must proceed by a union of theory and fact. Theory must be informed and tested by investigation. Facts must not only be illuminated by theory but must be selected out by theory for measurement and observation.

For the most part, American sociology has proceeded by the inductive method. Whether or not the attacks upon it as "blind empiricism" are justified, there has been a preoccupation with detail not coupled to any overarching theory of how the society works; that this is true remains clear even after one has read what most American sociologists have regarded as theory. American theory has been characterized by an abundance of "midlevel" theories, with the closest approach to a comprehensive view being the work of Talcott Parsons—whose intellectual roots, however, are more European than American. European sociology, on the other hand, has been relatively non-empirical. It has proceeded, for the most part, from the work of the three titans Marx, Weber, and Durkheim— though there is considerable dispute about whether the theory evolved by the Weberians is less comprehensive than the others, a dispute provoked in part by the opacity of Weber's writings.

Now Professor Inverarity and his colleagues have provided a first attempt to tie in grand sociological theory with what we have found out about law and the legal system. If for nothing else, the book is invaluable for its explanations of the thoughts of Marx, Weber, and Durkheim, making them comprehensible, rescuing them from their most simpleminded partisans and interpreters, and pointing up their ambiguities as applied to the development of a sociology of law. The result is that in each case a readable and faithful summary of the relevant ideas of the master comes through clearly, without real distortion, and with relatively little truncation of the grand social scheme.

Perhaps the most interesting question raised by this book is why a work of this kind has taken so long to appear before the American reader. One reason is the pragmatic American suspicion of overarching theory (our common law heritage is merely one aspect of our preference for inductive over deductive social thought); another is the preference for numbers caused by analogizing the social to the natural sciences; and yet another is the fact that detailed investigations of small phenomena are easier and safer than development of a theory that may be hard to test, or worse yet, that may predict results at odds with experience.

My contention here, however, is that a major part of the reason for the lack of application of grand theory in any systematic way to the sociology of law is that, for one reason or another, each of the major overarching theorists has been handicapped in his appeal to sociologists of law.

In the case of Marx, it is sometimes said that the problem is caused by his lack of attention to the issue. It is true that he spelled out no detailed theory of law, since he apparently thought law was an epiphenomenon and not particularly important. This is not as serious a problem as it might appear, however, since his general economic and social theory allows, as this book shows, the derivation of many insights into law.

Rather, the problems with Marx have been quite different. First of all, he happened to have been demonstrably wrong about some very important things. Most important, probably, has been the inaccuracy of his prediction of the decline of real wages in advanced capitalist societies and, related to this, the continued proletarianization of the working class. Moreover, though his predicted revolutions may have occurred, they have occurred in the wrong places. Though embarrassing, these problems are by no means fatal to the Marxian viewpoint. There are many ways of explaining where and how he went wrong without casting doubt on most of his ideas.

The more important problem has been the fact that Marx has been singularly ill-served by his adherents. Those who call themselves Marxists have often misunderstood what Marx was saying. Many have reified his concept of class, and railed against particular individuals and groups as themselves constituting the "ruling class," bent upon the domination and exploitation of society. Often Marxists have been guilty of a kind of reductionism in applying what is basically a structural view of society to specific interactions—such as between a particular employer and his workers, or between the police and a group of vagrants. Marx himself would have shuddered at this type of simpleminded theory which derives social causation from analyzing who benefits from any particular social arrangement. Indeed, this type of Marxism is more like turn-of-the-century midwestern agrarian populism—albeit sometimes with Germanic footnotes.

The second way in which Marx has been ill-served by some of his adherents is by their contention that truth is that which advances the interest of the working class. Their writings are then suspect to all who believe that there is such a thing as truth, independent of whether it does harm or good on a particular occasion. A writer who denies the usual assumption, that the loyalty of a scholarly writer is to the reader rather than to some social program, gives the entire effort a bad name. One can find many problems with the pretense of academic neutrality, but the complete abandonment of the ideal turns research into special pleading and brings upon the social scientist the obloquy that many reserve for the lawyer: the hired gun of a cause.

Finally, the Marxists have been tarred by the nature of their political successes. Whether in fact any government in the world today does put Marxist principles into effect, there is no doubt that those governments which derive from revolts in the name of Marx and which purport to rule by Marxian principles have virtually all become heavy-handed, bureaucratic dictatorships, brutal as well as inefficient. They are indeed such a bad advertisement that Marxists have often succumbed to the temptation to invent countries. During the height of the starvation caused by Stalin's collectivization, Lincoln Steffens returned from the Soviet Union announcing, "I have seen the future, and it works." After the revelations of Gulag, China followed as the model society—until, with the fall of the Gang of Four, information on its workings began to seep out; then for a while North Vietnam was the good society. Now many Marxists have fled intellectually to Cuba.

Despite this bad publicity, as this book demonstrates, Marx was right about many things and has allowed us insights into the nature of law, not only in society in general but also specifically in present-day American society. It is Marx, after all, who both explains the importance of formal equality as a consequence of an advanced capitalist system and who shows us why the South, because of the organization of its production, was the last American region to adopt this basic American ideal.

Weber, on the other hand, has been ill-served for quite different reasons. His works are not yet completely translated into English and not all of his translations are much more readable for non-German speakers than are the originals. In addition, the structure of Weber's writing militates against a comprehensive understanding by anyone who has devoted less than a lifetime to the task. His social theories are, in a sense, a dialog with Marx, attempting to show that it is not only economics and the organization of production that determine the nature of a society, but its values and ideals as well. In setting out his theory, Weber analyzed a number of societies—the ancient Chinese, the ancient Indian, the Reformation in Europe—and it is only by gathering together his insights throughout these works that one can discern his broad social theory.

Fortunately, this raises fewer problems for the study of the sociology of law than for other areas of Weber's thought, since one of his major themes, rationalization of decision making through bureaucracy, comes out loud and clear through a number of his writings and it is this theme which is especially important for an understanding of our legal system.

That is not to say that Weber has escaped a reductionism which has lowered his acceptance into American sociology—quite the contrary. Although his grand theory comprehends a rationalization of the moral order of all society and the institutionalization of bureaucratic values, many of his interpreters have looked in various corners of the legal system for total bureaucracies. In America, these are conspicuous by their absence—and indeed every study that has sought to find this completely rational, rule-bound structure has noted strong elements both of bureaucratic irrationality, wherein means and measuring implements are substituted for goals, and of informal decision processes which have subverted the mechanistic processes that Weberian reductionists had predicted.

Finally, acceptance of Durkheim's social theory into the sociology of law has been handicapped by several factors. First is its deceptive appearance of simplicity. His view—that a major purpose of criminal punishment is to draw formally the line between acceptable and unacceptable conduct and thereby reinforce both the solidarity of the group and the norms which have been violated—runs counter to the usual utilitarian view that the purpose of criminal punishment is to repress crime by deterrence, isolation, and so on. In addition, two specific criticisms have been leveled at the Durkheimian view. First of all, it seems to be inapplicable to the crimes we worry about most. One might argue that so far as homicide and mugging are concerned, we do not require the reinforcement of any moral boundary where everyone knows that the conduct is wrong. A second and quite different objection is that Durkheim's views of organic solidarity may be inapplicable to a modern, highly differentiated and complex society with many subgroups, all with differing norms.

The first of these criticisms is easier to answer. Although what we think of as homicide may be always regarded as wrong, the killing of a human being does not always violate our norms. We slay in war, administer capital punishment (though rarely), take life in defense of ourselves or our property, or kill accidently in pursuit of our business (as in traffic accidents). Similarly, there are many occasions when we recognize the right to deprive someone of his property. Denunciation and punishment reinforce our views as to which of many types of functionally similar conduct violate our norms.

The second of the objections is harder to grapple with (and therefore more interesting and provocative as well). First of all, while many social scientists seem aware of the noncontractual bases of the social contract, they have, in a sense, too often taken for granted the moral underpinnings of our social life. Even Durkheim thought this mostly missing in complex societies. In fact, concepts of majority rule, fairness, and allegiance to the group can be noted even in the complex American society of today. Moreover, though Durkheimian processes are more clearly visible in relatively non-differentiated societies than in a complex one such as ours, there are enclaves within our society that do function like tribal villages. To most of us, the most familiar of these is the university.

I observed one remarkable episode myself at Stanford, the explanation of which is strikingly and surprisingly Durkheimian. The events on the Stanford campus took place during what are now referred to as "the troubles," so long ago that it will seem incomprehensible to today's students—about 1972. At that time, some students who were displeased with the state of the world had developed a pattern of disrupting classes—marching, yelling, chanting—to vent their anger with the university and the Vietnam War. Often they were charged before the university disciplinary system, and convicted. The disciplinary system in essence said, "This is bad behavior; you shouldn't do this." However, the punishment was a term or two on probation or a suspension for the summer quarter, when they would not be attending school anyway. These punishments were hardly draconian; indeed they were seen as extremely light. The students and faculty on the disciplinary board, however, did say as clearly as they could, "Look, this is a university! Its essence is that people are coming here trying to learn. Those who disrupt classes are striking at the very heart of the educational process."

Finally, after several years of class disruption, the disciplinary system took real action. A group of students disrupted a class, as had happened many times before, but this time the board imposed a real punishment. Writing a long opinion in the name of the community and saying what the previous boards had said, it suspended them indefinitely and told them to reapply in two years so that it could be determined whether they were "ready to live in a civilized community." This banishment surprised many students because, although the university had said again and again that disrupting classes was a very serious offense, it had never before acted that way.

Knowing about deterrence, one would have expected that there would be a drop in the number of classes disrupted, and that, of course, happened; it did not take a Durkheim to predict that. Jeremy Bentham would have done the job perfectly well. What was interesting to me, however, and what changed my views as to the relevance of Durkheim's theory was something else.

For a long time members of the faculty had wondered why the great majority of students who disapproved of the disruptions nonetheless stood idly by while their classes were being disrupted. On simple deterrence principles one really wouldn't expect the increase in the severity of the punishments to change the behavior of these onlookers. They after all were not being threatened with anything. One would have expected merely a deterrent effect on the disrupters. In any event, to protest against punishing the original disrupters, another group of students disrupted another class. To their—and the faculty's—enormous surprise, the students in the class stood up and hooted and yelled at them, "Get the hell out of here! You don't belong here!" The disrupters left, literally in tears.

What happened? Throwing people out of school for misbehavior actually did what Durkheim said it would do: it reaffirmed the university's value that the classroom as a place for education was not to be interfered with. Moreover, what may be more remarkable, it influenced the group's conduct as well as its values.

Since then I have looked for other examples of this Durkheimian phenomenon in the university setting and have found a few. In one law school, somewhat more recently, there had been a problem with the library. Students had been taking out books that were on reserve and returning them very casually: a three-hour book would be returned a week later. Finally, after warnings of dire punishments seemed to do no good, the judicial system there suspended for a year the student who had been the most flagrant offender. It was a very harsh punishment seeing that nobody had ever been punished at all before—even though everyone knew such behavior was against the rules.

What happened then was very interesting. Not only did people start returning their books, which one would have expected on deterrence grounds, but in all other ways, people began to treat the library with more respect. For instance, the noise level in the library dropped, as did the number of abandoned coffee cups and other litter—and usage of the library went up. By punishing somebody for violating the library in one way, the community had reaffirmed to everybody that the library was an essential resource which everyone had to depend on, and that to make it work they had to pull together and observe certain ideas of right or wrong. It caught on, not only in terms of values, but in behavior as well.

Admittedly Durkheim's ideals apply much better to a tribal university community than to the larger society. Nonetheless, every once in a while, we can see this phenomenon writ large. The Watergate case provided an example of this. There were two positions the press and the courts as community institutions could have taken. They could have said, "Oh, well, a lot of politicians do this. So what!" Many people did say this; Ronald Reagan was widely quoted as saying that the Watergate offenders weren't "real criminals." Alternatively they could have treated it as an outrage, increasing the likelihood that such political behavior would be stamped as unacceptable.

Judge Sirica more than any other person had the decision whether these should be regarded as serious wrongs or as trivial misconduct and, by sending some people off to very stiff jail terms and acting with considerable vigor, he did his part to see that the matter was seriously regarded. Had he given the Watergate buggers (if you will pardon the expression), and those who covered up, a fifty-dollar fine each, that would have made it a very different kind of business. True, the judge apparently was also trying to get defendants to talk, but even that is an assertion of the importance of the matter. It is in general true that the only way to get things taken seriously is to treat them as if they were serious.

In any event, the outcome of "Watergate" is clear. We were deluged with political breastbeating; clean political campaign laws were passed; and Spiro Agnew, in resigning, referred to the fact that what he had done might have been wrong under the "post-Watergate morality"—as if somehow before then it was all right to take bribes.

It is interesting to note in all three of the grand theorists some attention to the concept of law as symbolism or even religion. In Marx, one can note the view that both are sideshows compared to the organization of the means of production—though through its mystificatory process law justifies and supports the existing organization. In Weber, law and religion are connected, arising out of and influencing a kind of union of values and economics. And

Durkheim regards the two as parts of the very same organic glue that holds the society together.

It is, moreover, interesting to speculate that each of the three grand theorists was influenced greatly by the nation in which he worked. The darkest hour of the industrial revolution in England, combined with the apparently rigid class structure of that nation, misled Marx as to the inevitability of the revolution. Weber's prediction of bureaucratic rationalization of society seems to have been fed by what one might regard as the discipline and sense of order of the Germans. And it is even possible that Durkheim's view that the moral solidarity of the tribe had been lost in modern society was based on too much reliance on his experience in France—a nation which, by American standards, is composed of a remarkable combination of individualism and compulsory conformity.

It may be, then, that none of the grand theorists is quite so universal as his followers would like to believe. Despite this, all are far, far more so than the usual run of contributors to the sociology of law. It is for this reason that what follows is so welcome.

John Kaplan
Stanford University Law School

Preface

The study of crime and deviance, long a staple of American sociology, has often been preoccupied with determinants of individual behavior. Why do some people rob banks? How do some people become marijuana users? Such social psychological concerns tended for many years to crowd out of consideration macro-level issues about the creation and administration of laws. Since the late 1960s there has been substantial growth in the literature concerned with such questions. Along with this growth of interest has come a rediscovery of the treatment of the same issues by the nineteenth-century sociological theorists for whom the relationship between law and society was a key to how societies are made possible and how they become impossible. The rediscovery of the classics in recent years represents more than an exercise in intellectual archeology; the classic tradition has provided modern investigators with a rich legacy of concepts and conjectures concerning legal institutions and their social bases.

This book surveys how some of these central ideas of Karl Marx, Max Weber, and Emile Durkheim have served contemporary writers as heuristics. Furthermore, by showing the common theoretical grounds underlying diverse empirical studies of law and society, this volume will make clearer the underlying coherence of contemporary research. The book is intended, however, as more than a survey of the literature; it attempts to characterize the way of thinking peculiar to the sociological perspective, to underscore the hazards that have beset less successful efforts, and to articulate the features of successful contributions to the field.

This book is divided into three parts. Part I contains four introductory chapters. Chapter 1 considers the methods sociologists use that set them apart from historians, novelists, lawyers, and artists who are also concerned with understanding the relationships between law and society. The next three chapters present central concepts and issues in the sociology of law formulated by Marx, Weber, and Durkheim. The purpose of these chapters is to provide working tools for examination of substantive problems.

Parts II and III present a sample of such substantive problems. Part II examines three cases of the creation of law: the status of youth, the regulation of opiates, and control of corporations. These three cases are chosen because they developed in law contemporaneously during the Progressive Era at the turn of the century; they therefore provide a particularly good opportunity to examine the relationship between major transformations of the legal system and social structural transformations.

Part III examines a selected range of issues concerning the administration of law. Chapter 8 shows how Weber's analysis of legal procedure can be used to integrate the results of several diverse empirical studies of the consequences of procedure. Chapter 9 reviews empirical studies of disparities in criminal sentencing and shows how the atheoretical character of this research literature has produced a morass of conflicting claims, which can, at least in part, be sorted out by a careful consideration of the theories of Marx and Weber. Chapter 10 examines, in light of the theories presented in Part I, variations in the form of the criminal sanction. We will use these theories to explain the invention of the penitentiary, the increased use of probation, and the decline of capital punishment.

Thus the book is organized in terms of basic problems in the sociological theory of law and society. It does not seek to provide a representative sample of all work included in "the sociology of law." While much of the information on "the police," "lawyers," "the courts," and other substantive topics one would normally expect to encounter in such a book will be found here, they appear in such a way that general sociological issues take priority over specific substantive content. We will demonstrate throughout the volume the utility of this approach. For the moment let us offer two justifications.

First, all research entails theoretical issues, whether explicitly or not. By overtly orienting our thinking around these issues, we hope to provide a more systematic understanding of law and society than could be obtained in the literature on a set of discrete substantive topics.

Second, factual "knowledge" in this expanding area of investigation has often proven highly elusive. The conventional wisdom of just a decade ago about deterrence, extralegal factors in criminal sentencing, or the history of marijuana criminalization—to name just three topics—has been undermined by recent, more competent analyses (see, respectively, Ehrlich and Redlich, 1979; Hagan, 1974; Galliher and Walker, 1977). It seems, therefore, far more important to present, as far as possible, a portrait of how sociologists invent hypotheses and evaluate evidence, than to convey a body of dead facts to be committed to short-term memory. Thus the emphasis on Marx, Weber, and Durkheim is based on a judgment that their works provide the most seminal sociological perspectives on law and society.

Finally, a brief note on authorship. Chapters without by-lines were written by James Inverarity. The order of authorship on the title page reflects the overall planning and editorial contributions.

ACKNOWLEDGMENTS

This book embodies the time, effort, and critical acumen of a number of individuals; we bear the responsibility for the various uses we have made of their contributions. Versions of the complete book were given critical examinations by Marc Berstein, Hal Finestone, John Hagan, Nancy Heitzig, John Kaplan, Candace Kruttschnitt, Wayne Kobbervig, and Steve Leonard; Donald Cressey, David Greenberg, Gerald Larson, and Marge Roden were particularly helpful in "educating the educators." Several anonymous reviewers made possible substantial improvements. We received valuable comments on individual chapters from M. A. Bortner, Ray Bradley, Gray Cavender, Dan Cooperman, Mary Jane Lehnertz, Robert Levy, John Modell, Pete Parilla, Joe Raiche, Andy Shapiro, Fred Grittner, Russ Winn, M. L. Rasmussen, and Rhonda Shapiro. Cindy Campbell, Cam Counters, Steve Clark, Dennis Reis, Karen Sederquist, Sandra Stein and Scott Wolin provided invaluable research assistance as well as insightful comments on earlier drafts of the manuscript. Students in several courses at the University of Minnesota and Arizona State University heard or read drafts of several chapters and we are grateful for their comments and questions. Professor Feld is indebted to Dean Robert Stein and the University of Minnesota Law Alumni Association for generous assistance and the opportunity to work on this volume. We wish to thank Lisa Thornquist, Dianne Murrer, Julie Ross, Pete Fire Dog, and Cindy Johns for the effort they made typing the various drafts of this work.

Contents

PART ONE: FOUNDATIONS OF ANALYSIS

Law and Society

*Sociological Perspectives
on Criminal Law*

PART ONE:

Foundations of Analysis

Introduction: The Emergence of the Sociology of Law

Law was central to the nineteenth century European founders of sociology. For Karl Marx, Max Weber, and Emile Durkheim the relationship between law and society was a critical nexus for unraveling the general features of society and social change. Curiously, the sociology of law has been neglected until very recently in American sociology, which became preoccupied in its formative years with social psychological issues surrounding crime, delinquency, deviance, and their cause, prevention, and cure. This chapter will provide a brief survey of the emergence of the sociology of law. While an exhaustive treatment of this history would clearly be out of place here, understanding the broad picture will make the content and direction of the remainder of the book more intelligible. The sociology of law today is not a discipline with clear logical boundaries and a commonly agreed upon agenda of research problems. Its diversity of content, its schisms, its multidirectional character are products of a special set of historical circumstances in which the field was formed.

To simplify this overview, we concentrate on the major stream of development, the emergence of the sociology of law out of the sociology of deviant behavior in the late 1960s. Our account ignores a large number of important independent developments, such as legal realism and sociological jurisprudence, which arose primarily in American law schools.[1] It is limited to a fairly narrow stream of academic work in the sociology of law. Again, to simplify the presentation, we divide our reconstruction of this development into three historical periods: societal reaction theories (c. 1963–1970), conflict theory (c. 1970–1979), and the revival of classical theories (c. 1966–present). While these divisions are neither exclusive nor exhaustive, they serve to highlight what we perceive as significant developments in the evolution of contemporary sociology of law.

SOCIETAL REACTION THEORIES (c. 1963–1970)

With a few isolated exceptions American sociologists have traditionally had little interest in legal institutions and their relation to society. Occasionally a lone investigator such as Edwin Sutherland would point to the neglected area of law,[2] but for the most part American sociologists were preoccupied with studies of individual law violators. The nature of their violations was cataloged in detail, while the biographies and life styles of the violators were scrutinized. Robert Merton's theory of *anomie* is typical of this approach. Merton held that deviance was the product of a contradiction in the norms of society, which held out certain goals as desirable and sanctioned certain means for their attainment as legitimate. Contradiction arose when classes of individuals had goals for which they lacked legitimate means. For instance, in the United States everyone shares the same goals of material success, which are reinforced by mass advertising. Only a small portion of the society, however, has access to the legitimate financial means of attaining these goals. Hence, Merton argued, a high rate of "innovation" occurs in the form of theft. Since low-income groups are more likely to be caught in the normative contradiction, higher rates of crime will appear in those groups, according to Merton. Since young minority males living in urban ghettos encounter few legitimate opportunities, rates of crime and delinquency should be high for this group. Merton's theory also explains why the United States has higher rates of crime than Western Europe, despite its material prosperity. Evidence suggests that occupational mobility is about the same in the United States and Western Europe; yet expectations of upward mobility are substantially higher in the United States (Lipset and Bendix, 1959). Hence, according to Merton's theory, the United States should have a higher crime rate. Merton's theory thus explains individual deviant behavior as a consequence of a social structure that "condemns individuals to pursue an objective they are forbidden to reach" (Unger, 1976: 18).

While American sociology and criminology have traditionally

emphasized the social psychology of the individual offender, a major reorientation in the field took place in the mid-1960s,[3] as a group of American sociologists began to suggest that the *deviant* was of less interest than the *societal reaction* to deviant behavior. This reaction was not to be understood as simple, automatic, natural, or inevitable, but was rather a phenomenon requiring analysis in its own right. Edwin Lemert, whose work inaugurated this approach, summed up the new perspective as

> a large turn away from older sociology which tended to rest heavily upon the idea that deviance leads to social control. I have come to believe that the reverse idea, i.e., social control leads to deviance, is equally tenable and the potentially richer premise for studying deviance in modern society. (1967: v)

While various proponents of the societal reaction approach differ in emphasis among themselves,[4] the following four themes have emerged as dominant in most presentations of the perspective.

1. Behavior Is by Nature Ambiguous in Meaning

Deviance and *abnormality* are not objective properties of certain actions or behaviors. Most unusual or rule-breaking behaviors are not defined as problematic.

> Apparently, many persons who are extremely withdrawn, or who "fly off the handle" for extended periods of time, who imagine fantastic events, or who hear voices or see visions, are not labeled as insane either by themselves or others. Their rule-breaking, rather, is unrecognized, ignored, or rationalized. (Scheff, 1966: 47–8)

It makes little sense, therefore, to attempt to distinguish between two types of persons—deviants and nondeviants—to attempt to study the differences in their personalities or their social environments, since deviant or abnormal behavior is prevalent throughout the society.

2. Social Control—The Identification and Labeling of Behavior—Is Selective

The behavior in itself does not automatically elicit or achieve a deviant label; "many are called, but few are chosen." Many people drink alcohol to excess; only a few of these are labeled as "alcoholics." Many people have had sexual relations with a partner of the same gender; only a few of these persons are called "homosexuals." The problem for societal reaction theorists therefore became one of figuring out how social control agents went about ascribing deviant labels and the consequences that these labels had for the self-concept and subsequent behavior of the persons so labeled.

3. Social Control Is Imposed in a Discriminatory Manner, Singling Out Rule Breakers Who Lack Social Power

The demographics of crime control have been well known for some time. The young males, the unemployed, the poorly educated and racial and ethnic minorities are all in high-risk categories for intervention by various social control agencies. Merton accounted for this high risk in terms of the contradictory normative demands placed on these individuals and the resulting inducements to crime and delinquency. The societal reaction approach asserts that this view is mistaken (or at least one-sided), since it ignores the roles of police, judges, social workers, psychiatrists, and other social control agents in discriminating against members of these groups in law enforcement and "treatment." The labeled individuals, on the other hand, typically do not have the financial or intellectual resources to contest the definitions imposed on their behavior or their character. Therefore while deviance is uniformly spread throughout the society, it only becomes officially and publicly recognized as a social problem when it is committed by powerless persons in the society.

4. Labels Amplify Deviance

Most rule breaking is episodic and situational; there are, according to the societal reaction approach, very few "natural" recidivists. Once a label has been imposed and a person has been defined as a "delinquent," a "homosexual," or a "schizophrenic," others begin to react differently to the individual, and the person eventually redefines himself or herself in light of the label.

This theme represents an inversion of the more commonly held notion of *special deterrence*, the idea that once a person has been punished, he or she will be less likely to engage in the behavior again. This is the basic principle of behavioral psychology used (for example) to housebreak a dog. But dog psychology, societal reaction theorists argue, does not work equally well for human beings. The imposition of punishment has the consequence of changing the person's identity. This singular feature of punishment is a continual source of irony, according to societal reaction theorists: prisons produce criminals, psychiatrists breed neurotics, and mental hospitals "manufacture madness" (Szasz, 1970).

Societal reaction theory may be seen then as a codification or formalization of a number of critiques of social control institutions. For well over 100 years reformers had characterized mental institutions as "snake pits," had complained of prisons serving as "seminaries for vice," and had exposed brutality and racism among law enforcement officials. The societal reaction position sees these as being basic central features of the social control system, rather than as isolated, incidental occurrences. It indicates, furthermore, that an examination of social control mechanisms will provide an explanation of many of the features of deviance (e.g., its frequency, its social location) that had previously been accounted for by looking at the nature of the "deviant" individual.

In the late 1960s and early 1970s the societal reaction approach attained dominance in the field. Two types of opposition, however, began to emerge. The first was essentially ideological in character, attacking the theory for its treatment of the deviant as a passive reactor to official actions and for its preoccupation with the social psychology of deviance, rather than the political economy of social control.

Becker's school of deviance is redolent of romanticism. It expresses the satisfaction of the Great White Hunter who has bravely risked the perils of the urban jungle to bring back an exotic specimen. It expresses the romanticism of the zoo curator who preeningly displays his rare specimens. And like the zookeeper, he wishes to protect his collection; he does not want spectators to throw rocks at the animals behind the bars. But neither is he eager to tear down the bars and let the animals go. The attitude of these zookeepers of deviance is to create a comfortable and humane Indian Reservation, a protected social space, within which these colourful specimens may be exhibited, unmolested and unchanged. The very empirical sensitivity to fine detail, characterizing this school, is both born of and limited by the connoisseur's fascination with the rare object: its empirical richness is inspired by a collector's aesthetic. (Gouldner, 1973: 37–8)

In addition to the ideological criticisms (Gouldner, 1973; Lia-zos, 1972) a number of empirical studies challenged most of the basic factual premises of the societal reaction approach. Societal reaction theorists had generally relied on anecdotes, one-shot case studies, or poorly executed experiments.[5] More carefully designed research increasingly tended to suggest that official bias played a far smaller role in labeling than societal reaction theory had claimed (we will examine this issue more carefully in Chapter 9) and that the label itself had relatively little to do with subsequent episodes of deviant behavior (Gove, 1980).

Whatever its deficiencies, the societal reaction approach set into motion concern with the origins and consequences of legal and moral rules. Becker (1973), for example, rather than asking a traditional type of question ("Why do some types of people become marijuana users?"), raised a fundamentally different set of questions ("How did marijuana smoking become illegal?" "What are the social consequences of maintaining this legal definition of the behavior?"). Once questions of this nature were posed, it became increasingly clear that an understanding of societal reaction to deviance required an understanding of society. Most of the labeling theorists, who concentrated on interpersonal interaction, did not have a coherent, serviceable theory of social structure. This deficit, then, led to the emergence of the second phase of development, conflict theory.

CONFLICT THEORY (c. 1970–1979)

Conflict theory, in simple terms, viewed society as a nest of competing interest groups (economic, ethnic, racial, gender) and essentially looked at law as an instrument of power. Representative statements of the approach include the following:

> The criminal is . . . first and foremost a reflection of the interest and ideologies of the governing class. (Chambliss, 1974: 37)

> In contrast to pluralist theory, [conflict] theory notes that the basic interests, in spite of concrete differences, place the elite into a distinct ruling class (Quinney, 1975: 194).

> The legal system is an apparatus that is created to secure the interests of the dominant class (Quinney, 1975: 192).

Acts are criminal because it is in the interests of the ruling class to so define them. . . . The lower classes are labelled criminal and the bourgeoisie is not because the bourgeoisie's control of means of production gives them control of the State and law enforcement as well. . . . Defining certain people as criminal permits greater control of the proletariat. (Chambliss, 1975: 168–9)

The core idea of this conflict theory position was hardly new. Francis Bacon had written in the seventeenth century that "the laws are like cobwebs, where the small flies are caught and the great break through." A few years earlier Machiavelli cast the same idea into a different metaphor when he wrote that "who steals a handkerchief goes to jail; who steals a country becomes a duke." Regardless of its ancestry, the "conflict perspective" was held to provide revolutionary insights into the sociology of law.

Opposed to the conflict theory of society in the minds of its proponents was a mirror image, "consensus theory." The mirror image character is revealed most clearly by Chambliss's chart, reproduced in Table I.1, which itemizes the eight points of difference. Researchers face a fixed choice between these two alternative perspectives. "There is, at the very least, a gigantic struggle between the previously dominant, functional paradigm and the emergent conflict paradigm" (Chambliss, 1976: 1). This issue, furthermore, is to be resolved by empirical investigation. For example,

there is little evidence to support the functionalist contention that criminal law is a body of rules which reflect strongly held moral dictates of the society. . . . By contrast, considerable evidence shows the critically important role played by the interests of the ruling class as a major force in the creation of criminal laws. (Chambliss, 1976: 9–10)

However "gigantic" this "struggle" had been in 1976, within three years it had apparently vanished.

There was a time, not too long ago as a matter of fact, when theories trying to answer the question of how laws are created followed rather directly from the two paradigmatic traditions discussed above. . . . One is hard pressed to find examples of modern social scientists defending the pure forms of either of these models. Everyone, it seems, recognizes that there is some truth to both claims. (Chambliss, 1979: 5)

TABLE I.1
Mirror Image of Theoretical Issues in the Conflict-Consensus "Debate"

Consensus Position	Conflict Position
1. Acts are criminal because they offend the majority of the people.	1. Acts are criminal because it is in the interests of the ruling class to so define them.
2. Persons are labeled criminal because their behavior has gone beyond the tolerance limits of the community's conscience.	2. Persons are labeled criminal because so defining them serves the interests of the ruling class.
3. The lower classes are more likely to be arrested because they commit more crimes.	3. The lower classes are labeled criminal and the bourgeoisie is not because the bourgeoisie's control of the means of production gives them control of the state and law enforcement as well.
4. Crime is a constant in societies. All societies need and produce crime.	4. Crime varies from society to society depending on the political and economic structures of the society.
5. As societies become more specialized in the division of labor, more and more laws will reflect contractual disputes, and penal laws will become less and less significant.	5. As capitalist societies industrialize, the division between social classes will grow, and penal laws will increasingly have to be passed and enforced to maintain temporary stability by curtailing violent confrontations between social classes.
6. Socialist and capitalist societies should have the same amounts of crime where they have comparable rates of industrialization and bureaucratization.	6. Socialist and capitalist societies should have significantly different crime rates, since class conflict will be less in socialist societies and therefore the amount of crime lower as well.
7. Crime makes people more aware of the interests they have in common.	7. Defining certain people as criminal permits greater control of the proletariat.
8. Crime creates a tighter bond between and leads to greater solidarity amongst members of the community.	8. Crime directs the hostility of the oppressed away from the oppression and toward their own class.

SOURCE: William J. Chambliss, "The Political Economy of Crime: A Comparative Study of Nigeria and the USA" in *Critical Criminology*, Ian Taylor, Paul Walton, and Jock Young, eds. (London: Routledge & Kegan Paul Ltd., 1975), pages 168–69. Copyright Routledge & Kegan Paul Ltd. Used by permission.

In the late 1970s dissatisfaction with conflict theory and the conflict-consensus dichotomy as ways of thinking about theoretical issues had begun to accelerate.[6] Anthony Giddens wrote bluntly that the conflict-consensus debate "not only rests on misleading interpretations of past theorists but is also a wholly inadequate way of conceiving our present tasks" (1976: 717). More specifically, conflict theories suffered from the following deficiencies:

1. Rather than investigating consensus as an empirical issue they postulated a false theoretical dichotomy between consensus theories of society and dissensus theories of society. This approach not only overlooked the embarrassing empirical evidence of societal consensus on crime (e.g., Rossi et al. 1974; Hindelang, 1974) but also overlooked theoretical efforts to account for it (see e.g., Femia, 1975; Mann, 1970)
2. Conflict theories tended to combine into an amorphous amalgam such distinct theories of society as Marx's class conflict analysis and Mosca's theory of ruling elites (see Balbus, 1971a)
3. Conflict theory generally adopted an empiricist concern with interest group politics and tended to ignore the structural constraints on visible decision makers (see Gold, Lo and Wright, 1975).

In concluding his study of eighteenth century English criminal law, historian E. T. Thompson takes note of the deficiencies in the conflict approach to explaining law. He observes that

We reach, then, not a simple conclusion (law = class power) but a complex and contradictory one. On the one hand, it is true that the law did mediate existent class relations to the advantage of the rulers; not only is this so, but as the century advanced the law became a superb instrument by which these rulers were able to impose new definitions of property to their even greater advantage, as in the extinction by law of indefinite agrarian use-rights and in the furtherance of enclosure. On the other hand, the law mediated these class relations through legal forms, which imposed, again and again, inhibitions upon the actions of the rulers. For there is a very large difference, which twentieth-century experience ought to have made clear even to the most exalted thinker, between arbitrary extra-legal power and the rule of law. And not only were the rulers (indeed, the ruling class as a whole) inhibited by their own rules of law against the exercise of direct unmediated force (arbitrary imprisonment, the employment of troops against the crowd, torture, and those other conveniences of power with which we are all conversant), but they

also believed enough in these rules, and in their accompanying ideological rhetoric, to allow, in certain limited areas, the law itself to
be a genuine forum within which certain kinds of class conflict were
fought out. There were even occasions ... when the Government
itself retired from the courts defeated. Such occasions served, paradoxically, to consolidate power, to enhance its legitimacy, and to
inhibit revolutionary movements. But, to turn the paradox around,
these same occasions served to bring power even further within constitutional controls.

The rhetoric and the rules of a society are something a great deal
more than sham. In the same moment they may modify, in profound
ways, the behaviour of the powerful, but, at the same time, they may
curb that power and check its intrusions. And it is often from within
that very rhetoric that a radical critique of the practice of the society
is developed: the reformers of the 1790's appeared, first of all, clothed
in the rhetoric of Locke and Blackstone. (1975: 264–5)

The conflict approach to law had been heavily, alghough partially, influenced by a series of essays by the German sociologist
Ralf Dahrendorf, who pointed out that conflict and consensus are
"two equally valid aspects of every imaginable society" (1957: 174).
Whereas Dahrendorf had criticized American sociologists for over-
emphasizing consensus and integration as a normal property of
society, American conflict theorists reduced Dahrendorf's discussion to a simple dichotomy. In so doing, they fell into what Theda
Skocpol has aptly described as the "mirror image trap," which

plagues any attempt to create a new paradigm through direct, polemic
opposition to an old one. Social science may, as is often said, grow
through polemics. But it can also stagnate—through them, if innovators uncritically carry over outmoded theoretical categories (e.g.,
"system") and if they define new ones mainly by searching for the
seemingly direct opposite of the old ones (e.g., "world system" vs.
"national system"). For what seems like a direct opposite may rest
on similar assumptions, or may lead one (through the attempt to
work with an artificial, too extreme opposition) around full circle to
the thing originally opposed. (1977: 1089)

RENAISSANCE OF CLASSICAL THEORIES
(c. 1966–Present)

As the inadequacies of conflict theory became increasingly
clear, both from the critics (Steinert, 1978; Greenberg, 1976; Beirne,

1979a; Hopkins, 1975; Inverarity, 1980; J. Young, 1975; Allen, 1974) and from some of its earlier proponents (Chambliss, 1979), a number of writers began turning to the sociology of law written by European founders of the field. Erikson's *Wayward Puritans*, published in 1966, was one of the first of the societal reaction studies to draw extensively on Durkheim's analysis of ritual punishment. The greatest proliferation of these studies, however, has been in the Marxist tradition. A renaissance over the past ten years has been under way, not only for Marx's own writings, but for those of a number of his followers (Renner, Pashukanis, Rusche and Kirchheimer) whose work on the sociology of law had long been neglected by American sociology.

CONCLUSION

While the connections between law and society were focal for the founders of the field, during most of this century sociology has been preoccupied with other substantive areas. This pattern began to change dramatically in the 1960s largely as a consequence of the interest in "societal reactions to deviance," which led researchers once again to raise serious questions about the relationships between legal institutions and social structures. As efforts were undertaken to understand societal reactions to deviance in its larger societal context, the treatments of law and society by Durkheim, Weber, and Marx began to take on a new significance.

Isaac Newton remarked in the late 1600s that "If I have seen further it is by standing on ye sholders of Giants"; the same notion was expressed two centuries later by Coleridge when he wrote, "A dwarf sees farther than a giant when he has the giant's shoulder to mount on." (Merton, 1965: 31, 260). In returning to the works of the founders of the field as points of departure for their own studies, contemporary researchers recognize the fundamental truth in this aphorism. This volume seeks to trace how the ideas of Marx, Weber, and Durkheim have sustained traditions of thought and investigation in the sociology of law. We will explore a sample of the directions these three traditions generate and survey some of the unanswered questions that they raise.

FOOTNOTES

1. Sociological jurisprudence in the United States was advanced by Roscoe Pound (1870–1964), who emphasized the distinction between "law in

action" and "law in the books." Law, according to this position, is one of several modes of social control; it cannot be understood detached from the social context in which it is formed. It was therefore necessary for the practice of law to be based not only on knowledge of legal statutes and precedents, but also upon an understanding of society and its operation, values, and interests.

A related school of thought, legal realism, is associated with the writings of Oliver Wendell Holmes (1841–1935), Karl Llewellyn (1893–1962), and Jerome Frank (1889–1957). They emphasized the need to examine the *real* bases of legal decisions, which were often obscured by appeal to formal properties of law. The appeals to precedents and principles, according to this school, were largely rationalizations of decisions made on other, extralegal grounds.

The development of these orientations within American law schools was all but ignored by American sociologists. In many respects the recent developments in the sociology of law represent rediscoveries of the ideas of these schools (for an extended discussion, see Hunt, 1978).

2. "An understanding of the nature of criminal law is necessary in order to secure an understanding of the nature of crime. A complete explanation of the origin and enforcement of laws would be, also, an explanation of the violation of laws." (Sutherland, 1924: 11)

3. The contagiousness of the societal reaction perspective among sociologists had little to do with the empirical evidence its proponents offered. Much of the evidence, which was sketchy and anecdotal, came in the form of parables (e.g., Chambliss, 1973; Lemert, 1962). The basic ideas of the societal reaction approach had been proposed by Tannenbaum (1938) but for thirty years received only polite, cursory citation. Interest in social control institutions was an idea whose time had come in the mid-1960s. Civil rights activists were dramatically contrasting segregationist laws with "illegal" human rights protests, and there was increasing confrontation between middle-class youth and the law over drug control and military conscription. The political climate supported a variety of antiestablishment novels and films (Ken Kesey's *One Flew Over the Cuckoo's Nest* and Anthony Burgess's *A Clockwork Orange* reechoed in fictional form many of the themes developed by societal reaction sociologists (cf. Pearson, 1975).

4. Contrast, for example, Lemert (1974) and Goode (1975).

5. For example, in *Pygmalion in the Classroom* Robert Rosenthal and Lenore Jacobson (1968) report the effects of labeling on IQ test scores of grade school children. Twenty percent of the children in grades K–5 in a California elementary school were randomly labeled by researchers as "latent bloomers." The students so labeled showed a significant increase in test performance the following year. Rosenthal and Jacobson suggest that teacher expectations were subtly communicated to students, thus boosting their achievement. By extension, expectations

created by the label affect both the behavior of the social control agent (teacher, policeman, judge) and ultimately the behavior and performance of the person labeled. A closer examination of the data discloses that the labeling effect actually appears in only three grades. More significantly, nine attempts to replicate their results have failed (Hirschi and Hindelang, 1978).

6. Many of these deficiencies had long been recognized by perceptive observers. For example, Robert Merton had earlier noted that

> generally, when the sociologist with a conceptual scheme stemming from utilitarian theory observes a patently untrue social belief, he will look for special groups in whose interest it is to invent and spread this belief. The cry of "propaganda!" is often mistaken for a theoretically sound analysis. . . . To be sure, vested-interests often do spread untrue propaganda and this may reinforce mass illusions. But the vested-interest or priestly-lie theories of fallacious folk beliefs do not always constitute the most productive point of departure nor do they go far toward explaining the bases of acceptance or rejection of beliefs. (1968: 160)

1

The Logic of
Sociological Analysis

Our understanding of the relationship between criminal law and society is constructed from a variety of facts, experiences, and interpretations. While we generally regard facts and experiences as the building blocks of our understanding, it is clear that more than an accumulation of such bits of information is necessary. Consider for the moment the following facts about inmates in American prisons in 1978:

- 306,602 persons were confined in state and federal prisons.
- 45 percent of these persons were black males.
- 5 percent of the general population of the United States consists of black males.

These three simple facts reveal something quite basic about the relationship between criminal justice and American society: the profound inequality in the imposition of the criminal sanction.

Bare statistical facts, of course, reflect the combined experiences of individuals. Much of our knowledge about law and society comes from the testimony and observations of such individuals. For example, prison activist George Jackson tells us that

> Black men born in the U.S. and fortunate to live past the age of eighteen are conditioned to accept the inevitability of prison. For most of us it simply looms as the next phase in a sequence of humiliations. (1970: 9)

Description—either narrative or statistical—is a necessary but not sufficient ingredient for understanding law and society. Facts and observations serve to raise, rather than answer, questions. In this case we are left with the question: What is it about being black and male in the United States in the late 1970s that causes the risk of imprisonment to be so high? What is it about American society that results in 5 percent of the population's taking up over 40 percent of the prison space?

Once we begin to raise such questions, we are no longer simple hunters and gatherers of facts. We now confront the tasks of interpretation, explanation, or theory construction. We must find some way in which explanations of inequality in the imposition of criminal sanctions can be formulated and evaluated. The formulation and testing of such explanations are the primary tasks of sociology. We will consider more fully explanations of inequality in the administration of sanctions in Chapter 9. This chapter will examine the general criteria required for adequate sociological explanation of such phenomena.

The relationship between law and society, first of all, is not the exclusive preserve of the sociology of law. Philosophy, literature, and art—not to mention legal studies—all explore the relationships between law and society. Sociological analysis is but one of several styles of thought, and as sociologist Vernon Dibble points out,

> there is clearly no reason to assume that scientific styles are somehow more legitimate or valid for all purposes than other styles, that all others are somehow departures from the scientific style, and that all other styles of thought are to be judged by a scientific model. (1973: 547)

What is a "scientific" model or style? How does the scientific style of thought differ from the other ways of thinking about law and society employed by lawyers, novelists, or philosophers? This chapter will examine some of the central issues raised by these questions. It first explores the unique manner in which the scientific style of analysis makes use of observable data to develop general explanations of phenomena. We will encounter in this volume several modes of such explanations (causal, functional, structural, and dialectic). In this chapter we will first see how these various modes share common features and how they are subject to similar error. Having a basic understanding of the scientific style, we will then examine the differences between scientific and alternative styles of examining the relationship between law and society.

THE SCIENTIFIC STYLE: GENERALIZATION SUPPORTED BY SYSTEMATIC OBSERVATIONAL EVIDENCE

To understand the scientific style of analysis, it is best to begin with a simple example. Explaining the motion of the planets is not only a relatively simple problem, but it was historically the first success of the scientific style. The following discussion will draw very selectively from the history of ideas about planetary movement. We will specifically consider some of the ideas propounded by five individuals (Ptolemy, Copernicus, Galileo, Sizi, and Leverrier) whose ideas will not provide us with a capsule history of the field of astronomy, but instead will serve to illustrate basic problems of evidence and inference that will confront us in more complicated forms in later chapters. In brief, we will be concerned here with how the scientific style deals with the following problems:

How does an abstract theory yield consequences about observable events?

What happens to a theory when its implications are disconfirmed by evidence?

On what basis does a theory gain acceptance over its competitors?

If we accept the idea that facts may be interpreted only through theory, how can we prevent the theory from becoming self-confirming?

While we cannot adequately treat the nuances of these issues here (for a good survey of the literature, see Keat and Urry, 1975), an understanding of these problems is basic to our comprehension of the substantive research issues in the sociology of law.

Explaining the Movement of the Planets

We begin with what we can see. In 1500 Western Europeans meticulously recorded the movement of the moon, Mars, Venus, and the other "wanderers" across the night sky. Today we can do so less tediously with time-lapse photography. If we leave the lens open on successive nights, the resulting negative will show streaks of light "objectively" recording the movement of the moon and planets. We might be tempted to think that the camera is a neutral recording device that embodies no theoretical assumptions about the behavior of planets. In fact, our time-lapse photograph has been taken in such a way as to adopt implicitly the theory that the earth is the stationary center around which the other planets move.

That theory was developed in detail by the Greek writer Ptolemy around 150 A.D. Ptolemy's earth-centered theory of the planets had two important implications. First, it asserted that the pattern we see in the night sky reflects the actual movement of the planets. In a time-lapse photograph we see a simple arc left by the moon, but the other planets leave an irregular and very complicated pattern. The second implication of Ptolemy's earth-centered theory, then, was that each planet had a unique complicated orbit.

By 1500 Ptolemy's followers had developed very intricate clockwork mechanisms that reproduced the spiral orbits implied by the theory. It now was possible to predict precisely the position of any planet at any given time by using these mechanisms. Despite the technical success achieved by advocates of Ptolemy's theory, a challenger appeared in 1543 who revolutionized the explanation of planetary motion.

This challenger, the Polish astronomer Copernicus, proposed a theory that the sun rather than the earth was the center of the planetary system. His theory implies (1) that the planets have simple, circular orbits and (2) that all planets move alike. This new theory received important indirect confirming evidence fifty years later when the Italian scientist Galileo pointed a newly invented device, the telescope, to the night sky. Galileo then saw for the first time that moons orbit the planet Jupiter. This confirmed the orbital paths predicted by Copernicus's theory.

When in March of 1610 Galileo published his discovery of moons revolving around Jupiter, a storm of controversy erupted. Among his critics is the fourth figure who is of importance for us. The Italian astronomer Francisco Sizi objected to Galileo's report with the following argument:

> There are seven windows in the head, two nostrils, two ears, two eyes, and a mouth; so in the heavens there are two favorable stars, two unpropitious, two luminaries, and Mercury alone undecided and indifferent. From which and many other similar phenomena of nature

> such as the seven metals, etc., which it were tedious to enumerate, we gather that the number of planets is necessarily seven. . . . Moreover, the satellites are invisible to the naked eye and therefore can have no influence on the earth and therefore would be useless and therefore do not exist. (quoted in Randall, 1976: 233)

Sizi and his contemporaries refused even to look at Galileo's telescope. In response, Galileo bitterly complained that "these people believe there is no truth to seek in nature, but only in the comparison of texts" (quoted in Randall, 1940: 233).[1]

By refusing to look through Galileo's telescope Francisco Sizi was not simply clinging irrationally to his beliefs about the number seven. To interpret the image produced by the telescope, it is necessary to have a theory of optics that explains how the small distant image is magnified by the ground glass. Without such a theory, Sizi was quite rational to reject Galileo's observations as probable mirages (Lakatos, 1978: 15). Arthur Eddington put this issue succinctly when he remarked, "You cannot believe in observations before they are confirmed by theory." In other words, observations become "facts" only after they have been interpreted by a theory. We encountered another version of this problem at the outset of this discussion when we found that a camera taking time-lapse photographs is not quite the neutral observer we generally imagine it to be. By placing the camera on earth we have implicitly accepted the assumptions of Ptolemy's theory, and the resulting photograph confirms the complicated, unique movements of the individual planets. Were we to take the time-lapse photograph from outer space beyond the orbit of Pluto, the picture would confirm Copernicus's model of planetary motion.

Now if observations depend upon theory for their interpretation, we have a paradox: "the model seems to dictate the selection of facts used to confirm it" (Elton, 1967: 38n). One resolution of this paradox of self-confirming theory may be found in contrasting the strategy used by Francisco Sizi in attacking Galileo with the strategy used by the nineteenth century French mathematician Urbain Leverrier in defense of Newton's gravitational theory. Applying Newton's theory to planetary orbits, Leverrier noted that Uranus failed to conform to the theory's predictions. Assuming that his measurements were accurate and that Newton's theory was correct, Leverrier explained Uranus's deviations by postulating the presence of a planet beyond Uranus. Using Newton's theory, Leverrier then calculated the size and position of this planet in such a way that its gravitational influence would explain the odd behavior of Uranus. Leverrier was thus able to predict the position of the planet Neptune, a prediction that was soon confirmed by telescopic observation. It is instructive to contrast the two general ways of thinking represented by Sizi and Leverrier. Sizi's position was that logic could do most of the work in establishing his case against Jupiter's having moons. He did not look for *testable implications* of his theory, but instead sought to weave a compelling web of abstract argument garnished with a few selected facts. Leverrier, while also refusing to take "the facts" of Uranus's deviations at their face value, drew additional implications from his theoretical argument that another planet was responsible. He reasoned, for example, that if one were to look at a certain position in the sky, one would (with a sufficiently powerful telescope) observe reflected light from the planet causing the misalignment of Uranus's orbit.

A brief glance at the history of the explanation of planetary motion thus reveals some of the salient features of the scientific style. This style seeks to formulate explanations of observable events, but does so in terms of abstract models that generally can only be tested by examining their implications. Thus Copernicus's theory predicts that when the earth changes its orbital position, earth-bound observers should see a slight shift in the location of stars. Consistency with the data, however, is not the sole criterion for a theory's acceptance, since a theory can be made to fit almost any set of observations by making appropriate amendments. In addition, it is generally possible to find any number of theories that will fit equally well a limited range of observations. Other criteria therefore enter into the choice. One such criterion is simplicity. The technical development of Ptolemy's theory in 1500 yielded accurate long-range predictions about the position of planets. Despite such confirmation the theory was unsatisfactory, since it required each planet to move inexplicably in a different fashion. The movement of any newly discovered planet therefore could only be accounted for by the theory ad hoc. In contrast, Copernicus's model of the solar system as a series of concentric rings provided a general explanation that applied to all cases.

In addition this capsule account alerts us to the complicated relationship between theory and observation. The theory must have implications for observation. Its scientific acceptability rests in large measure on its batting average in making accurate predictions.[2] At the same time observations must be interpreted in light of theory. To prevent the proliferation of simple ad hoc accounts, we require that the theory being defended give an adequate account of a range of phenomena. "Thus, the basic logical process of science is the elimination of alternative theories . . . by investigating as many of the empirical consequences of each theory as is practical, always trying for the greatest possible variety of implications tested" (Stinchcombe, 1968: 22).

THE SCIENTIFIC STYLE IN SOCIOLOGY

We next review the manner in which Karl Marx and Emile Durkheim sought to extend the scientific style of analysis to data on social organization. Both saw their work as constituting a fundamental break with prescientific thinking about social organization. We will briefly examine how their characterization of the role of observable evidence departs from philosophical treatments of social organization.

In *The German Ideology* Marx and Engels seek to establish a way of thinking about society in which "history ceases to be a collection of dead facts as it is with the empiricists (themselves still abstract) or an imagined activity of imagined subjects, as with the idealists" (Tucker, 1978: 155). By *empiricists* Marx and Engels have in mind writers who refuse to generalize beyond "the facts" they gather on the basis of inarticulate, implicit theories. By *idealists*, Marx and Engels refer to writers who confine themselves to the highest level of abstract concepts without connecting these concepts to observable events. Specifically, Marx and Engels in this essay object to a tradition of speculative philosophy at the time (1848) dominant in German academic institutions. This social philosophy begins with some set of assumptions about the nature of Man and proceeds to work out the logical implications of these assumptions for social organization. Typically, such treatments begin with a hypothetical, obscure "state of nature" out of which society sprang.[3] Marx and Engels complain that these writers emphasize

the interests of Human Nature, of Man in general, who belongs to no class, has no reality, who exists only in the misty realm of philosophical fantasy. (Marx and Engels, in Tucker, 1978: 494)

In so doing, these writers weave a

robe of speculative cobwebs, embroidered with flowers of rhetoric, steeped in the dew of sickly sentiment, this transcendental robe in which the German Socialists wrap their sorry "eternal truths," all skin and bone. . . . (Marx and Engels, in Tucker, 1978: 495)

Furthermore, they fail to

enlighten us as to how we proceed from this nonsensical "prehistory" to history proper; although, on the other hand, in their historical speculation they seize upon this "prehistory" with especial eagerness because they imagine themselves safe there from interference on the part of "crude facts," and, at the same time, because there they can give full rein to their speculative impulse and set up and knock down hypotheses by the thousand. (Marx and Engels, in Tucker, 1978: 156)

The problem posed by speculative philosophy for Marx and Engels was thus similar to the problem Sizi posed for Galileo. Both cases involve the use of systematic empirical observation to judge abstract theoretical propositions.

When we conceive things, thus, as they really are and happen, every profound philosophical problem is resolved . . . quite simply into an empirical fact. (Marx and Engels, in Tucker, 1978: 170)

The task, Marx and Engels argued, is to find some middle ground between arid fact gathering and fact-free speculation.

Emile Durkheim set a similar goal. In the following passage from his *Rules of Sociological Method* he similarly contrasts empiricist and idealist styles in terms of a distinction between history and philosophy.

For the historian, societies represent just so many heterogeneous individualities, not comparable among themselves. Each people has its own physiognomy, its special constitution, its law, its morality, its economic organizations, appropriate only to itself; and all generalizations are well-nigh impossible. For the philosopher, on the contrary, all these individual groupings, called tribes, city-states, and nations, are only contingent and provisional aggregations with no exclusive and separate reality. Only humanity is real, and it is from the general attributes of human nature that all social evolution flows.

For the former, consequently, history is but a sequence of events which follow without repeating one another; for the latter, these same events have value and interest only as illustrating the general laws inherent in the constitution of man and dominating all historical development. For the former, what is good for one society cannot be applied to others. The conditions of the state of health vary from one people to the next and cannot be theoretically determined; it is a matter of practical experience and of cautious research. For the latter, they can be calculated once and for all and for the entire human species. It seems, then, that social reality must be merely subject matter of an abstract and vague philosophy or for purely descriptive monographs. (1950: 76–7)

In the course of examining sociological work dealing with law and society we will have numerous occasions to examine in greater depth and detail the relationships between theory and observation. It is through experience in dealing with such substantive questions that a full understanding of the art of scientific inference develops.

FORMS OF SOCIOLOGICAL EXPLANATION

Having considered the role of empirical verification in sociological statements generally, we consider now the typical specific forms of sociological explanations. A basic understanding of the key issues can be gained by comparing two major types of explanation, causal and functional. While they differ in several respects, causal and functional explanations share similar elements and suffer common disorders.

Causal Explanation

Perhaps the most commonly encountered form of explanation in sociology is exemplified by the following assertions:

- Drunken driving causes highway fatalities.
- Cigarette smoking causes lung cancer.
- Powerful interest groups dictate the legal definitions of criminal conduct.
- Class and racial biases of law enforcement officials cause low-income minorities to be overrepresented in arrest statistics.

In each case an independent variable (e.g., interest) is asserted to cause some variation in a dependent variable (e.g., legal definitions of criminal conduct).

Despite nearly universal application of causal explanation,

sociologists often disclaim using causal expressions (see Hirschi and Selvin, 1966, for a collection of such denials). In large measure these objections spring from the misconception that causal statements are necessarily deterministic. Sociologists wishing (for whatever reason) to avoid determinism deny that the explanations they offer are indeed causal. Typically, the denial takes the form of couching cause-and-effect assertions in sanitary prose, as for example: X *influences* Y, X *sets limits on* Y, X *modifies* Y.

Causal relationships, however, do not necessarily imply that the independent variable is the "prime mover," the sole (or even the most important) cause of variation in the dependent variable. The only claim made by a causal explanation is that a variation or a change in an independent variable will produce some corresponding change in a dependent variable. A common species of causal explanation in the sociology of law takes *interests* as an independent variable. For example, Chambliss (1966) claims that as the composition of the English ruling class shifted from a predominance of landowners to a predominance of merchants in the 1500s, Parliament rewrote the vagrancy laws to control highway robbers rather than to keep serfs down on the manor.

Testing such causal connections is often difficult, since outside controlled laboratory environments the impact of any independent variable (such as a change in elite interests) will compete with a large number of other factors, both strong and weak. The combined influence of such factors will generally weaken the causal influence of any particular independent variable. We should therefore expect to observe routinely modest associations between independent and dependent variables. As Karl Marx pointed out,

> in the analysis of economic forms . . . neither microscopes nor chemical agents are of use. The force of abstraction must replace both . . . . Consequently, to the superficial observer, the analysis of these forms seems to turn on minutiae. The analysis typically does in fact deal with minutiae, but they are of the same order as those dealt with in microscopic anatomy. (1967: 8)

This orientation runs counter to the language of conventional imaginations, which consists of dramatic causes and effects. When we think about poverty *causing* crime, a number of bold vignettes leap to mind of vast numbers of "real people" being forced into criminal activity by their deprivation. If we are to believe that poverty does cause crime, we probably expect at least a majority of the poor to engage in criminal behavior.[4] The dramatic way in which the English language makes us think about causes and effects does not prepare us for the reality that is revealed by research. This reality appears as a large void of random variations within which small effects can be detected. Sociologists are rarely in a position to explain more than half of the variation they observe in the variables they attempt to explain. This situation is not unique to sociology; medical research is often in the same position. The data on carcinogens, for instance, are largely a matter of effects that are not only small, but delayed. Exposure to benzine may only cause cancer in a small number of persons exposed to the chemical, and the cancer may take several years to develop after the exposure. Inability to think in terms of small effects frequently leads to non-sensical analysis and catastrophic policy.

For example, Morris and Hawkins (1977: 82) argue that the death penalty is of "singular inconsequence" as a cause of reduction of homicides because only a small minority of convicted murderers have been executed. Morris' and Hawkins' argument assumes that only dramatic events can be causes. To see the implications of this assumption it is useful to conduct a mental experiment. Economist Isaac Ehrlich (1975a) on the basis of execution and homicide trends over the period 1933–1969 projects that each execution was followed on the average by a subsequent reduction of eight homicides. Using these projections in a mental experiment,[5] we may apply Ehrlich's estimates to the data for 1974, in which there were no executions, 21,465 homicides, and 6,980 convictions. If the rate of capital punishment in 1974 had been at the 1947 level (4.3 percent of convictions resulting in execution) the United States would have had 297 executions in 1974 rather than zero. According to Ehrlich's projections, then, these 297 executions would have saved 2,376 lives in 1975, or about 10 percent of all the victims of homicide in that year (Kleck, 1979: 883).

Several important lessons can be drawn from this mental experiment. First, for capital punishment to have significant deterrent effects it is not necessary to execute a substantial portion of the murderers. *If* the theory were correct, a 4 percent execution rate would result in saving over 2000 lives. Morris and Hawkins's view that the effect of executions is trivial because so few are executed is thus misleading. Second, executions may have a substantial deterrent effect even if fully 90 percent of the homicides remain unaffected. This means that one cannot decide whether capital punishment deters homicides by creatively imagining the state of mind of the "typical" perpetrator. It is beside the point that *most* homicides are crimes of passion in which the potential punishment is not rationally weighed. This may well be true for the 90 percent of the homicides unaffected by executions, but 10 percent of all homicides still amounts to a substantial number of lives.

In general, then, sociologists often deal with small effects, in complex situations in which both random and unknown nonrandom events affect what is to be explained. The standard imagery of dramatic effects, the reliance on images of "typical cases," the whole range of expectations imbedded in our minds by the English language (see, e.g., D'Andrade, 1965) must be overcome to engage in sociological analysis.

Having ruled out magnitude of association as a proper standard of evaluation for the presence of cause-effect connections, we now will examine some basic criteria that must be considered. For a claim that X causes Y to be substantiated by evidence, the following four conditions must be fulfilled:

1. The independent variable must in fact be independent, that is, it must not be a logical consequence of the dependent variable.
2. Independent and dependent variables must covary (that is, a change in the independent variable is associated with a change in the dependent variable).
3. The independent variable must precede the dependent variable both logically and in time. If the criminal law changes before the power or interests of the dominant group change, then powerful interests cannot be a cause of legal change.
4. The relationship between independent and dependent variables must be nonspurious. This means that the variation that fulfills condition 1 must not simply be a coincidence, a random fluke, or a consequence of a change in some third variable.

We will now consider these conditions in more detail.

1. Is the Explanation Circular? "When there are not enough jobs for people," President Coolidge explained, "unemployment results." This is certainly a true statement fully consistent with all observed facts, but it is uninformative. It is worth the trouble to figure out *why* Coolidge's explanation is uninformative, since more subtle versions of the same error are quite common.

The difficulty with Coolidge's statement is that its premise (not enough jobs) logically entails the conclusion (unemployment); too few jobs could never fail to "cause" unemployment, since unemployment is by definition the absence of gainful occupations. Like a puppy chasing its tail, Coolidge's explanation is circular. Many statements, in fact, have no empirical import; they tell us nothing about the observable world. Thus,

> This cube has six sides

is a statement that tells us nothing about this particular cube because, by definition, a cube must have six sides. The apparent factual claim about reality turns out on closer inspection to be nothing more than a definition. In contrast,

> This cube has six colors

or

> This Rubik's cube has no solution

may be tested by some observation, since color is not a definitional property of cubes, nor is solvability a necessary feature of a Rubik's puzzle.

While the above distinctions between definitions and propositions is straightforward, the practice of circular explanation is widespread. For example, Richard Quinney claims that, "The criminal law is an instrument of the state and ruling class (used) to maintain and perpetuate the existing social and economic order" (1974: 16). Is this statement circular? Circularity is not obvious when one looks at this assertion alone; the critical factor is the manner in which the alleged explanatory variable (ruling class interest) is defined. Who makes up this elite of the powerful? Quinney's answer is that it is composed of (1) members of the upper economic class (those who own or control the means of production) and (2) those who benefit in some way from the present capitalist economic system" (1974: 55). If we stick with the first of Quinney's definitions, his hypothesis about the criminal law is not circular. The second definition, however, creates very serious problems. "Those who benefit *in some way*" is so broad as to include virtually any group in the society. Quinney's hypothesis now becomes, in effect, a circular statement that "the powerful" make the laws, and the lawmakers are "the powerful." This form of circular argument is very dangerous; since such arguments seem to have an intuitive appeal, they seem to be, somehow, obviously true. Their power, however, is a mirage arising from a failure to make the causal variable logically independent of its alleged effect.

Circular arguments are not always easy to identify. One simple test that usually works is to ask the question: Is there any possible set of circumstances in which this explanation could be *false?* Finding supportive evidence for a hypothesis is no problem, since apparent support in a circular argument is created *by definition.* Therefore forget the *supporting* evidence. If by *ruling class* we mean those persons able to get Congress to pass legislation in the power holders' interest, then there is no possible way the argument can be false. Who is the ruling class? Those who get Congress to act. Why does Congress respond to their interests? Because they are the ruling class! We should reserve judgment on the explanation until its proponent can tell us how to independently measure the causal variable.

2. Covariation Between Independent and Dependent Variables. If the statement "Cigarette smoking causes lung cancer" is to be accepted as a valid causal statement, some evidence must exist linking variation in the two variables. Smokers must have a higher incidence of lung cancer than otherwise comparable people who do not smoke. If ruling class interests dictate the content of the criminal law, some correspondence between variations in interests of different types of ruling classes should be found to correspond to varying contents of the penal codes.

Two difficulties confront us in establishing covariation between independent and dependent variables. First, outside highly controlled laboratory environments we are apt to find exceptions to our causal arguments. A good many smokers, for example, never contract lung cancer. How are we to deal with such exceptions? Second, it is possible to find some case that supports virtually any generalization. What then is necessary to establish the existence of an association between two variables?

Rare is the causal statement in any field (physics or biology as well as sociology) in which exceptions are not encountered. "The great tragedy of Science," Thomas Huxley once remarked, "is the slaying of a beautiful hypothesis by an ugly fact." Encountering exceptions, however, seldom leads a researcher to abandon an otherwise promising hypothesis. Occasional exceptions may be attributed to errors in measurement or observation. Recurrent exceptions are often explained after the fact. This may be done two ways: by *ad hoc accounts* or by *scope conditions.*

To understand the distinction between these two strategies, consider the following simple problem: "Suppose that a group of physicists identified the temperature at which water boils in New York. Another group conducted the same research in Denver, and the results obviously turned out to be different" (Przeworski and Teune, 1970: 8). The ad hoc (to this case) approach would focus on the particular circumstances of the two observations, typically attributing them to the unique temporal or geographic locations. Denver and New York, however, differ in so many respects that the resulting qualification will be of limited predictive values (What, for example, could we say about the boiling point of water in Pittsburgh?) and of no explanatory value whatever. Much social science research that resorts to "regional differences," "national character," and similar global space- and time-bound factors has this limitation.

In contrast, *scope conditions* state a general set of conditions under which the generalization applies.[6] In the above case atmospheric pressure seems to be a promising candidate, since the elevation of New York is at sea level, while Denver is at 5280 feet. The statement "water boils at 100 degrees Celsius" therefore is qualified by the scope condition "at sea level."[7]

The more exceptions a theory encounters, the more elaborate its set of scope conditions. It should be remembered, however, that "purely negative criticism does not kill a research program" (Lakatos, 1978: 179). A theory will usually be forgiven its anomalies if it is more successful than its competitors in accounting for other phenomena. For example, the theory of aerodynamics, which is used to construct aircraft, long predicted that the bumblebee could not fly. Its weight, shape, and wingspan made it impossible for the bee to get off the ground, according to the theory. Clearly, something is wrong with the theory, but that has not led to its rejection. In fact thousands of the lives of airplane passengers have been routinely entrusted to the accuracy of this theory, known to yield inexplicably wrong predictions.

We therefore need to avoid the common temptation to reject a theoretical statement on the basis of some singular experience or observation that appears to contradict it. Exceptions are to be expected. The problem in evaluating a theoretical statement is not one of discovering exceptions, but of imagining alternative theories that explain the phenomena better.

While rejecting explanations on the basis of exceptions is a mistake, accepting them on the basis of unsystematic evidence is just as bad. Anthropologist Max Gluckman suggests that rather than examining systematic variation to demonstrate a general conclusion, we too often resort to "the method of apt and isolated illustration,"[8] which tends

> to write in terms of general statements and then from a mass of examples (to) select the apt and appropriate to illustrate specific customs, principles of organization, social relationships, etc. (Gluckman, 1965: 210)

Taking isolated instances as evidence of a general relationship is a dangerous procedure for two reasons. First, isolated examples can generally be found to support virtually *any* general proposition. Thus,

> astrologers are adept at the line of argument that all pseudo-scientists consider "evidence." The line would be something like this, "People born under Leo are leaders of men, because the lion is the king of beasts, and the proof is that Napoleon was born under the sign of Leo. . . ." But one-twelfth of living human beings, amounting to 250,000,000 individuals were born in Leo. [Is] the proportion of leaders among them significantly greater than among non-Leos? (Asimov, 1965: 62)

The fallacy of proof by isolated instances is widespread. For example, a standard "empirical" argument against the deterrent effect of the death penalty is the observation that in England in the 1700s pickpockets worked the crowds attending the public execution of pickpockets. This observation appears to demonstrate a general relationship (or more correctly the absence of a general relationship) between crime and capital punishment. The apparent evidence, however, is deficient because it only illustrates that public execution is not a perfect deterrent; it does not tell us anything about the presence or absence of a *general* effect. That question can only be addressed by comparing the *rates* of behavior across different situations; rate of pickpocket activity in crowds at executions versus crowds at county fairs, for example.

The second problem with apt and isolated illustration is that any observed events are subject to random, extraneous influences that often disguise the basic forces at work. Thus for any single occurrence, the actual sequence of events occurred only in one way—and that way, paradoxical as it may sound, was not necessarily the most probable way. Consider for example the assassination of President Kennedy. Even with the advantage of hindsight we might very well say that his election for a second term was more likely than his assassination. Many assassination attempts are, we are told, foiled each year by the F.B.I. so, with a little luck they might have stopped this one too. Moreover, if we accept the main findings of the Warren Report, we have to say that even the most expert marksman would not have given himself much of a chance of doing what Oswald did. This being so one would surely not be justified in condemning a simulation of U.S. politics in the 1960s in which President Kennedy was assassinated only, say one time in every ten plays. By the same token, given President Roosevelt's narrow escape in Chicago in 1932 when the bullet killed Mayor Cermack instead, a series of simulations of U.S. politics in the 1930s in which Roosevelt was never assassinated could be criticized as unrealistic. (Barry, 1965: 212–13)

Observed events thus combine random, circumstantial factors with underlying general processes. If we are interested in uncovering the latter, we must go beyond appearances. It is for this reason that historical, cross-cultural, and statistical comparisons play such a major role in sociology. As Durkheim noted,

> comparative sociology is not a particular branch of sociology; it is sociology itself, insofar as it ceases to be purely descriptive and aspires to account for facts. (1964: 139)

3. *The Causal Variable Must Precede the Effect.* For an independent variable, X, to affect a dependent variable, Y, it must occur prior to Y. This logical requirement is straightforward. However, serious problems arise when this condition comes to be regarded as a sufficient rather than a necessary condition of causality. So widespread is this error that it has been given a special name: the "post hoc, ergo propter hoc fallacy" (after this, therefore because of this). One sees this fallacy quite often in discussions of reforms. A change in some condition is observed after the reform is instituted; this change is then taken as prima facie evidence that the reform has succeeded. When, for example, traffic fatalities declined a year after Connecticut instituted a crackdown on speeding, the governor of the state told the press that the change in the law had obviously saved lives. In fact, the decline in traffic deaths could be

attributed to several alternative factors (Campbell, 1969). This possibility therefore leads us to ask the following question.

4. Is the Relationship Spurious?   Once a systematic relationship has indeed been established between two variables, it remains to be seen whether the covariation is causal or merely coincidental. For example, Piliavin and Briar (1964) published a study of the effect of demeanor presented by juveniles on the likelihood of their being arrested by the police. Piliavin and Briar argue that typically juveniles who have committed comparable offenses will be treated differently depending upon their degree of respect for the police officer. Piliavin and Briar, however, succeed only in providing a few apt and isolated illustrations of the role of deference in arrests of juveniles, while failing to demonstrate any general pattern. To demonstrate such a pattern, one must minimally compare juveniles who are similar in the seriousness of their offenses and the frequencies of their past police contacts. (It is quite likely that serious, chronic offenders will not display much deference toward the police.) Piliavin and Briar have an insufficient number of cases (only 66) to distinguish the effect of deference apart from these other variables. (For a study design with a better sample, see Black and Reiss, 1970.) Piliavin and Briar rest their case on a number of anecdotes and the systematic data in Table 1.1.

While there is a coincidence of demeanor and arrest in these data, no possible method (other than blind faith) exists for telling whether the demeanor is affecting the rate of arrest, apart from offense and past record.[9]

Observing a systematic relationship between the two variables, demeanor and arrest, is an important first step in establishing a causal connection between them. While it does not logically imply

TABLE 1.1
Relationship Between Deference and Arrest

	Demeanor	
	Cooperative	*Uncooperative*
Arrest	2	14
No arrest	43	7

SOURCE: Adapted from "Police Encounters with Juveniles" by Irving Piliavin and Scott Briar from *American Journal of Sociology* 70: 2 (September 1964), p. 210, by permission of The University of Chicago Press. Copyright 1964 by The University of Chicago.

causation, correlation is the first requisite of causality. The actual magnitude of the correlation is no guide to its causal status. In Western Europe, for instance, a strong correlation exists between the number of storks in a county and the (human) birthrate. Knowing the stork population of a given area allows one to predict quite accurately the human birthrate. While the correlation is consistent with the theory that storks bring babies, the implausibility of this theory inspires us to look for another factor affecting both the presence of storks and a high birthrate. Urbanization seems the most plausible candidate, since storks build their nests in rural areas and people in rural areas tend to have larger families.

While we are inspired in the stork–babies case to search for a "third" variable, in general we need to do so regardless of the plausibility of the causal connection between the variables. In other words, the only way in which we can have confidence in a hypothesis of the form "poverty causes street crime" is to search for a variety of other factors that affect street crime to determine if the relationship we observe is "spurious." The relationship between the number of storks and birthrate is spurious because urbanization affects both of them in the same way. Therefore, shooting down the storks is unlikely to affect the birthrate.

In general, then, it *is* possible to verify causal statements by examining correlations between such observed variables as deference and arrest. To do so sensibly, however, requires ruling out the possibility that we are merely observing a coincidence. This may be accomplished in several ways. One is to consider, as we did in the above case, plausible alternative explanations of the dependent variable. Another strategy is to establish that the observed correlation is consistent with some previously well-established theory. This strategy is typically carried out by searching for the intervening mechanism between variations in the independent and dependent variables. For example, in the case of the presumed causal link between cigarette smoking and lung cancer, we can increase our confidence in the causal nature of the observed statistical relationship if we have available biochemical studies of the effect of tar and nicotine on cancer in tissue samples.

Whether we pursue the strategy of examining "control variables" or the strategy of seeking out "intervening variables," it is important to recognize that all we ever do is increase our confidence in the hypothesis that the relationship is causal rather than coincidental. We will not, in this life, be in the position of knowing with certainty that we have given a valid interpretation of what we have seen.

Functional Explanation

In contrast to causal explanation, in which a prior event X influences a subsequent event Y, in functional explanations the effect Y is explained by its consequences C. For example,

> "Birds have hollow bones because hollow bones facilitate flight." (G. A. Cohen, 1978: 249)

> Legal equality persists in capitalist society because it legitimates existing distributions of power and resources.

> Public executions of felons persist because such rituals sustain social cohesion.

In each of these statements some dependent variable Y is alleged to exist because of some consequence it has for the larger system of which it is a part. More accurately, the occurrence of variable Y (public execution) at time T is explained by the positive consequences C (social cohesion) produced by an instance of public execution at an earlier Time T-1.

The functional explanation has commonly been used by anthropologists attempting to account for "irrational" institutions of preindustrial societies. For example, the Hopi Indians periodically perform a rain ceremony, which has no demonstrable meteorological significance. Rather than dismiss the ceremony as an instance of the primitive's irrationality, the functionalist accounts for its recurrence in terms of the latent but empirical consequences it has in "reinforcing the group identity by providing a periodic occasion on which the scattered members of a group assemble to engage in common activity" (Merton, 1968: 118–19).

Whereas causal explanations are superstitiously avoided because of the misconception that they entail determinism, many sociologists shun functional explanation (or at least shun acknowledgments of their use) because they seem to be teleological. For instance, British sociologist Percy Cohen contends that "critics rightly argue that functional explanation defies the laws of logic, for one thing cannot be the cause of another if it succeeds it in time" (1968: 48). Religious ritual can, Cohen argues, be explained by the effect it has on social integration only through a supernatural conception of future events shaping present practices.[10] This objection, however, is based on a misconception of the nature of functional explanation. Such explanation takes as the independent variable not future events, but present *dispositions* of the system.

> For example, in a hydra that has just had a tentacle removed, certain regenerative processes will promptly set in; but these cannot be explained teleologically by reference to a final cause consisting in the future event of the hydra being complete again. For that event may never actually come about since in the process of regeneration, and before its completion, the hydra may suffer new and irreparably severe damage, and may die. (Hempel, 1965: 325)

In general, the explanation of a current event (e.g., a rain dance) is explained not by the future consequence (increased community solidarity the day after tomorrow), since any number of possible events might prevent the normal consequence from actually taking place. The explanation of the current event resides in the presence of a disposition of the system to maintain solidarity, to regenerate lost organs, and so on. The principal task of functional explanation therefore is to provide compelling evidence for the existence of such dispositions in the system under investigation. This may be a difficult task, but it does not entail the logical absurdity of invoking future events to explain present behavior.

As in the case of causal explanations, functional explanations can be evaluated on the basis of four criteria: noncircularity, association, time order, and nonspuriousness.

1. Noncircularity. Again many convincing functional explanations achieve their intuitive, gut-level appeal by allowing the independent variable simply to rename the dependent variable. This fraud is particularly likely to arise in functional explanations when the need, function, consequences, or disposition is left undefined. The author presents to us a rain dance, a public execution, or an animal with a horn on its forehead and then postulates some need that the observed event or trait might conceivably serve. Without an independent assessment of that need and its variations, the functional explanation readily turns circular.

It may be logistically impossible to measure the need directly. Giving out questionnaires to a community before and after it performs a ritual is not often a practical alternative (however, see Lauderdale, 1976). In lieu of such direct observation, however, indirect manifestations of changes in dispositions can be used. For example, community solidarity responds to threats, which are often identifiable. An observed association between threats and rituals may therefore be used to break the chain of circularity in functional explanations of ritual.

2. *Association.* The "method of apt and isolated illustration" is as much a bane of functional explanation as it is of causal explanation. A small imagination can readily conjure up a plausible consequence for any existing state of affairs. The eighteenth century satirist Voltaire gave us the archetype of this mentality. In Voltaire's novel *Candide,* Dr. Pangloss teaches that "all's for the best in this best of all possible worlds." The earthquake, famine, rape, and pillage that afflict Candide and his friends are all explained by Dr. Pangloss in terms of positive consequences they have for society. Dr. Pangloss's counterparts in reality are numerous. Voltaire's contemporary, Albert Seybert, for instance, reasoned that swamps are necessary "to keep the atmosphere in a proper degree of purity . . . animals live too fast in atmospheres overcharged with oxygen gas" (cited by Matza, 1969: 56). Valid functional explanations, like valid causal explanations, require systematic evidence of association between independent and dependent variables.

3. *Is the Relationship Between the Variable and Its Consequence Spurious?* As with causal explanation, functional explanation faces challenges from plausible alternative accounts of the same association. For example, while a public execution may increase community solidarity, so might a religious revival or a foreign war. Any given disposition may be satisfied by a variety of "functional alternatives" or "functional equivalents." To the extent that for any given system a large number of interchangeable traits can perform the same function, little explanatory value will be had from a functional analysis.

Confidence may be increased in functional explanations, just as it is with causal explanations, by discovery of the mechanism connecting the variable and its consequence. This in essence was Charles Darwin's major contribution to biology. He took functional explanations of species characteristics and showed *how* the traits and their functions were established through the mechanism of natural selection. For example, the functionalist explains the chameleon's ability to change color from brown to green in terms of the consequence this ability has for camouflaging the lizard from its predators. Darwin showed that connections appear because of natural selection among competing organisms with varying traits. In the long run chameleons unable to change color (or with the capacity to change into inappropriate colors) were eliminated and failed to pass on their defective traits to subsequent generations. Darwin's *Origin of Species* is essentially an extended documentation of this process based on field observation.

While a similar process of natural selection may underlie functional explanations of social organizations, few sociologists have undertaken a serious examination of mechanisms connecting social institutions and their functions.

NATURE OF SCIENTIFIC EXPLANATION: SUMMARY

As we have seen, scientific statements are generally of a high order of abstraction. Unlike many abstract statements, however, scientific propositions must be sufficiently precise to be verified by observed events. The task of verification, however, is by no means simple. We have reviewed some of the main hazards that must be overcome to establish confidence in two common forms of scientific explanation. Given these hazards, the probability that any given statement about law and society (e.g., that executions reduce the homicide rate) is true, must be quite low. The conclusions of any particular study must be taken with a grain of salt (a series of undemonstrable assumptions about the reliability of the measure variables, seriously contaminating variables that have been left out of the analysis, etc.). The qualification must also include the specifics of the data employed, since it is dangerous to overgeneralize from a single jurisdiction or time period. The scientific explanation, then, is distinguished by a recognition of the uncertainty of knowledge, the realization that unknown, unexplained variance will often be substantial. In addition, scientific explanation forces us to recognize problems that have no solution. Unsolvable problems are unknown to conventional imagination, which is never at a loss to conjure up some ad hoc explanation. Scientific imagination is, in contrast, often constrained so that no solution to a problem is possible with the amount and type of information available. For example, we are familiar with impossible problems in algebra, which ask us to find the value of k unknowns but give us fewer than k equations. If $2X + 4Y = 20$, we cannot find a unique value for X or Y. Any number of combinations will satisfy the equation ($X = 8$, $Y = 1$; $X = 2$, $Y = 4$). While this problem is easily recognized in its simplest form, it reappears in more complicated disguises in social research. For example, it appears to be impossible to tell which of two explanations of high levels of violence in the American South is valid because of insufficient information. Cash (1941), Hackney (1969), and others have proposed that the South has historically had a "subculture of violence" that normatively supports the use of dueling, feuding, lynching, and other forms of aggression. The persistence of this tradition, according to these accounts, explains the recent regional variations in rates of violence. Against the subculture explanation, proponents of an economic model of crime causation contend that poverty, urbanization, education, and unemployment work the same way in all regions to affect the level of violence. The South is more violent simply because it is more extreme in these ordinary determinants; there is nothing else special about the region. Choosing between subculture and economic interpretations of Southern violence is difficult given the high correlation between region and economic position. Since most studies use states as the unit of analysis, the number of cases to examine is limited to 50. This limitation makes it impossible to test empirically which of these interpretations is valid on the basis of existing data. Unlike common sense which is seldom at a loss for an explanation, the sociological approach occasionally leaves us stuck with no reasonable solution: there are not enough variables to solve the equation; we do not have enough variability in the available data to draw any conclusions about the effects of one variable on another. Agnosticism is occasionally demanded by the sociological perspective. A critical eye is thus essential. A critical eye, however, is not the same as a cynical eye. Awareness of the hazards of scientific inference should not create a know-nothing attitude, for as philosopher Alfred North Whitehead has said "if men cannot live on bread alone, still less can they do so on disinfectants" (1925: 59). Future discovery of errors in present logic and evidence should be taken as a matter of course. As in the case of aerodynamics and the bumblebee, we learn to work with defective theories.

Having gained a better sense of the nature and limits of the scientific style, let us now consider two alternative styles of analysis that have addressed many of the same substantive issues that will occupy us in this volume. Sociology, as we stressed at the beginning of this chapter, has no monopoly over the subject matter of law and society. We contend, however, that it does provide a special way of thinking about these phenomena. To better understand the special nature of the sociological perspective, it will be useful to contrast it with two alternatives, the literary and ideological styles.

LITERARY APPROACH TO LAW AND SOCIETY

The issues that concern sociologists in their consideration of law and society attract writers of fiction as well. Rather than survey the variety of literary treatments, we will consider one exemplary novel, *The Trial*, by Franz Kafka (1883–1924). Kafka, trained as a lawyer, worked in a government office handling workmen's compensation claims. From this experience with bureaucracy Kafka had nightmare visions of isolated individuals ensnared in a web of meaningless bureaucratic control. The major character of *The Trial*, Joseph K., is a thirty-year-old bank manager who awakens one morning in his rented room to discover that he has been placed under arrest by three policemen. As the police prepare to depart, the Inspector tells K.,

> "You are only under arrest, nothing more. I was requested to inform you of this. I have done so, and I have also observed your reactions. That's enough for today, and we can say good-bye, though only for the time being, naturally. You'll be going to the Bank now, I suppose?"
> "To the Bank?" asked K. "I thought I was under arrest? . . . How can I go to the Bank if I am under arrest?"
> "Ah, I see," said the Inspector, who had already reached the door. "You have misunderstood me. You are under arrest, certainly, but that need not hinder you from going about your business. Nor will you be prevented from leading your ordinary life."
> "Then being arrested isn't so very bad," said K. going up to the Inspector.
> "I never suggested that it was," said the Inspector.
> "But in that case it would seem there was no particular necessity to tell me about it," said K., moving still closer. . . .
> "It was my duty," said the Inspector.
> "A stupid duty," said K. inflexibly.
> "That may be," replied the Inspector, "but we needn't waste our time with such arguments." (Kafka, 1964: 19–20)

Joseph K. thus awakens in a world where law has become an assembly line operation in which each functionary (police officer, lawyer, and judge) performs a highly specialized, detached role.

K. spends the remainder of the novel attempting to find someone in the court bureaucracy (lawyer, court portrait painter, prison chaplain) who can inform him of the reason for his arrest. K. discovers that each actor in the system has a circumscribed duty, which taken in isolation has no meaning whatsoever. The system has furthermore become so specialized that such basic legal concepts as "arrest" no longer mean the same thing within the legal system as they do to the lay individual.

Kafka the novelist has much in common with his contemporary, the sociologist Max Weber. Both drew upon experiences with the same Germanic bureaucracy. Both sought to describe the general features of rational bureaucratic organization. Both constructed abstractions: Weber, the "ideal type," and Kafka, the character Joseph K. However, the devices of characterization, plot development, condensation, and narrative employed by the novelist are quite different from the tools of abstraction employed by the sociologist.

> A literary structure is not a natural structure, like that of a snowflake whose symmetry is unintentional. Whatever relationships its parts bear to one another they bear because they have been deliberately placed in that particular juxtaposition. (Jaffe, 1967: 7)

Thus Kafka develops the exchange between K. and the police in order to create, in particular images, general types of situations in which the protagonist encounters an inversion of crime and punishment (the arrest has been made, but K. does not know for what reason) and in which the protagonist must deal with officials who are ignorant of all but a small fragment of their organization's purpose.

While the novelist and the sociologist differ in the devices they use to explore the general features of concrete human experience, a number of basic similarities underlie their crafts. Thus while statistical analysis of quantitative data appears on the surface to be an entirely different exercise of imagination than the construction of characters, settings, and dialogue, a closer inspection of what the researcher is actually accomplishing reveals a fundamental analogy. The researcher, as Paul Meehl insightfully points out,

> concocts statistically, by the making of certain algebraic "corrections," a virtual or idealized sample, the members of which are fictional persons assigned fictional scores, to wit, the scores the inves-

tigator algebraically infers they would have had on the output variable of interest if the alleged causal influence of the nuisance variable were removed. (1970b: 401)

The literary style of thought thus does not simply transcribe events, but abstracts and reconstructs observations; the difference between literary and scientific styles rests in the particular methodology employed to accomplish a fundamentally similar task.

NORMATIVE APPROACH TO LAW AND SOCIETY

Strictly speaking, a scientific statement only contains claims about facts, whereas a normative statement welds together assertions of fact and value, thus making it possible to move freely from statements about what is to statements about what ought to be. Scientific statements contain no such injunctions.

In contrast to scientific analysis, normative discourse combines both factual and normative styles through ideological concepts, such as *progress*.

> That concept combines certain cognitive assertions about directionality in human history and about the reasons for the directionality with the value assertion that the goal of history's movement is desirable and good. If the cognitive component were removed, there would be no concept of "progress," but simply the pure statement of value that some envisaged future would be desirable. If the value component were removed, there would also be no concept of "progress," but simply the value-neutral cognitive assertion that there is some sort of directionality in human history. The very meaning of the concept depends upon the combination of cognitive and value elements. (Dibble, 1973: 515–16)

Normative statements resemble in form scientific statements in that they are often expressed as generalizations. For example, the following generalizations from John Stuart Mills's essay "On Liberty" spell out implications of a normative position:

> the sole end for which mankind are warranted, individually or collectively, in interfering with the liberty of action of any of their number, is self-protection. That the only purpose for which power can be rightfully exercised over any member of a civilised community, against his will, is to prevent harm to others. His own good,

either physical or moral, is not a sufficient warrant. He cannot right-fully be compelled to do or forbear because it will be better for him to do so, because it will make him happier, because, in the opinions of others, to do so would be wise, or even right. These are good reasons for remonstrating with him, or reasoning with him or per-suading him, or entreating him, but not for compelling him or visiting him with any evil in case he do otherwise. To justify that, the conduct from which it is desired to deter him must be calculated to produce evil to some one else. The only part of the conduct of any one, for which he is amenable to society, is that which concerns others. In the part which merely concerns himself, his independence is, of right, absolute. Over himself, over his own body and mind, the individual is sovereign. (1962: 135)

The style of the analysis exemplified in this passage is altogether different from discussions of individualism that seek to explain the acceptance of the idea by a particular society. From the standpoint of a scientific analysis of the emergence of the doctrine of individ-ualism in Europe in the 1700s, Mills's discussion is too vague; it fails to ask the "right" kinds of questions. We recognize, however, that there is absolutely no reason to expect a compelling normative statement to serve simultaneously as a fruitful analytic tool; we would not ask Abraham Lincoln to make the Gettysburg Address more precise.

In practice, normative and scientific concepts and arguments are often mixed together in a single work. Their mixture, however, is more like that of oil and water than it is like that of oil and vinegar. By confusing ideological concepts (such as blame) with scientific concepts (such as cause) writers are led to mistake value connotations for validity of an argument. One form this error takes is the garden-variety logical fallacy of *ad hominem* argument (lit-erally "to the person"). Rather than examine the substance of the argument, one analyzes the person making the argument. The per-sonal values of many successful natural scientists often provide poor standards by which to evaluate the validity of their theories. Johannes Kepler, for example, was led to formulate an accurate theory of planetary orbits on the basis of his mystical faith in numerology. Newton saw his scientific work as a contribution to Christian theology.[11] The best rule in evaluating scientific argu-ments, it seems, was given by William James: "You shall know them by their fruits, not their roots."[12]

The fruits of the alternative position, which assesses the validity of scientific statements on the basis of their normative connotations, have proved in the past to be bitter. In Germany in the 1930s, the works of Albert Einstein were publicly burned by the Nazis, who believed that the notion of "relativity" was a typically Jewish concept, denying the absolute standards of truth and morality upheld by the German Reich. Moreover, Einstein's work was "Jewish physics," as to be distinguished from "Aryan physics." As German physicist Johannes Stark put it:

> It can be adduced from the history of science that the founders of research in physics, and the great discoverers from Galileo and Newton to the physical pioneers of our own time, were almost exclusively Aryans, predominantly of the "Nordic race." (quoted in Merton, 1968: 608)

Those German physicists who shared Werner Heisenberg's position that Einstein's work was an "obvious basis for further research" were condemned by the Nazis as "white Jews," Aryans who were tragically corrupted by impure ideas (Merton, 1968: 592). The basis of scientific claims was not, therefore, to be decided by testing the empirical consequences of the theory; to suggest this line of inquiry is simply to identify oneself as corrupted. The truth about the nature of the physical world was genetically bestowed on the master race.

About the same time a very similar episode of fact-free, value-guided scientific research was emerging in the Soviet Union. Trofim Denisovich Lysenko (1898–   ) became the administrative head of Soviet agriculture under Stalin. Lysenko, regarded by most biologists outside Russia as a crank, performed experiments in freezing the seeds of spring wheat in an effort to generate a new species of winter wheat. This work had catastrophic practical consequences for Soviet agriculture. It was, however, viewed by the government as being necessarily correct because it was seen to coincide with Marxist-Leninist emphasis on environmental determinants of species characteristics. The followers of Mendel were denounced as bourgeois geneticists; characteristics acquired in the environment *had* to be inherited, and no amount of data to the contrary was entertained from 1948 to 1962. (For more discussion, see Medvedev, 1969).

By evaluating statements according to the "race" of the author or according to the supposedly relevant implications of a political ideology one denies the value of empirical research as an arbiter of the validity of statements about the world.

In this volume we take the position that the validity of statements about facts is independent of value position; the writer's motives, political commitments, ethnic identity, race, and class have no bearing at all on the scientific validity of the argument.[13]

Karl Marx has become such an icon of left-wing polemicists that it comes as a great surprise to discover that he himself rejected the social origins of a theoretical proposition as a basis for determining its *validity*. Thus, Marx

> adopted the labor theory of value from the bourgeois economists
> . . . and made it a cornerstone of his political economy. Had he
> thought the bourgeois origin of this theory invalidates it, he would
> not have accepted it. Further, in the *Theories of Surplus Value* . . .
> Marx devotes nearly two thousand pages to thorough analyses of
> theories advanced mostly by bourgeois economists. Again, he would
> not have undertaken such analyses had he thought that the exposure
> of the social origin of these theories is sufficient to invalidate them.
> His procedure makes clear that whether a theory is acceptable or
> unacceptable must be settled by rational argument. (Husami, 1980:
> 55)

The use of *ad hominem* arguments is a relatively transparent contamination of normative and analytical styles and can generally be recognized and avoided. Much more problematic are the normative connotations of individual concepts. Throughout this volume we will encounter such concepts as "repressive justice," "rational law," "exploitation," "legal equality" and the like. Each of these concepts carries strong overtones of value and meaning that, for our purposes, will constitute excess baggage. To develop statements about the world that can be disconfirmed by evidence, it is necessary to make use of narrowly defined concepts whose meaning is far more restricted than ordinary language allows. We will see, for example, that Max Weber distinguishes *rational* law as that form which relies on explicit rules for arriving at decisions. Now, whether the law or a particular decision is "rational" in a broader sense is a question that must be put aside if we are to pursue Weber's analysis of the relationship between social structure and types of legal decision making. Removing the normative connotations for such words as "rational" or "repressive" and allowing them to denote narrow slices of reality is a difficult task, but one that is essential for sociological analysis.

SUMMARY

Sociology offers a distinctive perspective on law and society, a perspective that demands certain adjustments in the way we think about social phenomena. One criterion of evaluation that most laymen and many professional social scientists use as an arbiter of validity is "the common sense of operative participants in social life" (Matza, 1969: 93n). While willing to acknowledge that common sense was wrong in rejecting Pasteur's germ theory of disease, Copernicus's heliocentric theory of the solar system, and Einstein's theory of relative motion, they feel that common sense is a perfectly valid basis for judging statements about *social reality*, which after all is only subjective reality (e.g., Matza, 1969: 103).

The sociological perspective draws a very sharp distinction between knowledge about and experience of reality, a distinction that is equally significant for social and natural phenomena. We experience the earth as flat and as being the center around which revolve the stars, moon, and sun, even though we know that these perceptions are optical illusions.[14] The same is true, Marx points out, for social reality.

> The recent discovery that the products of labor so far as they are values are but material expressions of the human labor spent in their production . . . by no means dissipates the mist through which the social character of labor appears to us to be an objective character of the products themselves. (Marx, in Tucker, 1978: 322–3)

In other words, we see commodities being exchanged in a market ("having social relations") without any designation of the persons who created them, nor the nature and duration of their labor involved in the creation. The commodity exists on the store shelf totally independent of its human creators. Marx's labor theory of value, however, claims that the value of that commodity is determined by the now invisible amount of human labor that has gone into its production. Even after we accept in our hearts and minds the validity of the labor theory of value, we will, Marx suggests, continue to *experience* commodities as objects independent of human labor and social relations.

This point has two important consequences. First, personal experience is a very poor basis for developing theory. Appearances often have very little to do with reality. What appears to be an equal exchange in a free market may, as Marx points out, conceal the exploitation of worker by employer. What appears to be an attempt to deter wrongdoers by punishing an offender may, as Durkheim suggests, conceal the effort of a community to increase solidarity among its members. (We will examine both of these arguments in more detail later in this book.) Social reality, then, is not necessarily equivalent to experienced reality; by taking the common sense, the taken-for-granted assumptions of actors about their social existence, one is very likely to end up with a distorted conception of how that social organization works.

The second consequence of Marx's point is that having knowledge does not automatically alter experience. To take a simple example, Figure 1.1 shows two lines of equal length. No matter how many times we measure the lines, we will always *see* them as having different lengths.

Similarly, if we come to understand that the consequence of ritually punishing deviants is to shore up the solidarity of our community, there is no reason to assume that this knowledge will overcome our sense of indignation against those particular types of deviant individuals who threaten the groups to which we have strong commitments. Experience does not directly inform knowledge; neither does knowledge necessarily inform experience.

The sociology of law examines the relationship between such components of the legal system as sanctions or procedures and such features of society as stratification or solidarity. The ultimate objective of this discipline is

> a theoretical structure applicable to the laws of the Nazis as well as American law, to revolutionary law and colonial law as well as the cumbersome law of traditional China. (Black, 1973: 31)

It should be recognized that this orientation is but one of several equally viable paths to understanding the relationships between law and society. In this chapter we have sketched in very general terms the attributes that set the sociological approach apart from the alternatives. The next three chapters will develop this orientation by examining how three sociologists addressed specific problems.

FIGURE 1.1
Two Lines of Equal Length

SUGGESTED READING

The distinctive features of scientific explanation are stated clearly by Dibble (1973), whose contrasts among legal, ideological, and scientific styles of discourse are useful for anyone interested in law and sociology. The presentation in the chapter of the logic-of-analysis problem is motivated by Hirschi and Selvin (1966), a review of one variety of error that is recurrent in the delinquency literature. Smelser (1976) presents an accessible introduction to the core ideas of research design based on a presentation of the contributions (and mistakes) of Tocqueville, Durkheim, and Weber. Bierstedt's (1949) critique of empiricism remains one of the best succinct statements on the inevitable role of theory in research. This chapter touches on several complex issues in the philosophy of science. While this serves the purpose of sensitizing the reader to these issues in the later chapters, it falls considerably short in its breadth of coverage. For sociologists one of the best surveys of these issues will be found in Keat and Urry (1975). A very fine brief introduction by a natural scientist is provided by Ziman (1978). Blaug (1980) provides a lucid overview of the philosophy of social sciences. Merton (1972) develops an important argument regarding the role of value positions in social research. The contrast between literary and social scientific approaches is developed by Berger (1977) and Sagarin (1981).

FOOTNOTES

1. This novel insistence on the priority of observation over conjecture is perhaps most clearly epitomized by Isaac Newton, whose law of gravitation explained the orbits of the planets, the acceleration of falling bodies, and the effect of the moon on the tides.

   In developing this theory he saw clearly that the truth of his law depended on confirmation through a verification of its implications. In order to derive these implications, he had invented a new mathematical method, the differential calculus; but all the brilliancy of this deductive achievement did not satisfy him. He wanted quantitative observational evidence and tested the implications through observations of the moon, whose monthly revolution constituted an instance of his law of gravitation. To his disappointment he found that the observational results disagreed with his calculations. Rather than set any theory, however beautiful, before the fact, Newton put the manuscript of his theory into his drawer. Some twenty years later, after new measurements of the circumference of the earth had been made by a French expedition, Newton saw that the figures on which he had based his test were false and that the improved figures agreed with his theoretical calculations. It was only after this test that he published his law. (Reichenbach, 1951: 100–101)

2. Compare Lakatos (1978: 5–6):

   in a progressive research programme, theory leads to the discovery of hitherto unknown novel facts. In degenerating programmes, however,

> theories are fabricated only in order to accommodate known facts. Has, for instance, Marxism ever predicted a stunning novel fact successfully? Never! It has some famous unsuccessful predictions. It predicted the absolute impoverishment of the working class. It predicted that the first socialist revolution would take place in the industrially most developed society. It predicted that socialist societies would be free of revolutions. It predicted that there will be no conflict of interests between socialist societies. Thus the early predictions of Marxism were bold and stunning but they failed. Marxists explained all their failures; they explained the rising living standards of the working class by devising a theory of imperialism; they even explained why the first socialist revolution occurred in industrially backward Russia. They "explained" Berlin 1953, Budapest 1956, Prague 1968. They "explained" the Russian-Chinese conflict. But their auxiliary hypotheses were all cooked up after the event to protect Marxian theory from the facts. The Newtonian programme led to novel facts; the Marxian lagged behind the facts and has been running fast to catch up with them.

While Lakatos's critical evaluation of some Marxists may be accurate, the predictions he enumerates do not follow from Marx's theory in any clear fashion. Chapter 2 attempts to show that there is more in the Marxian tradition than myopic prophecy and limited ad hoc accounts. Lakatos's observation is useful, however, in calling attention to the fundamental feature of a scientific (or "progressive") research program: its ability to generate a range of testable implications that receive better confirmation than alternative plausible explanations of the same phenomena.

3. For example, English philosopher Thomas Hobbes (1588–1679) argued that human nature being selfish and violent naturally leads to a state of anarchy, "a war of all against all." Organized society therefore is the result of a social contract among people who willingly give up some of their autonomy to a coercive state (preferably a monarch) in order to avoid riot and mayhem. Some contemporary writers seek to trace sociological theories of Marx and Durkheim to their alleged roots in such social theories. Thus Horton (1966) links Marx to Hobbes and Durkheim to Rousseau (cf. Turk, 1976b). We agree with Giddens (1976) that this orientation neglects the major break with social philosophy that Marx and Durkheim made in their sociological work (cf. Kuhn, 1962: 75–6).

4. This standard is summarized by Hirschi and Selvin (1966) as "False criteria 2. Insofar as a factor is not characteristic of delinquents, it is not a cause of delinquency." The example they give is fairly representative of the form this fallacy frequently takes in the literature:

> Again, ecological studies showing a high correlation between residence and interstitial areas and delinquency, as compared with lower rates of delinquency in other areas, overlook the fact that even in the most marked interstitial area nine-tenths of the children do not become delinquent. (Barron, 1954: 86–7)

5. To determine the deterrent effects of capital punishment we must examine a large number of cases, which will allow for eliminating plausible alternative explanations of variations in the rate of homicide. This task is quite complex, and Ehrlich's (1975a) estimates should properly be taken as highly tentative conclusions. The point of this example, then, is not that Ehrlich's conclusions about the deterrent effects of the death penalty are correct, but that these conclusions cannot be intelligently judged on the basis of the fact that the estimated effect is small. (For discussion of the controversy surrounding Ehrlich's estimates, see Ehrlich and Redlich, 1979; McGahey, 1980; Blumstein, Cohen, and Nagin, 1978.)

6. Some sociologists labor under the mistaken impression that "science is a search for universally applicable propositions that can be refuted by tests" (Turkel, 1979: 29) or that natural science "seeks after universally valid, highly formalized laws" (Applebaum, 1978: 74). These writers suppose that such universal, exceptionless laws are common in the natural sciences and that their absence in social scientific investigations signals the need for altogether different methods, in which "the focus is on particular cases and careful comparisons and not on broad generalization" (Turkel, 1979: 729) or which "straddle the methodological schism between the ideographic and nomothetic approaches to social phenomena" (Applebaum, 1977: 72). These methods involve an abandonment of empirical research as a criterion for assessing theories, a reduction *ad absurdum* easily reached if one is unaware of the role of scope conditions in formulating generalizations.

7. Such scope conditions are used routinely without being labeled as such. This often creates confusion. For instance, Marx wrote that as capitalism developed, poverty increased. This tendency is "the absolute general law of capitalist accumulation. Like all other laws it is modified in its working by many circumstances." (Marx, in Tucker, 1978: 430). Failure to recognize that the second sentence is a scope condition has often created confusion.

> Anti-Marxists have always maintained the falsity of this law and have deduced from this the incorrectness of Marx's analysis of capitalism. Some Marxists, on the other hand, have been equally concerned to demonstrate the truth of the law, and so a controversy producing much heat and little light has raged for more than a half century. (Sweezy, 1942: 19)

The apparent contradiction in Marx's statement, Sweezy points out, arises from failure to recognize that by "absolute" Marx means "abstract" not "exceptionless" or "invariant." Like the laws of natural science, Marx's economic laws apply only within certain general circumstances.

8. The method of apt and isolated illustration has always been a problem in the social sciences. For example, Emile Durkheim criticized this device in a book on the Marxist theory of history:

Here is a law which pretends to be the key to history! To demonstrate it, a few sparse, disjoined facts are cited, facts which do not constitute any methodical series and the interpretation of which is far from being settled: primitive communism, the struggles of the patricians and the plebians, of the common people and the nobility, are advanced as having economic explanations. Even when a few examples borrowed from the industrial history of England are added to these rare documents, rapidly passed in review, they will not have succeeded in demonstrating a generalization of such magnitude. On this issue Marxism is at variance with its own principle. It begins by declaring that social life depends upon causes which escape awareness and conscious reason. But then, in order to get at these causes, one would have to employ procedures at least as indirect and at least as complex as those used in the natural sciences: all sorts of observations, experiments, and laborious comparisons would be necessary to discover a few of these factors in isolation, let alone to attempt to obtain at present a single representation of them. And here we are, in a twinkling, with all these mysteries clarified and with a simple solution to these problems which human intelligence appeared so hard pressed to penetrate! (1978: 129–9)

9. Failure to read the *tables* in the Piliavin and Briar article has over the years produced mythical overinterpretations of their results. For example, Joseph Gusfield condenses their findings this way:

    Juveniles apprehended by the police received more lenient treatment, including dismissal, if they appeared contrite and remorseful about their violations than if they did not. This difference in the posture of the deviant accounted for much of the differential treatment favoring middle class "youngsters" as against lower-class "delinquents." (1967: 179)

10. For example, Chambliss and Seidman (1982: 132) argue that "the consequence (function) of a social fact does not explain its existence, except teleologically."

11. These issues are, of course, the proper domain of intellectual history and biography. To assess the validity of a theorist's propositions on the basis of his philosophical or political positions is an open invitation to capricious and nonsensical judgments. For example, both Durkheim and Marx adhered to the prevalent nineteenth century doctrines of phrenology. "Karl Marx always judged the mental qualities of a stranger from the shape of his head" (Davies, 1955: 39) and Durkheim's opinions on the subject are well known (e.g., Durkheim, 1964: 57–8).

12. The controversy surrounding the relationship between value commitments and empirical analysis is complex and multifaceted. This discussion does not address these issues in any comprehensive fashion, but merely argues against the position that valid factual statements can be derived from value positions. As we will see later in examining "white collar crime" and bias in criminal sentencing, the practice of confusing empirical analysis with value positions is quite widespread, especially in its tacit forms. All three of our classical theorists rejected

this practice, and Chapter 1 seeks to outline the major objections contained in their work.

Rejecting the idea that fact statements may be derived from value positions, however, does not logically entail solutions to other facets of the fact-value relationship. For instance, Marx and Durkheim held that reliable statements of fact could provide the basis for choosing between competing value positions. Weber, however, maintained that value preferences can never follow unambiguously from valid statements of fact (for a clear presentation of this debate, see Giddens, 1971: 205–23).

Similarly, by arguing that validity of empirical hypotheses can be settled apart from the investigator's value position in principle does not deny the role that values play for particular investigators in the errors they make in observation and inference or in the nature of problems they select for investigation. Significant biases are frequently built into a body of knowledge by the hidden agendas in the selection of problems.

We leave to more comprehensive treatments discussion of this range of issues that surround the fact-value relationship.

13. Arthur Stinchcombe (1978) provides a good illustration of this fundamental principle. He contrasts the theories of revolution written by Leon Trotsky, organizer of the Red Army in the Russian Revolution, and Alexis de Tocqueville, a conservative French aristocrat. While totally opposite on the political spectrum and a century apart, both Trotsky and Tocqueville were competent analysts who drew surprisingly similar conclusions about revolutionary processes. In general, we would argue that to the extent analysts are competent, they will arrive at the same conclusion.

Becker and Horowitz develop this theme further in their discussion of the nature of "radical sociology." They suggest that

> good sociology is often radical. A sociology which is not good, however, cannot be radical in any larger sense. But moral sentiments do not determine scientific quality. The reverse is more often true: the quality of sociological work determines the degree to which it has a radical thrust.
>
> We insist on the isomorphism between radical sociology and good sociology in order to dissuade those who think political sloganeering can substitute for knowledge based on adequate evidence and careful analysis. (1972: 50)

14. Compare Durkheim's observation:

> Shall we say that the error will dissipate itself as soon as men are conscious of it? But we hardly know that the sun is an immense globe; we see it only as a disc of a few inches. This information can teach us to interpret our sensations; it cannot change them. (Durkheim, 1964: 101)

2

Substance of Law and Mode of Production: Some Contributions of Karl Marx to the Sociology of Law[1]

In 1954 the U.S. Supreme Court in *Brown* v. *The Board of Education* unanimously ordered the nation's public schools to desegregate their classrooms. The *Brown* decision has come to be viewed by many observers as marking the beginning of the Civil Rights Revolution, a combination of court decisions, legislation, and social activism that changed dramatically the status of black people in the United States and inspired imitative social protests among women, gays, American Indians, and other oppressed groups. The *Brown* decision furthermore symbolizes for many the power of law to institute major social change; it suggests that law is an effective instrument in the hands of those powerful enough or clever enough to gain control over it. If legal activism can produce quickly such major changes in the status of black Americans, there is seemingly no limit to the role law can play in eliminating discrimination, preserving the environment, or protecting consumers.

Such optimistic assessments of the success of civil rights law and of the potential role of law in effecting social change are, however, incongruent with both recent events and past history.[2] The Civil Rights Revolution produced a mixed pattern of success and failure. While the *Brown* decision serves as a symbolic turning point in civil rights, its actual impact on school desegregation has been mixed. While more dramatic changes in segregation were achieved by law in the areas of voting, public accommodations, housing, and employment, the success has been neither continuous nor uniform. The record of the recent past makes all the more ominous the lessons of the distant past. After the Civil War, Congress enacted Constitutional amendments and civil rights legislation designed to ensure equal protection of the laws for the former slaves. The language of these civil rights laws is in many cases virtually identical to the language of the civil rights laws of the 1960s. If law were an effective instrument of social change, why did the civil rights revolution of the 1870s fail? What is to prevent the civil rights laws of the 1960s from falling into similar misuse and neglect?

To begin to address such questions, we need a general understanding of the relationship between legal change and social change that goes beyond the naive belief that legal activism alone is sufficient to effect change. One source of such an understanding is the work of Karl Marx, who developed a general theory of the relationship between law and social structure and who, in addition, analyzed the sources and consequences of an earlier civil rights movement, the political emancipation of European Jews around 1800. This chapter outlines the basic ideas in Marx's approach to law. We will see how Marx explained the Jewish emancipation as a consequence of economic change. We will then apply this analysis to the civil rights revolutions of American blacks in the 1870s and 1960s. While we will not by this exercise be in a position to prophesy the fate of civil rights in the years to come, we will gain a better understanding of the social structures that sustain civil rights law. In addition we will explore some of Marx's seminal ideas, which, as we will see in Part II of this volume, will prove to be highly useful in thinking about other aspects of law and society.

BASE AND SUPERSTRUCTURE

For Marx, law is not to be understood as an independent entity nor to be explained in terms of ideas; instead, law is to be understood by examining its "roots in the material conditions of life." In an essay published in 1859 he concisely states the relationship between law and material conditions in the following terms:

The general result at which I arrived and which, once won, served as a guiding thread for my studies, can be briefly formulated as follows:

In the social production which men carry on, they enter into definite relations that are indispensible and independent of their will; these relations of production correspond to a definite stage of development of their material forces of production. The sum total of these relations of production constitutes the economic structure of society—the real foundation, on which rise legal and political superstructures and to which correspond definite forms of social consciousness. The mode of production in material life determines the general character of the social, political and spiritual processes of life. It is not the consciousness of men that determines their existence, but, on the contrary, their social existence determines their consciousness. (Tucker, 1978: 4)

Let us look more closely at the three central variables introduced in this passage: forces of production, relations of production, and superstructure.

Forces and Relations of Production

In Marx's terminology the mode of production, the way in which goods are produced and exchanged, consists of two components: forces and relations.

By *forces of production* Marx meant the material aspects of economic activity, including the nature of the task, the level of technology, and the type of skill. A productive force (a tool, skill, or resource) is thus some capacity that contributes directly to production. Some activities, such as police and fire protection, defense against foreign invasion, and the building of public highways contribute to economic production indirectly by making production easier. We will, however, avoid many dead ends by carefully distinguishing between directly "productive forces" and these secondary factors that do not play an immediate, necessary role in production.

The forces of production are "the material basis of all social organization" (Marx, 1967: 372n). In other words, the forces of production determine the *social relations of production*, the manner in which the forces of production are distributed and controlled. At the immediate site of production—the assembly line, the machine shop, the laboratory, the construction site—a characteristic pattern of social relations develops around such questions as: Who decides when to start and stop work? Who owns the tools, machines, and resources? Who decides when and how to modify the task being performed? Who determines the distribution of the economic rewards of the enterprise? Production creates issues of ownership and control, and the way in which those issues are resolved gives rise to a class structure. The first basic idea in Marx's model, then, is that forces of production of a given type will give rise to characteristic class structures.

For example, nineteenth century United States southern cotton agriculture was characterized by a low level of technology and a heavy reliance on unskilled labor. This combination of forces of production resulted in a class structure consisting of a small elite of landlords and a mass of subservient landless workers. At the same time, midwestern wheat farming utilized technology (such as the mechanical reaper introduced in 1834), which made possible efficient production by small, independent farmers. Beyond observing such correlations between forces and relations of production, Marx's analysis suggests that systematic variations will be found between these two variables regardless of political and social ideology (for examples, see Stinchcombe, 1961; Paige, 1975). Thus, although the Soviet Union is far from the American South ideologically, there are some very curious similarities between the cotton-growing regions of the two areas. The Soviet cotton region located north of Afghanistan is populated by Moslem Turkic groups who work the fields under the supervision of a minority of Slavic supervisors, a situation reminiscent of race relations in the American South (Hodnett, 1974). Marxian base-superstructure theory predicts that insofar as two such areas have the same forces of production, their social relations of production will be similar, and their superstructures will, in the long run, converge.[3]

Relations of Production and Superstructures

Relations of production give rise in turn to "noneconomic" superstructures of society: politics, religion, and law. The superstructure does more than reflect the relations of production; it exercises its own influence over the relations and forces of production. This influence is obvious when we consider the impact of a scientific invention or discovery, such as the semiconductor, on the economy. Marxists have always had a very difficult time thinking about how the superstructure could affect the base, while at the same time maintaining that the base determines the superstructure. Among the solutions proposed,[4] we find the following, by the British philosopher Gerald Cohen, to be the clearest:

> If production relations require legal expression for stability, it follows that the foundation requires a superstructure. This seems to violate the architectural metaphor, since foundations do not normally need superstructures to be stable. We must be careful if we are looking for a visual image to go with the metaphor. One slab resting on another would be inappropriate. One correct picture is the following.
>
> Four struts are driven into the ground, each protruding the same distance above it. They are unstable. They sway and wobble in winds of force 2. Then the roof is attached to the four struts, and now they stay firmly erect in all winds under force 6. Of this roof one can say: (i) it is supported by the struts, and (ii) it renders them more stable. There we have a building whose base and superstructure relate in the right way. (1978: 231)

Another way to look at the relationships between base and superstructure is in the form of a causal model,[5] as illustrated in Figure 2.1.

Marx's suggestion that the "relations of production correspond to material forces of production" is represented as a causal effect, arrow a. Similarly, Marx's argument that "the mode of production ... determines the [superstructure]" is represented as arrow b.[6] Note that superstructure and relations of production are influenced by exogenous variables e_s and e_r, which represent the factors that lie "outside" the variables specified by the model, which give rise to the exceptions or deviant cases. This model, then, claims that while major, systematic changes are determined in the manner specified, the base-superstructure model does not account for all of the variations in these variables.[7] This, in essence, captures Engels's statement, that

> without making oneself ridiculous it would be a difficult thing to explain in terms of economics the existence of every small state in Germany, past and present, or the origin of High German consonant shifts. (Engels, in Tucker, 1978: 761)

This acknowledgment of exogenous variables does not, however, mean that the model only claims that "everything is related to everything else." The causal directions a and b are asserted to be primary, while the exogenous factors are assumed to be unsystematic.

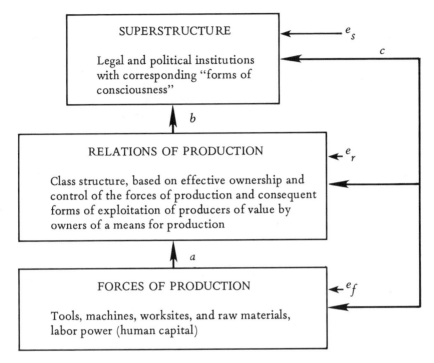

FIGURE 2.1
Marx's Base-Superstructure Model

The arrow labeled c represents the "feedback" from super-structural elements, such as law, to the economic base. While it is true that "the hand-mill gives you society with the feudal lord; the steam mill, society with the industrial capitalist" (Marx, 1963: 122), it is also true that changes in the law governing property rights over water power gives you society with waterpowered industrial mills. Concretely, the Massachusetts mill acts of the early 1800s gave mill owners the right to flood adjoining land, subject to annual payment of damages to the land owner for the loss of her or his productive value in the immersed land. The earlier common law rights of land owners (to sue for punitive damages or to tear down the offending dam) placed a roadblock to the development of productive forces in the form of large cotton and paper mills (Horwitz, 1977: 31–53). The base-superstructure model, thus, takes into account the potential for law to facilitate (or inhibit) the growth of the forces of production.

The effect of the relations of production on the superstructure (arrow *b*) will on the average be much larger than the effect of the superstructure on the base (arrow *c*). In other words, *major* social transformations will only occur through prior transformation of the economic base. Attempts to change the social formation through superstructural change—rewriting constitutions, passing statutes, and the like—will have no major effect on society.

Utopian Socialism

Since much debate revolves around various interpretations of the base-superstructure model, it may be useful to consider the general model in light of Marx' and Engels' specific critique of "utopian socialism."[8] In contrast to utopian socialism, Marx and Engels argued that scientific socialism begins with the "real factors," the mode of production, and builds its program of action on thorough analyses of the present system, its nature, operation, contradictions, and tendencies. The state of development of productive forces at any given moment in history sets limits on the range of political action that will be viable.[9] Just as "Don Quixote long ago paid the penalty for wrongly imagining that knight errantry was compatible with all economic forms of society" (Marx, 1967: 94n), so no one with a scientific understanding of capitalism in 1850 would spend the time and resources on remote utopian communes.

> Equally naive are the utopian socialists' belief that socialism is the expression of absolute truth, reason and justice and has only to be discovered to conquer all the world by virtue of its own power. (Engels, in Tucker, 1978: 693)

It is not enough, Marx and Engels argue, to be opposed to the capitalist social order. That opposition, to be effective, must be based on a scientific and objective appraisal of that order. The issues raised in this critique are by no means restricted to nineteenth century debates; utopian socialism remains a popular orientation, even among writers who claim to be Marxists. For our purposes, the polemics by Marx and Engels against utopian socialism are primarily of interest because they demonstrate how Marx and Engels applied the base-superstructure model. They believed that any successful political program had to be based on an objective understanding of the existing system. A socialist, for example, must understand how and where exploitation takes place in the capitalist system. A socialist lacking this understanding will chase after non-sensical goals and perhaps divert large segments of the working class toward quixotic adventures. More generally, for Marx and Engels a civil rights statute, a constitutional amendment, a court decision, or some other change in the superstructure will be effective only if there has been a corresponding change in the economic base. Otherwise, the law will become a "dead letter," a "law in the books."

The immediate cause of legal change may indeed be a popular movement, a journalistic exposé or some other event in the superstructure. For the change to succeed, however, the underlying economic base must be compatible. Political practice ignorant of the base and its corresponding superstructural requirements inevitably will be "utopian." Marx expressed the essential idea most succinctly when he wrote that

> men make their own history, but they do not make it just as they please; they do not make it under circumstances chosen by themselves, but under circumstances directly found, given and transmitted by the past. (Tucker, 1978: 595)

To provide a scientific basis for action, Marx contends, it is necessary to seek out those objective circumstances.

Modes of Production and Their Combinations

While *mode of production* is the key to understanding these objective circumstances, this concept is not fully developed in Marx's work and has been used in various ways by his followers. Many Marxists think of modes of production in terms of unilinear evolutionary sequences, such as ancient-feudal-capitalist-socialist. England after 1066 was feudal, according to this view, while France after 1789 was capitalist. Such dating may be a useful didactic device for retaining the theory in short-term memory, but it leads to wholesale misinterpretations of reality. Modes of production coexist and do not display any necessary time order of development.[10]

Table 2.1 surveys some of the principal modes of production in a schematic fashion. Each is defined in terms of the class relations surrounding the ownership of the means of production. This list is by no means exhaustive; the typology of mode of production will necessarily depend upon the concrete historical society in which one is interested. For example, Hechter and Brustein (1980) show

TABLE 2.1
Modes of Production: A Representative Typology

Mode of Production	Economic Actors	Owns Labor Power	Owns Means of Production (investments, resources)	Controls Labor Power of Others
Slavery	owner	yes	yes	yes
	slave	no	no	no
Feudalism	lord	yes	yes	yes
	serf	limited	limited	no
Capitalism	bourgeois	yes	yes	yes
	wage worker	yes	no	no
Petty Bourgeois	petty bourgeois	yes	yes	limited
	wage worker	yes	no	no
Primitive	independent producer	yes	yes	no

SOURCE: Adapted from Wright (1979: 40) and G. A. Cohen (1978: 65).

that by 1100 Western Europe had developed three distinguishable modes of production. In northeastern Europe a *sedentary pastoral* mode of agricultural production predominated. Here self-sufficient subsistence farmers lived in small hamlets, growing their crops on family plots. In southern Europe a *petty commodity mode* of production developed around villages and towns whose residents developed more extensive and diversified agriculture, use of a light scratch plow, and production for market rather than subsistence. In certain interior regions of Europe (the English Midlands, Burgundy, Madrid) the *feudal* mode of production emerged. Under feudalism, land was divided into strips cultivated by using a heavy wheeled plow; the technology and organization of production favored more consolidated landholding than the other two modes of production and corresponding superstructures.[11] In political development the feudal system gave rise to consolidated state power and eventually predominated over the other two modes.

The modes of production in medieval Europe illustrate that "region, a territory defined in terms of the homogeneity of its mode of production, is the optimal unit of analysis rather than any unit circumscribed by a political boundary—such as a state" (Hechter and Brustein, 1980: 1089). A persistent mistake of many writers is to take the nation state as the unit of analysis and, moreover, to equate one nation state (e.g., the United States) with "capitalism," ignoring not only the unique features of the United States that place it on a range of variation among capitalist nations, but also the regional variations in dominant modes of production that produce a wide range of internal variations in the forms of law.[12]

TRANSITION FROM FEUDAL TO CAPITALIST MODES OF PRODUCTION

Marx developed the general model of base and superstructure in his effort to understand the birth of modern industrial society. For Marx this birth involved a transition in the forces and relations of production from a feudal to a capitalist mode of production. Neither Marx nor any subsequent investigator has been able to explain adequately how this transformation took place.[13] Our primary concern, however, is not the antecedents of the transition, but its consequences for legal change. Around the late 1600s we see a very striking change taking place in the economic life of England and certain other regions within Western Europe. This change in production and commerce evolves into an era beginning in the late 1700s that we now identify as "the Industrial Revolution." We will concentrate on three features of developments: the revolution in productive forces, the revolution in relations of production, and the revolution in law. Following the logic of the base-superstructure model, we will see that the third revolution was a response to the other two.

Revolution in the Forces of Production: Pin Making as a Case in Point

The transition from feudal to capitalist modes of production involved first a transformation of the forces of production. Initially the primary change involved the organization of production or division of labor, which massively increased productivity and created the basis for the increasing use of machine technology. To comprehend the nature of these developments, it will be convenient to consider the transformation in a single trade, that of the pin maker (see A. Smith, 1976; Marx, 1967: 370–1; Pratten, 1980).

In the precapitalist, medieval economy of Europe prior to the 1600s people made pins out of wire as the need arose. In the advanced stages of the medieval economy, specialists engaged exclusively in the manufacture of pins. These highly skilled specialists could produce a superior product at a cheaper price than do-it-yourself pin makers working at home. They sold their pins, by and large, to a local isolated market: the town and its immediate vicinity. By the eleventh century the pin makers in the towns banded together into guilds, associations to protect the interests of the occupation by regulating entrance into the trade, setting prices, and establishing norms of quality control. The town guilds of pin makers and other crafts and merchants were sufficiently powerful in the medieval towns to prevent outside competitors from legally selling their particular product.[14] The guilds strove to perfect their crafts, to develop esoteric knowledge that could only be gained by someone training as an apprentice. "[E]ven down into the eighteenth century, the different trades were called 'mysteries'; into their secrets none but the duly initiated could penetrate" (Marx, 1967: 532). An average pin maker could produce no more than twenty pins in a working day; this was not a great number, but it was sufficient to keep the local market satisfied. Production was limited but of high quality.

By the 1660s such forms of economic production began to be undermined by an expansion of trade and commerce. Pin makers along with other producers faced a new situation in which the market for their goods was greatly expanded. As a result, the guild organization of production began to give way to a new form of production based on the division of labor. In place of the skilled workman who had spent years perfecting the craft of making pins, the production of pins was broken down into separate operations, each individual "detail worker" performing a single operation. Thus one person drew the wire, a second straightened the wire and passed it to a third worker who cut it, a fourth who put a point on it, and so on. One such operation employing ten detail workers in the 1770s produced in a given day twelve pounds of pins, which is equivalent to 48,000 pins (A. Smith, 1950: 4). A simple division of labor, then, could increase productivity dramatically. Ten skilled craftsmen producing 200 pins a day were replaced by ten unskilled workers who could each produce 4800 pins in the same time. Furthermore, this change required no new technology. Detail workers in the pin factory used the same tools, machines, and raw materials as the guild craftsmen, but with a division of labor the factory could greatly outproduce the guilds.

The economic consequences of this change are simple to see. Suppose that pins currently sell at $1 because the craftsman needs $20 a day to live. Suppose that Jones hires detail workers at $20 a day. His labor costs are, for ten workers, $200. These workers will produce in a day $4800 worth of pins. Two important points should be apparent. First, Jones is about to become rich overnight. Second, Jones may reduce his price to 90¢ and still make a fabulous profit. By so reducing his price he would drive the guild craftsmen out of the market, forcing them to work as detail laborers. With the guilds demolished, Jones could sell pins for whatever the traffic would bear.

Our fictional case of Jones the capitalist pin maker compresses, in fact, the early history of manufacturing in England. Such innovations in the organization or production, particularly in textiles, led to an explosive increase in production and made fortunes for the entrepreneurs overnight. For example,

In 1789 an ex-draper's assistant like Robert Owen could start with a borrowed 100 pounds in Manchester; by 1809 he bought out his partners in the New Lanark Mills for 84,000 pounds *in cash*. And his was a relatively modest story of business success. (Hobsbawm, 1962: 54)

As more entrepreneurs were enticed into the new economic system, competition became fierce. So many pins, for example, were produced by the capitalist manufacturer with his division of labor that not even the new expanding markets could possibly absorb them all. As the bottom fell out of the price of pins, they were transformed from luxury goods for the rich to commonplace possessions of the masses.

For the capitalist the only way to stay ahead of the game was to become more efficient. Detail workers were pushed to produce more. The fourteen-hour working day became the norm and whole families were recruited into the work of the factory. To remain competitive, however, further innovation was necessary.

The bourgeoisie cannot exist without constantly revolutionizing the instruments of production, and thereby the relations of production, and with them the whole relations of society. Conservation of the old modes of production in unaltered forms, was, on the contrary, the first condition of existence for all earlier industrial classes. Constant revolutionizing of production, uninterrupted disturbance of all social conditions, everlasting uncertainty and agitation distinguish the bourgeois epoch from all earlier ones. All fixed, fast-frozen relations, with their train of ancient and venerable prejudices and opinions, are swept away, all new-formed ones become antiquated before they can ossify. All that is solid melts into air, all that is holy is profaned, and man is at last compelled to face with sober senses, his real conditions of life, and his relations with his kind. (Marx, in Tucker, 1978: 476)

At this point technology became a major factor in the Industrial Revolution. The major technological innovations of the early Industrial Revolution were quite simple (Hobsbawm, 1962: 48; Marx, in Tucker, 1978: 391). The steam engine, to take the most famous symbol of industrial technology, was not a sophisticated product of the genius of James Watt. Centuries before Watt the Greeks had invented steam engines to open and close temple doors. Steam power was, for the Greeks, a toy capable of providing amusement and awe. Their economy, based on the efficient exploitation of slave labor, had no practical use for this clever gimmick.

Indeed, the whole frantic enterprise of the Industrial Revolution makes no sense to the precapitalist mind. The legal superstructure and social consciousness of medieval society worked in concert to prevent novel ways of organizing economic activities. With the rise of capitalism, economic action was no longer embedded in a larger way of life but became market-oriented, providing unparalleled wealth for the clever and imaginative.

Revolution in Relations of Production

Marx attempted to show that this shift from feudal to capitalist forces of production caused a corresponding shift in the social relations of production and to show how the economic transformation ultimately brought about changes in the form of law.

The first question to address, then, is, How do the social relations in a capitalist economic system differ from the social relations in feudal society? Marx noted that both feudal and capitalist societies have classes. Feudal society had masters and apprentices in the shops and lords and serfs on the land. The capitalist society has capitalists and workers. In feudal society the master owned the tools and machines; he made the decisions about what was to be produced and at what price it was to be sold. In capitalist society those basic production decisions are made by the capitalist.

In feudal society the subordinates were required to turn over a given proportion of their production to the master or lord. Craftsmen had to work for a certain period under a master; all their production belonged to him. After serving an apprenticeship they became masters in their own right. A similar arrangement developed for serfs working the land. A fixed amount of time or a fixed proportion of their crop belonged to the lord. The exploitation (that is to say, the appropriation of the product of one class by another) was clearly and explicitly defined in feudal society. Should a serf or journeyman object to these conditions, the master or lord resorted to force. Such coercion, however, was tempered somewhat by the long-term obligations that provided economic security in the guild or manor. Furthermore, the serf or journeyman was entitled to keep whatever additional goods were produced beyond the obligation.

The situation of the workers under capitalism is altogether different. As detail workers they are unskilled and own neither tools nor machines of production. The capitalist supplies all of this, organizes production, determines output, and sets prices. The detail workers sell their *labor power*, their capacity to provide so many hours of useful effort. If a capitalist pays for a day's labor power, "then the right to use that power for a day belongs to him, just as much as the right to use any other commodity, such as a horse that he has hired for the day" (Marx, in Tucker, 1978: 350). Whether the capitalist gets his or her money's worth (in the sense of making a profit) is dependent upon how the rented labor or horse power is used.

Suppose that Jones initially sold pins for $1 each and that he paid his unskilled workers $20 in wages, for, let us say, an eight-hour day, or $2.50 an hour. In an eight-hour working day Smith would produce, in conjunction with his fellow detail workers, $4800 worth of pins. The difference between Smith's $20 wage and the $4800 value he produced was what Marx referred to as *surplus value*, the true source of the capitalist's profit.[15]

For Marx, this particular form of exploitation is the key to understanding the peculiar features of capitalist law. Exploitation in capitalism is uniquely hidden from view, from both the worker *and* the capitalist.[16] Capitalism's exploitation is not clear and explicit in the way exploitation has been in feudalism. The working day, the year, or the career is not divided up into wage and surplus value periods "nor is the turning over of surplus value directly coerced. The silent compulsion of economic relations affixes the seal to capitalist rule over the worker. It is true that the immediate extra-economic force is still used, but only as an exception" (Marx,

1967: 737). The wage worker does not directly exchange the commodities she or he produces as did the feudal serf or apprentice. Rather, the wage worker sells a specified duration (e.g., eight hours) of labor power to the capitalist.[17] The capitalist then must employ that labor time in such a way as to both recoup the original labor cost and make a profit from the product of the worker's labor. The length of the normal working day therefore becomes the object of negotiation between worker as seller and employer as buyer of labor power. Beyond the normal working day lies "overtime," for which the worker generally is paid time-and-a-half or double-time wages. Workers are generally glad to get overtime, since they get paid more for the "same work."[18] While they also recognize that it is in management's interest to be paying them more, nothing in the wage contract, the time clock, or the W-2 form indicates to either workers or capitalists where the surplus value begins and the wage equivalent ends.

Marx makes a subtle point about the wage contract, which is absolutely crucial for understanding the economic basis of capitalist law: Capitalists and workers make these wage agreements in a free market.[19] Labor must be free to move to another employer to get a better wage. Capital must be free to hire and fire according to the demand in the market for its commodity. The value of all commodities is determined by the value of the labor invested in their production and in a free market *all* commodities exchange *at their value.* This means that the value of the labor power is not determined by the value that a worker produces during the working day. The amount of value a worker produces is determined by the use the capitalist makes of the labor power he or she has purchased. The value of the labor power is determined by the value of the goods and services that have gone into *its* production. In other words, in order to maintain a worker capable of putting in a full eight-hour day, a certain minimum amount of food, clothing, shelter, and recreation must be provided on a daily basis. This "daily bread," then, is the value of the labor power. The capitalist makes a profit not in the wage contract, since the capitalist pays the full value of the labor power. Profit arises in the process of production from the use of labor power. One key consequence of this fact is that the relationship of exploitation remains structurally hidden in capitalism. For the capitalist form of exploitation to succeed, it is therefore essential to have workers who are legally free and equal to the capitalist.

Revolution in Law

In England the new entrepreneurs were able to redirect state policy toward the ideal of *laissez faire* (literally "let alone"), the principle that the economy best serves the common good with minimal governmental interference or regulation. Adam Smith has given us the best statement of this ideal:

> Every individual endeavors to employ his capital so that its produce may be of greatest value. He generally neither intends to promote the public interest, nor knows how much he is promoting it. He intends only his own security, only his own gain. And he is in this led by an invisible hand to promote an end which was no part of his intention. By pursuing his own interest he frequently promotes that of society more effectually than when he really intends to promote it. (1950: 421)

In Adam Smith's social philosophy the greatest good for the greatest number paradoxically arises out of individual self-centeredness and greed.[20] The ideology of individualism and the free market, then, became a weapon in the battle between the rising capitalist class of manufacturers and merchants and the guilds, landed aristocrats, and other remnants of the feudal order.[21] The new mode of production, thus, gave rise to new political and legal ideals.

Marx's argument links modes of production to legal systems in two ways, functionally and causally. The functional relationships entail the ways in which a particular form of legality serves to maintain or reproduce the relationships between classes in a particular mode of production.

> The exchange of commodities of itself implies no other relations of dependence than those which result from its own nature. On this assumption, labour-power can appear upon the market as a commodity only if . . . its possessor, the individual whose labour-power it is, offers it for sale . . . as a commodity. In order that he may be able to do this, he . . . must be the untrammelled owner of his capacity for labour, i.e., of his person. He and the owner of money meet in the market, and deal with each other as on the basis of equal rights, with this difference alone, that one is buyer, the other seller; both therefore, equal in the eyes of the law. The continuance of this relation demands that the owner of the labour-power should sell it for only a definite period, for if he were to sell it rump and stump, once for all, he would be selling himself, converting himself from

a free man into a slave, from an owner of a commodity into a commodity. (Marx, 1967a: 186)

The free market in which labor power wages are exchanged at their value is, Marx writes,

a very Eden of the innate rights of man. There alone rule Freedom, Equality, Property and Bentham. Freedom, because both buyer and seller of a commodity, say of labor-power, are constrained only by their own free will. They contract as free agents, and the agreement they come to, is but the form in which they give legal expression to their common will. Equality, because each enters into relation with the other, as with a simple owner of commodities, and they exchange equivalent for equivalent. Property because each disposes only of what is his own. And Bentham, because each looks only to himself. The only force that brings them together and puts them in relation to each other, is the selfishness, the gain, the private interest of each. (Tucker, 1978: 343)

Individual equality is thus a functionally necessary precondition for the operation of a capitalist mode of production based upon the extraction of surplus labor through wage contracts. Freedom of the individual is a prerequisite for capitalist exploitation of labor power.

Engels subsequently stated succinctly the functional relationship between bourgeois economy and legal equality:

Trade on a large scale, that is to say, national and even more, international trade, requires free owners of commodities who are unrestricted in their movements and have equal rights as traders to exchange their commodities on the basis of laws that are equal for them all, or at least in each separate place. The transition from handicraft to manufacture presupposes the existence of a number of free workers—free on the one hand from the fetters of the guild and on the other from the means whereby they could themselves utilize their labor power: workers who can contract with their employers for the hire of their labor power, and as parties to the contract have equal rights to his. (1976: 115–16)

The medieval master craftsman could count on traditional obligations to ensure consistency in the behavior of his customers, suppliers, and workers. The capitalist lived in a world which "has pitilessly torn asunder the motley feudal ties that bound man to his 'natural superiors,' and has left remaining no other nexus between man and man than naked self-interest, than callous 'cash payment'"

(Marx and Engels, in Tucker, 1978: 475). This novel situation required changes in the nature of the actors involved in economic transactions. Capitalist law therefore reconstitutes the individual. "Much of the system of commodity exchange . . . is possible only on the basis of far-reaching personal confidence in the loyalty of others" (Weber, 1978: 306). As a consequence, the law of capitalist society places heavier emphasis on the legal conceptions of responsible actors.[22]

Ironically, legal equality in a capitalist system reproduces economic inequality. This paradox of legal equality and economic exploitation has received its best known expression in the ironic formulation by Anatole France:

> Our citizenship is another occasion for pride! For the poor it consists of supporting and maintaining the rich in their power and their idleness. At this task they must labour in the face of the majestic equality of the laws, which forbid the rich and poor alike to sleep under the bridges, to beg in the streets, and to steal their bread. This equality is one of the benefits of the Revolution. (1925: 91)

The functional connection between legal form and productive relations explains why the particular legal form tends to persist over time. In addition Marx offered a causal explanation of the form itself, which explains the peculiar contours of particular legal systems. Legal rules and categories are seen as transformations of corresponding structures in the economic base. To return to the example of bourgeois law, equality is generated by the nature of commodity exchange in a free market.

> Equality and freedom are thus not only respected in exchange based on exchange values but, also, the exchange of exchange values is the productive, real basis of all *equality* and *freedom*. As pure ideas they are merely the idealized expressions of this basis; as developed in juridical, political, social relations, they are merely this basis to a higher power. (Marx, 1971: 245)

Thus the emphasis that bourgeois legality places on equality is a reflection or transposition of equal exchange among free actors that constitutes the market system of the capitalist economy.

Marx's causal argument explains the derivation of bourgeois legal forms, while his functionalist argument explains why these forms persist over time.

MODES OF PRODUCTION AND CIVIL RIGHTS

The basic elements of Marx's theory of the relationship between economic base and legal superstructure thus explains how the transition from feudalism to capitalism transformed Western European law. One key element of that transformation was the creation of civil rights laws. This section will first discuss the Jewish emancipation of the early 1700s in light of Marx's theory and then turn to a more detailed discussion of the civil rights experience of American blacks viewed from this Marxian perspective.

The Jewish Question and the Bourgeois Revolution

Jews migrated to Western Europe in large numbers after Rome forced their diaspora (dispersion) from Palestine in 135 A.D. European Jews retained their separate cultural identity and communal institutions during this exodus. Prohibited by European law from owning land and from entry into many craft occupations, Jews were forced to become an urban people specializing in a narrow range of economic activities.

In the early medieval period the Christian church placed severe restrictions on usury (taking interest on loans) and on profit making in general by Christians. Consequently, Jews found few competitors in trade, commerce, and banking, and they soon came to occupy an important niche in the medieval economy. Kings and nobility, dependent upon the financial skills and resources of the Jewish community, provided protection from the religious prejudices and economic hostility of the general populace.

In the eleventh century this situation changed drastically. The Crusades to recover the Holy Land from Islam, begun in 1095, stimulated trade and commerce. As more European Christians entered banking and commerce, the special position of the Jews declined and, with it, their political protection. The change in their position is most dramatically marked by the decisions of the Fourth Lateran Council of 1215. This church assembly voted to force Jews to reside in ghettos, to enter only a few restricted occupations, and to wear yellow badges when venturing outside their segregated enclaves. In 1290 England expelled its Jewish population, as did France in 1392 and Spain in 1492. Jews joined Christian heretics as objects of mass persecution as Western Europeans came to believe that Jews routinely engaged in blood sacrifices of Christians, especially children. Thus, the belief that [the Jews] murdered Christian children was so wide-spread and so firmly held that not all the protests of popes and bishops—and there were many—could ever eradicate it. . . . And the other stock accusation brought against Jews in medieval Europe—of flogging, stabbing, pulverizing the host—has a similar significance. For if from the point of view of a Jew an atrocity committed on the host would be meaningless, from the point of view of a medieval Christian it would be a repetition of the torturing and killing of Christ. Here too, then, the wicked [Jewish] father is imagined as assaulting the good son; and this interpretation is bourne out of the many stories of how, in the middle of the tortured wafer, Christ appeared as a child, dropping blood and screaming. (Cohn, 1961: 86–7)

As late as 1612 Sir Francis Bacon recommended in his essay "Of Usury" that all Christian usurers "should have tawny orange bonnets, because they do judasize" (Trachtenberg, 1943: 192).

However, in the late 1700s the legal status of Jews in Western Europe changed markedly. They were now not simply accorded the occasional protection of individual patrons, but given full political and legal equality as citizens. Consequently, in 1867 Benjamin Disraeli (1804–1881) became Prime Minister of England, and the Rothschild family, famous for its international banking organization, was made a member of the Hapsburg nobility in 1823 (Hobsbawm, 1962: 234). Various forms of social and economic discrimination against Jews continued on a wide scale throughout this period, but the late 1700s marked a dramatic change in the legal status of Jews in Western Europe.

This change, moreover, was one symptom of a more fundamental legal revolution that occurred in Western Europe in the 1700s as equality replaced inequality as the foundation of law. So familiar is the idea of legal equality today that its recent historical origin is difficult to appreciate. Nonetheless most precapitalist legal codes elaborate status distinctions. One of the greatest philosophers in Western civilization, Aristotle (354–322 B.C.), argued that

it is clear, then, that some men are by nature free, and others slaves, and for these latter slavery is both expedient and right. . . . [Similarly], the male is by nature fitter for command than the female, just as the elder and fullgrown is superior to the younger and more immature. (1921: 1255a, 1259b)

If people are by nature unequal, it is only just that the law explicitly takes into account the inequality of their natures. Aristotle's position is a characteristic feature of most precapitalist law. One of the first legal codes, the Code of Hammurabi, written in Babylonia around 1750 B.C., carefully specifies appropriate differences in the way the law is to treat different social ranks.[23] For example,

> If a man strike another man of his own rank, he shall pay one mana of silver. . . . If a man strike a superior . . . he shall receive 60 strokes with an ox-tail whip.

Novel ideals of the late 1700s challenged these ancient principles of legal inequality:

> The end of every political association is the preservation of the natural and imprescriptable rights of man. . . . These rights are equality, liberty, security and property. (French Declaration of the Rights of Man, 1791)

> We hold these truths to be self-evident, that all men are created equal, that they are endowed by their creator with certain unalienable Rights, that among these rights are Life, Liberty and the pursuit of Happiness. (American Declaration of Independence, 1776)

In the late eighteenth century Western Europeans discovered these "universal rights of man." Proclaimed here in the French and American declarations, the same ideas found numerous expressions in constitutions, manifestos, and proclamations of this period. The authors of these statements—men like Thomas Jefferson in America and Abbé Sièyes in France—believed that they were describing timeless, universal, and natural values.

All of the late eighteenth century declarations of human rights conceive of the individual as the basic unit of society, an "independent, autonomous and thus (essentially) nonsocial being" (Dumont, 1965: 15). Men were no longer a king's subjects but were, rather, *citizens*, individuals born free and equal, at least in a legal sense. One paradox of this conception of equality that immediately strikes our attention is the failure of any of these documents to consider half of humanity—women. All *men* are created equal; women continued for over a century to be excluded from the political and property rights given to males; not until 1920 were American women even granted the right to vote. Equally significant is the failure of these declarations to mention slaves. Slave labor, which provided the economic basis of the American South and the French Caribbean colonies, was left untouched by statements that "all men are created equal."[24] Thomas Jefferson, perhaps the most eloquent spokesman for the ideas of individual freedom and equality was himself a Virginia slaveowner (Lynd, 1968).

In his essay "On the Jewish Question" Marx seeks to explain the emancipation of the Jews in Western Europe, the general trend toward legal freedom and equality and the peculiar blind spots in this new ideology. Marx argues that as Western societies moved from feudal to capitalist modes of production, the norm of legal equality began to supplant legal systems based on conceptions of natural differences among people.

> the [capitalist] state abolishes, after its fashion, the distinctions established by *birth, social rank, education, occupation,* when it decrees that [these factors] are non-political distinctions; when it proclaims, without regard to these distinctions, that every member of society is an *equal* partner in popular sovereignty, and treats all the elements which compose the real life of the nation from the standpoint of the state. But the state, nonetheless, allows private property, education, occupation, to *act* after *their* own fashion . . . and to manifest their *particular* nature. Far from abolishing these *effective* differences, the [capitalist] state only exists so far as they are presupposed. (Marx, in Tucker, 1978: 33)

In other words, the civil rights revolution is one legal consequence of the shift from a feudal to a capitalist economic system. Equality in the law is a by-product of the capitalist mode of production.[25] In general,

> it is only possible to achieve real liberation in the real world . . . by employing real means. . . . Slavery cannot be abolished without the steam engine and the mule and spinning-jenny, serfdom cannot be abolished without improved agriculture. . . . "Liberation" is a historical and not a mental act, and it is brought about by historical conditions, the development of industry, commerce, agriculture. . . . (Marx and Engels, in Tucker, 1978: 16)

As a consequence of the general emphasis on legal equality, the traditional forms of discrimination against Jews were eliminated. Jewish emancipation followed the French army through Europe and receded with their defeat. In Holland, where the capitalist class was highly developed, emancipation for the Jews was well established. As bourgeois revolutions advanced in Western Europe, the old barriers against the Jews were eliminated. Eastern Europe, however, remained largely untouched by the bourgeois revolutions, and there the medieval pattern of chronic discrimination and periodic persecution continued into the nineteenth century.

The close correspondence between the advance of capitalism and the emancipation of Jews follows from Marx's analysis of the manner in which the legal system reflects its economic base. In the next section we will examine this connection in more detail to see how well Marx's model explains the experience of black Americans with civil rights.

Civil Rights in the South: The Precapitalist Period

As in the case of Jewish emancipation, the emergence of civil rights for American blacks is to be explained from a Marxist perspective in terms of changes in the dominant modes of production. This discussion begins with an overview of the legal system based on slavery, examines the alterations that took place in the economic base of the South as a consequence of the Civil War, and finally examines the consequences of the economic transformation of southern agriculture in the twentieth century.

Slavery was concentrated in the Black Belt of the American South, a discontinuous band of fertile black soil stretching from East Texas to South Carolina. Within this belt, cotton has traditionally been the major crop. Marxian analysis of southern justice must begin with an examination of cotton agriculture, the social relations generated by this plantation mode of production, and the legal requisites generated by these social relations.

Until recent years several distinctive features characterized the forces of production in cotton agriculture.[26]

Confronted with the necessity of (1) having land plowed and planted, (2) having the plants individually weeded several times during the growing season (three to seven times) and (3) having the cotton picked by hand (three times), the cotton grower had to provide enough total working time to enough laborers to insure that a sufficient number would remain with him or be available when called. (Dillingham and Sly, 1966: 345)

These labor requirements produced in cotton plantations a characteristic form of class structure, consisting of a landowning elite and a mass of landless laborers. Inequality is typically extreme, since the cash crop is exported rather than consumed locally. Luxury goods for the elite are the primary imports, rather than mass consumer goods for the laborers. To preserve this system, land-owners seek to prevent labor from becoming a market commodity. Labor is closely supervised, often in work gangs. The antebellum slave labor system proved to be a highly efficient system for extracting the maximum labor power from numbers of unskilled laborers (cf. Ransom and Sutch, 1977). In the absence of slavery other class relations have appeared that are marked by restrictions on mobility, rights to organize, education, and political power of the production workers. Such systems are also characterized by rigid status distinctions between landowners and workers. Racial or ethnic status differences are frequently used as axes for this distinction; as E. T. Thompson (1975) observes, "plantations breed racism." In all such systems, Marxian theory predicts that the law will embody the status distinctions as a means of maintaining the relations of production, specifically ensuring the continued existence of a subordinate class of unskilled, permanent agricultural laborers.

> In Marxian terms the slave South was prebourgeois in essential respects, but it was far from being feudal. That is, the South rested on a distinct mode of production that was as different from the feudal as from the capitalist. ... That the world market bent the slave economy to its own ends is incontrovertible. In this sense the South certainly was part of the capitalistic world. Slavery ... raised to regional power a prebourgeois ruling class of formidable political strength and military potential. Capitalism may be able to absorb and use prebourgeois ruling economies, but it cannot readily digest prebourgeois ruling classes that are proud and strong enough to reject the role of comprador and retainer. (Genovese, 1972: 340)

The American South, dominated by the plantation mode of production in the cotton belt, sanctioned slavery in its legal institutions and legitimated slavery in its social consciousness.[27] It maintained an uneasy compromise with the other regions of the Union. The Constitution of 1789, which formed the federal union, was based on a compromise that banned further importation of slaves but preserved the ownership rights of existing slaveowners.

The northern and western states, whose economies were based on manufacturing and mechanized family farms, grew increasingly apart from the southern plantation economy, which was in its economic relationships more closely tied to Great Britain than to the other regions of the United States, supplying Britain with most of the cotton for its textile mills and importing cheap manufactured goods. This trade pattern undercut nascent industries in the North and created political conflict between regional economic interests that was combined with increasing opposition in the North and West to slavery (Moore, 1966). This opposition culminated in the Civil War.

Prior to the Civil War of 1861–1865 American law generally supported slavery.[28] Many American states enacted laws designed to restrict the legal rights of blacks, both slaves and free. The laws of slave states forbade teaching slaves to read and write. Slaves generally could not testify in court against a white person, although the courts had great difficulty with this issue (Tushnet, 1975). Persons discovering escaped slaves were required by law to return the slaves. Federal laws were enacted to ensure the return of fugitive slaves even from northern states whose legislatures had decriminalized aiding and abetting escaped slaves. The culmination of the legal definition of the status of slaves came in the 1857 Supreme Court decision, *Dred Scott* v. *Sanford*.[29] In this landmark case Dred Scott, a slave, petitioned for freedom on the grounds that he had illegally been transported into areas of the country in which slavery had been prohibited by law. Not only was Dred Scott's petition denied, but the Court went on to declare that no former slave could ever become a citizen with the right to sue in court and that Congress possessed no Constitutional authority to restrict the movements of slaveowners. While most of the American public remained ambivalent about the slavery issue, the two opposing camps regarded the conflict as a mortal contest. The abolitionist Presidential candidate, Lincoln, won the 1860 election, but he did so by winning only 25 percent of a popular vote split four ways.

The First Civil Rights Revolution: 1870s

The issue of slavery was ultimately resolved by four years of civil war costing over a half a million lives. The war created strong sentiment in the North to protect the newly freed slaves and to penalize the rebellious states. Between 1866 and 1875 Congress enacted eleven laws and three Constitutional amendments designed to secure civil rights for the former slaves. Thus the Thirteenth Amendment, ratified in 1865, made slave labor illegal. In 1868 the Fourteenth Amendment extended the civil rights to all citizens, providing in part that no state could "deprive any person of life, liberty or property, without due process of law; nor deny to any person within its jurisdiction the equal protection of the laws." The Fifteenth Amendment (1870) granted the right to vote regardless of "race, color, or previous condition of servitude." The comprehensive Civil Rights Act of 1875 granted blacks the right to "full and equal enjoyment" of all forms of public transportation, entertainment, and housing as well as the right to serve on juries.[30]

If one were to take constitutions and statutes—the legal superstructure—as descriptions of social reality or as sufficient causes of change in social life, it would seem that a fundamental alteration in the society had been accomplished. The formal grants of civil rights by statutes and Constitutional amendments, however, proved to have little permanent effect. Southern opposition to the laws was violent, the Ku Klux Klan being the best known and most organized form of southern white opposition. Terrorism was used to prevent blacks from voting, from purchasing land, and from attending school. After 1877, when the remaining Federal troops were withdrawn from the South, blacks were provided primarily with moral support from their northern allies and sympathizers. The Supreme Court in the 1880s began to interpret the civil rights laws in such a way that states and localities were given increasing discretion over sanctioning racial discrimination. The most important of these cases, *Plessy* v. *Ferguson* (1896) established that racially segregated transportation did not violate the Civil Rights Act as long as equal facilities were provided for both races. "Legislation," said the court, "is powerless to eradicate racial instincts." By 1900 most southern states had effectively eliminated black political power through a series of devices that deprived blacks of their right to vote. Poll taxes excluded the very poor, while literacy tests (selectively administered) prevented wealthier blacks from registering. Simultaneously, a new set of laws were passed—"Jim Crow laws"—which rigidly segregated virtually every aspect of social and economic existence. For the first time on a major scale there were

> Jim Crow cars on the railroads . . . and street railways. Also on all passenger boats . . . Jim Crow waiting saloons at all stations and Jim Crow eating houses . . . a separate Jim Crow dock and witness stand in every court—and a Jim Crow Bible for colored witnesses to kiss. (Woodward, 1957: 50)

The extensive Constitutional amendments and Congressional statutes passed immediately after the Civil War promised a great deal. The actual accomplishments, however, proved to be short lived. Within forty years blacks, particularly in the South, found themselves with very few of the Constitutional protections accorded citizens of the United States. They could not vote or serve on juries. They were required by law to submit to countless demeaning restrictions on their lives. While slavery had not been restored and while the legal guarantees achieved during Reconstruction had not been overtly repealed, the actual situation had largely reverted to the prewar condition.

From a Marxist perspective the failure of the civil rights amendments and accompanying legislation is to be understood in terms of the failure of the economic base to change. Ironically, this point was well recognized by at least one member of Congress. In the debate over the proposed Constitutional amendments, Illinois Congressman George W. Julian (1817–1899) asked

> of what avail would be an act of Congress totally abolishing slavery or an amendment of the Constitution forever prohibiting it, if the old agriculture bases of aristocratic power shall remain? (U.S. Congress 1864 Congressional Globe, 38th Congress, First Session; quoted by Wiener, 1980)

Indeed the Radical Republicans initially proposed what amounts in contemporary terms to a program of land reform (Moore, 1966: 145). The Freedman's Bureau was instructed to divide landholdings of 200 acres or more among independent family farm owners, both black and white. The promise of "forty acres and a mule," however, never materialized on any scale because President Andrew Johnson, sympathetic to southern landowners, granted amnesty from confiscation. The Republicans in Congress also began to have second thoughts about such a massive intervention into rights to private property. In the end, not only did the large southern landholdings remain intact, but transfers of land ownership after the Civil War appeared not to have been any greater than the prewar levels (Wiener, 1980).

Although slavery was prohibited by federal law, the large landowners sought to create new, equivalent forms of labor control. In most areas the plantation gave way to a sharecropping form of tenancy, in which family plots of land were leased annually in exchange for 50 percent of the crop. The laborer provided the labor power of himself and his family in return for a plot of land and provisions of food, tools, and animals. Illiterate sharecroppers found themselves continually in debt, and any attempt to escape could legally be prosecuted as a violation of contract. The sharecropping system did not exercise the same degree of control over laborers as slavery. There was worker mobility among plantations, and the possibility of migration was occasionally realized as employment opportunities expanded in towns outside the region. Southern "anti-enticement" laws, however, limited the activities of labor recruiters in the region.

The plantation's labor requirement of a large, permanent pool of unskilled labor was sustained as well through state educational policies. Typical of the pattern is one Black Belt county in Alabama, which spent in 1908 an average of $12.26 per white pupil for teachers salaries but only 37 cents per black pupil (Bond, 1939: 162). The state in various ways therefore served to maintain an immobile, largely black labor pool for a southern agriculture that remained labor-intensive.

While sharecroppers and other tenants enjoyed greater freedom than had plantation slaves in terms of both the supervision of their labor and their mobility, effective power remained in the hands of the landowners. The failure of the economic base to change in such a way as to give the farm laborers effective power rendered the Constitutional guarantees of their civil rights meaningless. Landowners did not oppose giving blacks the right to vote, as long as they voted for the candidates favored by the landowners. When threatened by independence on the part of their tenants, landowners supported the movement toward disfranchisement.

With its policy of racial segregation and black disfranchisement protected by law, the South was able to regain political power at the federal level. White voters, united behind the Democratic party, returned to Congress representatives who built up seniority on key committees. So powerful was the southern bloc that Congressional action on civil rights became virtually impossible, including federal antilynching legislation (Zangrando, 1980). Similarly, the ability of Solid South Democrats to deliver electoral votes in Presidential contests assured a friendly ear in the White House for concerns of Southern Democrats. Despite the commitment of Franklin Roosevelt and his New Deal reformers to institute basic economic reforms, the New Deal's government jobs, crop subsidies, and welfare programs were administered at "the local level," in such a way as not to upset the power of the local white power structure in the South (Pivan and Cloward, 1971: 76). When in 1940 Roosevelt was threatened with a march on Washington by blacks opposed to the federal policy of racial segregation, he established a Fair Employment Practices Commission to eliminate discrimination in federal employment. After the Second World War, President Truman began to press for expanding federal enforcement of civil rights. By executive order he desegregated the armed forces. Opposition to such policies within his own party almost cost him re-election in the 1948 campaign. However, the demographic shifts resulting from the modernization of southern agriculture were beginning to alter the balance of political power to reduce the power of Southern Democrats. This change is not without irony, since much of the modernization movement was stimulated by New Deal subsidies, which encouraged landowners to replace tenant farmers with tractors, fertilizers, and mechanical cotton pickers (see Fligstein, 1981).

No single factor explains the decline of the plantation mode of production in the twentieth century. A confluence of disparate events that cannot be neatly summarized in terms of Marxian theory contributed to its decline. This point is worth emphasizing, since many commentators take Marx's writings as a source of prophecy. Marx is alleged to have been able (or, for critics, to have failed) to anticipate the future direction of particular societies. For example, Marx is claimed to have failed to predict the Russian Revolution. In point of fact, foretelling the future is beyond the capacity of Marx's theory or any other scientific theory. Such theories may make predictions about specific changes (e.g., in the change in legal form with the introduction of a change in the mode of production) based on the occurrence of antecedent conditions. If, however, these antecedents fail to occur, no theoretical prediction can be made.

> We can predict with great accuracy the motions of a given pendulum as long as it is isolated from the influence of various disturbing factors, because the theory of pendular motion and the requisite factual data concerning that specific system are known; but the predictions cannot be confidently made far into the future, because we have excellent reasons for believing that the system will not remain immune indefinitely from external perturbations. On the other hand, we cannot predict with much accuracy where a leaf just fallen from a tree will be carried by the wind in ten minutes; for, although available physical theory is in principle capable of answering the question provided that relevant factual data are supplied about the wind, the leaf, and the terrain, we rarely if ever have at our command knowledge of such initial conditions. Inability to forecast the indefinite future is thus not unique to the study of human affairs, and is not a certain sign that comprehensive laws have not been established or cannot be established about the phenomena. (Nagel, 1961: 461)

Similarly, Marxian theory could not predict the transformations in the southern economy during the twentieth century; it can, however, explain the impact of the economic changes on the legal superstructure. Before turning to this issue we will briefly survey the sources of the transformation of the plantation mode of production in the American South.

Four basic factors do not provide an exhaustive explanation of the change but will suffice to give us a sense of the diversity of influences that were responsible. First, the demand for black labor in the North dramatically increased after 1914. The First World War shut off the annual flow of one million immigrant laborers. After the war a xenophobic Congress strictly limited the importation of more "hyphenated Americans." The resulting labor shortage led businesses to send labor recruiters to scour the South. The exodus of black tenants in some areas was massive; Georgia in the 1920s lost 45 percent of its young black male population (Mandle, 1978). Southern planters were powerless to prevent the migration, which greatly undermined their labor supply.

The second factor leading to the demise of the plantation system was the boll weevil, a beetle that first appeared in Texas in 1892 and gradually spread havoc throughout the cotton region. This plague encouraged agricultural diversification. Since soybeans, cattle, and poultry required much less labor than cotton, tenants were driven from the land. Additional incentives to eliminate tenant labor came from federal funds for farm machinery. The Agricultural Adjustment Program, begun in 1933, gave subsidies to farmers for limiting production as a means of driving up the market prices for farm commodities. Farm owners, rather than tenants, received the benefits of this New Deal program.

Finally, technological innovation greatly accelerated the pace of modernization in southern agriculture, particularly after the Second World War. Prior to these innovations, picking the cotton crop required hand labor. Around 1950 a practical mechanical cotton picker was adopted, and its use spread rapidly. The net effect of the opening of labor opportunities outside the South, the devastation of the cotton crop by the boll weevil, New Deal subsidies, and the introduction of mechanical cotton pickers was to destroy the tenant mode of production.

The elimination of the economic base did not turn southern oligarchs into champions of civil liberties. The superstructure, in other words, did not change automatically in response to changes in the economic base. It will therefore be instructive to examine the intervening stages between the destruction of the economic base in farm tenancy and the changes that subsequently occurred in civil rights law.

The overall demographic effect of the modernization of agriculture was a dramatic displacement of the southern rural population (Day, 1967). In 1940, 80 percent of the black population in the United States was concentrated in the rural South, where they worked primarily as tenants. Over the next thirty years the percent of the black population in the South fell to 53 percent. Nationally, the black population shifted from being predominantly rural to becoming more urbanized than the white population (Farley, 1977).

This demographic shift in turn had profound political consequences. Blacks "came to be located in states of the most strategic importance in Presidential contests" (Pivan and Cloward, 1971: 252; Glantz, 1960). John F. Kennedy's Presidential campaign in 1960 was the first attempt on the part of a Democratic candidate to build a coalition with urban ghetto votes in New York, Pennsylvania, and other key northern states, while surrendering the South to the Republicans. In contrast, Franklin Roosevelt, for all his desire to improve the civil rights position of blacks, could not afford politically to alienate his southern Democratic support. Even Kennedy was unable to deliver Congressional legislation on civil rights because of the entrenched power of southern congressmen on key committees. Lyndon Johnson's administration achieved the breakthrough that eluded Kennedy. The rediscovery of poverty served as a device for constructing federal political machines in the urban areas that dealt directly with the ghetto constituency, avoiding the established state and local government that were controlled by Republicans or old line Democratic machine hostile toward blacks (Pivan and Cloward, 1971: 262).

The Second Civil Rights Revolution: 1960s

Discrimination has been a daily fact of life for minorities in the United States. The *Brown* decision in 1954 was of major significance because it marked the end of institutionally sanctioned discrimination. Before *Brown*, many states adopted laws that required black children to attend separate schools, required black passengers to ride in separate railroad cars and in separate sections of streetcars and buses, and required black people to eat in separate sections of restaurants, to swim in separate swimming pools, to drink from separate water fountains. In countless ways the laws of segregation were manifest in daily life. The *Brown* decision held that such laws inherently violated Constitutional rights to "equal protection of the laws." Legally endorsed segregation, the Court argued, could never be anything but stigmatizing.

In the year following the *Brown* decision Rosa Parks, a Montgomery, Alabama, black woman, refused to leave the section of a bus reserved for whites. Her arrest sparked a year-long boycott of the city bus system, a protest led by a young, unknown minister named Martin Luther King, Jr. The Montgomery boycott brought racial segregation to the front pages and inspired a series of further nonviolent protests against segregation laws. In 1959 the sit-in demonstration was first employed at a segregated lunch counter in Greensboro, North Carolina. In the early 1960s such demonstrations, marches, and voter registration drives attracted large numbers of blacks and whites. From those protests arose a number of court cases challenging the constitutionality of state and local segregation laws and pressure increased on Congress to pass new national civil rights legislation, culminating in the Civil Rights Act of 1964, which guaranteed equal rights in the housing market, public accommodations, and voting.

The impact of this legislation and corresponding court decisions has not been uniformly successful. While the *Brown* decision was a symbolic turning point, its immediate effect on school desegregation was minor. By 1964 fewer than 3 percent of the black children in the Deep South were attending previously all-white schools (Rodgers and Bullock, 1972: 4). While dramatic changes occurred in voting and public accommodations, housing segregation has remained largely unaffected by the legislation. Employment opportunities have similarly had an inconsistent pattern of change. It is apparent that the civil rights movement and national legislation improved the economic position of American blacks as a whole; the increase in relative income for the black population from 1965 to 1969 was greater than the entire gain between 1947 and 1965 (Farley and Hermalin, 1972). The overall occupational gains of the 1960s were not reversed during the recessionary 1970s, contrary to common expectations ("the last hired, the first fired"). Economic indicators continued in the 1970s to record a convergence in the status of blacks and whites. Despite this trend, racial differences remain very large. For example, "the purchasing power of the typical black family in 1974 was equivalent to that of a white family twenty years earlier" (Farley, 1977: 206).

Moreover, the economic upgrading that followed the civil rights movement has not been uniformly experienced by the black population. The position of certain segments of the black population has, in fact, deteriorated during this period. For example, among blacks aged sixteen to nineteen, the unemployment rate in the late 1950s was between 16 and 19 percent; in the early 1970s the rate was between 29 and 34 percent (W. J. Wilson, 1980: 91). In general, employment opportunities for the urban, uneducated, and impoverished have progressively diminished.

An analogy between the historical experience of Jews in Western Europe and blacks in the United States, taken at face value, contains at least as many differences as similarities. Blacks in the precapitalist system were slaves, whose largely unskilled labor was a source of profit to the planters. Jews, on the other hand were free agents engaged in trade, commerce, and banking. Marxian theory, however, suggests that despite these surface dissimilarities there are "deep analogies" (Stinchcombe, 1978: 23) between the two cases.

Applying the base-superstructure perspective to the late eighteenth century discovery of the rights of man, Marx argued that legal equality, far from being universal and natural, was a historical aberration peculiar to capitalism. Legal equality was a norm that arose from the unique character of economic exchange under capitalism and was necessary for the maintenance of capitalist economic relations.

In both cases, then, the breakdown of the precapitalist mode of production led to the disintegration of legal boundaries between minority and majority populations. The economic changes further led to mass population displacement that had profound consequences on the development of the societies.

Attention to the changing modes of production in the American economy will enable us to explain the inconsistency in the aftermath of the civil rights revolution. The demise of the sharecropping system of agriculture undercut the political pressure to sustain segregation laws, which had been used to maintain coercive control over unskilled laborers. Parallel to the trend toward increasing mechanization of Southern agriculture was the continual expansion of technology in industry, which reduced the demand for unskilled and uneducated labor. Simultaneously, the increased capital intensity of the economy increased demand for professional, managerial, and service positions. Businesses thus began recruiting in the 1960s the best educated and the most talented blacks to fill these positions once the traditional barriers to blacks had been attacked by civil rights legislation and court decisions. The net result of the demise of the plantation economy and the expansion of technology in industry has therefore been to create two economic segments in the black population: an underclass of marginally employed or unemployed workers facing a declining market in unskilled labor and a middle class of educated and trained persons, competing in a market in which civil rights laws have created new routes of access (W. J. Wilson, 1980: 180).

While some contemporary Marxists (e.g., Reich, 1981) argue that the capitalist class uses a deliberate strategy of divide and conquer by encouraging racial and ethnic divisions among the working class, Marx's model of labor exploitation is more closely represented by Edna Bonacich's argument:

> Business, I would contend, rather than desiring to protect a segment of the working class supports a liberal or laissez faire ideology that would permit all workers to compete freely in an open market. Such open competition would displace higher paid labor. Only under duress [as in South Africa] does business yield to labor aristocracy [by imposing racial barriers on employment]. (1972: 556)

SUMMARY

This chapter has introduced some of the sociological ideas and methods of Karl Marx through an examination of civil rights law. This exercise has allowed us to see how Marx's central model of base and superstructure can be used to explain significant changes in law and to relate those changes coherently to developments in other historical periods. In part this examination serves to illustrate the subtlety of Marx's analysis of the law. His more recent followers have tended to overlook the manner in which he linked legal equality to the capitalist economic system and to treat his approach as a general form of conflict theory, in which legal inequality is a universal feature of all historical societies. (For a lucid elaboration of this approach, see Black, 1976.) For Marx, legal equality is linked to a particular mode of production. The link is by no means simple.

To overlook the link, however, is to invite utopian reformist visions as substitutes for effective action.

SUGGESTED READING

This chapter has presented some of the basic concepts and propositions in the Marxian tradition by demonstrating their power to explain a small set of historical developments. While we will bring to bear other facets of the Marxian tradition in later chapters, the interested reader would do well to sample at least some of the diversity of this tradition directly. For Marx, there is no substitute for a careful reading of the original texts. The best overall collection of original works is Tucker (1978); Cain and Hunt (1979) pull together diverse passages that address law, but the collection does not add up to a coherent Marxian perspective. In part, this is because Marx never elaborated a theory of law and the state. The occasional remarks he made on these topics directly are not consistent and give rise to diverse developments within the Marxian tradition; on the theory of the state, see, for example, Block (1977) and Gold et al. (1975). Commentaries on Marx are overwhelming in number and diversity. For sociologists one of the best is that of Gerald Cohen (1978), whose careful reading demonstrates a high degree of consistency among Marx's writings and suggests interpretations conducive to the forming of testable hypotheses from Marx's analyses. However, Cohen's interpretation should be read in light of the alternative readings (see, e.g., Rader 1979; Althusser, 1969). Until recently, few empirical studies were undertaken of mode of production. As Balbus (1971a) points out, studies of class interest and the law tended to veer off into elite-mass contrasts as radicals confused Mosca and Marx. This began to change with the contributions of Stinchcombe (1961) and Paige (1975), who do not adopt a Marxian perspective explicitly but whose work contributes in a major way to this tradition. Hechter and Brustein (1980) provides a suggestive study of the relationship between mode of production and state formation.

On the Jewish question, see works by Carlebach (1978), Hertzberg (1968), and Leon (1950). On American civil rights law the most comprehensive treatment will be found in Bell (1980). Briefer, more readable accounts of the main developments are given by Berger (1967), which is dated but still valuable, and Rodgers and Bullock (1972). C. Van Woodward's study (1957) of the historical origin of southern institutionalized segregation had a profound impact on historical studies of racism and continues to be an important work despite the critiques of more recent historical investigation (for review, see Woodward, 1971). On the effects on black people of recent changes in the mode of production, see Baron (1975), Willhelm (1971), and W. J. Wilson (1980).

Empirical research on law from a Marxian perspective has grown substantially in recent years. Two volumes bring together some of the best of these works, Greenberg (1981) and Beirne and Quinney (1982).

FOOTNOTES

1. This chapter departs from our central focus on criminal law by examining the implications of Marx's analysis for one branch of civil law. This departure is taken because, first, Marx never systematically examined the implications of his theory for criminal law. His occasional references to criminal law occur in his accounts of particular historical episodes and cannot be taken together to form a coherent analysis of criminal law. For example, his discussion of vagrancy law as a tool used by early capitalists to coerce masses of unskilled labor is a description peculiar to the period of "primitive accumulation"; efforts to apply this analysis to later periods of capitalist development (e.g., Quinney, 1977) are misplaced. Second, although the discussion centers on civil rights laws, this analysis has direct bearing on such questions in criminal law as the issue of discrimination in sentencing, which we will treat in Chapter 9.
2. The major casebook on civil rights law, by Derrick Bell, in large measure is devoted to documenting the failure of legal remedies in achieving the goals of racial equality. Thus, for example, Bell concludes that

   employment discrimination laws will not help millions of non-whites —the legal conflicts ... are sufficiently complex to guarantee that litigation on this subject could continue indefinitely. (Bell, 1980: 657; cf. Freeman, 1978)

3. The link between forces and relations of production can be clearly seen by considering the fundamental differences between two major contemporary industries, home construction and automobile production.
   Automobiles are produced on an assembly line in which the task of construction is broken down into hundreds of discrete operations performed by workers specializing in one operation. Each operation brings to bear various bodies of scientific and engineering knowledge (metallurgy, chemistry, mechanical engineering) that are beyond the comprehension of the worker performing the task. Basic decisions about the production process are made by distinct departments of production engineering, quality control, personnel, and cost accounting. These specialized administrative personnel supervise the flow of work, inspect the quality of the product at each stage, and determine the optimal method of performing each operation in the assembly.
   These relations of production are made possible by the nature of the forces of production peculiar to the manufacture of automobiles.

A corporation may in a given year produce over 2,000,000 identical units, each of which will require precisely the same sequence of operations. Consequently, automobile production is stable in both the volume and nature of tasks to be undertaken. It is therefore profitable for enterprises to be large scale, to produce mass quantities of automobiles to be sold at a small price, rather than to handcraft a small number of luxury vehicles. In such enterprises the skill level of the work force is continually being eroded by new methods of subdividing the task, but since productivity is so high, the organization can afford to pay high wages and benefits. Automobile production thus entails forces of production that give rise to a population of large firms with several layers of administrative and production workers.

In contrast, housing construction is carried out by small firms that hire skilled laborers and have a relatively small administrative component. This difference is due to the peculiar features of the forces of production in the construction industry. Construction is characterized by instability, since projects are short term, work is seasonal, and the market for any given firm is locally limited. The continual relocation of workers, tools, and materials presents problems of coordination that cannot be efficiently resolved by an assembly line organization. Instead, small contractors supervise an array of specialists (earthmovers, bricklayers, carpenters, electricians, steam fitters, woodworkers, painters, glaziers, etc.), each of whom plays a role in a particular stage of construction. The subdivision of tasks possible in a continuous-flow production of standardized products is impossible in construction, even in housing tracts. Decisions about work pace, coordination, and quality control must be made on site, rather than by a bureaucratic office removed from the actual production. This leads further to the requirement that workers have a high level of "craftmanship," which is ensured in symbolic fashion by licensing and union membership requirements.

As a result of these properties of the forces of production, construction enterprises are decentralized small-capital concerns. Not too long ago automobile production resembled the social organization of the contemporary construction industry. In 1903, when Henry Ford began making automobiles, the task was carried out by a handful of men who were, for the most part, machinists. The Dodge Brothers, who built the engine and chassis, had previously been famous for their bicycles. A small number of automobiles were assembled from immediately available parts to be sold to a wealthy clientele. Ford soon realized the potential for mass marketing of cheap cars if the assembly line were substituted for the casual work of skilled craftsmen. Between 1909 and 1920 Ford reduced the price of the Model T from $950 to $300, which boosted sales from 12,000 to 2 million and captured 50 percent of the market (Lanzillotti, 1971).

The elaborate stratification hierarchies that we see in automobile production do not appear in construction. It would be impossible for a single individual to enter into the automobile market with a new model; individual carpenters, however, routinely set themselves up as independent contractors. In Marx's terms the assembly line raises a much higher barrier between workers and capitalists. Construction gives rise to a class system that is more permeable (Stinchcombe, 1959).

4. A protracted controversy has developed among Marxists over the proper interpretation of this passage. We have opted in this chapter for a single line of argument that stresses the primacy of productive forces as essential to a distinctive Marxian position. In this we follow Gerald Cohen (1978). As Rader (1979) points out, however, there are at least two other coherent readings. The *dialectical* view stresses the interaction between base and superstructure. The *organic totality* view denies altogether the possibility of classifying social organization into discrete categories of base and superstructure. The former approach differs only slightly from the primacy-of-productive-forces position; we will attribute at least one version of this position to Max Weber in the next chapter. As to the organic totality position, we believe not only that it represents a misreading of Marx, but that it is ultimately useless as a basis for empirical research (indeed, proponents of this position typically deny the possibility of such research). The organic position contends that social relations of production are in fact superstructural in character and therefore it is senseless to suggest that the economic base determines the superstructure. *Ownership* of the means of production, after all, is a *legal* relation; law must therefore exist prior to the economic relations. Gerald Cohen (1978: 216–30), however, points out that Marx used such legal terms as *ownership* and *right* in a nonlegal sense and that one may routinely substitute the nonlegal term *power* without altering the meaning of the text. More important, we feel, than the proper interpretation of Marxist texts is the potential of the reading for furthering our understanding of law and economy. The organic totality approach leads ultimately to the sterile, descriptive truism that everything is related to everything else.

5. The advantages of representing the argument in this form are as follows: First, it forces us to be explicit not only about the relationships among central variables, but also about the role of factors that are not represented explicitly in the model. Second, the diagram may help to dispel at least some of the more common confusions about "rigid determinism" in the base superstructure model. This point is important to keep in mind because many writers assume that Marx's base-superstructure model entails the idea of "technological determinism": that social change results simply from an alteration in machinery. Not only is technology not the prime mover in Marx's theory, it is also historically a product rather than a cause of the Industrial Revolution.

6. Elsewhere Marx states that

social relations are closely bound up with productive forces. By acquiring new productive forces men change their mode of production; and in changing their way of earning a living, they change all their social relations. The hand-mill gives you society with the feudal lord; the steam-mill society with the industrial capitalist. (1963: 122)

It is always the direct relationship of the owners of the means of production to the direct producers ... which reveals the innermost secret, the hidden basis of the entire social structure and with it, the political form of the relation of sovereignty and dependence. (Marx, 1981: 791)

7. Compare Marxist historian Eugene Genevose's statement of the same idea:

To trace all historical events and changes to class structure and class struggle is to convert marxian analysis into a childish formula worthy of a particularly fanatic and simple minded religious cult. (1972: 350n.9)

8. Utopian socialism is the label Marx and Engels gave to a number of their contemporaries, including Robert Owen and Charles Fourier. These writers adhered to a variety of positions, but they all shared certain common themes. The utopians argued that the road from capitalism to socialism lay in creating model communities, isolated from the mainstream of industrial society. Experimental communities, such as Robert Owen's New Harmony, Indiana, or Fourier's "phalanxes" in New York State would, their founders believed, show by the example of their success that an alternative social order was possible.

9. Ignoring the distinction between scientific socialism and utopian socialism, some Marxists have argued that it is not the economic structure, but the class struggle that produces the characteristic features of the legal system. Thus

attainment of equality is not "inscribed" in the capitalist mode of production as an inherent functional necessity ... it is achieved only through popular struggle. (Zeitlin, 1980: 22)

This assertion is flawless if it is confined to the proximate causes of equality (cf. G. A. Cohen, 1978: 148–9); it says nothing, however, about the factors that affect the outcome of the struggle. There is a strong temptation to adopt a voluntaristic or utopian perspective as an alternative to the "rigid," "mechanistic," "nihilistic," and "fatalistic" base-superstructure conception. Thus

Politically it is crucial that a theory be developed which, while according primacy to structures, restores to people their dignity by acknowledging that they are capable of changing their world. (Cain and Hunt, 1979: xiii)

Behind a good many such sentiments is the notion that the validity of the theory rests on its conformity to standards of personal taste. If the theory has unpalatable implications for political activism (if, for example, it counsels against the political mobilization of housewives, students, and welfare recipients), then it lacks validity. While such concerns may legitimately motivate further inquiry, this position amounts to a choice of activism for its own sake, unguided by an adequate understanding of the social forces shaping political outcomes. The ghost of Robert Owen thus remains a continual presence.

It should be emphasized that a nonreductionist deterministic model does not eliminate the role of class struggle in producing change. The relations of production do not spontaneously generate corresponding superstructures. Scientific explanation—and its cousin, effective praxis—begin, however, with an understanding of the modes of production. Contemporary utopian socialists have reproduced almost verbatim the ideas and slogans of nineteenth century utopians. For example, Taylor, Walton, and Young in the conclusion of their book *The New Criminology* issue the call for a value-charged criminology:

> normatively committed to the abolition of inequalities of wealth and power, and in particular of inequalities in property of life changes. (1973: 281)

This argument restates point three of the 1875 program of the German socialist party: "The emancipation of labor demands . . . the co-operative regulation of the total labour with a fair distribution of the proceeds of labour." Of programs of income redistribution in general, Marx had this to say:

> I have dealt at length with . . . "equal right" and "fair distribution" . . . to show what a crime it is to attempt on the one hand, to force on our Party again, as dogmas, ideas which in a certain period had some meaning but have now become obsolete verbal rubbish, while again perverting, on the other, the realistic outlook, which it cost so much effort to instill into the party but which is now taken root in it by means of ideological nonsense about right and other trash so common among the democrats and French socialists. (Tucker, 1978: 531)

To see why Marx regarded the emphasis on income redistribution as "obsolete verbal rubbish" it should be remembered that

> If all of the privately held wealth were distributed equally among all residents of the United States, each individual would receive little over $4000 [c]omputed from census data of 1962. . . . Susan P. Lee and Peter Passel point out that "redistributing monopoly profit would shift only about 1 percent of income. . . . Total elimination of monopoly profit, even if every penny were diverted to poor people, would do relatively little to alter the lives of the bottom quarter of the population." (Mueller, 1973: 159)

10. Marx confined his systematic analysis of modes of production to the capitalist mode and feudal mode of production and the transformation of Western societies from feudalism to capitalism. This work was oriented to developing the general theory, rather than to elucidating

concrete historical developments. Tangentially, Marx discussed other modes of production (primitive communist, slave, ancient, Germanic, Asiatic), but he never formulated a consistent typology.

11. In religion, for example, the sedentary pastoral system led to conservative peasant beliefs, mixing Christian doctrine with earlier pagan myths; the petty commodity system gave rise to religious movements that were alternatively treated as reforms or heresies; and the feudal system gave rise to conservative orthodox Christian beliefs.

12. Thus Quinney (1974: 19) suggests that "a critique of the American political economy begins with the acknowledged assumption that life in the United States is determined by the capitalist mode of production." While claiming to engage in Marxian analysis, Quinney and American conflict theorists generally neglect altogether the mode of production. Instead, they engage in neo-Machiavellian discussions of political power in which the major division lies between some elite (e.g., the 1 percent of the population that owns 40 percent of the wealth) and the powerless masses. This may be a "radical" analysis, but it has very little to do with the theories of Marx (cf. Balbus, 1971a).

13. For examination of these issues see Anderson (1974), Wallerstein (1974).

14. Similar associations emerged in ancient Greece and Rome, the Islamic Middle East, India, and China. Where they attained political power, they served to prevent the emergence of rational capitalism, Weber argued. The same point is made by Marx (1967: 394).

15. "Exploitation" is another one of those terms (like "repressive justice" and "rational decision making") that social scientists use in a restricted way, but which have numerous connotations that may lead less vigilant readers astray. Marx defines "exploitation" as the ratio of surplus labor to necessary labor: "The rate of surplus value is therefore an exact expression for the degree of exploitation of labor power by capital, or of the laborer by the capitalist" (Marx, 1967: 241). Thus "exploitation" in Marx's sense only occurs when the product of the labor of one person is being expropriated by another beyond the production of necessary labor. Exploitation, in other words, is within Marxian theory a technical term confined to production that generates surplus value. As with all such technical terms, confusion is often generated by the global usage of the term to include a wide range of diverse phenomena. Thus the use of the same concept to describe relations between developed and underdeveloped nations introduces unnecessary and unresolvable contradictions in analysis (Bettelheim, 1972). Similarly, fairly representative of the muddled use of the concept by radical writers is Barry Krisberg's observation that "urban ghettos provide a classic example of exploited labor, exploitation of tenants by slum landlords and merchants selling inferior goods at high prices" (1975: 14). It is instructive to contrast Krisberg's use of the term *exploitation* with that of Marx. For Krisberg, *exploitation* is a term of moral con-

demnation to be freely applied to any situation in which one human being unfairly takes advantage of another. His usage thus combines sociological and normative analysis (see Chapter 1). In contrast, for Marx, exploitation is not a term of moral condemnation; it refers specifically to a carefully defined type of economic *production* in which the worker receives at the end of the working day only part of the value of the goods she or he has produced. To include all other forms of "unfair advantage" into the theoretical concept, Marx would argue, only serves to muddy the water (Recall Marx's attack on Proudhon's moralistic position, "property is theft".) Specifically, by taking Krisberg's definition of exploitation we could eliminate most of the evils described without having touched the basic source of exploitation in capitalism, the wage relationship. Indeed, Krisberg's moral indignation is rooted in bourgeois sentimentality: the evils of slum housing and overpriced and adulterated food are all evils that liberal capitalist society is committed to eliminate. The rhetorical use of concepts should be distinguished from their analytic use. Not even the bourgeois economists, according to Marx, had been able to diagnose correctly the source of profit in the capitalist system. Only the British economist Nassau Senior (1790–1864) in his argument against proposed laws to limit the working day to ten hours hit upon, in a crude way, "the secret of capital" (Marx, 1967: 224–30). The unfortunate popularity of the phrase *false consciousness* (invented by Engels after Marx's death) has had the consequence of creating the illusion that Marx saw the capitalist class as fully conscious of its interests and fully capable of deceiving the workers. A more accurate formulation of Marx's position is to be found in Antonio Gramsci's concept of *hegemony* (see Femia, 1975).

16. Cf. Marx:

> the analysis of the real, inner connections of the capitalist production process is a very intricate thing and a work of great detail; it is one of the tasks of science to reduce the visible and merely apparent movement to the actual inner movement. Accordingly, it will be completely self-evident that, in the heads of the agents of capitalist production and circulation, ideas must necessarily form about the laws of production that diverge completely from these laws and are merely the expression in consciousness of the apparent movement. (1981: 428)

17. Labor power is assumed to be a homogeneous quantity, measured by duration. Skilled labor differs not in quality, but as a simple multitude of unskilled labor. Marx (in Tucker, 1978: 310–11, 322–23) was not only making a simplifying assumption regarding measurement problems in the labor theory of value; he was, I argue, asserting the factual equality of all forms of labor in the capitalist market, which routinely reduces incommensurables to the cash nexus.

18. "Over the last thirty years the average work week in industry has remained almost constant. The standard work week has declined but

this has been offset by increased demand for overtime work and the companion willingness to supply it. . . . In 1941 the average work week in manufacturing was 40.6 hours; in 1969 it was 40.6 hours" (Galbraith, 1967: 349)

19. This argument is such a departure from common sense ideas about exploitation that it is worth emphasizing that Marx is not seeking to describe the particular exchanges between wage laborers and capitalists, but to characterize the essential nature of the exchange. Particular exchanges involve instances of force and fraud; the general pattern, however, consists of exchange of equivalents (wage for labor power). For Marx, exploitation occurs not in the wage settlement but in the process of production, over which there is no negotiation. Dario Melossi has recently published his misunderstanding of this argument. Since this misconception is widespread, it is worthwhile to consider the source of the difficulty. Melossi writes that

> freedom of contract is only for those who own capital—the freedom of a person under the civil and even the public and constitutional law of liberalism means property. Indeed legal fiction is fictitious only for the proletarian, who owns only his/her labor power. For the others, it is fair. They exchange commodities at their prices (sic). For them and only for them the sphere of circulation is a "variable Eden" of rights. This has never been true for the proletarian, for whom the only possible contract, inasmuch as he/she owns only the power of his/her body, is that labor contract at the core of which lies the "secret of production." (1980: 382)

Without entering into a discussion of the historical validity of this generalization, it should be apparent that his argument has very little to do with Marx's model of the exchange between labor and capital. Marx begins with the assumption that—all else being equal—commodities exchange at their value. This assumption provides the foundation for his analysis of exploitation and is central to his analysis of bourgeois law. At the same time Marx recognized that in real life the exchange-of-equivalents assumption is violated.

20. It takes little imagination to see why Smith's ideas found such a receptive audience among the new capitalists, but the "invisible hand" is more than an apology; it is the first discovery of a general sociological principle, that the collective result of individual behavior is not the same as the individual behavior. Personal greed is collective altruism; individual rationality results in collective irrationality.

21. The capitalists won this battle in England. They lost, however, in Germany. For a discussion of the consequences of the difference, see Moore (1966).

22. "Intention" in the criminal law and "good faith" in civil law become central to the law of capitalism, in a way unknown to medieval law. *Mens rea* was seldom an issue in feudal law, which emphasized the consequences of the act, rather than the character of the individual

committing it. Most harms were treated generally as a species of tort. If one person killed another, the offender was required to pay *composition*, monetary damages to the victim's family. Failure to pay entitled the family to retaliate by killing the offender or a member of his family. The system occasionally broke down, and blood feuds resulted. Generally, the *wergild* ("man's price") resolved problems of death or injury, the price to be paid based upon the status of the victim. Elaborate tables of compensation were worked out for the loss of life and particular limbs. (This system was common in medieval Europe and persists today in the Middle East and other precapitalist societies.) The market requirement of responsible actors who could be expected to live up to the terms of a contract without the existence of personal bonds was a novel way of thinking about individuals. Actors had to be equal to the participants in the market. Persons outside the labor commodity market (serfs, plantation slaves, children, etc.) did not participate in the legal reconstruction of the individual.

23. Medieval law is filled with similar prescriptions—for example, the *benefit of clergy*, an institution that evolved in England in the twelfth century to prevent priests and bishops accused of felonies from being tried before secular courts. Separate ecclesiastical courts were to have jurisdiction over cases involving clergy, thus preserving the independence of the church from secular rulers. There were, however, many advantages to the church courts over the secular courts; primarily, the church courts could not impose the death penalty, except in cases of heresy or sorcery. The nobility therefore moved to have the definition of "clergy" broadened so that they could enjoy the benefit when they ended up on the wrong side of the law. At first a literacy requirement was enacted (since priests were the only people in medieval society who could read), but many nobles found this skill impossible to acquire. Therefore the "test" of whether the defendant was a member of the "clergy" became the ability to recite the first verse of Psalm 51, a skill which almost any noble could acquire by hiring a tutor. The second medieval institution that embodied status differences as legitimate criteria was the doctrine of *coverture*. Put simply, this idea derives from the Biblical description of husband and wife as being one flesh. Since they are one person before the law, certain acts are impossible. A spouse cannot testify against the other spouse, since to do so would amount to self-incrimination. Rape cannot occur in the eye of the law in such a relationship. Furthermore, since the male is the head of the household, coverture respects the stratification of the marriage, subordinating the rights of wives to transfer property, enter into contracts, inherit wealth, and so on. Furthermore, under the doctrine of coverture, the husband is *responsible* for criminal acts his wife commits in his presence.

Similarly, inequality was inscribed in the laws of the slave states. In Virginia (a relatively liberal southern state), for example, five crimes were capital offenses if the defendant was white. If the defendant was a slave or a free black person, then seventy offenses could be punished by death. The criminal code prescribed a fine for forcible rape if the rapist was white and the victim was black. If, however, the victim was white and the rapist was black, then the law prescribed the death penalty for the offender.

24. As historian Eugene Genovese suggests,

> it is only through an appreciation of the duality of historical judgment that we can appreciate the tragic dimension of all human history. And at the risk of doing unintended violence to my radical critics and their assertion of absolute values, I must confess to believing that a man who cannot understand the inherent tragedy of history is not likely to be able to tell us much about the past, the present, or the future. (1972: 372)

Now, it could be, and generally is, argued that the development of slavery and other forms of servitude propelled human society from a primitive existence, which, in Hobbes's famous phrase, was "nasty, brutish, and short," toward civilization. How else could ruling strata, including those who were freed from manual work and could engage in art and science, emerge? Without those strata, how could civilization have developed, and with it the present possibilities for a long and full life for the masses themselves? The tragedy inherent in this ironical historical process has been lost on few who have reflected on history at all; it was certainly not lost on Marx (Genovese, 1972: 372–3).

25. While Marx views the legal equality of these bourgeois constitutions as historically limited and at times makes scathing references to the universalistic presumptions of their authors as "ideological nonsense about rights and other trash" (Marx, in Tucker, 1978: 532), he viewed the discovery of the rights of man in the late eighteenth century as an important historical development.

> Political emancipation certainly represents a great progress. It is not, indeed, the final form of human emancipation, but is the final form of human emancipation within the framework of the prevailing social order. It goes without saying that we are speaking here of real, practical emancipation. (Marx, "On the Jewish Question," in Tucker, 1978: 35)

This position has been restated recently by the American Marxist historian Eugene Genovese:

> The grim experiences of Russia, China, and other undemocratic socialist countries—whose revolutions and social systems we support in principle—ought to be enough to convince us that one of our major responsibilities is to guarantee that our own movement embody those great and living traditions of free and critical thought which are the glory of Western civilization and without which we have nothing to offer the American people or our comrades in the socialist countries who are today fighting with genuine heroism to humanize their own societies. (1972: 17)

26. Robert observes that

> the combination of tobacco raising with general farming discouraged large-scale operations. An analysis of the manuscript census returns for over five thousand tobacco-producing farms in the heart of the Eastern District indicates that by 1859 the average producing unit was marketing about 3,500 pounds, produced on some five or six acres. Of the major Southern staples, tobacco was characteristically grown on the smaller plantations. Sugar cane, incidentally, was at the other extreme and invited the largest plantation units. It is not surprising that the slaveholdings in the tobacco regions of the upper South were as a rule less extensive than those in the lower South. (1949: 61–62)

27. In Egypt, Syria, and Turkey cotton cultivation is also organized in sharecropping systems, and workers show similar patterns of political apathy. It seems that there must be some features of cotton sharecropping generally rather than the peculiar cultural circumstances of the southern United States that account for the passivity of southern plantation workers (Paige, 1975: 64).

28. Article 4, Section 1 of the Constitution provides that

> no person held to service or labor in one State, under the laws thereof, escaping into another shall, in consequence of any law or regulation therein, be discharged from such service or labor, but shall be delivered upon claim to the party to whom such service may be due.

This Constitutional protection for slaveowners was reinforced by federal laws passed in 1793 and in 1850. The law was difficult to enforce. In 1850 a Boston mob attempted to prevent the return of an escaped Virginia slave, requiring the presence of 1100 troops to escort him to the ship returning him to slavery.

29. Born in Virginia, Dred Scott was taken west to Alabama and Missouri. In 1834 he was sold to an army surgeon, who took his slaves along when he was transferred to posts in Illinois and Minnesota Territory. When the surgeon died, Scott became the property of his wife, whose brother J. F. Sanford was administrator of her property. In 1846 Scott sued Sanford on the grounds that, having been taken into free states and territories, he could no longer be held as a slave. After ten years of litigation the case finally reached the Supreme Court.

30. In addition to the Constitutional amendments, Congress passed a series of civil rights acts in 1860, 1870, 1871, and 1875. They were designed to ensure blacks the right to sue, to give evidence in court, to hold property, and to enjoy equal accommodations.

3

Legal Procedure and Social Structure: The Contribution of Max Weber

This chapter explores the wide range of legal procedures employed in human societies and examines the compatibility between these legal procedures and their social contexts. The problem of sorting out the types of legal decision making emerged for Max Weber in the course of his comparative study of economy and society. To get a sense of Weber's perspective, we will start by considering four different cases of legal decision making. We will then look at the manner in which Weber dissected such cases to reveal underlying types of legal procedure.

FOUR CASES OF LEGAL DECISION MAKING

1. King Solomon's Wisdom (Tenth Century B.C.)

Then came there two women, that were harlots, unto the king, and stood before him. And the one woman said, "O my lord, I and this woman dwell in one house; and I was delivered of a child with her in the house. And it came to pass the third day after that I was delivered, that this woman was delivered also. And this woman's child died in the night; because she overlaid it. And she arose at midnight, and took my son from beside me, while this handmaid slept, and laid it in her bosom, and laid her dead child in my bosom. And when I rose in the morning to give my child suck, behold, it was dead: but when I had considered it in the morning, behold it was not my son, which I did bear." And the other woman say, "Nay: but the living is my son, and the dead is thy son." And the first said, "No; but the dead is thy son, and the living is my son." Thus they spoke before the king.

Then said the king, "The one saith, 'This is my son that liveth, and thy son is the dead'; and the other saith, 'Nay; but thy son is the dead, and my son is the living'." And the king said, "Bring me a sword." And they brought a sword before the king. And the king said, "Divide the living child in two, and give half to the one, and half to the other." Then spake the woman whose the living child was unto the king, for her bowels yearned upon her son, and she said, "O my lord, give her the living child, and in no wise slay it." But the other said, "Let it be neither mine nor thine, but divide it." Then the king answered and said, "Give her the living child, and in no wise slay it: she is the mother thereof." And all Israel heard of the judgment which the king had judged; and they feared the king: for they saw that the wisdom of God was in him to do judgment. (1 Kings 3:16-28)

2. The Poison Oracle of the Azande (c. 1930)

The Azande are a tribal society in Sudan. To determine the guilt or innocence of a person accused of a crime, the Azande shaman prepares in a ritual ceremony a poison that is administered to a chicken. The poison, whose spirit is called *benge*, is then asked to reveal the guilt of the accused by letting the chicken live. If the chicken dies, the accused is guilty. The verdict is then confirmed by administering the same poison to another chicken. The criterion of guilt is reversed for this second chicken. If the first chicken dies, the second must live before the accused can be declared guilty. Occasionally, the verdicts are inconsistent: both chickens live or both chickens die. The Azande, however, do not regard such inconsistency as evidence of the arbitrariness of the procedure; rather, they explain these anomalies by pointing to some mistake made during the ceremony or by suspecting the interference of some outside magical power, much in the same way as a radio broadcast might be disrupted by static. When properly performed without outside magical interference, the poison oracle provides legitimate solutions to perplexing legal problems by referring them to super-natural powers (Evans-Pritchard, 1937).

3. The Trial of Anne Hutchinson (Boston, 1637)

Anne Hutchinson, a middle-aged woman in Puritan Massa-chusetts, became in the mid-1630s the leader of a religious dis-cussion group that met weekly in her home. She quickly gained notoriety for her attacks on the local ministers, who, she argued, did not by virtue of their education and status possess true Christian grace. After one of its members lost the election for Governor, Hutchinson's group became the object of criminal prosecution. The difficulty for the Massachusetts court was that Hutchinson and her followers had violated no clear law in criticizing the competence of the local ministers. The following exchange appears in the tran-script of her trial in 1637:

Mrs. Hutchinson:	What have I done or said?
Gov. Winthrop:	Why, for your doings, this you did: harbor and countenance those that are parties in this faction that you have heard of. . . .
Mrs. Hutchinson:	What law do they transgress?
Gov. Winthrop:	The law of God and of the state.
Mrs. Hutchinson:	In what particular?
Gov. Winthrop:	Why in this among the rest, whereas the Lord doth say honor thy mother and father. . . . This honor you have broken in countenancing them. (Erikson, 1966: 93)

In making this argument, Winthrop is saying that Hutchinson is guilty of violating the Fifth Commandment, since the ministers are to the community as parents are to the family. Guilt is deter-mined, then, neither by personal charisma nor by oracle, but by analogy between the facts of the case and the scriptural command.

4. McBoyle v. U.S. (1931)

In 1931 the U.S. Supreme Court heard on appeal a case in-volving the violation of a federal statute that prohibited the transportation of motor vehicles across state lines (*McBoyle* v. *U.S.*, 283 US 25). McBoyle had been convicted under this law for flying a stolen airplane from Illinois to Oklahoma. Having been sentenced to three years in prison and fined $2000, McBoyle appealed. The Supreme Court ruled that McBoyle was not guilty of violating this law, since the National Motor Vehicle Theft Act passed by Congress in 1919 contained no mention of "aeroplanes." The Court argued that when Congress passed the law, the intention was solely to protect automobile owners. Under the norms of due process the 1919 law did not contain "fair warning" to McBoyle that his act would be prosecuted. Note that there was no question about the facts of the situation: McBoyle flew an airplane he knew to be stolen across state lines. He could not, however, be found guilty of violating a law that did not specify that the concept "motor vehicle" includes flying as well as surface vehicles.

TYPES OF LEGAL DECISION MAKING

These four cases illustrate the range of procedures by which human societies resolve legal problems. Each society considers its procedure a just and reliable way of making legal judgments. Each procedure, however, contains characteristic flaws. Reliance on the insight of charismatic individuals to solve legal problems rarely produces the wisdom of Solomon. On the average a society can probably expect, at best, mediocrities for kings, presidents, and judges; were this not true, Solomon would not be such a legendary figure.

Reliance on direct intervention of the supernatural may be preferable to depending upon the capacities of mortal individuals, but the difficulty lies in finding a reliable method of invoking supernatural powers to make such mundane decisions. The Azande poison oracle is ingenious in its elaborate safeguards; but we suspect, even here, that whether a chicken lives or dies depends upon its state of health and the amount of food in its digestive tract before it is given the poison. To an outsider who does not accept the theoretical basis of the supernatural procedure it seems that the results are largely random in character. Indeed, Vilhelm Aubert (1965) has argued that it is precisely their randomness that provides them with their legitimacy: in the long run no one group is favored over another by the results of the supernatural legal decisions.

Reliance on written rules appears to have the advantage of

consistency and predictability. Scriptures (the Bible: "Honor thy father and mother!"; Chairman Mao: "Avoid mountain fortress mentality!"), while providing general rules, do not give clear solutions for particular cases. The Fifth Commandment, for example, refers specifically to parents; it may presumably be generalized to all authority figures, but as in the Puritan's case, this commandment may turn out to be too broad and may turn out to be of very little use if there is some disagreement among the authorities themselves.

Reliance on formal rules and concepts as a basis for deciding cases overcomes many of the problems with the other three types of procedure. The cost, however, is suggested by the McBoyle decision. Should factual evidence of guilt beyond a reasonable doubt be ignored on the grounds of some definitional technicality? Basing legal decisions upon precise definitions and arid logic strikes many people as being irrational.

The problem for Weber was not simply to collect such episodes and evaluate the relative merits of the procedure used. Recognizing the costs and benefits of each procedure will help us avoid the trap of ethnocentrism, that is, regarding our most familiar procedure as inherently superior to others. At issue sociologically is not such normative considerations, but rather why one procedure becomes predominant in certain social structures and remains rudimentary in others. In addition, we will also want to examine the consequences that having one procedure rather than another has on the manner in which the society reacts to crime. The task is to understand how these varied procedures are related to each other and to locate the social contexts in which they come to predominate. Any given society is likely, Weber argued, to employ a wide diversity of legal procedures. Different procedures may occasionally coexist. The problem is to see through such complex combinations to the essential, basic types of legal decision making.

Weber's solution to this problem is presented in Table 3.1. Procedures, Weber argues, can be related to each other in terms of two basic dimensions, rationality and formality. In his use of the term *rationality* Weber refers to the presence or absence of general rules as a means of deciding the outcomes of cases. *Rationality* does not mean "rational" in the general sense of "reasonable," "optimal," or "providing the greatest good for the greatest number."[1] By "rationality" Weber means the use of "explicit, abstract, intellectually calculable rules and procedures [instead of] . . . sentiment, tradition, and rule of thumb" (Wrong, 1970: 26). No such

TABLE 3.1
Weber's Typology of Modes of Legal Decision Making

		GENERAL LEGAL RULES USED TO DECIDE CASES ("Rationality")	
		Absent	Present
AUTONOMY OF LEGAL SYSTEM ("Formality")	**Absent**	SUBSTANTIVE IRRATIONAL *Example:* Solomon's wisdom. *Characteristics:* Case-by-case decision making on basis of insight of charismatic judge.	SUBSTANTIVE RATIONAL *Example:* Puritan use of Biblical commandment. *Characteristics:* Cases decided by applying rules from some extralegal source, e.g., religion, ideology, economic expediency, science.
	Present	FORMAL IRRATIONAL *Example:* Poison oracle. *Characteristics:* Specialized legal procedures are used, but *decisions* are not derived from general rules but are determined by supernatural forces.	FORMAL RATIONAL *Example:* McBoyle v. U.S. *Characteristics:* Cases are decided by applying logically consistent abstract rules that are independent of moral, religious, and other normative criteria. General rules require that all cases of the same nature be treated equally.

general rules, for example, were announced by Solomon to justify his decision. Similarly, the poison oracle reaches decisions without the application of rules to the facts of the case. General rules are, however, applied to the particular circumstances of the case in substantive and formal rational justice.

It well may be "rational" in the sense of sensible, desirable, or just to make decisions on a procedurally "irrational" basis. The term "rational" is used by Weber with specific reference to the form of procedure and says nothing whatsoever about the quality of the substantive decision. *Formality* refers to the existence of an autonomous system for deciding legal issues. If disputes are decided by distinctly legal procedures, the system will be "formal." If the decision is made on extralegal grounds (political, moral, economic), the procedure is "informal" or "substantive." Autonomy of the legal system may be institutionalized in several ways. For example, the United States Constitution provides that judges should "receive a compensation which shall not be diminished during their continuance in office" (Art. 3, Sec. 1), thus reducing the influence the legislature might otherwise have over court decisions.

Combining these two dimensions of rationality and formality yields four basic types of legal procedure (substantive irrational, formal irrational, substantive rational, and formal rational), which turn out to be a useful set of distinctions in comparing characteristics of legal systems and their manner of handling cases. It is important to remember in reading the following section that each type of procedure is an abstraction (in Weber's terms, "an ideal type"), which seldom—if ever—is encountered in its pure form in concrete historical societies. Consequently, attempts to neatly "pigeonhole" particular legal institutions may fail to provide satisfactory results in many cases. A particular historical legal institution is apt to combine in various aspects of its operation two or more of these ideal types. As we shall see later, however, the combination of incompatible ideal types in the concrete forms of legal decision making may explain the strains and conflicts we see in concrete decisions. Let us begin with the simpler problem of classifying the four cases we started with into Weber's types.

1. Substantive Irrational

Solomon's decision may be viewed, Weber suggests, as a special case of a general type of legal decision made legitimate by appealing to the charisma of a particular individual or group of individuals. This type of legitimacy is perhaps best exemplified by Jesus' statement: "It is written . . . but I say unto you. . . ." The crucial feature of this form of adjudication is that no systematic rules justify particular decisions. Few people could have anticipated Solomon's solution to the problem of the disputing mothers. In general, litigants are seldom in a very good position under substantive irrational legal procedure to anticipate in advance the outcome of their case. This inability is what Weber means by "irrational." Solomon's decision was not irrational in the sense of being arbitrary, incoherent, inappropriate, or suboptimal. Weber uses the term "rational" not to refer to these criteria for evaluating the quality of the decision; rationality for Weber refers simply to the application of general rules to the facts of a case in reaching decisions.

Substantive irrational procedure takes a variety of concrete forms. A partial but representative list follows.

Khadi Justice. In the marketplace of an Islamic town there sits a judge who arbitrates disputes that arise between buyers and sellers. The Khadi judge acts like Solomon in arriving at "insightful" solutions to disputes without any recourse to explicit rules or legal principles. Each decision is made on a case-by-case basis, the legitimacy of the judgment arising from the charismatic gifts of the individual judge.

Weber uses the term "Khadi justice" to refer generally to this style of adjudication. Thus he refers to Chinese judges as Khadis (1951: 149). In the United States the clearest example of Khadi justice is the juvenile court (see Matza, 1969: 118). The juvenile court is based upon the idea that youthful offenders should not be subjected to the laws and penalties of adult criminals. In fact, "almost one-fourth of the nation's 2,800 juvenile court judges are not trained in the law" (Kittrie, 1971: 160). The distinctive mission of the juvenile court is to help the child rather than impose impersonal standards of justice. The particular offense is taken as a symptom of a child's general problem that needs attention, rather than as being meaningful in its own right. Thus, depending upon the juvenile's past behavior and current environment, stealing an automobile may indicate a variety of problems. The juvenile court judge must exercise insight into each particular case to arrive at a correct decision; no rules exist to dictate whether the appropriate judicial response to auto theft is incarceration, psychotherapy, or parental supervision. Two individuals committing the same offense will probably, as a matter of course, receive quite different "treatments."

Juries. Substantive irrational judgments are issued by charismatic collectives in the American criminal justice system. The jury is a panel of laymen whose task it is to decide whether the evidence warrants prosecution of a suspect (grand jury) or whether the evidence is sufficient for conviction (trial or petit jury). In either case the individual jurors rely on personal insight to arrive at a satisfactory decision. Since few general rules guide the way in which the jury arrives at a decision, each decision is made on a case-by-case basis. By relying on the jury, English criminal procedure depended upon "the rough verdict of the countryside without caring to investigate the logical processes, if logical they were, of which that verdict was the outcome" (Pollock and Maitland, 1923: II, 660–1).

Parole Boards. Parole boards likewise have the task of deciding which inmates should be released from prison on a case-by-case basis without recourse to general rules (Talarico, 1980; Kastenmeir and Eglit, 1973). As in the case of Khadi justice, litigants find it difficult to predict the outcome of the procedure, since no general rules are acknowledged. Furthermore, it is characteristic of these systems that similar individuals receive very different dispositions. This, in turn, leads to a general sense of injustice among the clients of these collective charismatic bodies. In recent years, for example, prison unions have campaigned extensively for the elimination of parole boards in favor of fixed, determinate sentences to eliminate the gross disparities that the parole system creates among inmates.

Popular Tribunals. In several socialist societies, substantive irrational procedures have been institutionalized in the form of "comrades courts" or "popular tribunals." Some advocates of "participatory democracy" in the United States see in these institutions a means by which substantive justice may be achieved through overcoming the formalisms of professional lawyers (e.g., Pepinsky, 1978).

The "tribunals" operating in Cuba in the late 1960s and early 1970s are fairly representative of the organization of these institutions. The Cuban tribunals emphasized popular involvement in neighborhood meetings that were held at convenient times. The judges, primarily laypersons who were elected by the community, heard cases involving local problems. Witnesses usually presented personal knowledge regarding the situation and engaged in a dialogue with both tribunal officials and the audience. Finally, punishment was administered by unpaid members of the neighborhood patriotic organization. The state stressed the goal of teaching law to the people through these tribunals.

In general, the goals of popular justice vary considerably from one country to the next, and the stated goals may, in effect, depart radically from the actual operation.

State rhetoric may assert the principal objective of popular justice as the encouragement of local jural autonomy, but in operation these institutions may be used to facilitate the penetration of the national legal order. Conversely, tribunals designed to facilitate the implementation of national policies may in actual fact articulate local values and interests and cushion the impact of these policies. Secondly, there tends to be an ambiguity or lack of unanimity amongst a nation's ideologists as to the goals of popular justice. Policy makers may oscillate between the "policy implementation" and "self-management" conceptions of legal tribunals. Thirdly, the legal ideology of a society may be subject to shifts, as correspondingly popular courts acquire a new significance at different periods of time. State propagandists may at an early phase of the establishment of popular tribunals emphasize its conflict management function, but as the regime becomes more radicalized, place greater emphasis on its pedagogic functions. Fourthly, different popular tribunals may occupy contradictory positions in the legal ideological landscape. One popular tribunal by being empowered to dispose of minor crimes and anti-social conduct by the application of informal social pressure may represent the withdrawal of the central legal order, while another tribunal by being vested with coercive sanctioning power over a wide range of social behavior not previously subject to state regulation may represent a contradictory trend. (Tiruchelvam, 1978: 264)

Discretion on the part of individual decision makers exists in all legal procedures. Substantive irrational systems make a virtue out of this necessity; decisions are legitimate precisely because they reflect the personal inclinations and insights of the individual decision maker(s). Both benefits and costs are associated with this form of procedure. It allows the law to take into account the circumstances of the individual and to balance the benefits to the individual and to society in a way that would be impossible were some general formal rule to be applied across the board. "Substantive irrational" decisions are in this sense "humane," recognizing the special qualities of the unique individual. At the same time, to the extent that the litigant knows others who have the same problem or who have committed similar offenses, the case-by-case manner of decision making will often create a sense of arbitrariness and injustice among the population of clients.

2. Formal Irrational

The Azande poison oracle exemplifies a general type of legal procedure that Weber characterized as formal irrational. It is *formal* in the sense that distinctly legal procedures are used to reach a decision. For the poison oracle to work, certain ritual incantations must be made; failure to employ the proper procedure will result in an erroneous judgment. The oracle is *irrational* because, as with substantive irrational procedures, no general rules guide the decision. "The formal character of procedure thus stands in sharp contrast to the thoroughly irrational character of the technique of decision. Logical or rational grounds for a concrete decision were entirely lacking" (Weber, 1978: 762). The outcome is, in most instances, unpredictable and inexplicable.

A variety of formal irrational procedures are found in human societies. These procedures are usually invoked when the case poses difficult problems of evidence. Such procedures are used to resolve troublesome cases, particularly in those societies in which central authority is weak (Roberts, 1965). Since the central authority is unable to impose a solution to legal problems, the outcome is placed in the hands of supernatural forces. This may be done in several ways.

Oracle. In ancient Greece the Delphic Oracle was frequently consulted to resolve problems or plan the future. The oracle spoke through a priestess, who sat on a golden tripod and fell into a trance. Such oracles are widespread in various cultures. They often rely upon the interpretation of patterns of bones, flight of birds, or the content of dreams as signs to be interpreted by a magician or priest with expertise in the meaning of such signs.

Ordeal. The supernatural may resolve legal problems by directly intervening in a physical trial of the accused. Ordeals were once common legal procedures in Western Europe. Guilt could be determined by the inability of the suspect to hold a heated iron bar, the weight of the bar being proportional to the seriousness of the offense. Alternatively, it was believed that the guilty would be unable to swallow the consecrated Host or to recite correctly the Lord's prayer.

In the case of witchcraft, other ordeals were devised. Since water was one of the pure elements, it followed logically to the medieval mind that water would expel evil. Thus a guilty person thrown in a pond bound hand and foot would float to the top, whereas an innocent person would be embraced by the water and pulled to the bottom. The disadvantage of this procedure for the innocent is plain.

Trial by combat was another form of ordeal commonly employed in the medieval period; indeed, it remained open as a legitimate legal device in England as late as 1824. Here two disputants would choose weapons and fight to the death. God would intervene on the side of the virtuous. Should the virtuous person feel physically incapable of fighting in his own defense, he could hire a legal "champion" to take up arms for him. In Western Europe these ordeals were supervised and administered by the church until 1215. In that year the Fourth Lateran council eliminated the participation of the church, although ordeals persisted for several centuries.

Oaths. When a witness in a modern court swears on the Bible to tell the truth, the courtroom reenacts the last vestige of the formal irrational procedure in Western law. Originally, it was believed that God would directly intervene and strike down any person who gave a false oath. Far less reliance is placed today on this procedure as a method of ensuring the veracity of witnesses, although it has been retained as a ceremony.

These formal irrational devices are quite foreign to contemporary legal institutions. They have, however, played a major role in the legal systems of tribal and feudal societies. In the absence of a centralized state able to back up its decisions with force, the invocation of the supernatural has proven in a great many societies to be an effective method of obtaining compliance (Roberts, 1965). When in the twelfth century King Henry II attempted to reform the English system by eliminating oaths and ordeals, he ran into stiff opposition. When Henry sought to have legal cases decided by a jury, opponents argued vehemently that this change would corrupt the law by taking the judgment away from God and placing it in the hands of mere men.

As with the substantive irrational procedure, the failure to base decisions on explicit rules makes prior calculation of outcomes exceedingly difficult. If the Azande oracle is conducted without manipulation, for example, the result in the long run will be random. Making random decisions may be a rational way to resolve certain types of problems and disputes, but it is *irrational* in Weber's restricted sense of the decision being made in the absence of general rules. The procedure works only if properly performed. Hence legal specialists are necessary as well as a body of rules governing only the invocation of the supernatural. However, the legal decision (for example, guilty versus not guilty) is not determined by these rules for invoking the supernatural. The legal decision is dictated by the gods, fate, or chance.

3. Substantive Rational

Decisions are often made on the basis of general rules that are not specifically legal. The principles on which such a decision is based may derive from a religion, a system of ethics, a political ideology, or an economic program. The efforts of the Ayatollah Khomeini to rewrite Iranian law on the basis of the Koran's commandments is one instance of substantive rational law. Khomeini does not claim legitimacy as a charismatic law giver; the true law giver was the Prophet Mohammed. It is the task of Islamic leaders to return their societies to the commands of the Prophet.

In the United States, substantive rational decision making is to be found in a variety of situations. The use of psychiatric diagnosis in determining the ability of the accused to stand trial for a crime or in determining the nature of the sentence to be imposed on the convicted defendant is one example. The decision is based upon a systematic body of rules (e.g., the Diagnostic Statistical Manual); but although these rules are articulated and written, they are extralegal. They are not formulated or applied by legal specialists. The most celebrated introduction of substantive rational criteria into American law is the "Brandeis brief." This innovation by Louis D. Brandeis (1856–1941) in 1908 explicitly utilized data on the social and economic impact of law as grounds for assessing its constitutionality. While such considerations had entered court decisions before, the Brandeis brief legitimated substantive rational bases for Supreme Court decisions.

Systems that rely on substantive rational criteria for justifying legal decisions often encounter gaps between the rules employed and the situations encountered. The Bible, for example, has little to say about the appropriate legal response to real estate swindles; on the other hand, many Biblical commandments ("If thy hand or thy foot offend thee, cut it off," Matthew 18: 8) imply consequences that would be unpalatable if taken literally. In general, to go from religious, ethical, ideological, or pragmatic considerations to the circumstances of a particular legal case requires a set of auxiliary or bridging devices. We see this in the indictment of Anne Hutchinson. Having been unable to find a clear Biblical rule that Hutchinson had violated, Winthrop argued that her actions were violations of the Fifth Commandment. His argument rests on the principle of *analogy*. A given act is criminal if it sufficiently resembles an act explicitly condemned by the law. Disobedience to the ministers was not forbidden explicitly in Scripture but was, Winthrop argued, analogous to disobedience to parents.

Another case may make the principle of legal analogy clear. In the 1930s the Soviet Union was engaged in a campaign to destroy organized religion within its borders. The Islamic populations of the south central part of the Soviet Union were particularly troublesome. Rather than ban the practice of Islam outright (and blatantly contradict the freedom of religion provision of the Soviet constitution), the government sought other ways to undermine the power of tradition. Women, for example, were encouraged to enter the labor force, thus undermining the traditional Moslem patriarchal family authority. Circumcision, a rite central to the religion, was banned. To locate a legal basis for this prohibition, the government began prosecuting practitioners under the antiabortion law, the argument being that circumcision was analogous to abortion (Starosolskyj, 1954).

Substantive rational procedures are more consistent than irrational procedures, but there is still a large element of incalculability associated with them. The gap between substantive criteria and a legal problem is often wide and can only be bridged by the use of legal analogy. Only imagination and verve govern the content of analogy; the litigant is in large measure left in the dark, despite the reliance on formal, explicit rules in arriving at decisions.

4. Formal Rational

General rules may be used in quite a different way to arrive at legal decisions. To understand the distinction between substantive and formal rationality, we might best begin with a specific problem (Rheinstein, 1954: xliii–xliv).

Suppose two individuals decide to buy some lakefront property. Smith and Jones pool their money and buy "Lakeview"; they agree to split the land into West and East Lakeview and toss coins to determine which one gets the more desirable East Lakeview property on the water. Smith wins the toss but agrees to allow his friend Jones access to the lake. In legal terminology, Smith agrees to an "easement" on his land, a right of access to be enjoyed forever by Jones and all her seed. Figure 3.1 shows a map to keep things straight. Now imagine the following twists of events:

1. Smith sells East Lakeview to Green.
2. Green eventually sells the land to Jones, who now owns East and West Lakeview.
3. Unable to pay property taxes and her alimony, Jones sells West Lakeview to Brown.

Does the new owner, Brown, still have the easement on East Lakeview? If we base the decision on the legal concept of "easement" and follow logical rules, we conclude that he does not. An easement is a right in a property belonging to another. When Jones came into ownership of Lakeview, the easement ceased logically to exist.

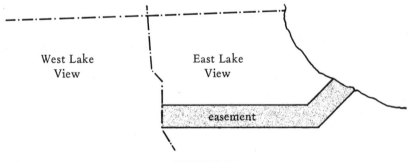

FIGURE 3.1
A Typical Easement Problem

We might address this question on substantive grounds, rather than logically formal grounds. Without access to the lake, East Lakeview is a much less desirable piece of property, since Brown has no convenient way to get to his sailboat. Such a decision might have adverse consequences for the real estate market. On the grounds of social, political, or economic criteria we might want to continue (or eliminate) the easement. Following the dictates of formal rationality, however, these substantive considerations are beside the point because the easement ceased to exist with the previous transfer of ownership.

In general, formal rationality is characterized by the application to legal problems of explicit, universal rules. The rules come from no external source, but are intrinsically legal. The doctrine of easement was developed, for example, by Roman jurists, who spelled out the logical consequences of the concept for various types of problems. Basing legal decisions on such abstract concepts and rules has a number of significant consequences. First, decisions are highly predictable. One need only know what "easement" means to inform Brown of the outcome of his case. Second, decisions will be made without consideration of the immediate needs of political or economic elites. The social "desirability" of a given action need not be weighed in evaluating the legality of an action. Being freed of substantive constraints, the jurists can discard concepts and rules that are contradictory or vague and—in principle—arrive at a fully consistent, logical system of legal rules. In a pure formal rational system

> The judge . . . is more or less an automaton of paragraphs: the legal documents, together with the costs and fees, are dropped in at the top with the expectation that the judgment will emerge at the bottom, together with more or less sound arguments—an apparatus, accordingly, whose functioning is by and large calculable or predictable. (Weber, 1978: 1395)

While Weber, in writing this around 1920, was taking this image figuratively, the introduction of computers into the legal process may make the image more literal. Computer predictions of court decisions, Julius Stone suggests, is not only technically feasible but

> holds much promise of relief from ills such as court congestion, backlog, inefficiency and delays. In advising clients, reasonable reliable prediction of future appellate holdings (particularly if behav-

iorist claims to accuracy as high as 90 percent were approached) could encourage settlement of many suits. It would do this, moreover, without thrusting excessive personal responsibility on to the advising lawyer. . . . This might be resorted to by inferior court judges themselves without serious countervailing risks. (1966: 687–95)

A distinguishing feature of the formal rational system is that the creators of the rules themselves become bound by the rules they create. Consider, for example, the situation in Figure 3.2, in which Union Army General Abner Doubleday (1818–1893), reputed inventor of the rules of baseball, is being sanctioned by a military subordinate according to the formal rational rules of his own creation. This position is paradoxical from the standpoint of the charismatic law giver, who is free to announce new standards according to the situation. The formal rational law giver, however, is not free to modify the rules once they have been established. In Doubleday's case, as depicted here, the result is role conflict; formal rational systems typically impose a price on the interests of their creators.

No legal system has ever been a fully formal rational one. Even with the technology to place such a system into operation, it is not clear that any society is willing to decide legal cases solely on formal rational grounds. Certain legal systems in Western Europe, however, have developed an unusual preponderance of formal

"General Doubleday, sir, you're out."

FIGURE 3.2
Dilemmas of a Formal Rational Law Maker
Drawing by Drucker; ©1978 The New Yorker
Magazine, Inc. Used by permission.

rational criteria in their procedures. This preponderence, Weber argued, has had significant historical consequences.

RATIONAL CAPITALISM AND FORMAL RATIONAL LAW

The typology of legal procedure emerged from Weber's comparative study of law and economy in Europe, ancient Israel, Islam, India, and China. Weber did not pursue all the lines of inquiry opened up by this comparison. He has very little to say, for example, about the circumstances under which oracles and ordeals will dominate a legal system. Weber's primary goal instead was to solve one problem: How did rational capitalism emerge in Western Europe? About 300 years ago Western Europe embarked on a period of sustained economic growth unparalleled in human history. Later joined by the United States and Japan, Europe has raised the levels of economic production, science, and technology far beyond those of any previous civilization. Weber attempts to explain why this particular portion of humanity at this particular period in history was able to launch such a period of growth.

In this section we will discuss Weber's analysis of Western capitalism and review this explanation of the affinity of rational capitalist economic systems with formal rational legal systems. Although the details of Weber's historical analysis are beyond the scope of this review, the main points are essential for understanding his sociology of law. Weber compares Western Europe with the other major civilizations to discover the unique set of circumstances that favored economic growth. For example, all these civilizations had at one time developed urban centers, monetary systems, centralized political states, written languages, and mathematical systems. While each of these factors is certainly a necessary ingredient for economic development, Weber argued, they do not in themselves constitute sufficient conditions. The profit motive, similarly, is commonly found in a variety of cultures. Thus the existence of *capitalists* was not a sufficient condition.

The conclusion Weber reaches is that a particular *form* of capitalism was necessary for economic development to take place and that this form had appeared only in Western Europe. Its appearance there was due to a variety of coincidences. The rational capitalist was, unlike the traditional capitalist, concerned with the deliberate and systematic calculation of long-term profits rather than making quick profits through daredevil speculation, piracy, or conquest. The affinity for long-run calculation was influenced by the legal, political, and religious institutions of Western Europe. The latter effect is the subject of Weber's most famous work "The Protestant Ethic and the Spirit of Capitalism". This essay, however, is a mere fragment of the larger comparisons of Western and non-Western institutions. Since our primary concern is with Weber's sociology of law, we turn now to his analysis of the relationship between rational capitalism and formal rational law.

To understand better the peculiar nature of rational capitalist enterprise, consider what is involved in the production of a new mass-produced automobile.

> In the spring of 1964, the Ford Motor Company introduced what is now called a new automobile. In accordance with current fashion in automobile nomenclature, it was called, one assumes inappropriately, a Mustang. The public was well prepared for the new vehicle. Plans carefully specified prospective output and sales; they erred, as plans do, and in this case by being too modest. These preparations required three and a half years. From late in the autumn of 1962, when the design was settled, until the spring of 1964, there was a fairly firm commitment to the particular car that eventually emerged. Engineering and "styling" costs were $9 million; the cost of tooling up for the production of the Mustang was $50 million. (Galbraith, 1967: 30–1)

For Weber the hallmark of rational capitalism is this propensity for systematic planning, careful advanced calculation of the costs and benefits, and reinvestment of returns back into the enterprise. For such an operation to succeed, the legal system must provide a climate for rational calculation. Both the capitalist enterprise and the capitalist state share a common character. Their authority relations are identical, despite the fact that they pursue different goals. One of the central features of the capitalist economy is the dispossession of the worker. Precapitalist workers (craftsmen, small farmers, knights) had generally owned "the tools, supplies, finances, and weapons with which they fulfilled their economic, political and military functions and maintained themselves" (Weber, 1978: 1394). Capitalism concentrated ownership of the means of production, so that the only means of production the laborer effectively owned was "human capital," the skills and motivations contained in his person. This concentration in the private sector of the economy was repeated in the state sector as well. The means of administration and means of violence are similarly concentrated in the hands of the centralized state.

> This all important fact: the "separation" of the worker from the material means of production, destruction, administration, academic research and finance in general is the common basis of the modern state, in its political, cultural, and military sphere, and of the private capitalist economy. (Weber, 1978: 1394)

Just as Marx draws attention to the functional necessity of legal equality in an economic system in which labor is a commodity, Weber suggests that the rational character of capitalist enterprise is functionally related to rational state administration and a formal rational legal system.

> The modern capitalist enterprise rests primarily on *calculation* and presupposes a legal and administrative system, whose functioning can be rationally predicted, at least in principle, by virtue of its fixed general norms, just like the expected performance of a machine. The modern capitalist enterprise cannot accept what is popularly called "*khadi*-justice": adjudication according to the judge's sense of equity in a given case or according to the other irrational means of law-finding that existed everywhere in the past and still exists in the Orient. The modern enterprise also finds incompatible the theocratic or patrimonial governments of Asia and of our own past, whose administrations operated in a patriarchal manner according to their own manner according to their own discretion and, for the rest, according to inviolably sacred but irrational tradition. (Weber, 1978: 1394–5)

One manifestation of the necessity of rational, predictable law for capitalist enterprise has appeared in the form of advertisements taken out by Aetna Life and Casualty to explain to the public the reasons for the escalating costs of insurance. In one series Aetna focuses on jury awards in tort cases. In recent years juries have awarded multimillion dollar damages in tort cases. In one case

> a 23 year old women was arrested, tried and found innocent of shop-lifting. In turn, she sued the store and its special policeman. To compensate her for "depression, anxiety, nervousness, phobia, fears, and nightmares" the jury awarded her $1,100,000 in damages. (Aetna advertisement, *Newsweek*, January 30, 1978)

The problem for insurance companies posed by jackpot jury awards is not so much the dollar amounts they must pay for these settlements since this additional expense is passed on to the consumer in the form of higher rates. The more basic problem with jury awards is their unpredictability. Swayed by emotion and circumstance, juries do not behave systematically and predictably in tort cases. The insurance business is based on careful calculation of actuarial rates of expected losses. With long-term investment decisions based on these calculations, the success of an insurance company rests in large measure on the accuracy of its actuarial calculations. The introduction of state-financed workman's compensation programs developed out of similar problems with jury awards in industrial accident cases (Friedman and Ladinsky, 1967; cf. H. L. Ross, 1970).

What is true of insurance is equally true of most large-scale enterprises from bakeries to automobile assembly plants. The law must in its very structure be coherent, consistent, and predictable. Any large enterprise employs a substantial staff of attorneys to ensure the legal position of the company either by advising on company policies or lobbying for laws favorable to the corporation's interests.

In addition to understanding the functional compatibility between rational capitalism and formal rational law, Weber was concerned with the historical role this form of legality had played in the emergence of rational capitalism. In contrast to Marx, Weber does not postulate an economic basis as a precondition for the emergence of forms of law. There is, Weber argues, a tendency toward mutual affinity between legal systems and economic systems, but the historical priority does not necessarily belong to the economic system. Formal rational procedure did not emerge as a consequence of economic change, Weber argues. Instead, the prior existence of rationality in the legal systems was a precondition for the emergence of rational capitalism.

The roots of formal rational law lie not in economic transformations, but in the centralization of political power. The political history of the medieval period consists largely of attempts by the monarchs to consolidate their power over the independent nobility. Given the nature of warfare, travel, and communication in Europe, this consolidation remained elusive. For example, just within the small east German state of Saxony "there were in the early seventeenth century upwards of two thousand courts of first instance possessed of criminal jurisdiction" (Langbein, 1977: 56). One of the early successful efforts to unify the legal system was made by King Henry II of England (1154–1189), who introduced major legal reforms that have had important roles in shaping our own legal institutions. Prior to Henry's reforms, each locality had its own courts and laws; difficult cases were tried by formal irrational procedures. To standardize the law, Henry introduced a system of traveling or "circuit" judges who appeared once a year to hear cases. The *assizes* did not attempt to impose a uniform written code; rather, they attempted to develop rules common to the various local traditions in their circuit (hence the term "common law"). Once established by Henry's political power, the assizes gained power and independence of their own. Around these courts there developed a guild of lawyers. As with the other craft guilds of the period the lawyers' guild, the *Inns of the Court*, recruited (largely from the nobility) and trained lawyers, set fees, and established professional norms. The judges came over time to be selected from the lawyers' guild. Thus the first of Henry's reforms established an independent, national judiciary allied with a professional body of legal specialists trained in the tradition of common law.

The second reform was the introduction of the jury. Initially, the jury was little more than a panel of twelve men whose task was to testify to the best of their knowledge the facts of a given case. Over time this role shifted from that of witness to that of evaluator. The jury retained a substantial amount of irrationality in that its decisions were not governed by systematic rules. It did, however, serve to reduce the reliance of the law on formal irrational devices, reinforcing the general tendency of the legal system toward a secular, professional orientation.

These changes in the legal system, it must be emphasized, did not result from previous modifications of the economic system. Legal change in this case was in large measure a consequence of the English kings' efforts to consolidate their power. Once a secular, national legal system was in place, an independent legal profession accelerated the trend toward rationalizing the law. Rational law, in turn, became a precondition for the emergence of capitalism in Western Europe.[2]

Both Marx and Weber subscribe to a common functionalist model of law and economy. Thus they both explain the persistence of such features of bourgeois law as equality by referring to the consequences such features of law have for the reproduction of capitalist economic relations. Both contend that legal equality in a capitalist society ironically serves to reproduce political and economic inequality.[3] In Weber's words,

> The propertyless masses especially are not served by the formal "equality before the law" and the "calculable" adjudication and ad-

ministration demanded by bourgeois interests. Naturally in their eyes justice and administration should serve to equalize their economic and social life opportunities in the face of the propertied classes. Justice and administration can fulfill this function only if they assume a character that [solves legal problems on the substantive merits of individual cases]. (1978: 980)

They differ, however, in this causal analysis of the origins of the characteristic features of the bourgeois legal order. Marx tends to view these features of law as outcomes of economic changes, whereas Weber contends that legal rationalization not only occurred prior to the economic transformation of Western Europe, but provided one of the catalysts for this change. The independent role of legal change in the transition from feudalism to capitalism is an empirical issue subject to debate; at least some modern research tends to favor Marx's interpretation over Weber's (cf. Tigar and Levy, 1977). However the debate over the origins of capitalist law is resolved, Weber's careful examination of formal rationality as a key property of capitalist law by itself represents a substantial contribution to our understanding.

SUMMARY

Two important themes stand out from Weber's analyses. First, his comparative strategy encompasses the range of diverse legal procedures found in various human societies. His typology represents the diversity of grounds for making legitimate legal decisions as combinations of a small number of elements. This view permits us to see analogies between legal systems that would be less apparent given our natural inclination to classify societies by place and time.

The second major theme is really a continuation of the line of analysis begun by Marx, namely, the relationship between the economic system and the legal system. Like Marx, Weber argues that law and economy are closely linked. Weber was specifically concerned with modern industrial capitalism and its unique application of rationality to economic production. Such an economic system, in Weber's view, was compatible with a narrowly circumscribed range of legal institutions. In the case of Western Europe, Weber argues, legal change antedated economic change. This view is at odds with that of Marx; it suggests the possible role of legal change in the development of economic growth. In fact, Weber's thesis has provided a point of departure for lawyers who have sought to assist developing nations in modifying their legal codes to further economic growth (Trubek, 1972b; F. G. Snyder, 1980).

SUGGESTED READING

Weber's work on law, most of which is contained in Weber (1978), is not accessible to most readers, owing to its detail and disorganization. Unlike Marx, it is better to begin with secondary sources. Rheinstein's introduction (1954) to a collection of Weber's work on law is excellent, as is the discussion of rational law and bureaucracy in Bendix's (1977) classic portrait of Weber. Hunt (1978) gives a more detailed summary. Trubek (1972a) presents clearly Weber's thesis on law and rational capitalism. Useful historical accounts include Kern (1939) and Baker (1977). Ladinsky and Silver (1967) examine the autonomy of American courts in the face of populist pressures, while Levin (1977) examines the consequences of variation in the relative autonomy of the courts. For a suggestive study of the consequences of greater formal rationality in penal policy, see Greenberg and Humphries (1980).

FOOTNOTES

1. Confusion is often created by failure to distinguish between the colloquial use of the term rationality and Weber's technical usage. For example of such confusion, see Marcuse (1968) and Hunt (1978).

2. The rationalization and systematization of the law in general and . . . the increasing calculability of the functioning of the legal process in particular, constituted one of the most important conditions for the existence of capitalist enterprise, which cannot do without legal security. (Weber, 1978: 853)

   If the formal rational ideal type provides the greatest realization of these rational properties, a major difficulty for Weber is the appearance of the Industrial Revolution first in England. In the English legal system "the degree of legal rationality is essentially lower than, and of a type different from, that of continental Europe" (Weber, 1978: 890). England has never had a written constitution; the constitution consists of a body of unsystematic traditions. While Parliament enacts statutes, much of the law consists of "common law," a body of precedents, past decisions made by courts. In essence common law treats as charismatic law givers the judges who have rendered decisions in the past. Moreover, the contemporary judge is free to select those aspects of previous cases that are "relevant" to the current case. For example, the United States Supreme Court in *Heart of Atlanta Motel v. U.S.* (1964) ruled that Congress had Constitutional authority to ban racial discrimination in public accommodations. In the civil rights cases of 1883 the Supreme Court had ruled unconstitutional a similar civil rights law enacted by Congress in 1875. The 1883 decision was not relevant, the Court argued, because the 1964 Civil Rights Act was based on Congress's power to regulate commerce, whereas the defunct 1875 law did not have that basis (M. Berger, 1967: 72–3). The reliance on past charismatic law givers and the freedom to use analogy and to employ precedent selectively places the common law under the rubric of "substantive irrational" justice. The extensive use of the jury, similarly, sets English law apart from Continental law as departing from the ideal type of formal rationality. The peculiar character of British law is largely attributable, Weber argues, to its development in a guild rather than a university.

> The guild style of legal training naturally produced a formalistic treatment of the law, bound by precedent and analogies drawn from precedent. Not only was systematic and comprehensive treatment of the whole body of the law prevented by the craftlike specialization of the lawyers, but legal practice did not aim at all at a rational system, but rather at a practically useful scheme of contrasts and actions, oriented towards the interests of clients in typically recurrent situations. . . . From such practices and attitudes no rational system of law could emerge, not even a rationalization of the law as such, because the concepts thus formed are constructed in relation to concrete events of everyday life, are distinguished from each other by external criteria, and extended in their scope as new needs arise by means of the techniques just mentioned. They are not "general concepts" which would be formed by abstraction from concreteness or by logical interpretation of meaning or by generalization and subsumption; nor were these concepts apt to be used in syllogistically applicable norms. In the purely empirical conduct of legal practice and legal training one always moves from the particular to the particular but never tries to move from the particular to general propositions in order to be able subsequently to deduce from them the norm for new particular cases. (Weber, 1978: 787)

This statement needs to be qualified to some extent, since American and British courts seek to follow the principle of *stare decisis* ("let it stand"). This maxim discourages deliberate overturning of past decisions, although it allows considerable flexibility of interpretation. Perhaps most important, while consistency may be produced from one case to the next following stare decisis, little incentive exists in common law to articulate a system of consistent general rules. In fact

> it is precisely some of those cases which have been decided on incorrect premises or reasoning which have become the most important in com-

mon law. . . . Our modern law of torts has been developed to a considerable extent by a series of bad arguments. (Goodhart, 1930: 16)

Weber never resolved the anomaly that the first European nation to industrialize was the one whose legal system least conformed to the ideal type of formal rationality. His major work, *Economy and Society*, contains several suggestions. Perhaps, Weber suggests, rational capitalism can develop without a fully rational legal system; perhaps the English religion, polity, technology, and labor markets were so conducive to rational capitalism that the legal system provided only a minor impediment. Alternatively, Weber suggests, the English legal system may have had some characteristics that were the "functional equivalent" of formal rationality. If the legal system were a tool of the economic elites, Weber suggests, anticipating American conflict theorists fifty years later, then the irrational legal system would have been conducive to the emergence of the capitalist economy. Alternatively, the emergence of due process rules provided a constraint on the court and introduced an element of formal rationality into the legal procedure without systematizing the law. It should be recognized that *Economy and Society* was at the time of Weber's death largely in the form of notes. Consequently, we have only some ideas about the England problem tentatively put forward by Weber. The England problem thus remains an issue requiring more work.

3. This is periodically rediscovered. For example, Herbert Marcuse makes a similar observation about the "repressive tolerance" characteristic of liberal society:

> The underlying assumption is that the established society is free, and that any improvement, even a change in the social structure and social values, would come about in the normal course of events, prepared, defined, and tested in free and equal discussion, on the open marketplace of ideas and goods. . . . Then the laborer, whose real interest conflicts with that of management, the common consumer whose real interest conflicts with that of the producer, the intellectual whose vocation conflicts with that of his employer find themselves submitting to a system against which they are powerless and appear unreasonable. The ideas of the available alternatives evaporates into an utterly utopian dimension in which it is at home, for a free society is indeed unrealistically and undefinably different from the existing ones. (1965: 92–3)

The concept of "institutional racism" (cf. Knowles and Prewitt, 1969) is a variation on this theme, in that policies that have the practical consequence of disadvantaging minorities may be carried out by unprejudiced individuals following formal rational criteria of decision making.

4

Sanctions and Solidarity: The Contribution of Emile Durkheim

On April 23, 1899, near the town of Newman in Coweta County, Georgia, 2000 persons witnessed the torture and burning of Sam Holt, a black farm laborer accused of murdering his white employer and of raping his employer's wife. The sheriff arrested Holt two weeks after the crime; as word of the arrest spread through the community, a crowd formed at the jail. The sheriff turned the accused man over to the crowd, which then marched him through the town to the scene of the crime. Despite pleas by a former governor of the state and a town judge, the mob pushed on to a site about two miles from town, where Holt was tied to a tree and his body was mutilated and set on fire. A confession of the crimes was obtained from Holt before he died. The participants and observers made no effort to conceal their identity, and no legal action was subsequently taken against any of Holt's killers.

Over 200 such lynchings took place in the United States annually in the early 1890s (Grant, 1975; Ginzberg, 1962). The public torture and execution of condemned criminals was until the eighteenth century a common form of punishment employed by even the most advanced states in Western Europe (cf. Foucault, 1979). Explaining what took place in Newman in April of 1899 therefore requires more than simply an examination of the peculiar institutions of the American South at that particular historical period. In the work of French sociologist Emile Durkheim we find one set of ideas that allow us both to understand such episodes and to view more coherently the relationship between these archaic forms of punishment and their contemporary counterparts. After examining Durkheim's thesis we will consider a specific case of ritual punishment and social solidarity (in Puritan Massachusetts) to explore some of the empirical consequences of Durkheim's thesis. Finally, we will consider the role of ritual punishment in contemporary society by examining how the present criminal justice system has been largely stripped of its role as the focal point of collective ritual, while it has continued to provide such ritual for subgroups within the society.

DURKHEIM ON PUNISHMENT
AND SOLIDARITY

Durkheim suggests that punishments serve, under certain conditions, as social rituals that bring together the "upright" members of the community and provide them with opportunities to reaffirm and intensify their commitment to shared values and a common identity. Rituals of all kinds strengthen social bonds; the act of punishment provides a dramatic forum for reaffirming the values of the community. Imagine, suggests Durkheim, a community of saints,

> a perfect cloister of exemplary individuals. Crimes, [commonly] so called, will there be unknown; but faults which appear venial to the layman will create there the same scandal that the ordinary offense does in ordinary consciousnesses. If then, this society has the power to judge and punish, it will define these acts as criminal and will treat them as such. (Durkheim, 1950: 68–69)

Within this parable are four important ideas:

1. Punishment is more proactive than reactive.
2. Ritual punishment and solidarity are functionally linked.
3. Criminality is the product of ritual punishment; it is not a property of the behavior punished, but a reflection of the solidarity needs of the community.
4. The behavior being punished need have no direct objectively harmful consequences for the community.

Let us examine these in detail.

Punishment Is More Proactive Than Reactive

Punishment is generally viewed as a simple, automatic response of society to crime. The greater the crime rate, for example, the higher we expect the prison population to be. This apparently simple, straightforward relationship between crime and punishment, Durkheim suggests, is deceptive. Communities punish offenders who violate their norms; but communities also ignore violators, warn them, divert them, and commute them. A great deal of filtering occurs between the breaking of a norm and the final fall of the axe or slam of the cell door. For example, anthropologist Bronislaw Malinowski observed the following episode in the Trobriand Islands:

> One day an outbreak of wailing and a great commotion told me that a death had occurred somewhere in the neighborhood. I was informed that Kima'i, a young lad of my acquaintance, of sixteen or so, had fallen from a coco-nut palm and killed himself.
>
> I hastened to the next village where this had occurred, only to find the whole mortuary proceeding in progress. ... I found that another youth had been severely wounded by some mysterious coincidence. And at the funeral there was obviously a general feeling of hostility between the village where the boy died and that into which his body was carried for burial.
>
> Only much later was I able to discover the real meaning of these events: the boy had committed suicide. The truth was that he had broken the rules of exogamy, the partner in his crime being his maternal cousin, the daughter of his mother's sister. This had been known and generally disapproved of, but nothing was done until the girl's discarded lover, who had wanted to marry her and who felt personally injured, took the initiative. This rival threatened first to use black magic against the guilty youth, but this had not much effect. Then one evening he insulted the culprit in public—accusing him in the hearing of the whole community of incest and hurling at him certain expressions intolerable to a native.
>
> For this there was only one remedy; only one means of escape remained to the unfortunate youth. Next morning he put on festive attire and ornamentation, climbed a coco-nut palm and addressed the community, speaking from among the palm leaves and bidding them farewell. He explained the reasons for his desperate deed and also launched forth a veiled accusation against the man who had driven him to his death, upon which it became the duty of his clansmen to avenge him. Then he wailed aloud, as is the custom, jumped from a palm some sixty feet high and was killed on the spot.

There followed a fight within the village in which the rival was wounded; and the quarrel was repeated during the funeral. . . .

It is an axiom of Anthropology that nothing arouses a greater horror than the breach of this [incest] prohibition, and that besides a strong reaction of public opinion, there are also supernatural punishments, which visit this crime. Nor is this axiom devoid of foundation in fact. If you were to inquire into the matter among the Trobrianders, you would find that all statements confirm the axiom, that the natives show horror at the idea of violating the rules of exogamy and that they believe that sores, disease and even death might follow clan incest. This is the ideal of native law, and in moral matters it is easy and pleasant strictly to adhere to the ideal—when judging the conduct of others or expressing an opinion about conduct in general.

When it comes to the application of morality and ideals to real life, however, things take on a different complexion. In the case described it was obvious that the facts would not tally with the ideal of conduct. Public opinion was neither outraged by the knowledge of the crime to any extent, nor did it react directly—it had to be mobilized by a public statement of the crime and by insults being hurled at the culprit by an interested party. Even then he had to carry out the punishment himself. (Malinowski, 1962: 77–9)

While Malinowski's case dramatically illustrates the lack of a simple connection between performance of a criminal act and societal reaction to it, much the same story emerges from studies of more routine episodes in contemporary American society. In particular, victimization surveys, in which a sample of the population is asked to report involvement as victims of various crimes, show that fewer than half of all rapes, robberies, assaults, and personal larcenies are reported to the police. Similar filtering of episodes is conducted at each point in the criminal justice system, as we will see in Chapter 8. Societal reaction to crime is thus complex and contingent on a variety of factors, not all of which are directly related to the immediate offense.

Punishment Is Functionally Linked to Solidarity

Crime brings together upright consciences and concentrates them. We have only to notice what happens, particularly in a small town, when some moral scandal has just been committed. They stop each other on the street, they visit each other, they seek to come together to talk of the event and to wax indignant in common. (Durkheim 1964: 19)

This pattern of "waxing indignant" in common is found across a wide range of collectives from small task groups (Lauderdale, 1976), to families (Vogel and Bell, 1968) to communities (Erikson, 1966). Some occupational groups, for example, enjoy a high level of commonality and identity, maintained in part by the ritual stigmatization of outsiders. Jazz musicians, for instance,

> derive a good deal of amusement from sitting and watching squares.
> . . . Every item of dress, speech and behavior which differs from that of a musician is taken as new evidence of the inherent insensitivity and ignorance of the square (thus fortifying) their conviction that musicians and squares are two kinds of people. . . . The jazz fan is respected no more than the other squares. His liking is without understanding and he acts just like the other squares; he will request songs and try to influence the musicians playing, just as other squares do. (Becker, 1973: 91)

Not only does the reaction to crime bring together the community, but conversely a disruption of the community's solidarity will lead it to seek out a crime to punish. Thus

> when going through circumstances which sadden, perplex or irritate it, society exercises a pressure over its members, to make them bear witness, by significant acts, to their sorrow, perplexity or anger. It imposes upon them the duty of weeping, groaning or inflicting wounds upon themselves or others, for these collective manifestations (and the moral communion which they show and strengthen) restore to the group the energy which circumstances threaten to take away from it, and thus they enable it to become settled. This is the experience which men interpret when they imagine that outside them there are evil beings whose hostility, whether constitutional or temporary, can be appeased only by human suffering. These beings are nothing other than collective states objectified; they are society itself seen under one of its aspects. (Durkheim 1948: 459)

Implicit in this argument is a model represented in Figure 4.1, which outlines a characteristic functional relationship among three key variables: solidarity, ritual punishment, and external threat (cf. Stinchcombe, 1968: 89). The positive arrow from ritual punishment to solidarity represents the argument that ritual causes integration.

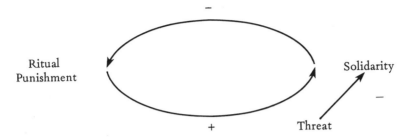

FIGURE 4.1
Durkheim's Functional Model of Ritual Punishment

The negative arrow from solidarity to ritual punishment represents the argument (not made by Durkheim, but implicit in his functional model) that high levels of solidarity inhibit the performance of ritual punishment. These two variables tend, according to the model, toward equilibrium, but solidarity is prone to disruption by the third variable in the schema, external threats. It should be kept in mind that the term *external threats* refers to threats outside the relationship between solidarity and ritual punishment, *not* necessarily to forces outside the community; these threats may be foreign or may be consequences of internal contradictions within the community. The model thus suggests that the disruption of solidarity by a threat leads the community to engage in some form of ritual punishment. Once the ritual has restored integration, minimal episodes of ritual will occur to maintain solidarity in equilibrium. One way to think about this functional model is by analogy to a central heating unit. At a given temperature (67 degrees) the thermostat kicks the furnace on until the critical temperature (68 degrees) is reached. Thermostat and furnace thus maintain an equilibrium, which may be broken in a dramatic fashion by an outside force (the opening of a door or window). Durkheim's theory of ritual suggests that solidary communities work in much the same fashion in performing periodic episodes of ritual punishment.

Crime Is Not a Property of Behavior

Apart from societal reaction to it, nothing else distinguishes crime. Crime is thus a creation of punishment rather than an instigator of punishment.[1] This is seen most clearly in those cases in which conventional notions of individual culpability for criminal acts is absent. For example, in the Roman practice of *decimation,* every tenth member of a legion was executed if the legion had performed poorly (Sykes, 1978: 61). More generally, some societies punish

> for the sake of punishing. . . . Thus, they punish animals which have committed no wrong act or even inanimate beings which have been its passive instrument. (Durkheim, 1964: 85–86)

For example, in September of 1750 one Jacques Ferron was charged with the crime of sodomy with a she-ass at Vanvres, France. Witnesses at the trial testified that they observed Ferron having sexual intercourse with the animal, and on the basis of this evidence Ferron was found guilty of the crime and executed. The animal was then tried, but acquitted on the ground that she was the victim of violence and had not participated in her master's crime of her own free will.

> The prior of the convent, who also performed the duties of parish priest, and the principal inhabitants of the commune of Vanvres signed a certificate stating that they had known the said she-ass for four years, and that she had always shown herself to be virtuous and well-behaved both at home and abroad and had never given occasion of scandal to anyone, and that therefore "they were willing to bear witness that she is in word and deed and in all her habits of life a most honorable creature." (Evans, 1906: 150)

It is a mistake, Durkheim argues, to take such rituals at their face value. To do so leads, in the case of decimation or animal punishments, to dismissal of these cases as irrational aberrations. In fact, such cases present in clear form an essential feature of repressive justice: ritual is a response to external social forces, rather than to the objective features of the object of the ritual itself. More recently, Rene Girard has suggested that

> if the modern mind fails to recognize the strongly functional nature of the scapegoat operation and all its sacrificial surrogates, the most basic phenomena of human culture will remain misunderstood and unresolved. (1977: 276)

Crime Need Have No Objective Correlation with Social Harm

> . . . the amount of harm that [a crime] does is [not] regularly related to the intensity of the repressions which it calls forth. In the penal

law of the most civilized people, murder is universally regarded as the greatest of crimes. However, a stock-market crash, even a failure can disorganize the social body more severely than an isolated homicide ... if we compare the significance of the charge, real as it is, and that of the punishment, the disproportion is striking. (Durkheim, 1964: 74)

Every so often, this consequence of Durkheim's theory is rediscovered (see, e.g., Chambliss, 1976). Often the discovery comes in the form of moral indignation over disparity between the penalty imposed and the economic loss for common law crime and white collar crime. Alternatively, when college athletes are caught taking bribes, their teams are suspended, whereas politicians convicted of receiving bribes are often reelected. Durkheim argues, in essence, that such contrasts surprise only the sociologically naive who view social control as some kind of antibody manufactured by society to counteract socially harmful behaviors.

EVALUATION OF DURKHEIM'S ARGUMENT

Having spelled out the rudiments of Durkheim's analysis, we need now to consider whether the argument is valid. How ought we to go about assessing the validity of this—or any other—sociological thesis? We might begin with intuition. The intuition of many people is that Durkheim is wrong. For example, in an article entitled "The Function of Crime Myth," Roshier argues that

to say that crime is functional and hence necessary for society's health is to say that we must always consciously retain a stock of people whom we humiliate, imprison or at the very least (or perhaps worst of all) regard as suitable cases for treatment. Next to that [conventional penology] looks positively enlightened. (1977: 323)

In short, for Roshier, Durkheim's argument about crime, punishment, and social solidarity violates our common sense understanding of crime and punishment and implies unpalatable consequences. Indeed, the image of criminal justice suggested by Durkheim's model rather resembles the dispensation of justice in Lewis Carroll's *Through the Looking Glass*.

"[the King's Messenger, the Mad Hatter is] in prison now, being punished: and the trial doesn't even begin till next Wednesday and of course the crime comes last of all."

"Suppose he never commits the crime?" said Alice.

"That would be all the better, wouldn't it?" the Queen said. . . .

Alice felt there was no denying *that*. "Of course it would be all the better," she said: "but it wouldn't be all the better his being punished."

"You're wrong *there*, at any rate," said the Queen. "Were *you* ever punished?"

"Only for faults," said Alice.

"And you were all the better for it, I know!" the Queen said triumphantly.

"Yes, but then I *had* done the things I was punished for," said Alice: "that makes all the difference."

"But if you *hadn't* done them," the Queen said, "that would have been better still; better, and better, and better!" (Carroll, 1960: 248)

The White Queen's law explicitly treats the criminal act as entirely secondary. The major determinant of punishment lies in the impulse of the social control agency to impose sanctions. Now we may, like Kafka, find this image intuitively representative of the true state of affairs in the criminal justice system, or we may alternatively share Roshier's qualms about its accuracy.

The task of sociology—or any other science—is to go beyond criticism and defenses based on personal intuition, preference, and desire in assessing the empirical validity of such arguments. A recurrent experience in the natural sciences, for example, is that theories containing intuitively absurd assumptions (e.g., that the earth is not stationary) turn out to provide the best explanations of the behavior of natural phenomena.

To understand how an empirical assessment of Durkheim's argument may be carried out, we turn to a book published in 1966 by the American sociologist Kai Erikson. *Wayward Puritans* is in part a historical account of how people in seventeenth century Massachusetts dealt with offenders. More importantly, Erikson seeks to use his historical account to assess the validity of Durkheim's argument concerning punishment and solidarity.

WAYWARD PURITANS: A TEST CASE

Setting

Erikson's choice of Puritan Massachusetts as a site for testing Durkheim's thesis was auspicious, since the Puritans created an unusually homogeneous society characterized by a high level of common commitment. Any relationship between changes in solidarity and changes in ritual punishment are likely to be extremely visible in such a setting.[2] We will first examine some background characteristics of this community and its inhabitants. We will then describe three "crime waves" that engulfed the community in the 1600s and seek to explain them by using Durkheim's model of ritual punishment.

Table 4.1 places the Massachusetts colony in historical context by providing a chronology of major events in England, America, and Europe that are central for Erikson's discussion.

The Puritans were a group of English Protestants who sought to "purify" the Church of England of its Catholic residues. When he severed the English church from Rome in 1534, King Henry VIII left intact the Catholic liturgy, sacraments, and church organization; only gradually did innovations of the Protestant Reformation in Europe begin to filter into the English church. A group of these Puritans led by John Winthrop departed England in 1630 in a bold move to establish reformed Christianity in America. Winthrop and his followers hoped to establish an ideal community, based on Biblical commandments, a community that would in time be so successful that all the rest of England would follow their lead.[3] Unlike the other colonies founded in the Americas during this period, Massachusetts Bay Colony did not attract men and women seeking to amass a personal fortune quickly, but drew a community with the purpose and expectation of founding a new order of Christian community, "a city upon a hill."

The Puritans were committed to Martin Luther's notion of "the priesthood of all believers"; each Puritan read and interpreted the Bible, minimally supervised by a church organization. Puritan theology assumed that each individual would arrive at more or less the same conclusions about matters of faith and morals. Since consensus among the elect would be spontaneously generated, "no resolution could be passed by the church unless some kind of working consensus was reached . . ." (Erikson, 1966: 79). John Winthrop had articulated very early the commitment to community solidarity that inspired Massachusetts Bay Colony in its early years of settlement.

"We must be knit together in this work as one man," he declared; "We must delight in each other, . . . rejoice together, mourn together, labor and suffer together, always having before our eyes our commission and community in the work, our community as members

TABLE 4.1
Chronology for *Wayward Puritans*

Europe	England	Massachusetts
1430 Joan of Arc burned for witchcraft		
1486 Publication of *Malleus Maleficarum*		
1517 Luther launches Protestant Reformation		
	1534 King Henry VIII separates church in England from Rome	
1536 John Calvin publishes his major work		
	1558–1603 Reign of Elizabeth, characterized by toleration of Protestants	
	1603–1649 Reigns of James and Charles Stuart	1630 Arrival of Puritans
1618–1648 Thirty Years War: major war between Protestants and Catholics ends in Peace of Westphalia, establishing principle of religious toleration		1636–1638 Antinomians
	1649–1659 Commonwealth of Cromwell and the Puritans	1656–1661 Quakers
	1660–1685 Charles II	1684 Charter Revoked
	1685–1688 James II	
	1736 Repeal of witchcraft law	1691 Royal colony imposed
		1691–1692 Salem witches

SOURCE: Kai T. Erikson, *Wayward Puritans: A Study in the Sociology of Deviance*. New York: John Wiley & Sons, Inc., 1966. Used by permission.

of the same body." Since each community was almost literally a "body," the individuals who composed it could neither logically nor practically regard themselves as autonomous creatures with their own "particular" interests. For a person to pursue such a self-determined course was as destructive and, ultimately, as absurd as for one part of the human body to pursue its own good: for a hand to refuse to release to the mouth the food it held in its grasp, for example, or the mouth to refuse to pass along that food to the stomach. "Self-interest" was like that. If left uncontrolled, it could result only in the failure of the community and of every person within it. (Boyer and Nissenbaum, 1974: 104)

The Puritans were not of one mind on every issue; diversity of opinion and debate were common, but always within quite definite limitations. Beyond those limits, the Puritans believed, one dare not venture. Like the ships that an earlier generation had viewed as falling off the edge of a flat earth, the true Christian could only venture so far in entertaining novel ideas and opinions. This fundamental feature of the Puritan world view is revealed in the diary of a Puritan minister written shortly after having a conversation with the President of Harvard College, one Henry Dunster. In Europe a new sect, the Baptists, had appeared, and Dunster was speculating about their doctrine that infant baptism is meaningless, having no reference in Scripture. Rather than entertain this argument as worthy of consideration, Rev. Mitchell tells us that

> these thoughts were darted in with some impression and left a strange sickliness on my spirit. Yet, methought, it was not hard to discern that they were from the Evil One. (quoted by Erikson, 1966: 52)

Diversity, then, was no virtue. Unorthodox ideas and practices were, quite simply, seen as the work of the Devil bent on destroying the Puritans' experiment in the New World.

New unorthodox ideas, however, were becoming commonplace in this age. The sixteenth century saw the birth of modern natural science. The Polish astronomer Copernicus published in 1543 his theory that the earth moved around the sun. This idea overturned the doctrine, virtually unquestioned for 1500 years, that the earth was at the center of the universe. Within the next 100 years Galileo had confirmed Copernicus's theory by using the newly invented telescope to make more precise observations of the heavens. Later, in 1687, Newton had published a general theory of universal gravitation, which explained precisely the movement of the planets and the behavior of falling objects with the same mathematical laws. Thus within a total span of 150 years Western Europeans were given a very dramatic demonstration of the power of human reason and observation to comprehend the natural world and ultimately to reshape it. Most people of the time, however, remained closer to medieval than to modern ways of thinking and arguing. For example, the British chemist and physicist Robert Boyle (1627–1691)—who we remember for Boyle's law of gases— also conducted a survey in which

> he interviewed English miners in an attempt to find out if they "meet with any subterraneous demons; and if they do, in what shape and manner they appear; what they portend, and what they do." (Stannard, 1974: 77)

Heaven and hell to Puritans were real places, closer in many ways than the distant places in Africa or Asia then being explored by Europeans.

The Puritans who came to New England in 1630, then, had a special sense of their enterprise as being part of a Divine Plan, a perfect Christian community made up of God's elect. They expected this New Israel to be challenged by Satan and were prepared for the forces of evil to attempt to undermine the true Church. They could not know in advance what forms the Devil would take.

The Puritan Legal System. The legal system of Puritan Massachusetts combined two diverse sources of law, Biblical commandments and English common law. King Charles I had granted a charter for the Puritan colony with the provision that the laws of the colony would conform to the laws of England. This requirement created an unresolvable conflict between two very different standards of justice. The following example will give a better idea of the problem:

> *Code of 1648:* If a man have a stubborn or REBELLIOUS SON, of sufficient years and understanding (viz) sixteen years of age, which will not obey the voice of his Father, or the voice of his Mother, and that when they have chastened him will not harken unto them; then shall his Father and Mother being his natural parents, lay hold on him, and bring him to the Magistrates assembled in Court and testifie unto them, that their Son is stubborn and rebellious and will not obey their voice and chastisement, but lives in sundry notorious crimes, such a son shall be put to death.

Deuteronomy 21: 18–21: If a man have a stubborn and rebel-lious son, which will not obey the voice of his father, or the voice of his mother, and that, when they have chastened him, will not harken unto them: Then shall his father and his mother lay hold on him, and bring him out unto the elders of his city, and unto the gate of his place; And they shall say unto the elders of his city, This our son is stubborn and rebellious, he will not obey our voice; he is a glutton, and a drunkard. And all of the men of his city shall stone him with stones, that he die. . . .

The Puritans repeatedly encountered difficulties in reconciling such laws based on Biblical commandments with the standards of pro-cedure that had emerged in the English common law tradition. The English common law was a body of rules that had emerged out of past court decisions. The governing principle of the common law is generally stated as *stare decisis* ("let the decision stand"). In essence this means that a court should follow the rule that had been applied to similar cases in the past and that this emphasis on legal precedent ideally produces consistency and fairness (see p. 124). The Puritans were thus faced with a legal tradition which at times was contrary to law revealed in the Scriptures. Most significantly, the common law had evolved a set of procedures, *due process of law,* designed to protect the rights of the accused.

According to this principle, no law should be arbitrary, capri-cious, or unfair. Persons should be subject to criminal sanction only if their behavior was prohibited by law. *Ex post facto* (after the fact) law defines as criminal an action that was not a crime at the time it was committed; such law was ruled out as illegitimate. Under due process the accused is given rights to notice of charges, public trial in which to contest the charge made against him, legal rep-resentation, cross-examination of witnesses, presentation of evi-dence and witnesses in his own defense, and exemption from self-incrimination. Similarly, if convicted, the defendant has the right to appeal the conviction to a higher court.

Englishmen in 1630 had won certain rights to a public trial and to appeal the decision of a trial court to a higher court. However, many of the due process procedures familiar to us today were yet to evolve. For example, habeas corpus[4] was not guaranteed until an act of Parliament in 1689. Similarly, prior to 1670 a judge could fine or imprison a jury that returned a verdict contrary to his own opinion. British common law thus provided some protections to a suspected criminal. These constraints, rudimentary by contem-porary standards, did serve to limit the Puritans' power of the pros-ecution, as we shall see when we examine the individual trials.

Erikson's Hypotheses

To move from the abstraction of Durkheim's theory to the concrete reality of social life in Puritan Massachusetts, it is necessary to recast the theoretical ideas in such a way that they can be tested with available data. This is not a simple task in this case, since the available data are limited. Measures of solidarity within the community do not exist, although there is good circumstantial evidence of a common commitment in the early days of the colony. To test the theory, Erikson therefore relies on the sequence of events. He argues that major dramatic episodes of repressive justice, which he calls "crime waves," should be preceded by disruptions of solidarity in the community, which he calls "boundary crises." A boundary crisis will not only precede a crime wave in time, but will affect the content of the particular crime wave as well. Erikson further suggests that "men who fear witches soon find themselves surrounded by them; men who become jealous of private property soon encounter eager thieves" (1966: 22). The burden of Erikson's analysis is thus to demonstrate systematic connections between crises in solidarity and outbreaks of repressive justice. We will consider how well the link is made in the three cases Erikson presents.

The Case of Anne Hutchinson: Crisis of Authority and the Antinomian Heresy

The first major crisis to affect the colony occurred in the 1630s, shortly after the Puritans arrived in Massachusetts. We need to consider this crisis at two levels. At the structural level the crisis may be viewed as the consequence of an internal contradiction in Puritan society between Protestant individualism and communal integration.

In addition to this contradiction, which Erikson discusses, we may identify another contradiction in Puritan Massachusetts by recalling Max Weber's 1958 essay, *The Protestant Ethic and the Spirit of Capitalism*, in which the Puritans play a central role. Weber contended that Calvin's doctrine of predestination led to tremendous anxiety over salvation. Since only a small fraction of humanity was destined to be saved and since no one could be certain of election, one means of resolving this anxiety was the notion, elaborated by later theologians, that success in one's calling was a sign of salvation. Calvin's theological innovation drastically transformed attitudes toward work and economic accumulation. Whereas previous societies viewed work as something to be avoided, for the Puritans wealth became a sign of election, while its consumption was regarded as sinful. Therefore profits were continually reinvested. The net result of this novel religious attitude toward wealth and work was an explosion of accumulated capital that provided the foundation for sustained economic growth.

Over time the unprecedented accumulation of wealth undermined religious commitment, and the work ethic became secularized. The Protestant Ethic, then, gave birth to the Spirit of Capitalism, exemplified in Weber's mind by Benjamin Franklin. Franklin had little concern with the afterlife, predestination, or salvation. Franklin was a practical businessman, inventor, and politician who sought a rational, successful existence in this world. His famous homilies such as "Time is money" and "A penny saved is a penny earned" are entirely secular and rational codifications of the work ethic. Thus the two centuries between Calvin's *Institutes of the Christian Religion* and Franklin's *Poor Richard's Almanac* marked a basic change that ironically transformed a fervent reformist religious doctrine into a rational secular ethic that accelerated the development of a new world "in which material goods have gained an increasing, and finally, an inexorable power over the lives of men as at no previous period in history" (Weber, 1958: 181).

Puritan Massachusetts was caught in the middle of this transition from Protestant Ethic to Spirit of Capitalism. While many members of the colony—particularly the residents of Boston and Salem Town—successfully engaged in commerce and trade, others were left outside of the expanding market economy. This resulted in divisions between town and country. Anne Hutchinson and her followers, for example, came from the merchant class of Boston, while the opposition was based among the landowners. The friction between landowners and merchants over the legitimacy of overcharging, usury, and the consequences of material success led to recurrent conflicts for which the colony was unprepared by its ideology (Bailyn, 1964: 41). This basic conflict will reappear in a different form when we examine the social bases of the witchcraft prosecution in the 1690s.

It is important to bear in mind that this diagnosis is one we can make 200 years later but was not likely to be made by the Puritans themselves. Since the Puritans allowed little room for differences of opinion, much less for contradictions in their way of life, the only departures from that way came from the machinations of the Evil One. On the one hand Protestant theology celebrated Luther's conception of "the priesthood of all believers." No priests or other authorities were necessary in a true Christian community. The natural consequence of this doctrine had been anarchy. In the hundred years since Luther broke with the Catholic church, European Christianity had splintered into a variety of sects, each based on a group of individuals reading the Scriptures in their own peculiar way. To maintain order and discipline in a church, on the other hand, some form of authority was necessary. Moreover, Erikson argues that since the Puritans were struggling to establish a viable society in a hostile environment,

> some form of external discipline was necessary if the colony were to survive at all, and few settlers seemed concerned that the earlier individualism of the movement was quietly disappearing. (1966: 73)

In 1634 a remarkable woman named Anne Hutchinson (c. 1591–1643) arrived in the colony. Hutchinson, a religious virtuoso,[5] soon began holding regular meetings in her home to discuss religious issues. Before long, the discussion turned to criticism of the character and competence of the local ministers. Hutchinson argued that it did not matter what kind of educational certificates a person had; faith alone is necessary for salvation. If the minister has not been saved through grace, no amount of work on his part can give him salvation or a special status within the community. Moreover, Hutchinson herself believed she could distinguish between ministers who adhered to "the convenant of works" from those who adhered to "the covenant of grace." Hutchinson soon began to attract a sizeable number of followers who carried her views into the congregations, freely criticizing certain ministers during their Sunday sermons.

Hutchinson embodied the contradiction in Puritan values between the tradition of individualism and the necessity for authority. Her followers briefly formed a major political faction, which included the colony's governor, Henry Vane. After Vane lost an election and returned to England, Hutchinson's opponents felt powerful enough to institute a prosecution against her. She was accused of heresy, but her opponents were uncertain about the grounds on which she could be convicted. It was difficult to find a Scriptural rule on which to convict her, particularly since she was as conversant with Scripture as any of her prosecutors. At one point

> Winthrop asked the defendant to cite a Biblical rule giving her the right to hold meetings in her house, and she answered smartly, "there

lies a clear rule in Titus that the elder women should instruct the young." (Erikson 1966: 94)

The outcome of the trial remained uncertain until Hutchinson faltered and impulsively confessed that she obtained her insights through direct revelation. "I bless the Lord, He hath let me see which was the clear ministry and which the wrong . . . by the voice of His own spirit to my soul." Moreover she warned the court that "if you go on in this course you will bring a curse upon you and your posterity, and the mouth of the Lord hath spoken it" (Erikson 1966: 98).

These statements provided the precise basis for conviction that the court had vainly struggled for days to find. For the Puritans the Bible contained all revelation; if Anne Hutchinson was hearing voices, they were the revelations not of God, but of Satan. Hutchinson therefore was found guilty of heresy and banished from the colony.

The conviction of Anne Hutchinson, Erikson argues, brought to a close the first boundary crisis of the Massachusetts settlement. It dramatically eliminated the strain of anarchy inherent in Protestant doctrine and established the legitimacy of a hierarchy within the Puritan church. The episode demonstrates Durkheim's thesis that episodes of repressive justice occur in response to organizational problems of solidarity. At the time the offense Anne Hutchinson had committed was by no means clear. As Erikson suggests

the two principals were trying to speak the language which had not yet been invented, to argue an issue that had not yet been defined. In a sense, the trial was an attempt to develop such a language. (1966: 93)

It is worth noting that the trial itself was a highly unpredictable event. For Durkheim's argument, however, the outcome of the trial is not of major importance. Of central importance is the relationship between the Puritan boundary crisis and the form of crime discovered by the community. To the extent that the trial is successful, the theory predicts solidarity will be restored. For nearly three decades the colony lived without a comparable crisis.

Toleration Crisis and the Quaker Invasion

"Quaker" was originally a derogatory term applied to members of "The Religious Society of Friends." The term arose from the tendency of members of this society to "quake" during their spontaneous religious services. The sect was begun in England around 1646 by George Fox, who preached that the essence of Christianity was "inner light," the direct experience of communion with God, rather than any outward trappings of sacraments or rituals.

Like the Puritans, the Quakers were seeking to restore New Testament Christianity by eliminating corrupting external influences. The Quakers pointed out that the standard names for the months (January, February) were all based on the names of pagan gods and therefore adopted a numerical system for naming the months; the Quakers used archaic modes of speech ("thee" and "thou"); Quaker men did not remove their hats in church. While these actions and beliefs were minor violations of Puritan norms, the Quaker innovations were viewed by the Puritans as major threats, regardless of their content. As Thomas Dudley remarked to the Quakers during one of their trials, "If ye meet together and say anything we may conclude ye speak blasphemy" (Erikson, 1966: 131).

Erikson suggests that, as in Hutchinson's case, the Quaker "crisis" was only the surface manifestation of a more fundamental problem confronting the Puritan community. By the 1650s the Puritans in Massachusetts were beginning to discover that England was drifting farther and farther away in its religious orientation. In 1649 English Puritans headed by Oliver Cromwell overthrew the monarchy and established a Commonwealth. After years of civil war the English had tired of theological conflict and a new mood of religious toleration was taking hold in the motherland. The Massachusetts Puritans were now viewed as being a bit odd, isolated, and out of touch with reality. This change was a great disappointment to the Massachusetts Puritans after twenty years of struggling in the wilderness to build Christ's kingdom.

Faced with a problem of identity, Erikson suggests, the Puritans responded swiftly and harshly to the new heresies propounded by the Quaker sect. In 1656 two Quaker women were discovered and quickly deported. As others entered the colony and converted followers, the magistrates increased the penalties to whipping and then to cutting off ears. Such punishments seemed only to attract more Quakers to suffer martyrdom. Following two executions, the Quakers increased the level of rule breaking. They disrupted church services, they argued with the magistrates during court hearings, and they paraded naked through the streets. The escalating conflict between Puritans and Quakers was brought to an abrupt halt by the intervention of the King in 1665. Charles II, firmly committed to the toleration of Protestant sects (Catholicism, in part because of the continued political conflict with the Pope, was proclaimed a form of treason) ordered the Massachusetts government not only to grant "freedom and liberty of conscience" but to extend voting rights to all eligible men, regardless of church membership.

Unlike the Antinominan crisis of Anne Hutchinson, which concluded with a resolution of the conflict favoring Puritan values, this second crisis ended—from the Puritans' standpoint—in failure. Note that nothing in Durkheim's theory says that a ritual *must* achieve a successful result. This theory, like any other, is limited to a small set of variables (threat, ritual, solidarity) operating in an isolated fashion with external (or "exogenous") variables held constant. In experimental studies the exogenous variables are held constant in a literal sense by manipulating the temperature, air pressure, amount of social interaction, magnitude of deprivation, and so forth. In nonexperimental research, where such control is impossible, allowances and adjustments must be made for these exogenous factors. We should no more expect Durkheim's model of ritual punishment and solidarity to fit completely Erikson's data on Puritan crime waves than we should expect the law of free fall to work outside a vacuum. The choice of Puritan Massachusetts, a relatively homogeneous community with strong collective commitments, meets the assumptions of Durkheim's model. Several events, such as the intervention of the King of England in terminating the Quaker prosecution, could not be predicted from the theory, since such an event is totally exogenous.

Puritan Massachusetts thus underwent a fundamental change in character between 1656 and 1665. The sense of identity, of common mission and unanimity, was greatly weakened. The effort of the colony in staging the ritual punishment of Quakers to recapture this solidarity failed. Before the final disintegration of the Puritan community, however, one more crisis was to appear.

Legitimacy Crisis and the Salem Village Witchcraft Episode

This third crisis is the most infamous. In 1692 twenty persons were put to death for allegedly practicing witchcraft, and scores of others were imprisoned on suspicion of engaging in the practice.

Few people in 1690 doubted the existence of witches or questioned their power. Witches and sorcerers are known to most cultures. Generally, they are not regarded as necessarily evil; the supernatural can, in most cultures, be conjured up for good or ill. In Western Europe, Christianity accommodated itself to the practice of magic, viewing it throughout the medieval period as a pagan nuisance rather than a major threat. About the middle of the fifteenth century, however, that attitude began to change. This change came at a time of great social turmoil. The feudal order was beginning to disintegrate, trade and commerce were expanding the horizons of Western Europeans, and the old certainties were being undermined by new discoveries and ideas. Along with the advances of art, literature, and the sciences came a deadly fear of supernatural forces. As a result, as many as half a million persons were put to death for witchcraft between 1484 and 1730. In some towns witchcraft charges were made against one-third of the inhabitants and one out of ten residents were executed (Stannard, 1977: 36). There appeared to be, after all, ample physical evidence of their malevolence. Life in general was, in the famous phrase of Thomas Hobbes, "nasty, brutish and short." The life expectancy of a British lord at birth was only thirty years (Stannard, 1977: 38). Food shortages and epidemic diseases were commonplace. Inexplicable deaths were often seen as the work of witches. The physical evidence was, in the minds of most people, confirmed by scriptural commandments: "Thou shalt not suffer a witch to live" (Exodus xxii: 18; Deuteronomy 24: 11; 23: 1).

While few people in Massachusetts questioned the reality of witchcraft, few persons were executed for this crime before 1692. This is quite remarkable, considering the number of executions being conducted in England during this same period. Particularly instructive is the case of John Broadstreet, who confessed in court to practicing witchcraft in 1672 (Erikson, 1966: 155) but was thrown out of court for lying. Twenty years later, similar confessions were routinely taken as grounds for capital punishment.

The witchcraft case began in the fall of 1691 when a group of teenage girls in Salem Village began to have fits, speak in tongues, and suffer convulsions. The afflictions began in the household of the village minister, Samuel Parris, and remained for some time undiagnosed. In late February 1692, three women were arrested for witchcraft. Among the three was Parris's black slave Tituba, a native of Barbados, who confessed in great detail to participating in a witch's coven. Despite the arrests, the symptoms prevailed, leading to further accusations. In June the first trials were held, and by September nineteen convicted witches had been hanged. Opposition by the principal ministers finally brought the prosecution to a close.

Erikson suggests that the cause of the witchcraft episode lies in the disintegration of the social structure. The Quaker crisis had not been resolved to the satisfaction of the Puritans, who had been required to acknowledge the legitimacy of the Quaker sect and of the established Episcopal church. Several events in the 1680s combined to undermine the confidence of the Puritans in the success of their "city upon a hill." By 1688 a contemporary observed that "the people were 'savagely factious' in their relations with one another and acted more out of jealousy and greed than any sense of religious purpose" (Erikson, 1966: 139). This state of affairs sharply contrasts with the earlier sense of community and common purpose.

Assessing Erikson's Analysis

While these crises fit Erikson's thesis, his study raises problems of evidence and interpretation. First, the extent to which members of the colony actually were involved in the three major trials is unclear. Much of our knowledge about these trials comes from the writings of members of the elite, who may have been projecting their own interests and orientations in describing the colony as a whole; the actual audience of the Puritan trials might have been quite limited. This became especially problematic during the seventeenth century, as the growing population began to include immigrants who were not members of the church. Second, Erikson provides no explicit criteria for selecting these three particular episodes in the colony's history as instances of boundary crises. If no other dramatic social strains had occurred during this period, the selection would be compelling, but the absence of explicit criteria weakens the empirical confirmation of the thesis.[6] Third, Erikson's analysis is limited to Puritan Massachusetts, and consequently it provides no clear idea about the domain or scope of the thesis. Do boundary crises produce crime waves only in theocratic regimes or in secular states as well?

Virginia, for example, was a colony organized around commercial interests rather than religious commitment (cf. Diamond, 1958; Breen, 1980); it is not clear that boundary crises in Virginia would have resulted in a reaction similar to that in Massachusetts. Little systematic work has been done so far in comparing the colonies; Rhode Island, however, appears to have been subjected to many of the same boundary crises faced by Massachusetts, but without having experienced crime waves, as one would expect if Erikson's thesis were universally applicable (Bernstein, 1975: 102). Massachusetts itself underwent major changes after the seventeenth century. The gradual disintegration of the Puritan experiment may have been partly a consequence of the failure to resolve satisfactorily the two earlier boundary crises. In the 1700s the Puritans were joined by members of other denominations. The immigration of the Irish in the 1800s totally changed the religious and moral composition of the state (see Thernstrom, 1964: 33–56). Massachusetts was transformed from a relatively homogeneous religious community into a diversified, pluralistic society. It is by no means clear that these different types of society would respond to deviance in the same way.

ELABORATION OF DURKHEIM'S THEORY: REPRESSIVE AND RESTITUTIVE SANCTIONS

Durkheim (1964) distinguished between two forms of social solidarity, which he called mechanical and organic. Mechanical solidarity is based on similarity of individual characteristics (for example, common race and region) and is characterized by a consensus on values, harmony (if not identity) of interests, and unity of purpose.[7] Strong ties bind members of mechanically solidary communities. Differences exist among members in their attributes, but such differences are regarded as secondary, not as bases for social organization.

In contrast, organic solidarity arises from diversity of individual interests and is characterized by interdependence and exchange.

> In a business firm, for example, though all managers may need some degree of commitment to common organizational goals, they also need different commitment to role values—the engineer to product quality, the accountant to cost, the personnel manager to industrial peace—for the survival and efficiency of the firm. Thus either role- or class-specific values may contribute more to social cohesion than general core values. (Mann, 1970: 425)

Organic solidarity consists of weak ties among members of the community (cf. Granovetter, 1973).

Mechanical solidarity generates repressive justice, which re-affirms a common value through diffuse forms of ritual punishment. The specific forms of punishment range from execution to ostracism. Despite the variations in the form of deprivation entailed in them, all forms of repressive sanctions have one key element in common: they change the status of the offender, increasing the social distance between normal and deviant actors. The imposition of all repressive sanctions is, in essence, a "status degradation ceremony" that

> brings about the ritual destruction of the person being denounced . . . recasting the objective character of the perceived other. The person [being denounced] becomes in the eyes of his condemners literally a different and new person. (Garfinkel, 1956: 421)

In the words of a nineteenth century English jurist, the criminal law says in effect to the offender, "You are not fit for this world; therefore, take your chances elsewhere."

The accomplishment of the status change, rather than simply the deprivation itself, constitutes a repressive sanction. This can best be grasped by contrasting the status of the *prisoner of war* and the status of the *convict*. Both may have been held captive in a degrading environment of deprivation. Both may have been (despite rules established by the Geneva Convention and the Eighth Amendment to the United States Constitution) subjected to brutalization and torture at the hands of their captors or fellow inmates. The nature of the physical deprivation may be similar (cf. Goffman, 1961), but the prisoner of war emerges with a social status uncontaminated by the stigma and ostracism of the convict.

Organic solidarity, in contrast, generates restitutive sanctions, characterized by efforts to restore the disrupted relationship, rather than stigmatize an offender. This restoration may take a variety of forms. *Restitution* restores the offender by compensating the victim for whatever loss has been incurred as a result of the offender's misconduct. For example, *torts* are injuries suffered by one person resulting from the acts or negligence of another, including personal injury, medical malpractice, libel, and consumer safety violations. When in 1978 Mrs. Shirley Brown fell on the icy sidewalk outside her Boston home, she successfully sued her husband for $35,000 for being "careless and negligent in his maintenance of the sidewalks" (*Time,* August 11, 1980: 23). While the monetary award may impose substantial deprivation on the defendant, the restitutive sanction differs from repressive sanctions in that the victim receives compensation for the loss, while the harm-doer returns to his or her original position in society, legally if not financially. *Rehabilitation* differs in character from restitution in that the focus is on changing the character of the offender through some form of treatment. Like restitution, however, the aim of rehabilitation is to restore social relations to their original state, rather than to exclude the offender as an outsider.

In actual practice a society's legal system may employ sanctions that are mixtures of repressive and restitutive elements, much in the same way that physical reality consists of combinations of hydrogen, oxygen, and other elements. Assault, for example, is both a crime and a tort. We therefore need to be careful in examining sanctions to see how they are actually used in specific circumstances rather than taking them at face value. Thus although mental hospitalization is ostensibly a restitutive sanction designed to rehabilitate aberrant behavior, stigma may attach to the medical diagnosis and treatment of certain problems. In recent years the Soviet Union has made systematic use of the latter consequence of psychotherapy by placing political dissidents in mental hospitals. Political activism is thus discredited as a form of mental illness. In 1970 Zhores Medvedev, an internationally famous Russian biologist who had long been critical of the government's involvement in Soviet science, was detained in a mental hospital for nineteen days, during which time he was diagnosed as suffering from

"Sluggish schizophrenia" accompanied by "paranoid delusions of reforming society" ... "split personality, expressed in the combining of scientific work in his field with publicist activities; an overestimation of his own personality ... lack of a sense of reality, poor adaptation to the social environment." (Medvedev and Medvedev, 1971: 39)

Because of his prominence, the protests of friends, colleagues, and the international community undermined the government's attempt to diagnose his actions as mentally abnormal; other dissidents have been less fortunate (Bloch and Reddaway, 1977). In general, the repressive or restitutive character of a sanction must be determined by the use to which it is put by the agencies of social control.

The solidarity of any particular society will be a mixture of mechanical and organic; its legal system, a mixture of repressive and restitutive sanctions. No existing society is integrated solely by mechanical solidarity. The horde, a mass of undifferentiated individuals, is "the protoplasm of the social realm, the natural basis of classification. It is true, perhaps, that no society corresponds to this description" (Durkheim, 1950: 83). While Durkheim's theory is written in terms of *types,* social reality is actually constituted by degrees of preponderance. While some societies, like Puritan Massachusetts, closely approximate the ideal type of mechanical solidarity, factions and divisions are not totally absent even there.

REPRESSIVE JUSTICE IN INDUSTRIAL SOCIETY

Durkheim's theory further postulates a change in the law as mechanical solidarity is replaced by organic solidarity. A massive replacement of this nature took place in the transition from feudal to capitalist society. Durkheim saw his own era as one of transition, in which the "old gods are growing old or already dead, and others are not yet born" (1948: 475). Whatever new forms mechanical solidarity was to take in industrial society, Durkheim suggested, the transition has several significant consequences for law.

First, Durkheim predicted that civil law would increasingly replace criminal law. As the division of labor increased the interdependence among unlike individuals, disputes would be resolved through restitutive measures, and the capacity of the population to engage in shared outrage would correspondingly diminish.

Second, Durkheim claimed that increasing organic solidarity made the state regularly independent of collective sentiments such that

> some actions . . . are more strongly repressed than they are strongly reproved by general opinion. There is nothing in us which protests against fishing and hunting out of season, or against overloaded conveyances on the public highway. . . . The state can become an autonomous factor in social life . . . treating as criminal, actions which shock it without, however, shocking the collective sentiments in the same degree. (1964: 82–83)

Finally, Durkheim suggested that the criminal sanction would not disappear altogether, but that its character would be altered.

The spirit of foresight which has been aroused no longer leaves the field so free for the blind action of passion. It contains it within certain limits; it is opposed to absurd violence, to unreasonable ravaging. More clarified, it expands less on chance. One no longer sees it turn against the innocent to satisfy itself. (1964: 90)

In other words, the criminal sanction undergoes a basic change when organic solidarity becomes predominant; it responds more directly to the behavior of the deviant, rather than to the state of the collective conscience.[8]

To what extent do these assertions about alterations in sanctions with changes in the dominant form of solidarity account for trends in punishment in industrial societies? We will consider the death penalty in more detail in Chapter 10. For the moment let us examine some broader implications of Durkheim's thesis.

The first issue we will review is the presence of mechanical solidarity and ritual punishment in the contemporary industrial society. Much of the literature concerned with this general issue focuses on political rituals, but the core problems are the same for both substantive areas. The discussion of this issue may be conveniently divided into three camps. The first position argues that in the United States, Britain, France, and other industrial nations, rituals of national integration reinforce mechanical solidarity. Edward Shils and Michael Young, for example, contend that Durkheim's analysis can be fruitfully applied to the British Coronation, which represents a "series of ritual affirmations of the moral values necessary to a well-governed and good society" (Shils and Young, 1953: 67; cf. Birnbaum, 1955). Other writers attribute such consequences to such political rituals as the public mourning over Kennedy's assassination (Verba, 1965; cf. Lipsitz, 1968). A second position taken by some writers is that Durkheim's theory logically applies to contemporary society, but that neither rituals nor mechanical solidarity is present in modern society and therefore the theory bites the dust (e.g., Chambliss, 1976). The third position, which we will discuss below, elaborates Durkheim's position on ritual in modern society, namely that it persists, but in attenuated form.

Durkheim argued that mechanical solidarity does appear in industrial society, but its character is substantially altered. Michael Mann, in reviewing the literature on class consciousness in Western industrial societies, suggests that a form of mechanical solidarity does exist in these nations, but that the commitment is to very general symbols, ideals, and values, which achieve a generally incoherent and inconsistent adherence. In such societies

> the ordinary participant's social relations are usually confined to a fairly narrow segment of society, and his relations with society as a whole are mostly indirect, through a series of overlapping primary and secondary groups. . . . Thus his normative connections with the vast majority of fellow citizens may be extremely tenuous, and his commitment to general dominant and deviant values may be irrelevant to his compliance with the expectations of others. As long as he conforms to the very specific role behavior expected of him, the political authorities may not trouble themselves with his system of beliefs. (Mann, 1970: 435)

Only occasionally will an extraordinary event sustain an integrative ritual. But Barrington Moore points out that although

> dramatic threat overcomes the atomization that the proliferation of different occupations creates in the city, this type of rapidly created solidarity breaks up again rather easily as individual interests reassert themselves. (Moore, 1973: 178)

This suggests that mechanical solidarity and ritual punishment will be found only in attenuated forms at the macro levels of organization. Thus, little connection should be expected between changes in criminal law and changes in collective sentiment. This prediction of Durkheim's theory has been sustained by research conducted by Richard Berk and his colleagues on changes in the California penal code between 1955 and 1971. They conclude that

> given the nature of piecemeal, incremental change in the Penal Code, often based on small and somewhat technical alterations, it is difficult to link public sentiment, whatever its nature, *directly* to legislative trends. Most legislative change received no publicity precisely because it bore little relation to the interests and competence of citizens. . . . In short, it seems inescapable that criminal law in California was enacted primarily by elite actors (public officials, organizational professionals, etc.). (Berk et al., 1977: 280)

Ritual forms of punishment may not simply lack integrative effect in a heterogeneous society, they may create divisiveness among the subgroups. Durkheim was well aware of this possibility as a result of the "Dreyfus affair," which dominated French political life at the end of the nineteenth century. Just as the state may impose sanctions without creating a ritual for the general public, a pluralistic society creates the possibility of a single sanction that serves two (or more) ritual functions. Durkheim was well aware of this possibility in his own time. Humiliated by defeat in the 1870 war with Prussia, France was electrified by the trial and conviction of Captain Alfred Dreyfus for selling military secrets to the Germans. The necessary ingredients for a ritual punishment were all there: the unmanageable external threat, the need for collective reaffirmation of solidarity. The standard scenario, however, did not unfold. Instead the nation split on liberal-conservative lines. Evidence began to appear that the real culprit was an officer named Esterhazy and that the army had been involved in a massive coverup to pin the blame on the Jewish captain. The trials lasted until 1906, when Dreyfus was finally exonerated. Far from uniting the country, the Dreyfus episode further widened the gap between liberals (academics, intellectuals, and workers) and conservatives (the military, the church, and the farmers). For Durkheim the crisis over Dreyfus was a significant manifestation of the disintegration of mechanical solidarity at the national level. In its place, however, one could find mechanical solidarity *within* the subgroups: the pro-Dreyfus and the anti-Dreyfus factions. This pattern is characteristic of politicized trials that produce simultaneously scapegoats and martyrs.[9] It suggests at the more mundane level of legal life the existence of mechanically solidary subgroups for whom the criminal sanction retains its ritual function.

Studies of the police, for example, stress the high degree of solidarity among members of the police departments. This solidarity is more than a preference for the company of fellow officers, *esprit de corps,* or the bonds of fellowship and mutual responsibility formed among persons who share danger and stress. It often includes the protective stance adopted regarding police misconduct. A criticism of one policeman is seen as a criticism of all policemen, and police thus tend to unite against complaining citizens, the courts, and other government agencies (Skolnick, 1975: 249).

Structurally, the urban police department approximates the conditions of Durkheim's ideal type of mechanical solidarity. To begin with, the police are socially isolated. A policeman, James Baldwin wrote, moves through Harlem "like an occupying soldier in a bitterly hostile country." (1962: 67) The urban ghetto is not unique; police face continual opposition to authority from the public. As a result, the social networks of police departments are unusually closed. Police are more likely to choose as close friends members of their own occupations than members of other occupational groups. More significantly, there is a much higher rate of participation among police in occupation-centered social events than is found among members of other occupations. This social isolation is combined with the perception of danger. While the occupational death rate is not highest for police work, the nature of the job gives danger particular salience. "Any profession which is continually preoccupied with the threat of danger requires a strong sense of solidarity if it is to operate effectively" (Janowitz, 1964: 175).

Given the special characteristics of authority and danger, Skolnick maintains, the police develop

> a perceptual shorthand to identify certain kinds of people as *symbolic assailants*, that is persons who use gesture, language and attire that the policeman has come to recognize as a prelude to violence. This does not mean that violence by the symbolic assailant is necessarily predictable. (1975: 45)

Symbolic assailants may include all residents of a high crime area (Skolnick, 1966: 218). Violation of the law, however, is not a sufficient condition; police, for instance, do not regard addict informers as being symbolic assailants, even though these individuals violate laws to which the police are personally highly committed. The existence of symbolic assailants as part of the police culture is consistent with Durkheim's theory and has certain structural parallels with the other social groups we have considered. All have a strong level of internal cohesion and are faced with external threats.

The ritual creation of deviants appears less frequently and is more localized in contemporary society. Although it occurs in law enforcement agencies, it is frequently limited by due process constraints. Unlike Puritan Massachusetts, repressive justice plays a subsidiary role in complex, industrial societies.

SUMMARY

This chapter has examined one way in which a sociologist attempted to study the connection between the legal system and society. For his analysis Durkheim took the nature of the legal sanction as the most salient feature of the legal system and sought to show that there is a systematic connection between the legal sanction and social solidarity.

Durkheim's ideas resemble the familiar notion of scapegoating, in which an individual is singled out for sacrifice as a means of satisfying some collective need.[10] In many religions the scapegoat figure provides supernatural benefits for the group. At a less conscious level we may observe the same process at work in the creation of social outcasts—minorities, deviants, the mentally ill. In each instance the rejection and stigmatizing of an individual provide a sacrifice for the group by allowing it to reaffirm its identity or to avoid intractable problems by displacing them on a manageable object of punishment. While such practices have been criticized and condemned as irrational, Durkheim suggests that we need to examine the social bases for such practices. This search, then, led to his formulation of the relationship between repressive justice—of which scapegoating is one special form—and social solidarity.

Having now explored the argument as it was tested by historical studies of the major episodes of repressive justice, we have seen that although the evidence supports the connection between repressive justice and solidarity, this relationship is not universal. Rather, like most general propositions, this one is conditional, limited to societies that are predominantly held together by mechanical solidarity. Where organic solidarity predominates, the legal system has quite different characteristics, which will be spelled out in more detail in subsequent chapters.

Durkheim's theory allows us to understand better recent trends in criminal law; what first seems like a series of isolated, fragmentary developments, the product of independent "reform" movements, can now be seen as a coherent pattern of structural change.

SUGGESTED READING

Durkheim's analysis of ritual and solidarity has spawned a wide range of treatments. An interesting, nonsociological discussion is provided by Girard (1977). Much of the literature is concerned with the role of ritual in complex industrial society. The best review of this issue is provided by Lukes (1977). Elaborations of Erikson's approach will be found in Inverarity (1976) and Lauderdale (1976). Cartwright and Schwartz (1973) draw out and test some conflicting hypotheses from the theories of Durkheim and Weber.

FOOTNOTES

1. Some confusion has arisen from Durkheim's repeated reference to the functions of *crime*. Roshier (1979) suggests that Durkheim was really talking about the functions of punishment. This problem was resolved, however, in an early criticism by Tarde, to which Durkheim responded by stating that "what is normal is the inseparable pairing of crime and punishment" (Durkheim, 1978: 185).
2. We focus here on Erikson's empirical study as an example of testing Durkheim's theory rather than another body of empirical studies that have been concerned with "legal evolution." These latter works attempt to test Durkheim's arguments by comparing relevant correlations among items in the Human Relations Area Files (HRAF), a compendium of ethnographic reports broken down by subject. For example, Spitzer (1975a) presents such a test based on materials from forty-eight societies ranging from the Trobriand Islands to "Georgia and the Soviet Union in Russia" (sic). We will not here review the difficulties with these efforts (see, e.g., Baxi, 1974; Turkel, 1979), but simply indicate some features of these studies that make them more suitable for more advanced presentations of research design. First, Spitzer divides his sample into two types of society, "simple" and "complex." The relationship between this division and the theoretically relevant distinction between types of solidarity is not apparent. A "simple society" such as the Trobriand Islands may, for instance, have a real predominance of organic solidarity. Consequently, a finding of a correlation between simplicity of the society and restitutive justice really has no bearing at all on Durkheim's thesis. In general this line of investigation fails to adequately operationalize either the concept of solidarity or the corresponding concepts of repressive and restitutive sanction.

   Studies of the "evolution" of penal sanctions, moreover, adopt a unilinear notion of societal development. Durkheim held inconsistent views on this position, which has generally been discredited by subsequent anthropological work. At any rate, the major theoretical propositions in Durkheim's analysis do not require acceptance of assumptions concerning the evolution of society from simple to complex forms.

   In general, the studies of legal evolution are largely empiricist works with only a very tangential operationalization of theoretical concepts. This difficulty is created by the nature of data available, and while these studies make the optimal use of the data, the HRAF do not appear to offer strategically promising research sites.
3. America was to become in the next three centuries the site of innumerable such experimental communities founded in the wilderness to escape the corruptions of conventional society. (A good sociological account will be found in Kanter, 1972). The latest, most dramatic attempt was Jonestown, Guyana.

4. "Habeas corpus" means literally "you have the body." Legally, habeas corpus is an order to bring a person who has been detained before the court to show cause for the detention. Prior to the Habeas Corpus Act the king's henchmen could arrest and detain persons with no other constraint than the possible political fallout of detaining someone who had poweful friends.

5. The empirical fact, important for us, that men are *differently qualified* in a religious way stands at the beginning of the history of religion. ... The sacred values that have been most cherished ... could not be attained by everyone. The possession of such faculties was a "charisma," which, to be sure, might be awakened in some but not in all. It follows from this that all intensive religiosity has a tendency toward a sort of *status stratification* in accordance with the differences in the charismatic qualifications. "Heroic" or "virtuoso" religiosity is opposed to mass religiosity. By "mass" we understand those who are religiously "unmusical" ... now, every hierocratic and official authority of a "church"— that is, a community organized by officials into an institution which bestows gifts of grace, seeks to organize the religiosity of the masses and to put its own officially monopolized and mediated sacred values in the place of the autonomous and religious status qualifications of the religious virtuosos (Weber, 1946: 287–288).

6. Erikson's use of crises as an independent variable is a widespread practice (cf., Balbus, 1973; Goldstone, 1980; Piven and Cloward, 1979). In most of these studies only face validity serves to classify a set of events as a crisis. For a good discussion of the dangers of circular reasoning created by this procedure, see Rule and Tilly (1972).

7. Ralph Turner suggests that the most familiar example of mechanical solidarity is romantic love.

> Several features of romantic love are relevant. First, romantic lovers insist upon unity of sentiment, and any evidence that the partners do not think alike in important matters threatens union. The couple often identifies in the romantic union. Second, the lovers must constantly demonstrate and reiterate their solidarity; merely relaxing their affirmations is often taken as a sign that love has cooled. Third, romance has its obverse emphasis upon privacy and retreat from the world; the honeymoon is to be enjoyed alone. Fourth, there is explicit repudiation of contractual and expediential considerations in the relationship; only sentiment can be acknowledged as its base. These patterns add up to a relationship governed by demands for the conspicuous enactment of mechanical solidarity. (Turner, 1967: 65).

Many of the same elements are present in nationalistic fervor, religious commitments, and other instances of intensified states of mechanical solidarity.

In *Wayward Puritans* Erikson ignores Durkheim's distinction between mechanical and organic solidarity. The last chapter of the book, "Puritanism and Deviance" contrasts the Puritan view of deviance as an inherent, incurable feature of certain individuals with the

Quaker view of deviance as a temporary, remediable condition. Erikson contends that these two seventeenth century philosophies shaped the discourse on correctional policy over the next several centuries. This contrast between Puritan and Quaker orientations could, however, be transcribed into Durkheim's contrast between repressive and restitutive sanctions, and thus made a more integral part of the sociological analysis. As it stands, the last chapter is simply an idealist and historicist account of penological ideals, rather than a sociological analysis of their underlying bases.

8. Viewed in this light, the application of Durkheim's concept of repressive justice to contemporary society made by Howard Becker and other adherents to the societal reaction school, misrepresents Durkheim's own characterization of industrial society as being deficient in such forms of collective ritual.

9. The Dreyfus trial had several parallels. In 1951 Julius and Ethel Rosenberg were convicted by a federal court in New York of conspiracy to commit wartime espionage. Ethel's brother, working in 1944 at the Los Alamos laboratory, had allegedly stolen plans for the detonating device in the atomic bomb. The Rosenbergs allegedly passed the secret on to the Soviet mission in New York. When the case came to trial, the country was confronted with a series of crises. The "secret" of the atomic bomb had been lost; the Soviet Union exploded its first device in 1948. Two years later the Communists took over China, and within a year the United States was sending troops to Korea for a "police action." The Rosenbergs became a symbolic focus, but a factional rather than a societal focus. Mass demonstrations in support of the Rosenbergs took place throughout the world between their trial and their execution in 1953. Far from being a source of unity, the Rosenberg trial generated controversy that continues thirty years later.

Public ritual arousing collective unity is thus rare in contemporary society. Justice is administered on an assembly line basis out of view of the general public. Those cases that do become the focus of public concern are more apt to result in polarization than in unification. Not only does criminal punishment *not* increase solidarity in this environment, but in this setting the converse of Durkheim's argument is equally invalid. Boundary crises do not result in crime waves. Variations in conviction rate have very little to do with boundary crises or external threats to the society.

10. Two social psychological explanations of scapegoating compete with Durkheim's social organizational account. Thomas Szasz, an American psychiatrist who argues mental illness is a myth, contends that witchcraft, mental illness, and other forms of deviance are manufactured as an irrational response to "vast, well-nigh insoluble problems" (1970: 274). Scapegoating may be eliminated, Szasz argues, by rational confrontation of problems of living, in the standard fashion of psychoanalytic therapy. It is not at all clear, however, that commitment

to rationality and scapegoating are incompatible. Ancient Greece provides examples of both flourishing simultaneously. At any rate, Szasz locates the phenomenon of scapegoating not in the social structure but in the irrational tendencies of the individual mind.

William Chambliss proposes an alternative explanation of scapegoating in terms of conflicts among groups. Deviance designation is a rational tactic employed by a self-conscious interest group to discredit its opponents. In the case of Puritan Massachusetts, Chambliss argues,

> the potential diversion of witchcraft served to give at least the appearance of a reaffirmation of authority in the hands of those who rule . . . Puritan society created crime waves to help the ruling stratum maintain control of the community. (1976: 14–15)

In considering this alternative explanation, it is instructive to compare the Salem Village case with that of Urbain Grandier, a French priest burned at the stake in the town of Loudun fifty years earlier. The historical record suggests fabrication of charges and orchestration of the prosecution by Grandier's personal and political enemies (Huxley, 1953). In contrast, in Salem Village the accusers did not attack their enemies directly, but "projected their bitterness onto persons who were, politically or psychologically, less threatening targets" (Boyer and Nissenbaum, 1974: 145–146). In short, while cases may be found in which deviance designation has been used as an instrument of a particular group in a rational struggle for power, in the case of Puritan Massachusetts the displacement of social conflicts into symbolic targets of collective condemnation is a process more congruent with Durkheim's structural theory of repressive justice.

PART TWO:

Creation of Law

Introduction
by James Inverarity
and Barry Feld

Having examined some basic sociological perspectives on law and society, we turn in this section to substantive research concerning the creation of law. Studies of law creation consist largely of isolated case studies of the enactment of particular laws (e.g., Becker, 1973; Chambliss, 1964; Hall, 1952; Timberlake, 1963). This case study literature—a collective contribution of sociologists, lawyers, and historians—has traditionally been segregated into discrete subject matter divisions: theft, drugs, sexuality, delinquency, and so on. Neither the case studies nor their subject matter classification have been conducive to the refinement of sociological theory in this area.

In fact, this has been one area in which the present state of the art clearly represents a regression. The empirical literature can best be described as "random fact gathering," a style of research that

> juxtaposes facts that will later prove revealing . . . with others . . . that will for some time remain too complex to be integrated with theory at all. Such a case study often omits from its immensely circumstantial accounts just those details that later scientists will find sources of important illumination. (Kuhn, 1962: 15)

The "immensely circumstantial accounts" provided by the case studies of legal change have, in large measure, been responsible for the sterility of theory in this area. The primary attempt to bring theoretical order out of this empirical chaos has been the conflict-consensus debate, which we reviewed in the Introduction to Part

163

One. Weber's discussion of the sources of law (Weber, 1978) is far more refined than this crude dichotomy and points up the need to rethink scattered observations concerning legal change in light of the fundamental concepts and issues we reviewed in Part One.

The next three chapters will be concerned with a set of changes in criminal law that took place during a watershed period in the development of American capitalism. A large number of case studies concern legal changes that took place during "The Progressive Era" (cf. Hagan, 1980). The juvenile court, probation, indeterminant sentencing, federal regulation of drugs, food, quality, and the environment are all major legal innovations that have a common origin in the age of reform, from about 1900 to the First World War. The next three chapters—on the changing status of youth, the legality of drugs, and the legitimacy of corporate transactions—will examine the interrelationships among these changes and locate the source of their coincidental appearance in the underlying transformations of American society.

Before considering the particular changes in the law, we need to give some consideration to these underlying transformations.

THE PROGRESSIVE ERA AS A CRITICAL PERIOD

The Progressive Era, roughly 1900–1916, was a period noted for its diverse reform movements, ranging from city government, to environmental protection, to urban welfare. Sociologically, the Progressive Era constitutes a "critical period" in the transformation of capitalism, akin to the major transformation from feudalism to capitalism that preoccupied the nineteenth century theorists.

Many profound changes occurred simultaneously in this period: The juvenile justice system was invented and quickly diffused. Probation emerged from being an isolated experiment to being a dominant mode of penal sanction. The federal government began to move increasingly to regulate and control business organization and the consumption of commodities. The standards of laissez faire capitalism were increasingly giving way to control by a "welfare state."

Sociologists who have studied the legal changes during this period have tended to examine them in isolation both from other changes and from the underlying changes taking place in nonlegal institutions. To get a better sense of what these changes involve, we briefly outline some changes in particular indicators that occurred during this period.

1. Capital Concentration

The Industrial Revolution is often described as a transformation from an agrarian economy to an industrial economy. This description is accurate in summarizing the change in the occupational structure. In 1870, 52 percent of the American labor force was employed in agriculture. A century later, less than 5 percent of the labor force was growing the food to feed a population five times as large as the nation had in 1870. At the same time the agrarian-to-industrial terminology is misleading. First, far from being eliminated, agriculture remains a major component of the economy. Second, the changes in agriculture that made possible the reduction of the labor force and the increase in production were precisely the same forces that were at work in manufacturing. The Industrial Revolution was thus primarily a revolution in capital. The accumulation of capital made possible the reorganization of production. The early stages of this process were discussed in Chapter 2. We take up here a very brief overview of how this process of capital accumulation accelerated in the last quarter of the nineteenth century.

The family farm and the small firm remained the major economic actors in the United States before the Civil War. The 1860 Census shows that

> in the major industrial center of Pittsburgh with 17 foundries, 21 rolling mills, 76 glass factories, and 47 other manufactories, not a single manufacturing enterprise was incorporated. (Means, 1970: 7)

Except for the textile industry, most manufacturing enterprises were small firms. For instance, traveling the 300 miles between Buffalo and Albany by rail required tickets on ten different railroads.

After the Civil War the size of the average firm dramatically increased, and the corporation became the dominant form of business organization. The corporation (or "joint stock company") had played a major role in the trade and commerce of Holland and England during the 1600s. The Puritan colony in Massachusetts was one of many such organizations that pooled the financial resources of a large number of individuals while allowing them limited responsibility for the organization's failures. Such corporations appeared in American industry quite late. In the 1890s the pace of incorporation accelerated to include not only textiles and railroads, but virtually every commodity from public transportation to patent medicines. Mergers began averaging 400 per year, the peak of 1200 mergers being recorded in 1899. By 1929 the industrial sector of the economy had become highly concentrated. The largest 100 firms that year controlled 44 percent of the assets of all manufacturing corporations in the country, a distribution that is only slightly different today.

Within the space of a few decades, therefore, a major change in the organization of the economy took place, as small independent firms increasingly gave way to large corporate organizations. This development was accelerated by the phenomenal growth after the Civil War of both population and transportation.

> The demands and opportunities of selling in a market that grew from less than 25 million relatively isolated people in 1850 to 100 million people bound together by rails and highways in 1915 led to the rise of industrial giants. (Cochran, 1972: 152)

Several additional critical changes in the economy and society accompanied this rise of industrial giants.

2. Immigration

The expansion of industrial production based on large-scale division of labor required substantial amounts of unskilled and semiskilled labor. These job opportunities attracted immigrants from Europe, many of them young, single males who sought to make a nest egg and return in a few years to their homelands. The pace of immigration accelerated after 1880 and, as was noted in Chapter 2, averaged over one million persons per year between 1900 and the First World War.

While this massive immigration solved the economic problem of labor shortage in the expanding industries, it simultaneously created complications for political life, labor union organizations, and—as we will see in the next three chapters—the criminal law. The problem posed by the dramatic increase in the numbers of immigrants was further complicated by their diverse social origins. The industrialization of northwestern Europe removed much of the incentive to migrate for the populations that had originally settled into the New World. The migration after 1880 largely came from southern and eastern Europe. Before 1890 this area had accounted for less than 20 percent of the immigration; in 1900 it accounted for more than half, and by 1910, nearly three quarters (Ralph and Rubinson, 1980: 946).

The changes in the numbers and ethnic origins of the immigrants entering the United States made the processes of assimilation increasingly difficult. The new immigrants, primarily peasants, differed in language, religion, political heritage, and culture from Anglo-Protestant Americans. The clash of cultures posed basic problems for social cohesion and stability (Hofstadter, 1955: 8). These "alien hordes" were disproportionately concentrated in the cities of the Northeast and Midwest, swelling the ranks of the poor in large urban slums and living in desperate conditions of poverty in cities that grew so rapidly that services were inadequate to provide for basic needs. These changing patterns of immigration threatened to alter irreversibly the relative cultural and ethnic homogeneity of rural, Anglo-Protestant America.

3. Expansion of a New Middle Class of Professional and Technical Workers

A new class of professionals, engineers, and managers was associated with these changes in the forces of production. Weber regarded the emergence of large-scale corporations as the principal feature of the rationalization of the economy under capitalism. For Weber the major characteristic of both modern society and Western capitalism was the process of bureaucratic rationalization. Only bureaucratic organizations could efficiently coordinate and distribute goods and services in the new national marketplace. He regarded bureaucratic organization as technically superior to any other form of administration in the same fashion that machine production is superior to nonmechanical production. The growth of the corporate economy reflected the fusion of machine production with a "concentration of the means of administration" in the corporate bureaucracy.

The new form of economic enterprise—the heavily capitalized corporation—revolutionized commerce and industry. The hierarchical corporate structure required personnel with a managerial, bureaucratic orientation and created a demand for more highly educated workers. Corporate enterprise required careerists who could work in a cooperative atmosphere and implement rational, scientific solutions to economic problems.

4. Class Conflict

In 1848 Marx and Engels had observed that

> with the development of industry the proletariat not only increases in number; it becomes concentrated in greater masses, its strength grows and it feels that strength more. . . . The growing competition among the bourgeois, and the resulting commercial crises, make the wages of the workers ever more fluctuating. . . . Thereupon the workers begin to form combinations (Trade Unions) against the bourgeois. (Marx and Engels, in Tucker, 1978: 480)

This passage describes fairly well the development of class warfare in the United States in the late 1800s. Competitive capitalism produced the typical pattern of business cycles, in which periods of prosperity gave way to periods of depression. During the latter, workers found themselves without any means of support or with reduced wages. The first major reaction to such conditions on a national basis came in the great railway strike of 1877, in which workers in a loosely coordinated fashion seized control of the railroads and destroyed rolling stock. Throughout the 1880s and 1890s major armed confrontations between capitalists and workers broke out. While unions remained weak and worker demands were ignored more often than not, it was becoming increasingly apparent to most parties concerned that the existing system of production could not long remain viable. The threat of working class opposition was thus a dominant factor in the Progressive reform movements and, as we will see in the next three chapters, had a substantial impact in shaping the changes in criminal law during this period.

SIGNIFICANCE OF THE PROGRESSIVE ERA

Sociologically, the Progressive Era marks a major shift in terms of the principal variables discussed in Chapters 2–4.

Mode of Production

It is now generally recognized that the form of capitalism that was the object of Marx's analysis gave way around the turn of the century to a new form of *corporate capitalism*. Indeed, in his later works Marx briefly considered the appearance of new forms of corporations concentrating large shares of market, and he loosely suggested that such concentration might pave the way for socialism. While Marx was correct in predicting the demise of competitive capitalism, he did not realize that its contradictions would be resolved by its metamorphosis into another form of capitalism rather than into socialism.

Competitive capitalism and corporate capitalism are two distinct modes of production that differ in several interrelated dimensions. Foremost is the concentration of economic production by a single firm (monopoly) or a small number of firms (oligopoly). Competitive capitalism is characterized by a plurality of firms producing in any given industry. In Chapter 2 we saw how the rudimentary organization and technology of early capitalist enterprise permitted large numbers of individuals to enter the market as petty capitalists. For some industries this condition remained true into the twentieth century. For instance,

Entry into the [meat] packing industry was, and still is, comparatively easy. The raw materials were freely available and could be produced virtually anywhere. The major difference in profits was the exploitation of the by-products of meat. Local slaughterers had less expense per head for refrigeration and freight, and usually had lower administration, sales, and accounting expenses as well. For identical grades of meat, local meat often commanded higher prices than Western meat. Liabilities were many as well, ranging from the cost of slaughtering to economics of mass purchase of animals, but the assets were sufficiently important to create serious competition. (Kolko, 1963: 53)

Competitive capitalism is also characterized by low technology, since ease of market entry means that little initial capital is required. Faced with stiff competition from other firms and little technology to increase productivity, competitive firms tend to be under great pressure to maximize the amount of surplus value they extract from workers. This, in turn, gives rise to highly antagonistic labor relations in which the firms resist labor organization as far as possible. To the extent that labor costs can be kept down, these firms will continue to utilize labor-intensive low technology in small-scale operations.

In *corporate capitalism* a large number of small competing

firms is replaced by a single firm or a small number of firms that conduct large-scale production using high levels of technology. The resulting efficiencies of scale and high level of per-worker productivity combine with the lack of market pressure to cut prices and create a climate in which labor relations are less combative. Wages are negotiated rather than determined by market forces. Labor unions become institutionalized mechanisms of resolving grievances and negotiating wage levels. Collective bargaining replaces union busting. Costs incurred in providing wages and benefits may, because of the firms' market position, be "externalized," that is, passed on to the consumer.

In addition, competitive and corporate capitalism differ significantly in the relations between firms and the state. Under competitive capitalism the state has the relatively circumscribed role of maintaining conditions for the free market, preventing conspiracies in constraint of trade, and providing the infrastructure (transportation, communication, military) necessary for commerce. The state also undertakes to finance high-risk, large-scale enterprises such as the construction of the railroads. In corporate capitalism the state comes to play a more regulative role in the economy. It becomes a major consumer of goods and services. These purchases are furthermore planned in order to even out the boom and bust cycle that has been endemic to capitalism. It provides social services, training educated workers and providing economic assistance to the unemployed. The state, in other words, increasingly takes on an active role in maintaining the social and economic conditions necessary to ensure the profitability of private enterprise.

The Progressive Era marks the beginning of the transition between competitive and corporate capitalism in the United States, not a complete change. It is important to bear in mind the argument made earlier (p. 61) that a plurality of modes of production exist simultaneously. Major regional differences still persist in the dominance of corporate capitalism, and corporate firms exist side by side with competitive firms.[1]

Examining the relationships between economy and law given this mixture of modes of production will necessarily be a very complex undertaking. The relationships may be seen more readily in the transition period during which corporate capital first emerged. The next three chapters will spell out some of the legal implications and consequences produced by this shift in the dominant mode of production from competitive to corporate capitalism.

Rationalization

The expansion of the scale of production and the corresponding changes in the concentration of administration represent, in light of Weber's analysis, expansion of the rationalization of production. Economist John Kenneth Galbraith has more recently characterized this shift as an increase in "planning."

> Economists have anciently quarreled over the reasons for the great size of the modern corporation. Is it because size is essential in order to reap the economics of large scale production? Is it, more insidiously, because the big firm wishes to exercise monopoly power in the markets? . . . The size [for example] of General Motors is in the service not of monopoly or the economies of scale, but of planning. And for this planning—control of supply, control of demand, provision of capital, minimization of risk—there is no clear upper limit to the desirable size. (Galbraith, 1967: 88–89)

Following Weber's discussion, the next three chapters will show how the expansion of rationalization in production spread beyond the workplace and influenced the direction of legal change during the Progressive Era.

Mechanical/Organic Solidarity

The expansion of technology brought with it a further increase in the division of labor and economic demands for more specially trained laborers. The net result of this influence was to increase the development of organic solidarity and restitutive forms of justice in the Progressive Era. This took on the particular form of widespread adoption of the medical model in corrections and social work.

At the same time a countercurrent of mechanical solidarity arose from the infusion of the large numbers of immigrant workers drawn by the expanding economy. Differing fundamentally in religion and culture from the more recent arrivals, the new immigrants provoked a strong wave of nativism. The reforms of the Progressive Era thus reflect a mixture of restitutive tendencies resulting from the transformation of the economy and ritualistic repressive sanctions stemming from the increased mechanical solidarity of "unhyphenated Americans" reacting to the threat of foreign immigrants.

SUMMARY

The next three chapters, then, will attempt to show that the variety of legal changes (creation of the juvenile justice system, federal regulation of drug consumption, regulation of corporations) that occurred around 1900 are related. These changes appeared at the time when the major characteristics of the present form of corporate capitalism were emerging. Using the sociological perspectives outlined in Part One of this volume, we will develop interpretations of this critical period. While the analyses here are far from definitive, they should indicate the value of moving beyond descriptive historical accounts of legal changes to a general perspective that links varied legal changes and shows their relationships to underlying transformations of social structure.

FOOTNOTE

1. Hodson (1978) estimates the labor force is divided as follows:
   Monopoly sector: 27%
   Competitive sector: 49%
   State sector: 18%
   Construction, agriculture, etc.: 5%

5

Progressivism and the Control of Youth: The Emergence of the Juvenile Justice System

by Barry Feld

The contemporary juvenile justice system enforces a host of laws that regulate everything from child labor to compulsory school attendance, and it reinforces the dependent status of children. Less than one hundred years ago, specialized juvenile courts assisted by psychiatric and social work professionals, welfare and child protection agencies, and youth correctional facilities did not exist. The emergence of the juvenile justice system reveals the relationship between social change and the social control of children, as the cultural and legal positions of youth changed with industrialization. The emergence of the juvenile justice system, while significant in its own right, reflects an even more fundamental change in social and legal views of childhood as a distinct human developmental stage from an earlier conception of children essentially as small adults (Aries, 1962; Bremner, 1970; DeMause, 1974). Although harbingers of change associated with the creation of the first separate institutions catering to youth appeared within fifty years after the War for Independence,[1] the fundamental structural and legal revolution took place during the Progressive Era.

Of particular significance in the transformation of youth during the Progressive Era was the concomitant modernizing of the nuclear family, a process that began a century earlier. Changes in family structure and function were reflected in the decreasing size of the family, the transfer of economic functions from the family to other agencies, and modifications in the roles of women and children.

The preindustrial family was the basic unit of economic production. Children's labor was integral to this family economic unit linking several generations and branches under one household. Childhood was therefore not the distinct, highly valued social status based on age that we take for granted today. Beyond infancy, children were regarded for most purposes as miniature adults who interacted, worked, and played with people ranging across the entire age spectrum. Stages of life were not age-graded categories marking common experiences, but gradual progressions from dependence to semidependence to independent adulthood. For example,

> the gravity of a Cheyenne Indian family ceremoniously making a feast out of the little boy's first snowbird is at the furthest remove from our behavior. At birth the little boy was presented with a toy bow, and from the time he would run about serviceable bows suited to his stature were specially made for him by the man of the family. Animals and birds were taught him in a graded series beginning with those most easily taken, and as he brought in his first of each species his family duly made a feast of it, accepting his contribution as gravely as the buffalo his father brought. When he finally killed a buffalo, it was only the final step of his childhood conditioning, not a new adult role with which his childhood experience had been at variance. (Benedict, 1938: 163)

Children in preindustrial societies generally were economic assets, since they prepared for adulthood by assuming increasingly adult roles. In colonial America children were a valuable source of labor and services. Traditional practices of apprenticeships and binding out to neighboring farmers or tradesmen served both educational and economic functions—training children, adding to the skilled labor force, and providing masters with additional workers.[2] Children thus contributed to their own support and provided their parents with social security, unemployment insurance, and support when their parents could no longer work (Kett, 1977: 23).

> In pre-industrial times, when the family was an economic enterprise in which two or three generations shared both the work and its fruits, each member could play a productive role from early childhood to

old age. Mutual economic exchange took place over the whole life span, so that if infants took from their parents more than they gave in return, they could reciprocate as they grew into adults and their parents lost strength. (Stern et al., 1975: 104)

Formal education of children was subordinated to their other activities and was reserved for sporadic seasonal attendance during the winter. Necessary education was supervised by adults within the family household.[3]

As the family farm began to be supplanted by factories and shops that utilized division of labor and machinery, demand for unskilled labor hastened the decline of the familial apprenticeship system (Finestone, 1976: 23). Youths previously dependent upon paternal authority for economic opportunities began to migrate from the country to the towns to enter the wage labor market. Indeed, by the early nineteenth century, "the adolescent came to be recognized as having the legal capacity to bargain for full autonomy . . ." (Marks, 1975: 85).

The new industrial economy also had profound effects on family life and organization. The increasingly private character of the nuclear family and the erection of barriers between the family and the society outside created a "new conception of the family as a refuge from the highly competitive and often brutal world of commerce and industry" (Lasch, 1977: 5). As parents' own economic future was rendered increasingly uncertain by the processes of industrialization, the preparation of children for adulthood took on greater significance.

The status of children changed with these modifications of family life. Children were increasingly perceived as corruptible innocents whose growth and development required special attention and highly structured physical, social, and moral environments rather than early and rapid integration into adult roles and activities. Parents became increasingly responsible for their children's education and moral upbringing. The idealized conception of the child provided a benchmark both for evaluating parental success and for detecting youthful deviance. Parental supervision and discipline were critical to instill morality, character, economic diligence, respect for authority, and self-control.

STATE-ADMINISTERED SOLUTIONS

Progressive solutions to social problems characteristically enlarged and expanded the power of the state at every level as they resorted to or created governmental agencies to rationalize and structure economic and social reforms. While Progressivism drew its values for social reform from a more stable, traditional society, it characteristically adopted modern managerial and organizational solutions. Progressive reforms generally sought rational and scientific solutions devised by experts and administered by the state (Rothman, 1980: 6). The processes of economic rationalization and corporate growth provided the model for organizational solutions —specialization, hierarchy, and bureaucratic discipline.

> The more complicated and specialized modern culture becomes, the more its external supporting apparatus demands the personally detached and strictly "objective" expert. . . . (Weber, 1958: 216)

Progressive managers and professionals used bureaucracy to cope with the fluidity and indeterminacy of life in a constantly changing urban industrial society (Wiebe, 1967: 145). For Weber the Progressive's adoption of bureaucratic solutions was an almost inevitable concomitant of the bureaucratic rationalization of the economy. The increasing specialization and division of labor in all spheres of social life, not simply the economy, dictated the use of comparable forms of administration.

The Progressives' expansion of state bureaucracy to rectify social problems reflected their trust in the benevolence and legitimacy of public authority. They were sustained by a moral consensus and confident of their own values. They were convinced of the benefits of the American economic and social order and the desirability of enabling the less fortunate to become upwardly mobile participants in that prosperity. "Americanization" meant becoming sober, virtuous, middle-class citizens, and the Progressives were oblivious to the possibility of conflict when they attempted to "aid" the immigrant or the poor. Progressives created a variety of agencies to expedite assimilation and acculturation. Since they viewed individual and social welfare as identical, they saw no need to impose procedural impediments to protect individuals from state benevolence (Rothman, 1978: 77).

Many Progressive programs shared a unifying child-centered theme. Child labor laws, compulsory education, playground supervision, the expansion of kindergartens, and the juvenile courts were intended to structure child development and increase children's dependency, to simultaneously control and model children and protect them from exploitation (Rothman, 1980: 106).

If humanitarian Progressivism had a central theme, it was the child. He united the campaigns for health, education, and a richer city environment, and he dominated much of the interest in labor legislation. . . . The most popular versions of legal and penal reform also emphasized the needs of youth. Something more than sympathy for the helpless, or even the powerful influence of women in this portion of Progressivism explained this intense preoccupation. The child was the carrier of tomorrow's hope whose innocence and freedom make him singularly receptive to education in rational, human behavior. Protect him, nurture him, and in his manhood he would create the bright new world of the Progressive's vision. (Wiebe, 1967: 169)

Child labor and compulsory attendance laws that prolonged and protected the dependency of childhood also required a specialized legal agency to enforce them, and the juvenile court provided the mechanism to define and control youthful deviance and to reinforce the other Progressive child-saving activities. All three of these legal reforms reflected the central Progressive assumption that the ideal way to prepare children for life was to strengthen the nuclear family, shield the child from adult roles, and formally educate him or her for upward mobility.

EXPANDING EDUCATION FOR CHILDREN

As corporations increasingly dominated the economic base in the early twentieth century, formal education became a functional prerequisite to white collar, middle-class careers. In a traditional agricultural economy children were welcomed as extra hands and contributed significantly to the family's enterprise (Stern et al., 1975: 95). Since their career expectations were similar to their parents', their economic education could be completed at home. The removal of work from the home altered both children's economic value and their preparation for economic participation.

One of the principal consequences of the bureaucratic rationalization of the economy and society is the increasing salience of education. As children's careers diverged increasingly from their parents' with increasing specialization and technical differentiation, employment opportunities were increasingly dependent upon formal qualifications. The demands of office work and a complex machine technology required more than rudimentary skills. The business community, professionals, and educators advocated that schools assume new responsibilities to instill industrial discipline and prepare children for technical roles and a specialized division of labor. As bureaucratic administration increasingly meant administration by experts, educational certification replaced privilege as the basis for personnel recruitment. A diploma served not simply as a testament to literacy or technical skills but also to discipline, manners, and decorum.

At the same time that educational certification assumed greater significance for participation in the corporate and managerial sectors of the economy, the waves of southern and eastern European immigrants arrived as unskilled laborers. Assimilating their children and enabling them to acquire the requisite skills and discipline for an industrial society became principal responsibilities of public education.

As the corporate economy increased the salience of education for success, schools became a primary agency of Progressive reforms. The forces of bureaucratic rationalization and administrative efficiency that pervaded American society also altered the structure of schools as they expanded their role as agencies of social change. The standardization of curricula, the development of norms for evaluating student performance, and the introduction of tracking on the basis of ability all reflected the influence of specialization and bureaucratic rationalization on education (DeLone, 1979: 59). The bureaucratic-corporate economy required workers to possess certain attitudes, values, and disciplines—diligence, cooperation, efficiency, and the ability to function interdependently within a segmented organization. The industrial discipline required to participate in the new economic order demanded people who could report for work punctually, concentrate on repetitive tasks, and adhere to schedules. Schools, functioning as specialized bureaucracies, reproduced the organizational characteristics of the corporate order and created an institutional environment to socialize children for their future roles in complex organizations.

As prolonged schooling became a prerequisite for a middle-class career, it had major implications for families and children, deferring economic productivity and increasing the dependency of youths. The prolongation of education forced families to forgo their children's economic contribution as part-time and random school attendance became incompatible with a more structured, systematic, and age-graded process of education. Throughout the course of the twentieth century, increasing numbers of adolescents graduated from high school. While prior to the First World War only ten percent of youths graduated from high school, by the Second World War nearly half did. There was a corresponding decline in the number of children under sixteen who were gainfully employed during this period, with the biggest decimal drop occurring between 1910 and 1920 (Stern et al., 1975: 99).

The financial opportunity costs of prolonged secondary education had a significant class component, since middle-class families could afford the sacrifices associated with extended education that working-class and lower-class families could not. Parents sufficiently wealthy to forgo the economic contributions of their children during early and middle adolescence guided their offspring through a more prolonged period of schooling and qualified them for desirable jobs. Poorer parents who had to rely on the labor of their children for support could not as readily afford the opportunity costs of more prolonged education[4] (Kett, 1977: 151). As a result, extended education and social mobility were correlated with racial and ethnic differences as parents of native stock absorbed the costs of prolonged education that immigrant parents could not (Kett, 1977: 152).

The importance of education for later success led Progressive reformers to adopt compulsory education laws as a device to assure that youths would not be deprived of those opportunities. While only six states had compulsory attendance laws in 1871, by 1900 virtually all of the states in the North and West had adopted them (Wiebe, 1967: 119). The enforcement of compulsory education laws through the truancy jurisdiction of the juvenile court introduced an inevitable class bias in its administration.

CHILD LABOR LAWS

Progressive reformers, appalled by the economic exploitation of children, mobilized a crusade against child labor that coincided with the movement for compulsory education. They were joined in their efforts by labor unions, which wanted to protect the jobs of working men from young children.

In opposing the entrance of children into the nonagricultural labor force, labor unions were seeking not only to protect children, but also to protect the economic authority of fathers, which was being threatened by industrialization. Although a man had historically been manager of the family economic enterprise, he found himself being compelled to compete with children for his job as work was removed from the home to the factory. (Stern et al., 1975: 103)

Child labor legislation shared many of the policy assumptions undergirding the juvenile court movement—preserving the family, alleviating the effects of urban industrialism on vulnerable children, and avoiding the deleterious social consequences of inadequate preparation for adult roles. Child labor laws were designed to remove children from the marketplace back to their homes and school and to prevent their economic exploitation until they were adequately prepared for success in later life (Marks, 1975: 87). By the beginning of the twentieth century, twenty-eight states had passed laws restricting child labor as well as requiring children to attend school (Empey, 1979: 15).

While protectionist in intent, child labor laws effectively excluded children from productive economic activity, denied them economic roles or self-sufficiency, isolated them from adult work role models, and further prolonged their period of financial dependency. At the same time, compulsory education laws isolated children from adults, deprived them of satisfying economic or social roles, and confined them in school with age-graded peers. Both compulsory education and child labor laws reflected similar Progressive assumptions about the disadvantaged position of the children of the poor and immigrants, the undesirable circumstances under which they lived, and the need to prolong and structure dependency as a prerequisite to responsible adulthood. The children of the urban poor were defenseless against immediate exploitation and vulnerable to being trapped in poverty as adults. Progressive reformers were prohibitionists who used the coercive power of the state to prevent premature autonomy and to institutionalize the economic and social dependence of youth within a nuclear family (Platt, 1969: 99).

SCIENTIFIC CRIMINOLOGY REPLACES RETRIBUTION WITH REHABILITATION

Progressives introduced a number of criminal justice reforms at the turn of the century—probation, parole, indeterminate sentences, and the juvenile court. All criminal justice policies reflect underlying ideological assumptions about the causes and cures of deviance, and these assumptions were dramatically reformulated by new social science theories about human behavior. Criminology rejected the classical formulations of crime as the product of free will, asserted a scientific determinism, and sought to identify the causal variables producing crime and deviance (Matza, 1969: 4; Lauderdale and Inverarity, 1980: 16). The view of criminal behavior as a product of external and antecedent forces rather than individual choice reduced individual moral responsibility for crime and focused on reforming the offender rather than punishing the offense. The notion that punishment should be tailored to fit the criminal rather than the crime came into vogue.

In the late nineteenth and early twentieth century, intellectuals aspired to scientific status and tried to strengthen the similarities between the determinism of the natural sciences and those of the social sciences. In Weber's formulation, scientific rationality was one of the primary determinants of economic rationalization in the West. Science facilitated the application of technology to production and imposed a dynamic of innovation on the economy. The impact of this revolution on technology, production, and medicine provided a model for other fields of endeavor.

The Progressives' emphasis on science and expertise was part of their continuing quest to subject all social problems to rational technological solutions from "scientific" management to the cure of crime. At the turn of the century, seeking scientific legitimacy, criminology borrowed both its methodology and its vocabulary from the medical profession. Medical metaphors and concepts such as "pathology," "infection," "diagnosis," and "treatment" were popular analogies for criminal justice professionals who prescribed an individualized case-by-case approach to the diagnosis and cure of each offender (Rothman, 1980: 56; Platt, 1969: 18).

Although early positivistic criminology attributed criminal behavior to hereditary and biological factors, criminal justice professionals increasingly emphasized environmental explanations of deviance, which allowed for greater possibilities of intervention and cure (Platt, 1969: 30–32). Although explanations of deviance varied substantially, most attributed criminality to the social and economic conditions associated with immigrant ghettos and urban slums (Rothman, 1980: 53). The emergence of service professions based in psychology, sociology, and social work provided outlets for the new professionals and graduates of colleges and universities. These professional practitioners purported to apply scientific principles to individual circumstances, although the primitive state of the social sciences often left them free to impose their own conceptions about the causes and cures of deviance (Ryerson, 1978: 99).

The conjunction of positivistic criminology, medical analogies in the treatment of criminals, and the burgeoning number of social pathology professionals provided the undergirding of the "rehabilitative ideal," a prominent feature of all Progressive criminal justice reforms.

> The rehabilitative ideal . . . assumed, first, that human behavior is the product of antecedent causes. These causes can be identified. . . . Knowledge of the antecedents of human behavior makes possible an approach to the scientific control of human behavior. Finally, it is assumed that measures employed to treat the convicted offender should serve a therapeutic function; that such measures should be designed to effect change in the behavior of the convicted person in the interests of his own happiness, health, and satisfactions and in the interest of social defense (Allen, 1964: 26).

A variety of Progressive criminal justice reforms, including the juvenile court, were premised on these assumptions.

A flourishing rehabilitative ideal requires both a belief in the malleability of human behavior and a moral consensus about the appropriate directions of human change (Allen, 1978). Progressives believed that the new social sciences provided them with the tools for systematic human change. They also believed in the virtues of the bountiful American social order and the propriety of imposing a middle-class life style on immigrants and the poor (Rothman, 1980: 53).

The emergence of the rehabilitative ideal coincident with the vastly increased division of labor in the economy would seem to confirm Durkheim's interpretation of the relationship between organic solidarity and a restitutive law designed to restore cooperation in the social order. At the same time the influx of foreign immigrants evoked a more repressive nativist reaction in conjunction with boundary crises regarding the core values defining the society. It is not accidental that the increased indeterminacy and discretion associated with rehabilitative social control practices corresponded with the increasing volume and changing characteristics of offenders.

Weber would see in the rehabilitative ideal the probability, given a number of other qualifying factors, particularly the English common law tradition, of the predominance of a substantively irrational legal order. In Weber's formulation a substantively irrational legal order prevails when "law-making and law finding . . . is influenced by concrete factors of the particular case as evaluated upon an ethical, emotional, or political basis rather than by general norms" (Weber, 1954: 63). Substantive irrationality prevails when decisions are not guided by any systematic rules or general norms but are decided by a reaction to the individual case. The principles of "scientific" rehabilitation served to justify discretionary decision making, since identifying causes and prescribing cures requires an individualized approach which precludes uniformity and maximizes professional expertise (Rothman, 1980: 54). The forces of bureaucratic rationality that were altering the economy and education increased the likelihood that the implementation of law would be bureaucratized as well.

THE JUVENILE COURT—CULMINATION OF PROGRESSIVE REFORMS

In its conception the juvenile court was a typical Progressive reform—a specialized, bureaucratic agency designed to serve a specific clientele, the young offender. It was to be staffed by professionals making discretionary, individualized treatment decisions based on scientific expertise "in the best interests of the child" and the welfare of the state. First introduced in turbulent Chicago in 1899, within the first two decades of the twentieth century it revolutionized social policy toward youth (Rothman, 1980: 205).

The legal justification for intervention was *parens patriae*— the responsibility of the state to substitute its own control over children for that of the natural parents when the latter were unable or unwilling to meet their responsibilities or when the child posed a community crime problem. Although the *parens patriae* doctrine originated in feudal property law to preserve the estates of minor heirs, its expanded version in the nineteenth century legitimated state intervention in the lives of problem children—orphans, offenders, and street urchins. Under the *parens patriae* doctrine no distinctions were made among youth on the basis of their criminal or noncriminal conduct, and this provided the rationale that juvenile court intervention was civil rather than criminal in nature.

One goal of the juvenile court movement was to remove children completely from the adult criminal justice system as part of the general differentiation of children from adults. Progressives were appalled that the criminal law still treated youths and adults as moral and psychological equals.[5] While classical criminal law prescribed retributive punishment for intentionally evil choices subsumed in the doctrine of *mens rea*, the common law recognized that some young children did not possess the requisite awareness of consequences, the capacity to make evil choices that justified punishment. Accordingly, children below the age of seven were conclusively presumed to be incapable of committing crimes—to lack the mental capacity to make blameworthy choices—while those above fourteen were regarded as adults for purposes of imputing criminal responsibility. Between the ages of seven and fourteen, youths were legally presumed to lack criminal capacity, but if that presumption could be rebutted, then they could be punished as adults. Although the ideal of separating juveniles from adults animated the earlier "house of refuge" movement, the continued commingling of juvenile with adult offenders forced Progressives to advocate creating a completely separate system of juvenile justice (Ryerson, 1978: 36).

"STATUS" JURISDICTION

The juvenile court sought to aid children as well as to regulate their criminal behavior. It was intended to provide treatment rather than punishment as well as to enforce the other laws that institutionalized the dependent status of children. It provided Progressives with a middle ground between punishing behavior through the criminal process and ignoring it altogether (Rothman, 1980: 213). Because the juvenile court theoretically eschewed punishment, it brought within its ambit of control behavior that had previously been ignored or handled informally. Its jurisdiction encompassed not only the activity of children who committed crimes or violated local ordinances, but also behavior by children that was not criminal if engaged in by adults: truancy, immorality, "stubbornness," habitual vagrancy; living a "wayward, idle, and dissolute life," and other symptoms of premature adult autonomy.[6]

The juvenile court's status jurisdiction was thus normative and so reflected the Progressive reformers' conception of the dependent conditions of childhood. They envisioned the court as a benevolent surrogate parent substituting for ineffective families and ameliorating the influence of corrupting communities (Platt, 1969: 135). The juvenile court simultaneously affirmed the primacy of the nuclear family and expanded state power to intervene in instances of parental inadequacy (Rothman, 1980: 212). Child rearing had become too complex to relegate to unsupervised family control. These reformers used high standards by which to gauge the socializing competencies of lower-class families. Immigrant families, caught in the conflict of cultures, could not be expected to "Americanize" their children adequately, and state supervision was imposed to assure that the next generation adopted an acceptable middle-class way of life (Rothman, 1980: 206). The juvenile court provided the agency through which the Anglo-Protestant Americans defined the norms of family and childhood to which the outsiders had to adhere (Ryerson, 1978: 48).

SCIENTIFIC ANALYSIS OF DELINQUENCY— KHADI JUSTICE

Progressives responded to many social problems by creating specialized bureaucracies staffed by professionals (Wiebe, 1967: 150). The juvenile court movement envisioned an expert judge assisted by social service personnel, clinicians, and probation officers. The role of the juvenile court judge reveals the characteristic Progressive reliance on professional expertise, individualized discretion, and administrative specialization. The job called for a specialist trained in the social sciences and child development whose empathic qualities and insight into human behavior were more important than any legal skills (Rothman, 1980: 217).

Juvenile court judges enjoyed enormous discretion with which to make individualized dispositions in the "best interests of the child" (Rothman, 1980: 238). The medical model analogy to the treatment of delinquency provided a powerful rationale for discretion, since no physician could prescribe a treatment without first conducting a thorough examination (Rothman, 1980: 59). Progressives substituted discretion for decisional rules to maximize flexibility in diagnosis and treatment (Rothman, 1980: 50). The Progressives' major contribution to criminal justice reform was the expansion of discretionary decision making. Since their aims were benevolent, their solicitude individualized, and their interventions guided by science, there was no reason to narrowly circumscribe the coercive power of the state.

The juvenile courts' methodology encouraged collecting as much information as possible about the child, since a rational, scientific analysis of facts would reveal the proper diagnosis and prescribe the cure (Rothman, 1980: 50). In the factual inquiry into the whole child—his or her life, character, environment, and social circumstances—the specific criminal offense was accorded minor significance, since it indicated little about a child's "real" needs (Rothman, 1980: 215). The principles of psychology and individualized case evaluation allowed clinicians to dispense with formal rules, since their professional expertise provided such consistency as was deemed necessary (Rothman, 1980: 242).

Individualized justice in the best interests of the offender represents a significant departure from formal rational legal decision making based on general rules, since many more factors are relevant to the ultimate decision. Chapter 3 describes some of the forms that legal decision making can assume. In the individualized justice of the juvenile court the substantive factors influencing decisions were not generally applicable rules of law, but considerations drawn from psychology, social work, and the facts of the case. As the criteria of individualized justice became more inclusive, diffuse, and subjective, the relationship between the criteria of judgment and the ultimate dispositions became more obscure.

A system of decision making in which literally everything is relevant to the ultimate disposition necessarily depends heavily on sound judgment and professional expertise. Juvenile court decisions were "substantively irrational," each case being resolved on the basis of unspecified considerations that were not necessarily applicable to the next. In this regard the juvenile court judge is like Weber's Islamic Khadi in the marketplace, freely deciding each case on the basis of an evaluation of its ethical and practical merits without reference to general rules, norms, precedents, or consistency. Indeed, the fundamental issue of juvenile jurisprudence throughout the twentieth century has been the inherent conflicts between individualized discretionary decision making and the rule of law. The United States Supreme Court's decisions in the 1960s and 1970s extending constitutional procedural safeguards to juveniles can be viewed as an effort to impose formal legal rationality and a modicum of equality of outcome on a system which, from its inception, was designed to ignore legal considerations in favor of individualization.

JUVENILE COURT PROCEDURES

In separating children from adult offenders the juvenile court also rejected the jurisprudence and procedures of criminal law prosecutions. It substituted a sympathetic, benevolent therapeutic regime for an adversarial, punitive one. A specialized separate bureaucracy and a euphemistic vocabulary were introduced to avoid the stigma of adult prosecutions. Courtroom procedures were modified to eliminate any implication of a criminal proceeding. Since delinquency determinations were defined as civil cases, criminal procedural safeguards were dispensed with. Juries and lawyers were excluded as unnecessary constraints on the discretionary determination of the child's best interests. Since the important issues in juvenile court proceedings involved the child's background and welfare rather than the commission of a crime, judges dispensed with technical rules of evidence and procedural formality to obtain all the available information about the whole child (Rothman, 1980: 216). To avoid stigmatizing the youth, reformers insisted on confidential and private hearings; the public was excluded, access to court records was limited, and their disclosure to other courts or agencies was prohibited. To make proceedings more personal and private, the judge was supposed to sit next to the child, rather than being elevated above the child in formal black robes. Youths were found to be delinquent rather than guilty of a specific offense. Following adjudication, the court developed a treatment plan to meet the specific needs of the child. Dispositions were indeterminate and nonproportional; fixed sentences were rejected as retributive and crude. The delicts that brought the child before the court affected neither the intensity nor the duration of intervention, since each child's needs differed and no limits could be defined in advance (Rothman, 1980: 69). The court's jurisdiction continued for the duration of the minority, although offenders always held the key to their own release from supervision simply by reformation.

As envisioned by Progressive reformers, the juvenile court would seem to closely track Durkheim's description of restitutive law. Emerging during a period of economic and social differentiation, it was a specialized organ whose proceedings were defined as civil rather than criminal. Its dispositions were rehabilitative and intended to reestablish the natural state of affairs that should have prevailed, rather than to punish specific wrongs. Its interventions were designed to be nonstigmatic in order to facilitate reintegration. At the same time, however, the boundaries of America's common culture were threatened by the economic changes accompanying rationalizing capitalism and the floods of immigrants seeking new lives. They came from alien backgrounds and shared few of the values of native Americans, particularly with regard to the proper raising of children. Durkheim's analysis, then, suggests a dispositional dilemma for the juvenile court—would its intervention be restitutive consistently with economic and social differentiation, or would it be repressive as an instance of mechanical solidarity on the part of native Americans in defense of their cultural boundaries?

DISPOSITION OF YOUNG OFFENDERS

Probation was the disposition of first resort in the juvenile court for the vast majority of delinquents. Although some offenders were placed on probation before the invention of the juvenile court, its use was systematized, expanded, and institutionalized in juvenile court legislation and practice. Probation was envisioned as an alternative to dismissal rather than to institutionalization, and its use expanded the scope of formal control over youths who might otherwise have been left alone (Rothman, 1980: 255). It also permitted the court to supervise the wide range of noncriminal status offenders or minor misdemeanants who might otherwise have escaped control (Ryerson, 1978: 45). The roles of probation officers evolved with the juvenile court and included supervision of a child's physical, moral, and spiritual development; delinquency prevention; and community organization.[7]

While probation was the disposition of first resort, Progressive reformers recognized the necessity of institutional confinement as a last resort as well. They elaborated on the cottage plan model already in use in reformatories to create "noninstitutional" family and community living within an institution (Rothman, 1980: 265). Surrogate cottage parents were to promote individual development by normalizing a youth's institutional experience. Reformatories were relabeled as "vocational schools" or "industrial training schools." Under the influences of psychiatry in the late 1920s and 1930s these institutions grafted a hospital therapy regime onto their family model. Despite the euphemisms the institutional experience of incarcerated youth remained essentially custodial[8] (Rothman, 1980: 267). "The closer the scrutiny of juvenile confinement, the more inadequate and, indeed, punitive the programs turned out to be" (Rothman, 1980: 268).

Modernization thus posed a threat to Anglo-Protestant Americans, who responded in a mechanically solidary fashion by supervising their own with probation while dispatching "the foreign" to institutions.

> The exercise of judicial discretion helped to effect a dual system of criminal justice: one brand for the poor, another for the middle and upper classes. Judicial discretion may well have promoted judicial discrimination. (Rothman, 1980: 103)

Indeed, in its conception the juvenile court was deliberately designed to exercise its broad powers more extensively over lower-class and immigrant populations than over the middle class and native born (Rothman, 1980: 252). The problems of the poor were simply seen as more deeply rooted and intractable. The poor were more likely to come into contact with agencies of control—police, welfare, or schools. They were less likely to respond to the inadequate and ineffective services available and thus were more likely to filter quickly through the benevolent system into the more punitive one.

SUMMARY

At the beginning of the nineteenth century most children still lived in small, homogeneous, traditional communities in which the value of their labor assured them a degree of equality, autonomy, and integration into the social system. By the end of the century the transition to an industrialized, urban society fundamentally altered the character of the work force and the prerequisites for economic participation. A machine technology, bureaucratization, and a complex division of labor required more extensive preparation for economic participation. The family system was altered to devote greater attention to the structured socialization of children to prepare them to fit into modern society.

During this same period the fundamental character of Anglo-Protestant America was threatened by an influx of immigrants who did not share their language, religion, or culture. One aspect of the Progressive response was the creation of agencies to define the common culture. Strategies for socializing and controlling children, the carriers of the next generation, were one of the battlegrounds on which the cultural struggle took place.

By the turn of the century the juvenile court emerged as one of the principal institutions defining and enforcing the norm of childhood dependency. Its jurisdiction encompassed both children and their parents as it enforced the host of laws that institutionalized the dependent status of children. Reflecting the more complex divisions in society, its social control responsibilities were defined as therapeutic rather than as punitive. It was intended as a reintegrating mechanism to reform children and supervise their families. Its social welfare functions were implemented through a bureaucratic structure administered by professionals who based their decisions on their presumed expertise to determine the "best interests of the child."

The recent history and "constitutional domestication" of the juvenile court reflects some of the inherent contradictions in the Progressives' conception of the juvenile court.[9] Beginning with *In re Gault* (387 U.S. 1 [1967]), the United States Supreme Court has extended to juvenile court adjudications virtually all of the criminal procedural safeguards adults receive prior to punishment.[10] In its Constitutional decisions the Court has emphasized the stigma of a delinquency conviction, the discriminatory consequences of discretionary intervention, and the punitive reality of the conditions of institutional confinement for the young. The substantive irrationality of juvenile court intervention has become increasingly inconsistent with the formal rationalization of law occurring in so many other areas. Indeed, legal changes and policy recommendations within the past decade have eroded most of the features that originally distinguished the juvenile court from its adult criminal counterpart, and there are an increasing number of calls for its outright abolition (Feld, 1978, 1981).

Despite these more recent legal developments, the legal dependency of children that the Progressive reforms institutionalized have been amplified during the course of the twentieth century. Compulsory education laws have increased and systematized the amount of time that youths are required to spend in schools. Child labor laws have excluded children from meaningful economic roles, consigned them to part-time, ultimately dead-end jobs and substantially increased their economic dependence. By the mid-twentieth century the possibility

> that a child upon reaching puberty could assume a status independent of his parents had virtually disappeared. The state compelled the

extension of childhood—enjoining longer supervision, more protracted education, and the postponed assumption of adult economic
roles. . . . The myth had emerged that a new incremental preparatory
period was necessary for success in later life. And, more important,
active state participation in this preparation had been legitimated,
and an at least implicit standard about the "right" way to raise
children had been formulated. (Marks, 1975: 88)

The Progressives' solicitude has resulted in unparalleled age segregation with rigorously age-graded, lockstepping cohorts of successive generations moving through specialized child-serving institutions in which young people interact almost exclusively with
their peers (Empey, 1979; Kett, 1977). The juvenile court remains
the universal fixture of the specialized, age-segregated handling of
children and a primary mechanism in reinforcing their modern,
legally dependent position.

SUGGESTED READING

David Rothman, *Conscience and Convenience: The Asylum and its Al-
ternatives in Progressive America* (1980);
Ellen Ryerson, *The Best-Laid Plans: America's Juvenile Court Experiment*
(1978);
Anthony Platt, *The Childsavers: The Invention of Delinquency* (1969);
Joseph E. Kett, *Rites of Passage: Adolescence in America 1790 to the
Present* (1977);
Robert H. Wiebe, *The Search for Order 1877–1920* (1967);
LaMar Empey, ed., *Juvenile Justice: The Progressive Legacy and Current
Reforms* (1979);
David Greenberg, "Delinquency and the age structure of society." *Contem-
porary Crises* 1: 189–223;
Mark Lipschutz, "Runaways in history." *Crime and Delinquency* 23: 321–
32.

FOOTNOTES

1. The most important of these innovations was the "house of refuge,"
   an institution intended to incarcerate and reform "predelinquent"
   youth. Established in New York City in 1825, the refuge movement
   remained limited in its adoption and impact but provided a model
   for later Progressive reforms. See treatments by Pickett (1969), Finestone
   (1976), and Mennel (1973).

2. A youth's entry into the labor force occurred between age seven and puberty. Following a centuries-old practice, children were often placed out to live in the homes of other people, to work in their homes as servants, woodchoppers, and water carriers and to prevent undue emotional attachments between parents and children that might interfere with their disciplining (Kett, 1977: 17; Aries, 1962). High birth rates often forced the placement out of older children to other homes to make way for younger successors (Kett, 1977: 30). Orphaned children and those experiencing household disruption were traditionally placed out with other families (Kett, 1977: 29).

3. This description of the American colonial family and economy corresponds closely to Durkheim's analysis of a traditional society in which consensus and social stability are maintained by mechanical solidarity, a solidarity based on resemblance with minimal individual differentiation (Durkheim, 1964). Colonial communities were characterized by ethnic, religious, and cultural homogeneity and integrated by shared values. They were segmented communities, in Durkheim's terminology, both in the sense that the individual was tightly incorporated into the social group and because each of the groups were locally situated, economically self-sufficient, and relatively isolated and separated from other groups. In Durkheim's mechanically solidary society, as in colonial America, the family was the primary legislator and transmitter of law and ethics (Durkheim, 1964). The early and extensive integration of children into economic and social roles is another aspect of a mechanically solidary society in which individuals are conceived of as being identical regardless of their "objective" differences along such dimensions as age.

4. With the decline of apprenticeship as an entree to careers, more young people remained at home longer, imposing a drain on family resources (Kett, 1977: 170). Until the end of the nineteenth century, urban teenagers had been an economic asset, contributing significant proportions of their family's incomes by working in factory production and as unskilled labor (Kett, 1977: 169). In 1900, one of every six children aged ten to fifteen worked, and even more among the children of immigrants.

> Immigrant parents did not understand that removing their children from the classroom and putting them to work as common laborers doomed them to a permanent place in the factory and subjected them to grave risks of injury. Therefore, reformers moved to ban children from the labor force and to compel them to attend schools. (Rothman, 1980: 207)

5. Historically, controlling youth through the criminal law presented the stark alternatives of a criminal conviction and punishment as an adult or an acquittal or dismissal, which freed the youth from all supervision. Particularly for minor offenders, jury or judicial nullification to avoid

punishment excluded many youths from effective control. A desire for greater supervision and control, rather than leniency, animated many reformers who sought a system that would allow the law to intervene in the lives of young offenders to treat them and reintegrate them and not simply impose punishment (Ryerson, 1978: 33).

6. The status jurisdiction assumed that certain aberrant conditions of childhood were precursors to adult criminality and authorized pre-delinquent intervention to control those criminal tendencies (Ryerson, 1978: 47). The status jurisdiction extended judicial authority beyond that of traditional criminal courts and enabled them to supervise the moral upbringing of youths.

> It was not by accident that the behavior selected for penalizing by the child savers—drinking, begging, roaming the streets, frequenting dance halls, and movies, fighting, sexuality, staying out late at night, and incorrigibility—was primarily attributable to the children of lower class migrant and immigrant families. (Platt, 1969: 139)

7. Probation was initially conceived as a source of social change and community uplift, a successor to "friendly visitors" that would uplift the child and transform the family and the cultural milieu of the lower-class ghetto (Ryerson, 1978: 50; Lubove, 1967). The probation officer was envisioned as a "friend" and law-abiding adult role model whose relationship with the delinquent would solve the child's problems through "spontaneous moral regeneration" (Rothman, 1980: 66; Ryerson, 1978: 53). During the first two decades of the twentieth century, probation became more professionalized as psychological research and Freudian psychiatry strongly influenced both social work practices and the juvenile court. Probation adopted the techniques of mental testing, introduced more intensive therapeutic relationships between client and worker, and expanded the role of the juvenile court as a social services agency (Ryerson, 1978: 104–5).

8. The repressive characteristics of juvenile confinement suggest the inherent incompatibility between simultaneously promoting custody and rehabilitation. For staff, maintaining order and control for their own immediate protection and to forestall external criticism necessarily takes precedence over more amorphous goals like treatment. The need to maintain discipline necessarily entails the use of backup sanctions and further punishment to maintain institutional order at virtually any cost (Rothman, 1980: 283). When coupled with inadequate budgets, ill-trained staff, and the primitive state of the art of psychology, psychiatry, and social work, the repressiveness of institutionalization became almost inevitable. Indeed, in the ensuing seventy-five years the conditions of juvenile incarceration have changed depressingly little (Feld, 1977).

9. Progressive reformers did not appreciate the potential conflicts between protecting children and protecting society. They did not recognize the

difficulties of fusing social welfare services with a legal institution. Their belief in their own benevolence and the superiority of their vision of childhood and society blinded them to the possibility of cultural conflict in defining and controlling youthful deviance. They also failed to perceive the operational contradictions between treating and punishing, between *parens patriae* and coercion, or the rapidity with which rehabilitative considerations could be subordinated to custodial concerns (Rothman, 1980: 144). They did not understand the organizational tensions in a multipurpose court where the voluntarism of a therapeutic relationship is coerced, while the rule of law is subordinated to discretionary professional expertise (Ryerson, 1978: 141).

10. *In re Gault*, 387 U.S. 1 (1967), guaranteed juveniles the procedural safeguards of due process in delinquency adjudications. These procedural rights included notice of charges, the right to counsel at the hearing, an opportunity to confront and cross-examine witnesses, and the privilege against self-incrimination. Subsequently, in *In re Winship*, 397 U.S. 358 (1970), the court ruled that the same constitutional standard of "proof beyond a reasonable doubt" was required to convict a juvenile of an offense as would be required to convict an adult similarly charged. In *Breed* v. *Jones*, 421 U.S. 519 (1975), the Supreme Court decided that juvenile court proceedings were sufficiently like criminal prosecutions that the constitutional limitations on double jeopardy barred a youth's criminal prosecution as an adult following a delinquency adjudication. Indeed, the only criminal procedural safeguard to which juveniles are not constitutionally entitled is the right to a jury trial. In *McKeiver* v. *Pennsylvania*, 403 U.S. 528 (1970), the court held that the potential impact of jury trials on juvenile proceedings might so totally impair the informality and flexibility of the juvenile court as to result in its elimination.

6

The Creation and Growth of Opiate Regulation

by Pat Lauderdale

American attitudes toward drugs are an odd mixture of acceptance and rejection. Consider, for example, such phrases as "wonder drug" and "drug fiend." The boundaries between those drugs viewed as having "medical value" and those seen as "dangerous" have typically been ambiguous. Reliable scientific information about the effects of drug consumption has been difficult to obtain. Mixed with the scientific issues are matters of personal taste and economic interest. When, for example, the Surgeon General announced that epidemiological research suggested a higher risk of lung cancer among cigarette smokers, the American Tobacco Institute quickly countered with arguments about correlation and causation.[1] In earlier debates the basis of the argument over drugs was theological rather than scientific. Some of the first prohibitionists argued for abstinence from alcoholic beverages on the grounds that persistent abuse was a sign of demonic possession.

Despite the controversies, drugs are major items of consumption in American society. The Stanford Research Institute discovered that the average household had some thirty different drugs, both prescription and over-the-counter (Ray, 1974). Annually, Americans consume 16,000 tons of aspirin; over 400 million dollars are spent every year in attempts to persuade consumers that one brand of $C_9H_8O_4$ is a superior remedy for headache, arthritis, the aches and pains of colds and flu, and existential angst. More than 230 million prescriptions are filled each year, including five billion doses of tranquilizers, three billion amphetamine pills, and five billion barbiturate capsules. The consumption of alcohol is staggering, and its abuse costs $25 billion annually in the United States alone.

While it is beyond the scope of this chapter to explain American consumption patterns, we will present an overview of the creation of drug regulations and the stigmatization of drug use in the United States. In order to investigate the conditions under which the social structure may be conducive to drug regulation, much of the following discussion centers around the emergence of opiate laws. As with other drug studies (Anslinger and Thompkins, 1953; Becker, 1963; Duster, 1970; Conrad and Schneider, 1980: 73–143), the prevalent belief is that opiate regulations simply reflect the interests of moral entrepreneurs or a few organized groups. These individuals or groups, however, were able to organize and compete under certain conditions. The Marxian perspective presented in Chapter 2 is particularly relevant here. The immediate cause of legal change regarding opiates was, in part, a popular movement; however, the movement succeeded when the underlying structure was compatible. The opiate issue emerged as an important national concern only with the corporate market interest in international trade and the shift to a more regulated economy.

As the Progressive Era ushered in the rationalization and regulation of corporations, it also turned to the items that citizens consumed. The emergence of the Pure Food and Drug Act in 1906, the Harrison Act in 1914, and Prohibition in 1920 coincided with the regulation of railroads, children, education, settlement houses, and "good" municipal governments. It is probably no coincidence that these three regulations appeared with increasing specialization, hierarchy, and bureaucratic discipline. This bureaucratic rationalization was developed as a means of organizing the rapidly changing national and international marketplace as well as stabilizing fundamental problems emerging from sudden changes caused by industrialization and urbanization. The specific legal developments following the three regulations parallel the Weberian predictions regarding the expansion of formal rational procedures. Subsequent decisions on drug regulation increasingly became governed by distinct legal procedures and rules that were explicit, abstract, and intellectually calculable.

It is important to note, however, that once regulations are enacted, they may have unintended consequences. Recall, for example, the discussion in Chapter 2 of the fate of the civil rights laws enacted immediately after the Civil War. Here again we will see that legislative history alone does not illuminate very well the subsequent significance of a change in legal definitions. Additionally, the stigmatization associated with drug use has been a major mechanism in separating deviants from nondeviants. From a Durkheimian view the drug laws have typically aided community integration through the increase or maintenance of solidarity.

This chapter will focus upon the remarkable transformation of opiates from a commodity operating in the competitive market to a social problem of such magnitude that the most extreme criminal sanctions were accepted as necessary for its control. We will pay particular attention to the structural bases of the transformation.

THE BEGINNING OF OPIATE REGULATION

Opium has a long and varied history of use. It was consumed by the Sumerians in 4000 B.C., and ancient art relics depict its use for various religious rituals in Egypt as early as 3500 B.C. Parents in ancient Egypt mixed it with dirt, strained it to a pulp, passed it through a sieve, and gave it to their crying babies (Scott, 1969: 109). Hippocrates legitimized its use for medicinal purposes in Greece. Records from Cyprus, Crete, and the Aegean Islands made frequent reference to the drug.

The modern international commerce in opium began around 1815. Faced with a massive balance of payments deficit with China, Great Britain began to monopolize and expand the export of opium from India to China. Although the Chinese had used opium for medicinal purposes with little known addiction for a thousand years, use of the drug increased sharply during the nineteenth century. Tobacco smoking was introduced at that time, which stimulated a shift from medical administration of opium to recreational smoking of the drug. The upper classes smoked opium during social and business occasions, while the lower classes used it as a means of overcoming fatigue. Addicts in China during the nineteenth and twentieth centuries numbered in the millions.

The Chinese government was the first to attempt to control the use of opium in the eighteenth century. Total prohibition alternated with heavily taxed legal importation, but consumption and importation continued (cf. Scott, 1969; Musto, 1973). In addition, the Chinese government attempted to improve domestic opium production despite official prohibition in order to decrease the costs of importation, but without success.

Although Britain had waged opium wars against China in 1842 and 1856 to ensure importation rights, by the latter part of the century the English government began to alter some former policies and acknowledge Chinese requests to cease importation from India (Scott, 1969). The Phillipine Commission in 1905 signified the onset of international cooperation to control opium. An agreement was reached at the Hague Conference in 1912. This series of international events directly affected the emergence of drug laws within the United States, especially the noted Harrison Act of 1914. However, before examining American drug laws, it will be useful to consider the relationship between the patent medicine industry and opiate addiction before 1914.

American Opiate Addiction Prior to 1914

In 1803 a German chemist derived from opium a meronic acid and an alkaline base, which he called morphium (Terry and Pellens, 1970). This discovery initiated a shift from the use of pure opium in folk medicine to a complex technology of other derivatives such as codeine, dionin, and heroin.

The opiate derivatives became popularly prescribed for virtually every sort of ailment. One doctor, for example, reported that opium could be used for relief of pain in venereal disease, cancer, and nervous headaches; for relief of palpitations; and in intestinal disorders such as vomiting, colic, dysentery, and diarrhea. Another was quoted in 1832 as maintaining, "There is scarcely a disease in which opium or its products may not, during some of its states, be brought to bear, by the judicious use by physicians, with advantage" (Terry and Pellens, 1970: 60). Morphine was believed to benefit anemia, angina, asthma, blepharospasm, bronchitis, carcinoma, cardiac diseases, cholera, chorea, continued fevers, convulsions, cystitis, delirium tremens, diabetes, epilepsy, gastric catarrh, hepatic ulcer, incontinuence of urine, insanity, insomnia, itching, lead colic, lumbago, malaria, meningitis, nymphomania, pleuritis, pneumonia, renal colic, shock, sprains, tetanus, vaginismus, and vomiting of pregnancy (Terry and Pellens, 1970: 71). Since medical remedies were directed at symptoms rather than at cures during that time, a drug that apparently suited such a range of medical situations became widely administered and enthusiastically used.[2]

The Patent Medicine Industry

In 1624 the British Parliament granted the first patent on a drug. The patent guaranteed the producer legal rights to a certain combination of ingredients. Over time, however, what came to be patented was not the formula for the drug, but its trademark. The special advantage of this arrangement was that the actual ingredients need never be revealed. The sale of patent medicines was a major industry in the United States in the 1800s.

From 1859 to 1904 the sales from patent medicines increased from about 4 million dollars to 75 million dollars. The mass media of nineteenth century America introduced seductive advertisements for painkillers, cough mixtures, soothing syrups, "women's friends," consumption cures, and other similar concoctions.[3] Patent medicines were effective as far as consumers were concerned. Opiates were often the main ingredient of such secret formulas, and dependency on the drugs increased.

The industry attracted an odd assortment of promoters, several of whom amassed large fortunes. For example:

The Rockefeller fortune was begun by Nelson's great-grandfather William Avery Rockefeller, a nineteenth-century dealer in drugs who, like modern narcotics dealers, dressed in extravagant silk costumes, used aliases, and never carried less than a thousand dollars in cash on his person. "Big Bill," as he was commonly called, hawked "herbal remedies" and other bottled medicines which if they were like other patent medicines being sold in those days, contained opium as an active ingredient. Long before opium—the juice from the poppy—became the base of patent medicine in America, it was used in Asia as a remedy for dysentery and as a general pain-killer. Because it was a powerful analgesic, hucksters on the American frontier made quick fortunes selling their various "miracle" preparations. (Epstein, 1977: 35)

While occasional fortunes were made, the market was highly competitive. A trade journal in 1905 listed some 28,000 brands. They were sold freely in drugstores and through the mails. Since ingredients were trade secrets the presence of alcohol and opiates was generally unknown to the consumer. Not all companies, however, were se-cretive about including opiates. A leading headache remedy, for example, came with "H" or "C" stamped on each pill to indicate heroin or codeine varieties.

The widespread use of opiates in commercial medications re-sulted in an incidence of addiction in virtually every social stratum.[4] In 1889 in a survey of 260 physicians who were asked "What classes of people mostly use [opiates]?" 30 percent of the responses designated all classes; 22 percent specified the upper class; 3 percent specified the middle class, and 6 percent specified the lower class (Terry and Pellens, 1970: 488). Further evidence of widespread addiction was recorded by a Joint Legislative Committee in New York in 1917:

> It has been further stated by competent authorities before your Com-mittee that drug addiction is not confined to the criminal or defective class of humanity. This disease, however contracted, is prevalent among members of every social class. (Terry and Pellens, 1970: 495)

The use of opium or its derivatives was not considered socially "respectable" in late nineteenth century America, particularly after chronic use was linked with addiction. Because the physiological and chemical effects of drugs on the human body were not fully understood, both physicians and the public generally assumed that opiate addiction signified only a lack of willpower or a flaw in character. Dr. John V. Shoemaker expressed the philosophy popular in 1890:

> The treatment of chronic morphine poisoning, or opium eating, is often more moral than medical. In such cases the will of the unfortunate victim is so weakened by self-indulgence that the acquired taste for the drug can not ordinarily be resisted, and he will acquire means for its gratification at any cost, or if it is not obtainable, he may destroy himself. (Terry and Pellens, 1970: 142)

While opiate addiction lacked respectability, it did not carry the stigma that it bears today. Addicts continued to participate fully in the life of the community and were indistinguishable from other community members in terms of occupation, appearance, and public behavior. Children of addicts were not removed from the home by the state. Little popular support existed for legislation to ban the use of opiates, and they were not viewed as a menace to society. Since the addict had inexpensive, legal access to the drug and was able to maintain equilibrium, no distressing behavioral effects occurred.

By 1900, medical and public health professionals estimated a population of between 200,000 and 400,000 addicts in the United States (Musto, 1973: 254). Thus the rate of addiction was apparently higher in 1900 than it is today (cf. Ray, 1974). Paradoxically, opiates were popularly regarded in much the same way as nicotine is starting to be looked upon by the public in our own time: potentially hazardous to health, but a legitimate drug. However, the situation changed as economic conditions led to preoccupation with one particular group of users, Chinese laborers.

DRUG LAWS REGULATING OPIATE USE

A wide variety of drug regulations were passed around the turn of the century in America; however, two specific laws are of special interest. The San Francisco Ordinance of 1875 was the first law to legislate opium use in America. This ordinance was primarily an outgrowth of an attempt to control a minority group that appeared to threaten the majority working class. The second regulation, the Harrison Act of 1914, put controls on the dispensing of opiates. The catalyst for this act was the attempt by a group of professionals to rationalize the marketplace and symbolically enforce their class values. The Harrison Act has had far greater impact than any other drug law. Although it was originally enacted as a tax measure to record opiate distribution, it has been interpreted and altered to make opiate addiction a criminal offense (for an analysis of the symbolic aspects of this stigmatization, see Gusfield, 1963).

The San Francisco Ordinance of 1875

The San Francisco Ordinance prohibiting the smoking of opium in dens was enacted in 1875, though impetus for its passage began with the arrival of Chinese immigrants in California in the 1850s. The Chinese laborers, suffering from a variety of economic and financial crises at home, were initially lured to the California gold boom to develop small mining claims. By the early 1860s "as surface mining close to natural waterways became scarce, the independent miner-prospector was replaced by Chinese indentured workers employed by quartz and hydraulic mining companies" (Takagi and Platt, 1978: 3). Those Chinese who had intended to develop their own claims and were unable to invest in the necessary equipment returned home, leaving the indentured workers. Between the arrival of the first immigrants in 1850 and the partial departure in 1863, use of opium was not specifically linked with the Chinese.

In 1867 a second wave of Chinese immigrants arrived in California. These newcomers usually financed passage to America with borrowed money and were anxious to accept any employment available upon arrival in America. Construction of the transcontinental railroad offered employment to the bulk of the immigrants. This immigrant group brought the recreational smoking of opium, but no public concern was expressed.[5] Indeed, labor contractors offered an allowance of one-half pound of opium per month in addition to regular earnings specifically to attract the reputedly industrious Chinese laborers.

Railroad construction and all other industry suffered a sharp decline in the early 1870s; San Francisco was severely affected. Widespread unemployment unexpectedly ensued with the "change from steamship to railway transportation" and "the completion of the Central Pacific Railroad" (Takagi and Platt, 1978: 4). The depression precipitated anti-Chinese agitation as the Caucasian labor force attributed the slump to Chinese competition; exclusion of that minority group became the rallying cry throughout the white working class. The use of opium by the Chinese was focused upon, creating hostile stereotypes and obscuring economic motivations. The negative reaction was compounded by the increasing urbanization of the Chinese; the percentage in San Francisco increased from 7 to 29 from 1860 to 1880; since they continued to immigrate, this amounted to an increase from approximately 2,500 to 22,000 people (cf. Takagi and Platt, 1978: 6). The ensuing crusade was not simply concerned with opium, but with the characterization of opium smoking as a Chinese habit.

In 1875 the city of San Francisco adopted an ordinance prohibiting the smoking of opium in dens. Following this enactment, many Chinese were heavily fined or imprisoned as a result of unrestrained and arbitrary police raids and searches. A number of other local ordinances were passed to restrict the occupational chances of the Chinese, and the California Supreme Court even held that the Chinese could not give evidence against white citizens (Takagi and Platt, 1978).

Although the ordinances greatly reduced the Chinese labor force in San Francisco as a result of extensive imprisonment and arrest, the labor unions, who had pressed for enactment, were not satisfied. At the first meeting of the Federation of Organized Trades and Labor Unions (later called the American Federation of Labor) in 1881, the Chinese Cigarmakers of California were formally condemned, and a boycott of nonunion cigars was launched. Samuel Gompers, President of the American Federation of Labor and an articulate leader of the anti-Oriental crusade, focused his campaign for exclusion on the newly created image of the Chinese as opium fiends. Largely as a result of AFL lobbying efforts, Congress enacted the Chinese Exclusion Act in 1882, barring any further Chinese immigration into the United States and effectively reducing labor competition.

The San Francisco Ordinance initiated a nationwide trend: in 1883, Congress raised the tariff on opium prepared for smoking; in 1887, Congress outlawed the importation of opium by Chinese persons entering America; 1890 marked the passage of a law that limited the manufacture of smoking opium to American citizens. In 1909, following the Shanghai Conference, the importation and manufacture of opium was prohibited altogether; by 1914, twenty-seven states had enacted laws similar to the San Francisco Ordinance to control the use of opium.

Despite this rash of legislation, the use of opium apparently increased. From the first legal prohibitions in 1870 to the ban on importation of smoking opium in 1909, the amount of opium imported for smoking increased from 49,000 to 149,000 pounds (Brecher, 1972: 45). The estimated number of opium smokers increased from 20,000 to 60,000 during the same period.

In sum, the earliest drug laws were not simply motivated by the potential harmfulness of the drug or any commitment to social welfare, but rather by desire for economic stability and political control (cf. Bonacich, 1972). The application of a negative label to Chinese opium smokers was the harbinger of modern attitudes about opiates.

The Harrison Act of 1914

While several of the inventors and promoters of patent medicines were doctors, in general a clear conflict of economic interest existed between the purveyors of self-administered remedies and the professional physician. This conflict was made all the more acute by the simple fact that the average patient could gain more comfort from an opiate-laced patent medicine than from any treatment the nineteenth century physician had to offer. Medical knowledge throughout the nineteenth century was rudimentary. As late as 1870 the head of the Harvard Medical School refused to give written examinations because few of the students could write well enough to pass (Larson, 1977). Since physicians had no reliable understanding of the causes of most diseases, the patent remedies containing opiates offered at least relief from the symptoms. Even those medicines that were totally inert (for example, sugar pills) elicited testimonials to their success; since many physical disorders are temporary, any form of intervention will thus be followed by a "cure." Drug companies, consumers, and physicians in the nineteenth century were without any conception of scientific testing, for example, the necessity of control groups and the dangers of a patient's anticipations in assessing the impact of a drug. This problem persists down to our own time with the continued proliferation of quack remedies for cancer or unscientifically tested "miracle" drugs for which unsystematic testimonial evidence abounds.

To make matters more complicated, the medical profession in the nineteenth century not only competed with a technically superior home remedy industry, but faced a problem of oversupply in its own ranks. The United States had four times as many practicing physicians per capita as Germany during this period.

Around the turn of the century, medicine became more rationalized along with most of the other institutions in corporate capitalist society. Before 1910 professional medicine had a few isolated successes, like the smallpox vaccine, but not until the late nineteenth century was medicine placed on a scientific basis. Pasteur's germ theory of disease and the physiological work of Helmholtz in Germany became the basis of professional training in American medical schools around 1900. Using its newly found scientific basis, the medical profession began around the turn of the century a process of upgrading.

> Somewhere between 1910 and 1912 in this country, a random patient, with a random disease, consulting a doctor chosen at random, had for the first time in the history of mankind, a better than fifty-fifty chance of profiting from the encounter. (Lawrence J. Henderson, in Strauss, 1968: 302)

Educational requirements and licensing regulations were made more stringent. As part of this effort, the American Medical Association (AMA) stepped up its campaign against "quacks" and quack remedies. Particular attention was devoted to the harmfulness of patent medicines whose principal active ingredients were opiates and alcohol.

The AMA thus became a leading lobby in the passage of the Harrison Act, which limited access to opiates by requiring a doctor's prescription.

In general the medical profession benefited greatly from its involvement in the struggle with the patent medicine industry and the subsequent passage of the Harrison Act.

> Public health and psychiatry have long been concerned with social behavior and have functioned traditionally as agents of social control (Foucault, 1965; Rosen, 1972). What is significant, however, is the expansion of this sphere where medicine functions in a social control capacity. In the wake of a general humanitarian trend, the success and prestige of modern biomedicine, the technological growth of the 20th century, and the diminution of religion as a viable agent of control, more and more deviant behavior has come into the province of medicine. In short, the particular, dominant designation of deviance has changed; much of what was badness (i.e., sinful or criminal) is now sickness. Although some forms of deviant behavior are more completely medicalized than others (e.g., mental illness), recent research has pointed to a considerable variety of deviance that has been treated within medical jurisdiction: alcoholism, drug addiction, hyperactive children, suicide, obesity, mental retardation, crime, violence, child abuse, and learning problems, as well as several other categories of social deviance. (Conrad and Schneider, 1980: 34)

The medical profession in addition to its own increase in legitimacy received support for opiate control legislation from the American business community. In 1900 the United States began— as it was to do again seventy years later—to look at China as a major market for American industry and agriculture. The brief, popular Spanish American War had made the United States a Far Eastern power. The United States had also gained possession of the Phillipines and several intermediate Pacific outposts. Having arrived late in the China trade, in 1899 the State Department promulgated an open door policy, respecting the territorial integrity of China, which had by this time been divided by the Europeans into spheres of influence. The Chinese were hostile to American trade, in large measure because of restrictions placed by the United States on Chinese immigration and because of a history of atrocities committed against individual Chinese within the United States. Faced with a boycott of American goods by the Chinese, the State Department set about trying to improve relations. A key part of this policy became control over the opium traffic. Having lost the Opium Wars to the British, the Chinese lost control over the trafficking of opiates in their own country. The British found the trade of opium highly profitable and were unwilling to give it up only to have a competitor move into the market. The problem required some international agreement on controlling the opium trade. The United States sought to accomplish this through a series of international conferences, beginning in 1909.

Passage of the Harrison Act followed several international attempts to control opiate traffic. The Shanghai Conference was attended by representatives of thirteen countries. Opium smoking was the common concern. The conference resolved that each government would attempt to control the manufacture, sale, and distribution of smoking opium. The smoking habit in China was considered a major problem, and it became the task of each government holding Chinese territories to close their opium dens. The United States applied the provisions of the resolution at home, and opium smoking was prohibited by Congress that same year. Opium smoking, however, was not the most popular form of opiate consumption; those relatively few addicts affected presumably switched to other forms of consumption.

The Hague Convention in 1912 marked the advent of international control of opium and all major derivatives. Each contracting nation was bound to adopt provisions of regulation and distribution for raw opium and prepared opium, medicinal opium, morphine, heroin, and codeine. Import or export was to be made only by authorized persons, and each contracting country was required to limit the ports or cities through which import and export were to be permitted. Export to countries prohibiting import of raw opium was to be prevented and controlled instead by those countries where importation was restricted. The manufacture, sale, and use of opiate derivatives was to be limited to medical and legitimate purposes (Anslinger and Thompkins, 1953).

The State Department found itself in the awkward position of advocating international restrictions on opium trade while at home trade flourished virtually uncontrolled (Musto, 1973: especially 54–61). To maintain credibility in negotiating international agreements, then, the State Department entered into lobbying efforts (aimed against, for example, the southern resistance to any invasion of states' rights) that resulted in the Harrison Narcotic Act. Those efforts focused attention on the relatively large number of addicts and "an impression that the problems posed by this fact were not being effectively met" by local regulations (Lindesmith, 1965: 4–5).

The Harrison Act of 1914 attempts to incorporate the basic intent of the Hague Agreement into domestic practice. Section 1 of the Harrison Act provides:

> That on or before July 1 of each year every person who imports, manufactures, produces, compounds, sells, deals in, dispenses, or gives away opium or coca leaves, or any compound, manufactive, salt, derivative or preparation thereof, shall register with the collector of internal revenue of the district of his place of business and places where such business is to be carried on and pay the special taxes hereinafter provided. . . .
>
> It shall be unlawful for any person to purchase, sell, dispense, or distribute any of the aforesaid drugs except in the original stamped package or from the original stamped package; and the absence of appropriate tax paid stamps from any aforesaid drugs shall be prima facie evidence of a violation of this section by the person in whose possession some may be found. Provided, that the provisions of this paragraph shall not apply to any persons having in his or her possession any of the aforementioned drugs which have been obtained from a registered dealer in pursuance of a prescription, written for legitimated medical uses, issued by a physician, dentist, veterinary surgeon, or other practitioner registered under the act; or to the dispensing or administration, or giving away of any of the aforesaid drugs to a patient by a registered physician, dentist, veterinary surgeon, or other practitioner in the course of their professional practice, and where said drugs are dispensed or administered to the patient for legitimate medical purposes, and the record is kept as required by the Act of the drugs so dispensed, administered, or given away. (Terry and Pellens, 1970: 983–984).

The original purpose of the act was to record opiate distribution for tax purposes. However, two provisions of the act remained subject to crucial interpretation: Drugs could now be prescribed only for "legitimate medical purposes," and physicians could prescribe opiates only "in the course of professional practice." No statutory definitions of these terms or phrases were provided.

Passage of the Harrison Act left the status of the addict almost indeterminate. The act did not make addiction illegal, and it neither authorized nor denied doctors the discretion to regularly prescribe opiates to addicts. The act only required that the opiates for addicts be obtained by prescription from physicians and pharmacists and that the securing of drugs be appropriately recorded.

Three significant Supreme Court rulings drastically altered the intent of the Harrison Act. In the 1919 case of *Webb* v. *U.S.* (241 U.S. 394) the Court ruled that the prescription of drugs with the purpose of maintaining sufficient morphine to keep an addict comfortable rather than professional treatment to cure the addict's habit "was not a prescription within the meaning of the law and was not included within the exemption for the doctor-patient situation" (Lindesmith, 1965: 6). In the *Jin Fuey Moy* v. *U.S.* (254 U.S. 189) decision of 1920 the Court ruled that the doctor could not legitimately prescribe drugs "to cater to the appetite or satisfy the craving of one addicted to the use of the drug" (Lindesmith, 1965: 6). The *U.S.* v. *Behrman* (253 U.S. 280) case heard in 1920 involved a physician who was prescribing vast quantities of opiates. The Court ruled that prescriptions for an addict were illegal regardless of the purpose of the doctor. This decision deprived physicians of the defense that they had acted in good faith. The Court did suggest that in view of the fact that the practices of Behrman were clearly not typical, a single prescription or even a number of prescriptions would not necessarily bring criminal charges upon other physicians. This qualification was ignored by enforcement agents, and after the Behrman decision the addict was denied all access to legal drugs. The risk of arrest and prosecution was recognized by physicians, and many severed all relationships with addicts. In addition, in the early 1920s the AMA, fearing federal domination in other areas, reacted strongly against any perceived expansion of the Harrison Act (cf. Musto, 1973: 58).

Three years after the Behrman decision the Court appeared to make a major modification in its judgment in *Linder* v. *U.S.* (268 U.S. 5). Dr. Linder gave an addict, apparently suffering withdrawal symptoms, four tablets of an opiate. The addict, an informer, notified police, and Linder was arrested and indicted in a lower court. Upon a successful appeal the Supreme Court held that Linder, unlike Behrman, had not been involved in flagrant abuse of opiate prescriptions. Linder was seen as acting reasonably, and the Court ruled in his favor. In the context of the Linder decision the Justices commented on the Harrison Act.

> It says nothing of "addicts" and does not undertake to prescribe methods for their treatment. They are diseased and proper subjects for such treatment. . . . What constitutes bona fide medical practice must be determined upon consideration of evidence and attending circumstances. (*Linder* v. *U.S.*, 268 U.S. 5, 1923: 18)

And in reference to the Behrman decision, the Court went on to note that the opinion cannot be accepted as authority for holding that a physician who acts bona fide and according to fair medical standards may never give an addict moderate amounts for self-administration in order to relieve conditions incident to addiction. Enforcement of the tax demands no such drastic rule and if the Act had such scope it would certainly encounter grave constitutional difficulties. (*Linder* v. *U.S.*, 268 U.S. 5, 1923: 22)

Initially, law enforcement officials enforced regulations consistent with the Behrman decision; however, the expected revisions of the regulations following the Linder decision did not materialize. The Treasury Department assumed responsibility for enforcement of the Harrison Act as a revenue measure but based the opiate regulations on the Court rulings prior to Linder. The literature of the Narcotics Bureau made no reference to the Linder decision. Harry Anslinger, the first commissioner of the Bureau, addressed the constitutionality of the Harrison Act and its enforcement in the book of which he is coauthor, *The Traffic in Narcotics* (1953). The Linder decision does not appear in the book, though the Webb and Behrman decisions are presented as proof of the illegality of addiction to opiates (Anslinger and Thompkins, 1953).

More importantly, the legal profession accelerated the trend toward the rationalization of the drug laws. With the interpretation of the Harrison Act shaped by the pre-Linder Court decisions and the vigorous labeling by the Bureau of Narcotics of the addict as criminal, the pattern of legal efforts to control opiates continued. In 1922 the Narcotic Drugs Import and Export Act was passed by Congress. In 1924 the manufacture of heroin was prohibited, and cultivation was controlled by the 1942 Opium Poppy Control Act. (The best estimate of the number of doctors arrested on narcotics charges in the twenty-five years after the Harrison Act is 25,000; cf. Goode, 1972.) The year 1951 marked the passage of the Boggs Amendment, which greatly increased the budget of the Bureau of Narcotics in order to provide more agents and more money to purchase illicit drugs as evidence in court proceedings (Lindesmith, 1965). In 1956 Congress passed the Narcotic Drug Control Act, which required less evidence to secure convictions and provided much harsher penalties for narcotics violators. The 1956 measure imposed the death penalty for the sale of heroin by an adult to a minor.

In order to enlist popular support for these measures the Bureau of Narcotics regularly disseminated sensational publicity on the need for such legislation and staunchly opposed publication of information not sponsored by the Bureau (Anslinger and Thompkins, 1953). The desire of the Bureau to maintain control of the public definition of the addict as deviant stemmed from the need to justify and sustain specialized enforcement agencies. Although the Bureau was created to destroy illicit drug traffic, the structure of the underworld organization proved almost impenetrable. By shifting their efforts toward the addict, a much easier target, the vast array of enforcement agencies were legitimized.

Throughout the history of opiate usage in America a variety of actors benefited economically, organizationally, and morally from the addiction of a small group. The author and addict Alexander Trocchi offers a perceptive summation in *Cain's Book*:

> It's [drug addiction] a nice tangible cause for juvenile delinquency. And it lets a lot of people out because they're alcoholics. There's an available pool of wasted-looking bastards to stand trial as the corruptors of their children. It provides the police with something to do, and as junkies and potheads are relatively easy to apprehend because they have to take so many chances to get hold of their drugs, a heroic police can make spectacular arrests, lawyers can do a brisk business, judges can make speeches, the big peddler can make a fortune, the tabloids can sell millions of copies. John Citizen can sit back feeling exonerated and watch the evil get its desserts. . . . (1960: 77).

THE CONSEQUENCE OF THE DRUG LAWS

Prior to the Harrison Act morphine was more commonly used than heroin. After 1914, however, this trend reversed, and heroin remains the more prevalent. With the enforcement of the law and the subsequent restrictions upon physicians, pharmacists, and drug manufacturers, the previously sporadic illicit traffic became well organized and continues to rank as the primary supply source. Heroin is particularly suited to illicit trade, since it is more highly concentrated than morphine; a kilo of heroin is equivalent to 2.5 kilos of morphine. Consumption patterns shifted accordingly.

With the elimination of legal sources of opiates, addicts were forced to seek drugs elsewhere. Underworld outlets flourished as a new demand created attractive economic gains for those willing to provide a supply for the addict despite the provisions of the Harrison Act that specified that only registered persons could dispense drugs.

Since it was also a violation of the Harrison Act as interpreted to receive drugs for relief of addiction, the addict assumed the risk of detection and a criminal status in pursuing a supply of opiates.

The average age of the addict decreased rapidly. Between 1885 and 1915 the average age of the addict decreased from about 60 to 50 (Terry and Pellens, 1970: 476). The percentage of youngsters addicted prior to 1914 was presumably quite low because they had fewer medical problems. When data concerning narcotics offenders were first published in 1932, only 15 percent of apprehended addicts were under twenty-five, and only 3.3 percent were under twenty-one. Although current reliable data concerning the number of addicts are unavailable, it is likely that a decline in the average age of the addict indicates an increase in the total number addicted (Lindesmith, 1965, 1968).

Prior to 1914, most addicts in America had legal, social, and economic access to drugs, and the life of the addict continued to be much the same in spite of reliance upon opiates. With the advent of drug laws, both accessibility and life styles changed drastically. Addicts were relieved of employment, and drugs became available only through illegal, expensive sources. As a result of (1) a dire physiological need for drugs, (2) exposure to criminal suppliers, and (3) the risks of prosecution already assumed by illegal transactions, post-1914 addicts increasingly turned to criminal activities to support the costs of addiction. Apart from any statistical estimate, it appears that addicts commit a higher proportion of crime than their numbers should warrant (Lindesmith, 1965).

There are, however, few, if any, indications of direct criminogenic effects from the use of opiates. Instead, social policy functions as the link between addiction and crime when it bans opiates. A variety of conferences on narcotic addiction have arrived at similar conclusions: (1) drug addiction does not seem to be connected with crime except where there is legislation to prohibit nonmedical use, and (2) efforts to control addiction probably will not reduce the number of addicts but may increase the amount of crime (Lindesmith, 1968).

In addition, the prohibitive drug laws precipitated the rise of a distinct addict subculture. Since addicts are prohibited socially and legally from participation in the conventional world, opiate users gravitate toward other users, that is, similar outcasts. Besides providing support for the legitimacy of the addict as a person, association with other users also provides crucial information concerning drugs and police activity.

SUMMARY

By 1900 the dangerous addictive properties of opiates had been recognized by medical science, if not fully understood. The public was by and large opposed to addiction, but the problem was generally conceived as being medical in nature, much like the diabetic's reliance on insulin. Despite the medical recognition of the dangers posed by these drugs, they were employed widely by physicians and sold by commercial drug enterprises.

The first attempts to control legally the use of opiates did not come in response to this increase in per capita consumption, but were directed instead against a single form of opium consumption, opium smoking. Most Americans did not consume opium by smoking, but rather took it in the form of a medical syrup or bitter. Opium smoking was, for the most part, confined to the Chinese population, and the movement to ban it was largely a manifestation of the anti-Chinese nativism that swept the country in the latter part of the nineteenth century. The completion of the transcontinental railroad in 1869 reduced the demand for Chinese laborers, who then competed with Caucasians for jobs. An anti-Chinese riot in San Francisco was followed by local ordinances restricting employment of Chinese. The fear, suspicion, and hatred of the Chinese population provided the climate for local regulation of "opium dens," in which the drug was smoked, accompanied (in the popular imagination) with a variety of other vices and crimes. By 1909 sufficient sentiment induced Congress to pass a law banning the importation of opium prepared for smoking. Importation of other forms of opium was left unregulated. The economic depression, the increasing urbanization of the Chinese, and the resulting reaction of the majority working class led to the first major regulations.

Most of the legislation designed to regulate the sale and distribution of opiates was limited to state and local control. In part, the failure of Congress to enact legislation was due to questions about the Constitutional authority of Congress to regulate what could be sold in the marketplace. Proponents of states' rights, in particular, feared that a dangerous precedent would be established by introducing federal control over drug distribution. Nonetheless, with the overriding importance of regulating the marketplace and posing as responsible in the international arena, Congress passed a series of new drug regulations; the Pure Food and Drug Act, the Harrison Act, and Prohibition.

The Harrison Act led to a new legal system of control. A number of abuses developed under the new system, however. Some doctors instead of writing prescriptions for individual patients began writing prescriptions for wholesale distributors. The Federal Bureau of Narcotics, charged with collecting the one cent per ounce tax from manufacturers, began prosecuting doctors who did not use the drugs for legitimate medical reasons. These prosecutions led to the Supreme Court's ruling in *Webb* v. *U.S.* (1919) that redefined restrictively the meaning of legally valid prescription as one used in the attempted cure of the habit, not "providing the user with morphine sufficient to keep him comfortable by maintaining his customary use." In effect the Supreme Court took opiate addiction out of the realm of medical control and placed it in the ambit of criminal law. The medical control system begun after *Harrison* in 1914 was not unlike the British system of treating opiate addiction as a problem for physicians' discretion. Webb and related decisions put a temporary end to that system and moved opiate control from a medical to a criminal justice problem. In so doing, the state created the conditions for a black market by levying a de facto protective tariff.

The expansion of the black market, the inability of the criminal justice system to eradicate the addict problem, and the pressure to institute some form of rehabilitation for the addicts in the 1950s and 1960s has led to a control system that presently vacillates between the criminal regulatory agencies and the medical profession (cf. Conrad and Schneider, 1980). From the history of the regulation of opiates it is clear that the evaluation of medical programs such as methadone will not directly settle the issue of proper control.

In summary, this chapter suggests that the variation in stigmatization and regulation of opiates was contingent upon numerous forms of economic organization, labor control, and symbolic concern. Specifically, researchers built professions by proclaiming the virtues of opium; physicians extended practices by converting patients to addicts through indiscriminate prescriptions; patent medicine grew into a major industry by concocting miracle drugs from the opiates; the American Medical Association expanded its profession and enhanced its legitimacy by controlling the use of these drugs; unions discovered that application of a deviant label to smokers of opium eased labor competition; and enforcement agencies depended upon opiate users for their existence. Nonetheless, those various interest groups operated and were successful under a vastly changing economic and social order. Otherwise, like most interest groups, they would not have been heard from, much less been successful (Lauderdale and Estep, 1980; Vago, 1981: 146–153).

The first United States law regulating opium use (the San

Francisco Ordinance of 1875) rose out of economic instability and carried with it the symbols of solidarity maintenance central to "unhyphenated" Americans. The most noteworthy law (the Harrison Act of 1914) emerged only with the beginnings of corporate, market interest in international trade of opium and the shift to a more regulated economy. Increased rationalization ensued as professional organizations became more involved in upgrading educational requirements for licensing. This process increased specialization, hierarchy, and discipline, leading to more distinct legal procedures and rules as well as laying the foundation for the expansion of regulatory agencies and further centralization of the state.

This increased rationality in legal developments regarding drug use has contributed to the division of society in which there are normal versus deviant individuals, drug laws being viewed as symbols of the boundary maintenance of nonusers. Ironically, these legal definitions do not accurately reflect more encompassing divisions within society, divisions that transcend formal legal boundaries and extend to the distinctions among prescription, over-the-counter, and illicit drugs. Despite the proliferation and ostensible preciseness of legal boundaries, the moral boundaries differentiating drug use within American society grow increasingly obscure.

FOOTNOTES

1. These attacks rehearse the fallacies concerning causal arguments we reviewed in Chapter 1. For further discussion, see Hirschi and Selvin (1966) and Brown (1978).
2. In 1843 the hypodermic method of injecting drugs directly into the bloodstream was discovered. This method was quickly adopted throughout France and England and was introduced to American medicine in 1856. Ray (1974: 18) argues that the use of the hypodermic syringe was one of the major factors leading to the unusually high level of dependency on some form of opium around the turn of the century. The undisputed effectiveness of hypodermic administration was thought to relieve the "opium appetite." The development of the Pure Food and Drug Act in 1906 coupled with greater appreciation of the dangers of continued administration of morphine might conceivably have alleviated the widespread addiction. However, prior to the act, in 1893, diacetyl-morphine, or heroin, was produced (Terry and Pellens, 1970). Consistent with the previous pattern of opium technology, heroin was proclaimed as free of the addictive qualities inherent in morphine. It appears that most products of opium technology followed a similar

pattern. A new discovery was followed by research experiments, publications, and public use. Reactions were initially favorable, and the product gained wide support. When the addictive qualities of the drug were recognized, use continued until a new discovery was hailed as a cure for the product and replaced it.

3. A typical American product, advertised in *Harper's Weekly* on December 7, 1867, claimed to be a cure for consumption (tuberculosis). "Piso's Cure" the ad says

> has CURED THOUSANDS . . . multitudes who without it would have filled untimely graves. . . . It cannot be asserted that every case of Consumption may be cured with this medicine, but . . . a neglect to try this great remedy is a foolish—a criminally foolish act.

A small firm, Hazeltine and Co., of Warren, Pennsylvania, sold this concoction in bottles ranging in price from twenty-five cents to one dollar. The principal active ingredients of Piso's Cure were alcohol, chloroform, opium, and hashish. The effect of these ingredients on the tubercle bacillus that produces tuberculosis is questionable, but Piso's sold well. The Hazeltine concern is fairly representative of the industry. It offered home remedies for diseases and ailments, relying heavily upon opiates as a source of their perceived effectiveness.

4. Physicians and pharmacists were somewhat overrepresented in the addict population, presumably because of proximity to drugs. Females also seem to have outnumbered males in addiction to oral morphine preparations, but not in the hypodermic administration of heroin. This probably resulted from the high incidence of gynecological problems for which oral morphine was predominantly prescribed.

5. Smoking opium is relatively weak, containing only 9 percent morphine. Only a portion of this percentage enters the bloodstream when inhaled. The opium smoking dose is consumed over a long period of time rather than being absorbed instantly as in hypodermic injection.

7

The Political Economy of
Corporate Regulation:
The Structural Origins of
White Collar Crime

by Barry Feld

Rape, robbery, murder, environmental pollution, price fixing, transporting adulterated foods, and maintaining an unsafe workplace are all law violations. The first three offenses clearly represent serious crimes for which punishments—fines and imprisonment— may be imposed. The latter violations also authorize punishment— including fines and imprisonment—but are not as readily viewed as real crimes. They are some of the violations of the expanding body of business and economic regulations that are often referred to as "white collar crimes." Typically perceived and enforced differently from common law criminal offenses, these "white collar crimes" are by-products of the proliferation of administrative agencies that regulate an increasing number of aspects of modern life. Understanding how and why some actions are defined as criminal while others are proceeded against in an administrative manner requires an exploration of the relationships between social change and the political and legal processes that define some behaviors as deviant.

THE "WHITE COLLAR CRIME" DEBATE

Sociologists and lawyers have devoted considerable attention to the questions "What is white collar crime?" and "Is 'white collar crime' crime?" The white collar crime debate is symptomatic of the shift in definitions of offenses that has occurred, primarily within the past century, as part of the processes of economic modernization.

The concept of "white collar crime" was first introduced by Edwin Sutherland[1] (1940, 1945, 1949). Sutherland contended that while white collar crimes such as price fixing and frauds involved real social injuries—oftentimes more serious harms than conventional crimes—the perpetrators were neither perceived by others nor conceived of by themselves as real criminals. He suggested that the social status of white collar offenders and the cultural homogeneity among legislators, judges, and businessmen made it difficult for the law definers to conceive of corporate law violators as "real criminals."[2] He also attributed the lack of stigma attached to white collar violations to an ambivalence about the behavior proscribed, since many violations of economic regulations involve statutes that have only recently been adopted to meet the requirements of a changing industrial society.[3] Finally, he observed that violators of economic regulations were the fortunate beneficiaries of fundamental changes in law enforcement practices. The special administrative procedures adopted for their enforcement help to obscure their criminality by concealing the nature of violations, minimizing their stigmatic consequences, and conveying the implication that there are differences between economic offenses and conventional crimes[4] (Sutherland, 1949: 39).

In arguing that white collar crimes were real crimes Sutherland advocated a change in the normative underpinnings of these laws so that their violators would be perceived and condemned as other criminals. In asserting that economic offenders should be stigmatized like common law criminals, however, they were caught in a sociological "chicken versus egg" dilemma: is it the stigma, the preexisting moral condemnation, that results in the denouncing of certain behaviors as criminal, or is it the criminalization and condemnation that socializes people to regard a particular type of behavior as blameworthy?

Critics of Sutherland's efforts to equate criminal offenses with administrative violations argued that only those behaviors specifically

defined by the legislature as criminal and prosecuted accordingly
were crimes (Tappan, 1947; Burgess, 1950; Caldwell, 1958). For
them, equating violations of administrative or economic regulations
with common law crimes was an exercise in "moral entrepre-
neurship" rather than criminological analysis.[5]

> The rebel may enjoy a veritable orgy of delight in damning as criminal
> most anyone he pleases; one imagines that some experts would thus
> consign to the criminal classes any successful capitalistic businessman;
> the reactionary or conservative, complacently viewing the occupational
> practices of the business world, might find all in perfect order in this
> best of all possible worlds. The result may be fine indoctrination or
> catharsis achieved through blustering broadsides against the "existing
> system." . . . This can accomplish no desirable objective, either po-
> litically or sociologically. (Tappan, in Geis and Meier, 1977: 276–7)

The Sutherland-Tappan debate is revived periodically. The 1970s
in particular saw renewed efforts to define *crime* independently of
the "state" definitions (e.g., Liazos, 1972; Pepinsky, 1974; Schwendinger and Schwendinger, 1970). For example, the Schwendingers
ask:

> Isn't it time to raise serious questions about the assumptions underlying
> the definition of the field of criminology when a man who steals a
> paltry sum can be called a criminal while agents of the state can,
> with impunity, legally reward men who destroy food so that price
> levels can be maintained while a sizable portion of the population
> suffers from malnutrition? (1970: 149)

Such arguments over what properly should be called *crime* are
examples of the mixture of ideological and analytic issues discussed
in Chapter 1. As Dean Clarke points out, this

> human rights perspective is diversionary because it detracts from the
> *specificity* and *politicality* of crime. It is a measure of the theoretical
> impotence of left-radicals who have no firm grounding in Marxism
> that all they can do is label as "criminal" everything in sight of
> which they disapprove. These radical criminologists are stuck both
> in an idealist and narrowly criminological mode of thought. Idealist,
> in the sense that they feel the need to judge social phenomena from
> the perspective of justice and right; criminological, in that they do
> not feel able to study social phenomena before labelling them criminal.
> Such a criminology is ultimately meaningless since it becomes a
> discipline divorced from reality. (1978: 44)

This controversy and the narrowly descriptive character of much of the work on "white collar crime" has inhibited exploration of the relationships between changes in social structure and political economy and the differences in legal definition and enforcement of white collar crimes (Lauderdale et al., 1978). Why, for example, were administrative agencies created to regulate complex economic activities around the turn of the century? Indeed, succeeding generations have entered the normative-ideological debate of white collar criminality virtually without reference to the relationships between social change and the legal order.[6] The ideological dispute over whether or not administrative violations are crimes has obscured the more sociologically interesting issues of how and why offenses are defined and enforced as they are, particularly why these economic regulations are defined and administered differently than are conventional crimes.

This chapter will focus primarily on the Sherman Anti-trust Act and Federal Trade Commission laws regulating economic and competitive activities that were adopted around the turn of the century in response to the social and economic dislocations associated with the rise of corporate capitalism. It will analyze the political economic changes that produced these hybrid violations. The process is illustrative of the broader structural changes that have resulted in increased administrative regulation of many sectors of contemporary economic life.

Some of these "white collar crimes" proscribe conduct in the strictest common law sense of crimes, although the majority of economic offenses involve violations of administrative regulations that dispense with many of the characteristics and procedural trappings of crimes. For the sociologists (Sutherland, 1949; Hartung, 1950; Newman, 1958) it was harmful social consequences rather than the technicalities of enforcement that were the distinguishing characteristics of crime, whereas for the legalists (Tappan, 1949; Burgess, 1950) crimes differed from administrative offenses in some fundamental ways that did not justify calling the latter type of violations "crime." Identifying some of the similarities and differences between common law crimes and violations of economic regulations provides the basis for exploring how these latter offenses are located and enforced as they are.

Traditional common law crimes entail the doing of a prohibited act or causing a proscribed result when accompanied by a criminal intent (*mens rea*) (J. Hall, 1960). It is the *mens rea* that provides the primary distinctions for purposes of grading punishments. The common law has presumed that individuals are morally responsible actors with free will and punished those who made evil choices. The essence of crime is punishment for making blameworthy choices, and criminal prosecutions involve the solemn moral condemnation of the actor with all of its associated drama and stigma. Those harms defined as criminal contravene a strong normative consensus whose underlying moral basis is often rooted in an even earlier equation between crime and sin. It is the formal condemnation rather than the details of punishment that distinguish the criminal law from civil proceedings. Thus common law crimes reflect many of the characteristics of Durkheim's repressive law in a mechanically solidary society in that they call forth an intense, passionate reaction on the part of all who are aware of a violation.

Since the beginning of the present century the growth of corporations and concurrent governmental efforts to regulate their behavior have taxed traditional conceptions of crimes and provoked the white collar crime debate. The prohibited economic behaviors are frequently defined as civil violations rather than criminal offenses. Even if they are defined as criminal, any common law requirement of *mens rea* is often dispensed with, since corporations have no "will" and can only act through their agents. Some of these regulations impose strict liability simply for causing a prohibited result regardless of intent. Crimes of strict liability are typically punished only as misdemeanors—"technical violations"—rather than as felonies. Unlike most common law crimes, which are *mala in se* (manifestly evil in their essence), many of the newer corporate crimes are simply *mala prohibita*—bad because they are administratively prohibited rather than intrinsically wrongful (Clinard, 1946; Hartung, 1950). Since economic violations often have a continuing and cumulative impact, many of these regulations are characterized as remedial and preventive rather than punitive. With the expansion of economic regulation in the twentieth century, many white collar crimes were manufactured from what were previously legitimate business activities. Since these laws regulate conduct that literally did not exist before the advent of large-scale corporate enterprises, the normative and moral stigma undergirding conventional crimes is less developed and does not attach to nearly the same degree to the perpetrators of economic violations. Differences are also reflected in the administrative procedures used and the sanctions imposed, and these differences further diffuse the stigma associated with economic violations. These features all correspond closely to Durkheim's description of restitutive law in an organically solidary society, law to maintain cooperation and restore harmonious relations, in which many violations are offenses against the central agencies of enforcement rather than against a broadly held collective consciousness.

Although the early analysts of white collar crime identified some of the similarities and differences between economic violations and conventional crimes, virtually none systematically traced the relationships between changes in the social structure and political economy and the legal control mechanisms that produced differences in their definition and procedural implementation (see, for example, Kolko, 1963, 1965; Weinstein, 1968). Our examination of the political economy of corporate regulation will focus on the relationships between structural changes and the political processes that determine the content of laws.

POLITICAL ECONOMY: CORPORATE AND GOVERNMENTAL GROWTH AT THE TURN OF THE CENTURY

The industrial corporation provided a vehicle for the concentration of risk capital as well as the organizational structure for economic coordination and bureaucratic rationalization. Corporations provided an investment outlet for small as well as large investors, with limited personal liability dispersing the risks and transferable ownership increasing their speculative attractiveness. State governments, through the legal chartering of corporations and their later judicial "personification," created a form of private government in which investors voted for a board of control, which delegated routine administration to an executive committee and created a permanent structure in which the owners profited from the economic surplus generated by the labor of an effectively disenfranchised working class (A. S. Miller, 1976). The growth of corporate industry increased the social distance between those who owned and controlled the means of production and those who sold their labor. The rise of the corporation also intensified the struggle of organized labor, and the end of the nineteenth century was marked by recurring strikes and industrial violence.

The growth of the large corporations continually reflected the increasing importance of economic rationality and efficiency. Following the Civil War, western expansion stimulated the growth of the railroads, the first industry to seek more efficient forms of organization during the transition from small-scale to large-scale business. A major challenge to capital coordination and industrial management was structuring large organizations so that orders from the top would be implemented at the bottom. The railroad corporations adapted the table of organization from the military command structure to the new problems associated with large-scale economic coordination.

Corporate growth was associated with integrated transportation, the Industrial Revolution, and the imperatives of technology. During the latter third of the nineteenth century, growth in population and aggregate demand, the diffusion of new technologies, the availability of foreign and domestic capital, and the fundamental alteration in the structure of manufacturing encouraged substantial growth and expansion in many sectors of the economy. By integrating the entire country into a single marketplace, railroads made manufacturing and retailing highly competitive. Opening the country stimulated both mass consumption and mass production as firms expanded in the growing marketplace. By the turn of the century the direct marketing of consumer goods to the public reshaped the marketplace as big mail-order catalog companies like Sears, Roebuck and Montgomery Ward opened branches to serve customers in local markets. Chain stores began to integrate retailers, wholesalers, and jobbers, offering assured supply, uniform products, services, and credit. Advertising increased as manufacturers communicated directly with consumers to sustain aggregate demand and force distributors to carry particular product lines (Cochran, 1972).

By the turn of the century there were about 1000 companies whose scale and diversity posed unique managerial problems as they attempted to expand the range and continuity of their power through bureaucratic means (Wiebe, 1967: 181). The formation of a national as distinguished from local marketplace became a major factor stimulating corporate development, since only the efficiency of bureaucratic organization could routinize the coordinated distribution of goods and services. Administering the giant corporations with hundreds of subunits and an internal structure with its own life called for new managerial skills (Cochran, 1972: 160). The expansion in numbers of professional executives was accompanied by the growth of a body of middle-managers and functional and technological specialists. The administrators of these complex social organizations attempted to integrate long-range projections and compute remote contingencies to produce immediate gain. They required predictability and stability to mobilize capital, equipment, technological talent, and labor over the extended periods associated with modern industrial production (Galbraith, 1967). They tried to include the effects of the economic, political, legal, and social environments in their calculations. Combining capital, technology, and managerial skills, corporations attempted to control and manipulate an ever increasing range of the factors of production—raw materials, labor, market demand, prices, legal conditions, and public opinion. Maintaining price levels and market shares through cooperative practices, financing internally from profits to avoid financial markets, integrating horizontally and vertically to assure the availability and price of materials, and maintaining aggregate demand through advertising were all part of the corporate strategy to insulate itself from competitive market controls to facilitate rational planning. Under the influence of the Social Darwinian ideology that associated growth with progress there was an admiration of size per se and a naive belief that any increase in size produced a corresponding increase in efficiency and competitive advantage.

"CUTTHROAT" COMPETITION

One of the most critical issues facing corporate capitalists at the turn of the century stemmed from their chronic inability to rationalize the marketplace, to organize, stabilize, and integrate the economy in a way that would "allow corporations to function in a predictable and secure environment permitting reasonable profits over the long run" (Kolko, 1963: 3). For the many firms in each sector of the economy, including the largest and most heavily capitalized, competition threatened profitability and even survival. Corporate economic stability required the elimination of both "cutthroat" competition and market fluctuations, predictability required an environment conducive to long-range planning and large-scale capital investment, and security required a political environment that permitted profitability free from the dangers of political radicalism or unpredictable governmental actions (Kolko, 1963: 3).

The extraordinary economic upheaval that powered corporate growth also inhibited efforts at rationalization. Rapidly expanding markets and exploitation of the vast natural resources on a national scale led to a loss of "geographical privileges" and a breakdown in patterns of local or regional cooperation and ushered in a period of intense, harsh competition characterized by risk and uncertainty. Previously adequate tacit agreements to control prices or price leadership by a dominant firm in a local or regional market broke down under the pressures of producing and selling in a national market (Cochran, 1972: 152).

The diffusion of new technologies, the availability of capital, and the virtually unlimited demand associated with urban growth constantly induced many new firms into the economy. Moreover, rapidly changing technology attracted innovative entrepreneurs who were risk takers, as expanding economies provided opportunities for managerial innovators (Cochran, 1972: 5). Even as firms merged and grew in size, others entered the new nationwide marketplace.

> The first decades of this century were years of intense and growing competition. They were also years of economic expansion and, in a number of industries, greater internal concentration of capital and output. But neither of these phenomena were incompatible with increased competition. (Kolko, 1963: 26)

While on one hand, heavy fixed costs imposed some barriers to new entrants, on the other, capital availability encouraged competitors.

Once capital was transformed into plants and equipment and "in place," it was no longer readily transferable to other sectors. In a competitive economy, businesses with heavy fixed costs quickly discovered that using existing facilities for the short-term, even at a loss, to partially cover fixed overhead costs was still preferable to not operating at all. Mass markets and the technological efficiency of mass production generated an oversupply, which drove prices down and threatened both immediate profitability and long-range stability. Even as the size of enterprises grew, competition intensified and periodic price wars raged to drive out competitors. Predatory practices, rebates, false rumors, exclusive dealing contracts, and bribing legislators and judges for advantages were all aspects of the corrupt and ferocious competitive struggles (Thorelli, 1954: 68).

Virtually every sector of the economy faced comparable crises of instability due to competition. In those sectors of the economy based on technological innovations, established firms faced threats to their market shares as new entrants entered the burgeoning fields (Kolko, 1963: 53). Where capitalization requirements were relatively low, there were few structural entry barriers to new companies induced by the successes of their predecessors (Kolko, 1963: 54).

Even in the absence of new entries, competition between the larger firms continually threatened existing market shares owing to overcapacity (Kolko, 1963: 54).

PRIVATE EFFORTS TO STIFLE COMPETITION

At the end of the nineteenth century, as businessmen's ability to control their rapidly expanding economic environment declined, they introduced a variety of strategies to achieve stability and profitability through interbusiness cooperation. These efforts were intended to control production, limit competition, allocate markets and market shares, assure stable prices and profitability, and facilitate long-term planning. At the root of the drive toward efficient marketing was the desire to escape the rigors and uncertainties of competition and impersonal market conditions they could not control. Many of the anticompetitive techniques that businessmen adopted were first developed by the railroads and later refined by the oil companies; but as other industries faced similar crises, they employed similar strategies.

Efforts to rationalize the economy and stifle competition progressed through a variety of forms from pools to trusts to holding companies to interlocking corporate directorates (Thorelli, 1954; Wiebe, 1967). The pools, first adopted by railroads, were loose trade associations that attempted to fix profitable rates, allocate business among competing lines, and end the destructive competitive practice of rebating. Pools almost invariably floundered as individual members sacrificed longer-term profitability to maximize short-term gains. Indeed, pools carried the seeds of their own destruction, since the artificially maintained prices tempted some members to cut prices openly or secretly to increase their market share, thereby causing the agreement to collapse. Moreover, free market ideology and judicial hostility to these "gentlemen's agreements" to restrain trade left them legally unenforceable and practically unreliable, since not all price fixers were gentlemen (Cochran, 1972: 153).

Businessmen subsequently turned to corporate trusts and holding companies to create boards of trustees to coordinate the economic activities of the various member corporations, who voluntarily surrendered their individual autonomy to a centralized authority. Due to legal uncertainties and limitations of many state corporation laws, however, their initial efforts to systematize and rationalize economic endeavors to stifle competition and assure profitability were often unsuccessful. It was unclear, for example, under some early state corporation laws whether one corporation could even own the stock of another (Thorelli, 1954: 83). Even when trust agreements became more common, the waves of corporate "combinations" and the growing concentration of capital failed to achieve the rationality and stability necessary for long-term economic planning.

Complicating efforts at economic rationalization were opportunistic, unethical, and sharp business practices that businessmen used to maximize their short-term advantage under competitive pressures (Cochran, 1972: 158). New types of enterprises, rapid population movements, physical distances, transactions between corporate intermediaries, and legal uncertainties in many areas of economic behavior all combined to supplant the older, personal ways of doing business with impersonal, market-oriented decisions that favored maximizing short-term gains over cultivating ongoing stable relationships.

EFFORTS AT STATE REGULATION OF CORPORATE EXCESSES

The appearance of the giant national corporations created as many political and legal problems as it solved economic ones. The political and economic power of the corporate "person" posed for states and the federal government the legal dilemma of how to effectively regulate this new form of private government. When the Constitution was adopted, there had been only two types of entities— natural persons and the state—and the Constitution defined the relationships between them (A. S. Miller, 1976: 19). When the corporate "person" became a significant economic and social force a century later, this collective enterprise—bureaucratic, hierarchical, economically rational, goal-oriented—did not fit neatly within the legal framework that structured other relationships (C. D. Stone, 1975; A. S. Miller, 1976). While the Constitution provided a legal framework for restraining the activities of public bureaucracies— government—no corresponding mechanism other than the marketplace constrained the actions of private economic governments— the corporations (A. S. Miller, 1976; C. D. Stone, 1975).

Two additional considerations constrained public efforts to

make private organizations accountable. One was the power of corporations. The issue of governmental regulation arose because the traditional market economy was increasingly inadequate to deal with organizations that dwarfed it. In the view of many at the time, legal restrictions were required to supplement the normal restraints of market forces. The political-economic reality, however, was that the same corporate characteristics that called for regulation—size, permanence, social impact, economic power—also provided these organizations with disproportionate influence over the eventual legislation that emerged.

There was also a basic ambivalence about bigness and corporate power. While the bigness was perceived as a threat, it was also seen as a source of economic efficiency, increased employment, growth, capital formation, and a rising standard of living. While some degree of regulation was obviously required and enforcement mechanisms had to punish violations sufficiently to maintain the legitimacy of the state as the ultimate political authority, regulations could not be so stringent as to curtail seriously the desirable economic activities of corporate capitalism. These laws adopted in response to the social and economic dislocations associated with the rise of corporate capitalism to regulate economic and business activities reflect the tensions of these legal dilemmas.

While increasingly concentrated capital sought stability and industrial harmony through informal agreements later superseded by formal legal devices, some states adopted legislation to curb their abuses, regulate the increasingly disproportionate influence of corporations, and reassert local controls over the distant and impersonal forces transforming community life (Wiebe, 1967). Midwestern farmers' movements, like the Grangers and Populists, and merchants and commodity dealers agitated to regulate railroads and grain elevators. States, through the exercise of their "police power"— the general authority to legislate to promote public health, safety, and welfare—created regulatory commissions to reconcile the power of railroads and grain elevators with the interests of shippers, farmers, and other constituencies. By the early 1880s, United States Supreme Court opinions like *Munn* v. *Illinois* (1876), which authorized the individual states to regulate corporate activities without federal interference, allowed them to impose maximum rate limitations and other restrictions on businesses that were "affected with a public interest."

The result of the initial judicial approval of Granger laws as in *Munn* was a proliferation of inconsistent and contradictory state provisions confronting businesses that were national in scope. Just as national corporations sought a predictable economic environment for rational planning, they also required a predictable and preferably favorable legal one. Indeed, the experience of the following decades was first the emergence of federal laws to supersede individual state variations and then an increasingly formal legal rationalization of those laws as the Federal Trade Commission provided a specialized administrative agency to supplement the more general provisions of the Sherman Anti-trust Act.

JUDICIAL NULLIFICATION OF STATE REGULATION

By the 1890s a significant changeover in judicial personnel resulted in the Supreme Court's taking an increasingly restrictive view of the states' authority to regulate interstate business activities. Continuing challenges to state legislation by national businesses led the Court to assert its authority over state regulatory activities that affected interstate commerce (Thorelli, 1954: 103). During this period, interstate commercial regulation came to be reserved exclusively to the federal government, and contrary state legislation was invalidated. On the basis of interpretations of the Commerce Clause and the Due Process Clause of the Fourteenth Amendment the Justices elevated corporations to the status of "persons" for purposes of extending constitutional protections to them and then passed upon the "reasonableness" of the economic regulatory policies adopted by the states. Through a judicial doctrine of economic substantive due process that prevailed until the mid-1930s the Supreme Court undertook an independent evaluation of the wisdom of states' legislative encroachments on private property and systematically struck down economic regulations that did not comport with its own model of a laissez faire economy. Through its interpretation of the Due Process and Commerce Clauses it became increasingly evident that the Court intended to review and oversee state legislation attempting to regulate or control the ownership or operation of private property (Thorelli, 1954: 107). Constitutional restrictions on states' regulation of interstate commerce laid the groundwork for federal laws governing nationwide economic activities.

FEDERAL REGULATION AND ANTI-TRUST

The Granger and Populist laws of the 1870s and 1880s proved to be inadequate to offset the political power and interstate character of the railroads, grain elevators, and national corporations. In the period before 1890, political agitation in the South and West expanded as trade unions and other groups joined the farmers in their opposition to the excesses of the railroads. After the United States Supreme Court decided in the *Wabash* case (1886) that regulation of interstate railroads was exclusively a federal task reserved to Congress, federal legislation regulating interstate commerce became imperative. The Interstate Commerce Act was adopted in 1887 and quickly provided a model for later federal agencies to regulate particular sectors of the economy.

During this same period, political agitation was gradually extended from monopolistic practices by the railroads and grain elevators to industrial combination in general. Political opposition to the corporations was provoked by the manifold examples of product adulteration, antisocial business conduct—price rigging, stock watering, and outright bribery—and the failure of state common law antimonopoly doctrines to cope effectively with economic issues on a scale for which there were no precedents. Standard Oil perfected the trust device, which was quickly adapted in many other industries (cotton oil, linseed oil, sugar, whiskey, cordage, lead, etc.) and provided a popular political target.

The Sherman Anti-trust Act (1890) was passed without extensive debate, apparently in response to the antimonopolistic clamor of southern cotton growers and midwestern grain farmers who fueled the agrarian protests of the Grangers and Populists. The Sherman Act made combinations in restraint of trade (anticompetitive conduct) and monopolization (structural domination with anticompetitive consequences) offenses against the federal government.[7]

There was little by way of prior experience to guide Congress in its novel experiment to control the operation of economic life or to inform them as to how the courts would interpret the Antitrust Act. Congress therefore wrote a short and deceptively simple general statute to govern a complex subject. Without itemizing any specific prohibited practices, Congress simply delegated to the courts the unpleasant and difficult task of defining illegal activities in an area with relatively few common law precedents.

The law contained both criminal and civil provisions. For the

first time it made combinations in restraint of trade and monopolization federal offenses that could be prosecuted as misdemeanors
in federal courts. The act authorized injunctions to prevent further
misconduct. It also allowed any private person who was adversely
affected by corporate misconduct to bring a civil suit and to recover
treble damages for any injury suffered. In these latter provisions
the Anti-trust Act reveals many of the characteristics of restitutive
law that Durkheim associated with societies integrated by organic
solidarity. For Durkheim, social differentiation provided the context
within which individual contractual relationships are formed. The
Sherman Anti-trust Act represented a legislative conception of the
permissible and prohibited conditions under which individual contracts could be entered.

Initial efforts to enforce the Sherman Act were meager and
unsuccessful; few suits were filed by a succession of Attorney Gen-
erals who had previously represented corporations in their own
practices. In an effort to sustain the constitutionality of the act
under the Interstate Commerce Clause, the Supreme Court limited
the applicability of the statute. In *United States* v. *E. C. Knight Co.*
(1895) the Court construed "restraints of commerce among the
several states" narrowly so that the American Sugar Refining Company's 98 percent monopoly of the total sugar refining capacity in
the country was deemed to be manufacture within a single state
rather than commerce between states. Despite the limited scope
accorded to Congress's power to regulate interstate commerce, the
Court's subsequent decisions upholding the constitutionality of the
Sherman Act as well as the authority of the Interstate Commerce
Commission to regulate interstate carriers laid the groundwork for
national laws and administrative agencies to regulate business.

Passage of the Sherman Act had virtually no impact on the
waves of corporate mergers that occurred around the turn of the
century or on the growth of holding companies that emerged as
the successor device to trusts to facilitate economic coordination
within an industry. Although the Supreme Court initially ruled
that every restraint of trade was prohibited, regardless of its reasonableness (*Trans-Missouri Freight Association* [1897]), that view
was subsequently repudiated in the Standard Oil case (1911), which
reinstated the common law "rule of reason" that allowed combinations to restrain trade provided they were not "unreasonable,"
with the Court serving as the ultimate arbiter of reasonableness
(A. S. Miller, 1976: 66). The Court in the Standard Oil case held
that whether an agreement or combination restrained trade could

only be determined "by the light of reason, guided by the principles of law and the duty to apply and enforce the public policy embodied in the statute . . . " (221 U.S. 64 [1911]). The result of the Standard Oil decision was to increase the substantive irrationality of judicial economic regulation, since the outcome of each case was determined by a judicial assessment of its merits in light of reason and economic and social policy. Within two decades the antitrust legislation that had apparently been adopted to prevent business consolidation and corporate concentration had become the vehicle that institutionalized and sanctioned it.

The initial enforcement of the Sherman Act further detracted from its effectiveness as an antidote to corporate consolidation. To the extent that punishing rule violations reinforces the values underlying the law, the enforcement pattern of the Sherman Act diluted whatever moral opprobrium may have existed at the time of its adoption. While initially vigorous prosecution of corporate combinations might have been anticipated following its passage, a specialized antitrust enforcement division in the Department of Justice was not created for a decade, nor were extra funds appropriated for prosecutions (Thorelli, 1954). Until 1903 there was only one successful criminal prosecution of a corporate defendant, and it was not until 1960 that a corporate executive was actually imprisoned. Antitrust prosecutions were initiated more frequently against labor organizers than against business firms.

> During the crucial period in which the Sherman law required massive, visible enforcement for it to become established as instrumental policy, only feeble token efforts were made. In consequence, corporate combination, consolidation, and monopolization not only continued, but increased, particularly near the turn of the century. (McCormick, 1977: 32)

The lack of enforcement failed to create a group of stigmatized convicted offenders, which in turn affected societal reactions to illegal corporate activities. The lack of stigma associated with antitrust violations provides further evidence of the law's restitutive rather than repressive character. As social differentiation progresses, centralized administrative agencies assume greater responsibilities to regulate those activities that are withdrawn from the common experience (Durkheim, 1964). The Sherman Act created a new category of offenses and symbolically affirmed a legal commitment to free competition while institutionalizing consolidation and regulation. Its almost immediate nullification by the judicial and executive branches demonstrated the dramatic influence of concentrated capital on public policy.

THE DILEMMAS OF CORPORATE CAPITALISM: RATIONALITY AND LEGITIMACY

By the beginning of the twentieth century the various corporate efforts to achieve economic order and stability, assure profits, and limit competition had all proved unsuccessful. While the economic ideologies of laissez faire capitalism and Social Darwinism furnished an appealing justification that exalted the successful businessman as the "fittest survivor" in the competitive struggle, they also contributed to insecurity and instability in the marketplace. Using the political and legislative processes could provide an alternative mechanism for economic rationalization to the failed efforts of the private sector (Kolko, 1963: 58).

Federal regulation could also provide a device to avoid unpredictable and potentially harmful state legislation. Despite the Supreme Court's nullification of states' efforts to regulate the corporations, businessmen realized that political changes and democratic reforms espoused by Grangers, Populists, and Trade Unionists posed a continuing threat and that antibusiness sentiments could lead to detrimental legislation (Kolko, 1963: 58). A federal regulatory solution provided an institutional mechanism remote from, and therefore less responsive to, local grievances.

The development of political solutions to economic problems was a familiar strategy to Progressive industrialists, who had already learned that money and campaign contributions provide political leverage as well. From the 1880s onward, corporate leaders took an increasingly active role in politics. McKinley's 1896 presidential victory was widely regarded as a tribute to the fund-raising and organizational skill of the steel industry's Mark Hanna (Thorelli, 1954: 249). Moreover, there was a functional unity between business and political leaders who shared familiar social origins and had extensive ties that reinforced a common outlook to the problems of economic rationalization (Kolko, 1963: 284).

Businessmen also realized that federal regulation could create a buffer by preempting the field against more restrictive state laws. Regulatory centralization was not only more responsive to corporate controls; it also diverted criticisms of business practices from the corporate perpetrators to the federal regulators (Kolko, 1963: 58). Federal regulation also legitimized anticompetitive business practices designed to stabilize markets and increase profitability.

Business's initial experiences with federal regulation did not counsel restraint; the government was a useful source of subsidies, resources, stability, and profits. From the inception of the first regulatory agency in 1887—the Interstate Commerce Commission, created to regulate the railroad industry—the buffering and legitimating functions of regulation became apparent to industry. As United States Attorney General Richard Olney, a former corporate attorney, wrote to his friend Charles Perkins, President of the Chicago, Burlington, and Quincy Railroad in response to Perkins's criticisms of the commission,

> The Commission, as its functions have now been limited by the court is, or can be made of great use to the railroads. It satisfies the popular clamor for a government supervision of railroads, at the same time that the supervision is almost entirely nominal. Further, the older such a Commission gets to be, the more inclined it will be found to take the business and railroad view of things. It thus becomes a sort of barrier between the railroad corporations and the people and a sort of protection against hasty and crude legislation hostile to railroad interests. (quoted in Miller, 1968: 66)

The history of the relationship between business and government at the turn of the century was one that could only inspire confidence in the minds of businessmen.

PROGRESSIVE REGULATORY REFORM

Earlier, we considered the structural and intellectual sources of Progressivism and their role in the creation of the juvenile justice system. Many of the features that led them to adopt innovations emphasizing bureaucratic rationality, scientific solutions, and specialized administrative agencies were also reflected in their economic regulatory reforms. At the national level the Progressive movement was more than an expression of public hostility to corporate abuses, although people clamored for governmental assistance to cushion the shock of industrialization. Control of the large corporation meant different things to the various members of the Progressive coalition— small businessmen wanted to restrict the impact of corporate growth on their own enterprises; the new professionals accepted the inevitability of growth and wanted to enable corporations to be more rational and efficient; the managers of the largest firms realized that giant firms with large fixed costs could not tolerate the vicissitudes of a free marketplace. They temporarily submerged their differences, however, in a host of movements to provide an orderly transition to urban industrialism and corporate capitalism. The goal of the Progressives was to rationalize all of the manifestations of chaotic modernization. Progressivism, which was fundamentally conservative, developed the political economic model for nearly all subsequent efforts at corporate regulation. The inability of the corporate giants to stabilize the economy through private efforts led the more sophisticated corporate leaders to turn to the federal government to provide the necessary stability (Kolko, 1963). Progressive political economic reforms were largely dominated by the large firms that enlisted the assistance of the federal government to create an orderly and stable economy in which cooperation and coordination superseded competition, and in which the state played a prominent and centralized role in the guidance and rationalization of various sectors of the economy (Kolko, 1963: 3; Weinstein, 1968: 3).

The fusion of science, technology, and manufacturing was another aspect of the rationalizing economy and the shifting economic base. It was associated with the emergence of a managerial, professional, and technocratic class that favored corrective and ameliorative planning to the harsh discipline of competitive capitalism. This first generation of scientific, technical, and managerial experts believed that the rational application of knowledge could achieve economic efficiency and that a government of expanded functions could provide an administrative process that would allow professionals and experts to make public policy decisions without the distortions of political strife or special interests' importunings.

FEDERAL TRADE COMMISSION RATIONALIZES
THE SHERMAN ANTI-TRUST ACT

While many governmental regulatory efforts were associated with public scandal and received popular support and enthusiasm, regulation occurred most frequently at the behest of the regulated industries themselves.[8] Many businessmen used the language of popular democracy to support campaigns for economic reform and efficient business practices.

The passage of the Federal Trade Commission Act (1914) is a legislative example of the continuing efforts to rationalize and stabilize the marketplace, legitimate anticompetitive practices, and insulate corporations from state political controls. The Federal Trade Commission Act and the companion Clayton Act were proposed to address the ambiguities and uncertainties associated with the earlier Sherman Anti-trust Act. While substantively irrational Khadi justice may have been adequate for juveniles, businessmen required a more formal rational legal order to enhance planning and predictability.

Although aggressive enforcement of the Sherman Act had been abated by earlier executive and judicial decisions, corporate mergers and consolidations around the turn of the century fanned antitrust sentiments. During the first decade of the twentieth century, corporations under the leadership of the National Civic Federation pressed for antitrust reform and either federal corporate chartering or a trade commission to facilitate national regulation of the economy (Kolko, 1963; Weinstein, 1968). The Bureau of Corporations established in the newly created Department of Commerce had not provided the desired rationality and predictability. Theodore Roosevelt's reputation as a "trust buster" did not cause undue apprehension among corporate leaders, although his adherence to an imprecise distinction between "reasonable" and "unreasonable" trusts was a source of continuing ambiguity, susceptible to subsequent reinterpretation. Roosevelt and his close business advisors had reached an informal accommodation with corporate capitalists that assured moderate antitrust enforcement policies (Kolko, 1963). Indeed, it was a more vigorous antitrust enforcement policy by Roosevelt's successor, Taft, that demonstrated the need to institutionalize the relationship between business and government, rather than to depend upon the idiosyncracies of a particular person or political party to provide a stable, rational, and predictable business environment (Kolko, 1963: 212).

Following the Supreme Court's Standard Oil decision (1911), which held that "reasonable" combinations would be permitted, trust regulation again became a major legislative issue. By the election of 1912 the Republicans, Democrats, and Progressives all made reform of the antitrust laws part of their platforms. Woodrow Wilson was aware that the business community was apprehensive about the enforcement of the Sherman Act, was uncertain about the meaning of the "Rule of Reason," and desired greater predictability and security (Kolko, 1963: 259). Wilson had recommended that uncertainty about the meaning of the Sherman Act could be eliminated by legislatively itemizing the prohibited practices that reduced competition. The National Civic Federation (NCF) and other corporate interests sought a federal regulatory mechanism that would provide a federal shield to preempt and transcend state regulations, clarify the ambiguities of the Sherman Act, and sanction anticompetitive actions in the pursuit of stability and predictability in a fluid economic environment (Kolko, 1963: 262). Similarly, the NCF under Mark Hanna's leadership sought stability in the workplace and cooperated with labor unions that accepted the basic capitalist framework; the AFL's Samuel Gompers was an NCF vice-president and legislative ally.

The passage of the Federal Trade Commission Act and the Clayton Act (1914) represented major accomplishments for big business.

> The provisions of new laws attacking unfair competitors and price discrimination meant that the government would now make it possible for many trade associations to stabilize for the first time prices within their industries, and to make effective oligopoly a new phase of the economy. (Kolko, 1963: 268)

The Federal Trade Commission Act legitimized the common laws' "reasonable" restraint of trade and created an information-gathering, accounting, and reporting system that contributed to planning and coordination. Supported by the National Civic Federation and the Chamber of Commerce, the act sought to eliminate the "unfair competition" that interfered with rational planning.[9] Although Congress could not agree on a comprehensive list of prohibited monopolistic practices, the Clayton Act proscribed certain specific types of anticompetitive corporate conduct: tying and exclusive dealing arrangements that restricted freedom of contracts, interlocking directors from competing firms, price discrimination, and the like.[10] Labor unions failed to achieve an antitrust exemption for their organizing efforts. However, clarifying the limits of corporate competition relieved some business uncertainty. The Clayton Act and the Federal Trade Commission provided a regulatory mechanism and predictable legal ground rules for corporate competition so that antitrust policies would not change with each judicial or presidential succession. While the ambiguities inherent in condoning "reasonable" restraints remained, some degree of uncertainty permits flexibility even in nominally prohibited areas of conduct.

The new laws prohibiting "unfair competition" allowed trade

associations to informally control "cutthroat" competition and stabilize prices within their industries. The Federal Trade Commission meanwhile provided a mechanism to stabilize the economy and protect against public attacks (Kolko, 1963: 268). The initial members of the commission were all men whose business backgrounds and sympathies quickly transformed the agency into an effective buffer against public hostility toward corporate prerogatives.

SUMMARY

The foundations of the parallel and intertwined growth of monopoly capital and the federal government were laid during the Progressive Era. Known by a variety of labels—political capitalism (Kolko, 1963: 279), corporate liberalism (Weinstein, 1968), and the corporate state (A. S. Miller, 1976; Fusfeld, 1972)—the growth of the federal government reflected an acceptance of the Progressive conceptions of the state's responsibility to create and maintain economic conditions conducive to rationality and corporate growth. Adopted to redress imbalances in the marketplace, the federal regulatory mechanisms of the Progressive period helped to rationalize and stabilize the economy and provide the structure of contemporary political economy. Contemporary administrative agencies continue to rationalize and legitimize the corporate economy through a fusion of the power of the private sector with the legitimacy and authority of the public sector. This influence of corporate power over federal policy stems from the concentration of economic power and from federal policies since the Progressive Era that have contributed to and perpetuated that concentration.

Our brief examination of the white collar crime debate at the beginning of this chapter suggested that the real issue was not the criminality of administrative offenses as such, but rather the structural forces that result in some offenses' being defined and enforced as they are. This analysis of the emergence of one type of administrative offense has attempted to trace some of the relationships between the increasing complexity of corporate economic life and the requirement of legal predictability as an adjunct to rational economic planning. The particular forms that the legal regulations assumed reflected the changing economic base and the legitimating functions of law, the increased social differentiation that relegates issues of public regulation to specialized agencies with a corresponding diminution in collective condemnation, and the transition to formal rational legal procedures as an adjunct to rational capitalism. Ultimately, the bureaucratic rationalization of law and the creation of new administrative agencies and sanctions are explicable only in relation to political power, which in turn is rooted in the class basis of economic power. The crucial feature of the American political economy of business regulation is the role of economic power in creating political and legal tools to rationalize economic activity.

SUGGESTED READING

Gabriel Kolko, *The Triumph of Conservatism: A Reinterpretation of American History 1900–1916* (1963);

James Weinstein, *The Corporate Ideal in the Liberal State 1900–1918* (1968);

Robert Wiebe, *Businessmen and Reform: A Study of the Progressive Movement* (1962);

David F. Noble, *America by Design: Science, Technology, and the Rise of Corporate Capitalism* (1977);

Thomas C. Cochran, *Business in American Life: A History* (1972);

Arthur S. Miller, *The Modern Corporate State: Private Governments and the American Constitution* (1976);

Edward D. Berkowitz and Kim McQuaid, *Creating the Welfare State: The Political Economy of Twentieth Century Reform* (1980);

David F. Noble, *America by Design: Science, Technology and the Rise of Corporate Capitalism* (1977);

James Stars, "The regulatory offense in historical perspective." In Gerhard Mueller (ed.) Essays in Criminal Science (1961).

FOOTNOTES

1. Sutherland defined white collar crime *"approximately* as a crime committed by a person of respectability and high social status in the course of his occupation" (1949: 9). Sutherland's interest in "white collar crime" stemmed from his desire to develop a general theory of criminal behavior—differential association (Sutherland and Cressey, 1970)—that did not see crime as exclusively "associated with poverty or with social or personal pathologies which accompany poverty" (Sutherland, 1949: 10). Sutherland's thesis was that while upper-class people commit crimes, their criminality is obscured by the prosecution of their violations in nonstigmatic administrative proceedings (Sutherland, 1949:

9). He tabulated a variety of corporate violations—price fixing, patent infringements, unfair labor practices, frauds, and other miscellaneous offenses—and concluded that the corporate criminals were "habitual offenders" with many of the same characteristics as the professional thief (Sutherland, 1949: 217–33).

2. Legislators were caught in a self-fulfilling prophecy. Since businessmen did not conform to their popular stereotype of "criminals," they were not prosecuted as criminals, and enforcement strategies were tailored to the characteristics of the probable violators (Sutherland, 1949: 46). Sutherland (1940) also asserted that by virtue of their social status, power, and respectability, businessmen enjoyed a substantial influence over the legislative processes that determined how criminal conduct was defined and enforced, although he never systematically demonstrated how that influence was actually exerted.

3. Sutherland suggested that where the prohibited conduct is complex and the relationship between the behavior and mores is attenuated, the legal prohibitions may not be congruent with general norms of corporate conduct. The "criminalization" of previously legitimate business practices and shifting definitions of proscribed conduct are difficult (Burgess, 1950; Clinard, 1946). The commission of offenses by corporate organizations also influences attitudes toward white collar crime, since many of the norms associated with interpersonal interaction are attenuated in relations with impersonal, large-scale bureaucratic organizations (Smigel and Ross, 1970). Responsibility for corporate behavior is more difficult to assign in a multilevel bureaucratic structure, and thus culpability and accountability are more widely diffused and difficult to ascribe than in relations with an individual actor (Sutherland, 1949: 229; C. D. Stone, 1975; Galbraith, 1967). Finally, many economic violations can only be established by sifting through masses of documentary evidence; they lack the immediacy or obviousness of personal victimization. Sutherland also attributed differential enforcement policies to a relatively diffuse public attitude toward these violations, which resulted from both the nature of the violations and the degree of public awareness of them. Economic crimes are more complex, and their ultimate impacts are less readily apparent than in simple common law crimes (Sutherland, 1949: 50). Sutherland also suggested (1949: 50–51) that public condemnation of white collar criminality is diminished by the lack of awareness of its prevalence, since the mass media do not provide extensive coverage of economic violations. He noted that mass media are structurally similar to likely economic offenders—concentrated economic corporations, owned and managed by business people, regulated by a specialized administrative agency—thus, being self-interested, are unlikely to recognize or report white collar crime extensively (Sutherland, 1945). Sutherland asked rhetorically whether public opinion against thieves would be as well mobilized if information about them was provided by pickpockets (Sutherland, 1945).

4. Reflecting the social structural changes at the turn of the century, there were parallel developments in both the increased use of nonpunitive administrative procedures in response to conventional crimes—probation, parole, indeterminate sentences, the juvenile court—and similar bureaucratic mechanisms to regulate the emergent economic violations. Although differing in important details, the creation of a specialized juvenile court to administer to the problems of youth reflects many of the same Progressive assumptions that were embodied in the agencies that regulated corporate economic behavior (Sutherland, 1949:44) (see Chapter 6). Both relied upon nonstigmatic administrative procedures implemented by professionals and experts, who imposed nonpunitive sanctions to solve the problems of deviance without actually acknowledging its criminality. If the essence of a crime is a stigma—the moral condemnation of culpable behavior and the expression of that opprobrium through punishment of the responsible actor—then many economic violations do not evoke the characteristic "criminal" moral outrage.

5. The legalists contend that crimes are crimes only by legislative definition and that the designation of behavior as criminal must precede its criminological analysis as crime. For them, only a legislative determination of criminality provides an adequate standard of normative proscription, since using a vaguely defined "social norm" concept of white collar crime frequently results in a subjective venture into moral outrage that quickly degenerates into polemics (Tappan, 1947). For the critics of the concept of white collar crime (Tappan, 1947; Burgess, 1950; Caldwell, 1958), only the criminal law represents a precise definition of legally proscribed behavior that embodies a significant departure from a social normative consensus.

6. Following Sutherland's contributions, other sociologists have attempted to define and account for the differences in perception and treatment of "white collar crime." Clinard (1946) analyzed causation, attitudes, and enforcement of OPA price and rationing laws during the Second World War. Hartung also analyzed violations of World War II pricing regulations and argued that these "white collar crimes," which he defined as "violation of law regulating business, which is committed for a firm by the firm or its agents in the conduct of its business," were functionally indistinguishable from other crimes (Hartung, 1950: 25). Newman's (1958) review of the white collar crime debate defined the critical characteristic of the offense as "a part of or deviation from, the violator's occupational role." Subsequent efforts to define and identify the distinguishing characteristics and criminal nature of white collar offenses and offenders have persisted without resolution (see, for example, Bequai, 1978; Conklin, 1977; Clinard, 1979). While some definitions of white collar crime focus on the social status of the perpetrator, others emphasize the economic benefit derived by the corporation or the method of perpetrating the violation as the distinguishing char-

acteristics. The only consensus in the definitional debate regarding white collar crime concerns the existence of a legally proscribed, socially harmful consequence for which some type of sanction or remedy is available, typically through an administrative proceeding rather than a routine criminal prosecution (Sutherland, 1949; Hartung, 1950).

Indeed, even the more recent collections of readings on the subject simply perpetuate the sterile debate and present some case studies of organizational, governmental, or professional deviance devoid of this social-legal context (see, for example, Geis and Meier, 1977; Johnson and Douglas, 1978; Geis and Stotland, 1980).

7. The Sherman Act, 15 U.S.C. SS 1–7 (1890) provides that:

> Sec. 1. Every contract, combination in the form of a trust or otherwise, or conspiracy, in restraint of trade or commerce among the several states, or with foreign nations, is hereby declared to be illegal. Every person who shall make any such contract or engage in any such combination or conspiracy, shall be deemed guilty of a misdemeanor. . . .
>
> Sec. 2. Every person who shall monopolize, or attempt to monopolize, or combine or conspire with any other person or persons, to monopolize any part of the trade or commerce among the several states, or with foreign nations, shall be deemed guilty of a misdemeanor. . . .
>
> Sec. 7. Any person who shall be injured in his business or property by any other person or corporation by reason of anything forbidden or declared to be unlawful by this act . . . shall recover threefold the damages by him sustained, and the costs of suit, including a reasonable attorney's fee.

8. Indeed, many of the legislative struggles around the turn of the century were between smaller and medium-sized businesses and their trade associations and the few large firms seeking to monopolize a market. An example of the contradictory aspects of Progressive legislative reform illustrates the relationship between political economy and business regulation. Passage of the Federal Meat Inspection Act (1906) is often attributed to Upton Sinclair's exposure of the unsanitary and oppressive working conditions documented in *The Jungle*. The coincidence of the public outrage associated with this book and the passage of the Meat Inspection Act, however, ignores the fact that some aspects of the industry had been regulated for decades and that the largest packing houses in the industry, which had achieved preeminence as suppliers during the Civil War, supported both the earlier legislation and the Meat Inspection Act.

By the 1880s the American meat industry was a highly competitive one because slaughtering and packing did not create significant capital entry barriers, the raw material was readily available, and there were no substantial economies of scale (Kolko, 1963: 51–53). At the turn of the century the six largest firms in the industry processed less than

50 percent of the cattle sold and experienced severe competitive pressures from hundreds of smaller packers in the industry and whose numbers were increasing (Kolko, 1963: 102).

The original impetus for meat inspection and regulation came from the larger packing houses in the 1880s to protect their access to the European export market. Import restrictions were imposed on American pork in Italy (1879), France (1881), and Germany (1883) because the United States lacked an inspection system that satisfied European standards (Kolko, 1968: 98). Other meats were also barred from Europe during the 1880s. The largest packers, adversely affected by the loss of export markets, lobbied for federal meat inspections and certification. The federal government instituted meat inspection in 1891 and later extended it to all meat in interstate commerce in 1895. However, the inspection system affected the major packers, but failed to reach many of the smaller packers, who gained a competitive advantage over the major packers (Kolko, 1963: 101). As the hearings on the 1906 act revealed, the big packers endorsed additional meat inspection and regulation in order to bring the small packers under control (Kolko, 1963: 107). The public support generated by *The Jungle* provided a democratic legitimacy to a form of governmental regulation sponsored by the larger firms, who advocated standards of production that they could meet more readily than their smaller competitors. If the smaller firms could not meet the federal standards that the larger packers supported and were forced out of the industry, Armour and Co. and Swift and Co. would not object (Kolko, 1963: 107).

9. The Federal Trade Commission Act, 15 U.S.C. SS 41–58 (1914), created a regulatory commission with the power to define and prohibit "deceptive business practices." Many of the catalog of practices that were not incorporated into the specific prohibitions of the Clayton Act were subsumed under the general Federal Trade provision that "unfair methods of competition in commerce are hereby declared unlawful."

10. The Clayton Act, 15 U.S.C. SS 12–27 (1914), dealt with price discrimination, merger activity, tying arrangements, exclusive dealing contracts, corporate acquisitions of competitors, and interlocking directorates. These practices were not prohibited absolutely, but only if the effect of the practices would "substantially lessen competition or tend to create a monopoly."

PART THREE:

Enforcement of Law

8

Some Consequences of Variation in Types of Legal Procedure

In 1953 President Eisenhower appointed as Chief Justice of the Supreme Court a liberal California Republican, Earl Warren. Between 1953 and his retirement in 1969 Warren presided over a revolution in criminal justice procedure. In *Mapp* v. *Ohio* (1961) the Warren court made the exclusionary rule binding on states; *Gideon* v. *Wainwright* (1963) extended the right to legal counsel to state felony cases; *Miranda* v. *Arizona* (1966) limited the power of police interrogation; and *Chimel* v. *California* (1969) constrained search and seizure to the immediate location of the arrest and required search warrants for broader searches. During the period in which the Warren court made these changes in criminal procedure the rate of crime increased substantially. Conservatives in particular and the public in general seized upon this coincidence as evidence that the liberalization of criminal procedure was "coddling" criminals, hampering the police in making arrests and gathering evidence, and slowing down the courts with appeals based on nit-picking technicalities.

The view that the Warren court's decisions contributed in a major way to the rise in the crime rate in the mid-1960s generally fails to take notice of the other factors contributing to this increase. The mid-1960s, for example, also happened to be the period in which the postwar baby boom children reached the crime-prone age. Crime grew concurrently with secondary schools and the youth-oriented popular music market. This fundamental demographic change was accompanied by major economic transformations that accelerated rates of teenage unemployment. It is thus by no means clear how much of an impact liberalization of criminal procedure had on the crime rate. Such an assessment must be further tempered by the recognition that *Mapp, Miranda,* and other decisions did not create new rights, but by and large extended to the states restrictions that had already been placed on federal police powers; furthermore, many of the states had already made similar reforms in their criminal procedure. The controversy over the Warren court's due process revolution, while largely uninformed by such considerations, does pose an interesting general problem: To what extent do variations in criminal procedure affect the operation of the criminal justice system?

This chapter reviews research on procedure in light of Max Weber's analysis presented in Chapter 3. We will first sample some of the ways in which recent writers have discussed the nature and consequences of procedural variations. We first examine law professor Herbert Packer's (1968) distinction between due process and crime control models of justice, which has become the standard work for examining the tensions between two conflicting standards within the American legal system. A second, more empirical, line of analysis seeks to compare legal organizations that embody distinct procedural norms. Representative of this mode of analysis are Elliot Currie's (1968) comparison of English and Continental witchcraft prosecutions and James Q. Wilson's (1968a, 1968b) comparison of fraternal and professional police departments. After reviewing the substance of these presentations by Packer, Currie, and Wilson we will show how they represent special instances of Weber's more general types of legal procedure. We will next turn to a more intensive empirical analysis of the role of formal rational legal procedure in American criminal courts provided by Isaac Balbus's (1973) study of the reaction of American courts to urban riots in the 1960s. This study permits a more extended examination of how legal procedure operates in conjunction with the nonprocedural demands on the courts to produce a distinctive pattern of criminal sanctions during crisis situations. We then return to the current controversy over the impact of Supreme Court rulings on law enforcement: To what extent and under what circumstances do procedural rules make a difference in the way law is enforced?

PACKER: DUE PROCESS VERSUS CRIME CONTROL MODELS OF JUSTICE

In 1966 the United States Supreme Court heard on appeal the case of Ernesto Miranda, who had been convicted by an Arizona court of kidnapping and rape. The case was appealed on the grounds that the conviction was based on a confession obtained by the police without Miranda's full knowledge of the nature and consequences of his statement. The Supreme Court overturned the conviction on the grounds that Miranda had been deprived of his right against self-incrimination. Subsequently, the police have generally adopted the practice of "reading his rights" to the suspect before interrogation begins. Suspects must not only be told, but must understand, that they have the right to remain silent, that their statements may be used against them in court, and that they have the right to have an attorney present during the questioning. The purpose of the Miranda ruling was to ensure that all suspects, including the poor and uneducated, received equal protection of the law. For many observers, however, the Miranda ruling was little more than a further impediment to efficient law enforcement (cf. Inbau, 1962).

This conflict between equal protection of the law and efficient law enforcement is examined in detail in Herbert Packer's (1968) contrast between due process and crime control models of justice.

"Limitation of official power" is the central theme of the due process model. Since power is open to abuse and fact-finding is inherently error-prone, proponents of the due process model argue that constraints ought to be placed on the discretion exercised by officials of the state. Thus a person is legally guilty only when proof beyond a reasonable doubt has been established on the basis of evidence that has been properly gathered. Hearsay evidence, evidence that has been seized illegally, and coerced confessions are not to be taken into account. The due process model draws a strict distinction between legal and factual guilt, between information and evidence. For example,

> a murderer, for reasons best known to himself, chooses to shoot his victim in plain view of a large number of people. When the police arrive, he hands them his gun and says, "I did it and I'm glad." His account of what happened is corroborated by several eyewitnesses. He is placed under arrest and led off to jail. Under these circumstances, which may seem extreme but which in fact characterize with rough accuracy the evidentiary situation in a large proportion of criminal

cases, it would be plainly absurd to maintain that more probably than not the suspect did not commit the killing. But that is not what the presumption of innocence means. It means that until there has been an adjudication, the suspect is to be treated, for reasons that have nothing whatever to do with the probable outcome of the case, as if his guilt is an open question (Packer, 1968: 161).

According to the doctrine of the legal presumption of innocence,

a person is not to be held guilty of crime merely on a showing that in all probability, based upon reliable evidence, he did factually what he is said to have done. Instead, he is to be held guilty if and only if these factual determinations are made in procedurally regular fashion and by authorities acting within competencies duly allocated to them. Furthermore he is not to be held guilty, even though the factual determination is or might be adverse to him, if various rules designed to protect him and to safeguard the integrity of the process are not given effect: the tribunal that convicts him must have the power to deal with his kind of case ("jurisdiction") and must be geographically appropriate ("venue"); too long a time must not have elapsed since the offense was committed ("statute of limitations"); he must not have been previously convicted or acquitted of the same or a substantially similar offense ("double jeopardy"); he must not fall within a category of persons, such as children or the insane, who are legally immune to conviction ("criminal responsibility"); and so on. None of these requirements has anything to do with the factual question of whether the person did or did not engage in the conduct that is charged as the offense against him; yet favorable answers to any of them will mean that he is legally innocent (Packer, 1968: 166).

In contrast, the underlying assumption of the crime control model is that state power is not inherently evil. Rather than placing roadblocks in the way of police, prosecutors, courts, or administrative agencies, the law should be streamlined to increase the efficiency of sorting out the guilty from the innocent. Due process is an irrelevant practical consideration in the open-and-shut case. The problematic cases are best treated as technical problems to be solved by professionals who have expertise in determining the facts. That the system may be subject to abuse is not reason to turn the criminal process into an obstacle course.

The crime control model in the United States finds a particularly warm reception among many police officers who have complained, particularly in recent years, that an undue emphasis on due process by the courts has hampered their ability to fight crime effectively.

(Indeed, it is argued, at least part of the reason for the increase in crime in the 1960s was the court imposition of "impossible" new due process guidelines governing search and seizure of evidence and the interrogation of suspects.)

The crime control model is analogous in some respects to the doctor-patient relationship in that the physician is assumed to have a monopoly of expertise and may inflict pain if it is deemed professionally necessary to arrive at a diagnosis or cure. No adversary relationship exists in the examining office; no contest between consulting physicians is expected. To the extent that disagreements arise between consulting physicians, the medical model is undermined. The role of forensic psychiatrists is instructive in this regard. Both defense and prosecuting attorneys frequently introduce expert testimony from psychiatrists to buttress their cases; the resulting conflicts in testimony have eroded the credibility of psychiatry in the courtroom (Ennis and Litwack, 1974; Meehl, 1970a). The crime control model seeks to avoid such contests and to turn law enforcement from an adversarial to a technical process, in which expertise and resources are concentrated in the hands of a professional enforcement agency.

Basic due process norms are enshrined in the Constitution (see Table 8.1) and have received elaboration in court cases. These norms have always been binding on federal courts; individual states, however, have until recently had wide latitude in the standards they apply to their own courts. The situation is further complicated by the absence of clear norms for the crime control model. One can glean these norms (as did the Supreme Court in the Miranda decision) from training manuals for police officers; but unlike legal rules, the crime control norms lack codification. Police and prosecutors, in the process of exercising wide discretion, develop bench rules of professional craftsmanship (Skolnick, 1975), which are often at odds with the standards of adversarial procedure.

Packer's Dichotomy and Weber's Typology

Packer's dichotomy is a useful place to begin thinking about the contradictions between legal procedures. The dichotomy between crime control and due process only scratches the surface, however. Weber's typology provides a richer basis for examining the composite character of procedures in the American criminal justice system. Packer's discussion draws our attention to one aspect of Weber's

TABLE 8.1
Constitutional Amendments Pertaining to Criminal Procedure

Fourth Amendment (1791)   The right of the people to be secure in their persons, houses, papers, and effects, against unreasonable searches and seizures, shall not be violated, and no warrants shall issue, but upon probable cause, supported by oath or affirmation, and particularly describing the place to be searched, and the persons or things to be seized.

Fifth Amendment (1791)   No person shall be held to answer for a capital, or otherwise infamous crime, unless on a presentment or indictment of a grand jury, except in cases arising in the land or naval forces, or in the militia, when in actual service in time of war or public danger; nor shall any person be subject for the same offense to be twice put in jeopardy of life or limb; nor shall he be compelled in any criminal case to be a witness against himself, nor be deprived of life, liberty, or property, without due process of law; nor shall private property be taken for public use without just compensation.

Sixth Amendment (1791)   In all criminal prosecutions, the accused shall enjoy the right to a speedy and public trial, by an impartial jury of the State and district wherein the crime shall have been committed, which district shall have been previously ascertained by law, and to be informed of the nature and cause of the accusation: to be confronted with the witnesses against him; to have compulsory process for obtaining witnesses in his favor and to have the assistance of counsel for his defense.

Eighth Amendment (1791)   Excessive bail shall not be required, nor excessive fines imposed, nor cruel and unusual punishment inflicted.

Fourteenth Amendment (1868)   Section 1. All persons born or naturalized in the United States, and subject to the jurisdiction thereof, are citizens of the United States and of the State wherein they reside. No State shall make or enforce any law which shall abridge the privileges or immunities of citizens of the United States; nor shall any State deprive any person of life, liberty, or property, without due process of law; nor deny to any person within its jurisdiction the equal protection of the laws.

typology that is often overlooked: If an organization combines more than one type of legitimate decision making, the resulting dissonance will create strains and contradictions within the organization. This, in effect, amounts to a dialectical perspective (see Elster, 1978: Chapter 4), which we will examine later in reviewing Balbus's study of the reaction of American courts to urban riots.

Weber's typology suggests that the contradictions within the American legal system are far more varied than are portrayed by Packer's distinction between due process and crime control. For example, the due process model combines formal rational, substantive irrational, and formal irrational elements. The formal rational elements consist of rules of evidence, rights, and privileges afforded defendants (see Table 8.1). These serve primarily as constraints rather than as foundations of the decision-making system. Ostensibly, the decision is made through a contest of advocates, a survival of the formal irrational procedure of trial by combat. The result of this combat depends upon the skill of the attorney. This feature is incompatible with the formal rational component, since it produces more favorable outcomes for those in a position to control the resources of advocacy (Galanter, 1974). The Constitutional guarantee to the right to an attorney extends only to criminal cases, and even there it does not guarantee more than competent counsel. The jury trial introduces a substantive irrational element into the proceedings by allowing the final decision to be made by a lay body. The ideal type of Packer's due process model thus consists of a variety of procedures having quite different bases for legitimating decisions. Later in the chapter we will examine some examples of the consequences of such incompatibility.

CRIMINAL PROCEDURE AND WITCHCRAFT PROSECUTION, 1481–1730

While Packer examines the strain between the existence of conflicting procedural standards, Elliot Currie examines the consequences of legal procedure variations in the nature and extent of witchcraft prosecutions.

For Western law witchcraft posed special problems of evidence. The crime itself involved a secretly signed compact between the defendant and the Devil. In exchange for their souls, witches received special powers, such as "bilocation" (being in two places at the same time). Normal rules of evidence could not be applied, since witnesses to the signing of these pacts or to the witches' Sabbath rituals were rare. Successful prosecution therefore depended heavily on confessions. Criminal procedure in England and Continental Europe differed substantially in its capacity to respond to the challenge posed by this crime. We will review here Currie's discussion of the consequences of procedural differences in the legal systems of England and the European Continent in light of Weber's typology.

English versus Continental Legal Procedure

We saw in Chapter 3 that England and the continent of Europe underwent distinct lines of legal development and that Weber devoted considerable attention to these differences as a source of understanding general relationships between law and society. Currie suggests that the legal systems of the two regions may similarly explain at least part of the differences between them in the pattern of witchcraft prosecution.

It will be worthwhile first to recall the source of the diversity of legal traditions and then to consider in more detail the implications of these differences for criminal procedure. Prior to 1215 England and the continent shared similar legal institutions, a predominant role being played by such formal irrational devices as ordeals and trial by combat. In the minds of the participants these devices ensured that legal decisions were made by God rather than by fallible men. The virtual abolition of ordeals by the Church in 1215 forced Europeans to find legitimate secular methods of resolving legal disputes. In England this was accomplished by the use of the jury to determine the facts of the case. In Weber's terms the English courts moved from a basis of formal irrationality to one of substantive irrationality. In Continental courts the jury played less of a role; instead, the court became an inquisitorial tribunal bound by formal rational laws of evidence, the "Roman canon law of proof," which required for a guilty verdict either two eyewitnesses or a confession. No amount of circumstantial evidence (a "smoking gun," bloody dagger, possession of stolen goods) was sufficient to convict a defendant of a crime.

This stringent law of proof, which remained in force until the 1600s, served to legitimate secular adjudication. At the same time it made convictions extraordinarily difficult. Consequently, torture was introduced as a means of obtaining a confession if the court had "half proof" of guilt. Elaborate specifications of this latter condition were developed, but essentially a court had to possess strong circumstantial evidence or one eyewitness. Furthermore, torture could only be used for capital offenses, since otherwise the pain of the investigation for the suspect would surpass the pain of the punishment inflicted on those found guilty. While constrained by procedural safeguards, the use of torture still gave prosecutors enormous power. Suspects were to be tortured not simply to confess to a crime, since sooner or later confessions would be forthcoming. Instead, the purpose of torture was to induce the suspect to incriminate himself and others by revealing information that only the guilty could know. Prosecutors, however, found it difficult to refrain from asking leading questions, since they "did not want to get a reputation for being outwitted by criminals" (Langbein, 1977: 148n. 19).

England, on the other hand, never developed torture as a component of its criminal procedure. Torture was employed only by special warrants of the Crown, and then primarily for cases of sedition (Langbein, 1977: 73). The failure of English criminal courts to use torture in the same manner as Continental courts was due to the lack of constraint placed on the courts by formal procedure. Indeed, "to this day an English jury can convict a defendant on less evidence than was required as a mere precondition for interrogation under torture on the Continent" (Langbein, 1977: 78).

Two other procedural differences were of significance in explaining their differential rates of witchcraft prosecution. In England not only were determinations of guilt in the hands of lay jurors, but the decision to prosecute was essentially a lay decision. The state could not, in principle, initiate prosecution.

> The need for an indictment was a constitutional principle of some importance, because it meant that the king and his ministers could not of their own motion put a man on trial for a felony . . . in matters of life and limb there existed between the Crown and the subject a shield borne by his neighbors. (Baker, 1977: 18–19).

While on the Continent criminal prosecution was actively pursued by the courts as inquisitorial tribunals, in England witchcraft prosecution fell into the hands of free-lance professional "witchfinders" hired by individual communities.

Currie suggests another procedural difference of some significance. Convicted felons in England forfeited their property to the state. On the Continent the courts themselves received the property of the defendants they successfully prosecuted. Currie suggests this feature as an explanation of the higher rate of witchcraft prosecutions among the wealthy on the Continent.

The overall higher rate of prosecutions on the Continent may be traced, at least in part, to the greater efficiency of the formal rational legal system. Witchcraft prosecution ended abruptly on the Continent when elites terminated the inquisitorial proceedings. Prosecution in England lingered into the 1700s as a consequence of the primary role played by local initiative in the indictments. Overall, Currie suggests, major divergent patterns of witchcraft prosecution may be explained by differences in legal procedures. This study is suggestive, and as we will see, its conclusions are reinforced by more recent analogies.

PROCEDURAL VARIATIONS AMONG POLICE DEPARTMENTS AND THEIR CONSEQUENCES

While four centuries separate James Q. Wilson's comparisons from the subjects of Currie's analysis, the same central contrast emerges in both studies. Wilson, comparing the organization of police departments in the United States, isolated two ideal types of law enforcement styles: the "professional" and the "fraternal." The former he found approximated most closely by the police department of "Western City," and the latter by the department in "Eastern City."

The "professional" police department in Western City places heavy emphasis on general impersonal rules, both in managing the internal affairs of the department and in dealing with the organization's "clients." Thus the departmental norms dictate that (1) recruitment of officers should be based on "standardized formal entrance examinations, open equally to all eligible persons" followed by formal training; (2) rules should be maintained "independent of circumstances of time, place or personality"; (3) authority should be attached to the role of the officer with "essentially bureaucratic distribution of authority" to "ensure rewards based on achievement rather than incumbency"; and (4) departmental focus should be "outward to universal, externally valid, enduring standards" of conduct (J. Q. Wilson, 1968a: 11–12). Police officers working in such departments typically give out "traffic tickets at a high rate; arrest a high proportion of juvenile offenders, act vigorously against illegal enterprises, and make a large number of misdemeanor arrests, when public order has not been breached" (Packer, 1969: 1315). Officers are trained to act the same toward juveniles as adults, blacks as whites, and rich as poor.

The "fraternal" department of Eastern City, on the other hand, operates quite differently. Recruitment and training of officers are typically much less formal, and rules are to be handled flexibly to fit particular circumstances. In addition, promotion comes with seniority, and departmental focus is upon community standards as well as the informal standards of particular groups within the organization. Fraternal departments "have a less formal sense of justice, either because the system of which they are a part encourages favoritism or because (and this is equally important) officers believe it is proper to take into account personal circumstances in dispensing justice." Whatever the case may be, Wilson maintains that the fraternal department will have a lower arrest rate than the professional ones, yet the ratio of blacks to whites arrested will be higher.

Wilson tests his ideas in the two cities by examining police contact, arrests, and subsequent court action of juvenile delinquents. He concludes from his data that a juvenile is almost twice as likely to come into contact with the police in Western City and that, independent of contact, the chance of arrest rather than simply a reprimand is over twice as high (1968a: 17). In addition, although Wilson finds little difference in frequency of arrests between black and white juveniles, he argues that the data indicate that "in Eastern City the probability of court action (rather than warning or reprimands) is almost three times higher for Negroes than for whites" (1968a: 14).

DIALECTICS OF LEGAL REPRESSION

The comparison of two legal systems embodying different procedures provides an empirical basis for assessing the effects of legal procedure on rates of processing and extralegal biases in decisions. The studies by Currie and Wilson are suggestive, but they fail to provide enough information to rule out with confidence alternative explanations of the differences in rates of conviction or arrest. We turn next to a study that does explicitly take into account the nonprocedural factors affecting the behavior of legal systems, Isaac Balbus's *The Dialectics of Legal Repression* (1973).

American criminal courts were faced with an unprecedented crisis in the mid-1960s as one city after another exploded in rioting. Some indication of the scale of the crisis is given by the following statistics (Horowitz and Liebowitz; 1968: 287):

Date	Location	Duration	Number Arrested	Number Injured	Number Killed
Aug. 1965	Watts	5 days	4000+	1000+	35
July 1967	Chicago	4 days	500+	100+	2
July 1967	Detroit	5 days	2600+	1500+	36

More generally, 169 cities with populations over 25,000 experienced a total of 341 disturbances involving 30 or more participants in the period 1961 to 1968.

Isaac Balbus (1973) attempts to explain the responses of the legal system to such riots in three cities: Los Angeles, Chicago, and Detroit. By examining the responses of these courts to serious threats, Balbus hopes to be able to further our understanding of the functions of the criminal sanction in contemporary society. In so doing, Balbus challenges two prevalent views of state power. The *liberal* view sees state power as generally exercised for the benefit of all in that it seeks to eliminate violent and predatory behavior. State power is furthermore held in check by due process procedures. Occasionally, these procedures have broken down, and discriminatory and arbitrary exercises of power have been inflicted on minorities, political dissidents, labor unions, and other groups. These breakdowns, however, are aberrations that can be corrected within the framework of the Constitution. In contrast, the *radical* view of state power holds that due process procedures are a thin disguise for the exercise of force in the interests of a ruling class. Typical statements of this position include the following:

> The criminal law is . . . first and foremost a reflection of the interests and ideologies of the governing class. (Chambliss, 1974: 8)

> Obviously, judicial decisions are not made uniformly. Decisions are made according to a host of extra-legal factors including the age of the offender, his race, and social class. (Quinney, 1970: 142)

In this radical conception, since law is an *instrument* in the hands of the powerful, it follows that the severity of the response of the legal system will be "proportional to the magnitude of the threat confronting the elite, i.e., that the state is far more likely to respond severely to a major revolt . . . than to a minor revolt" (Balbus, 1973: 252). Put another way,

> as the contradictions of capitalism became more apparent and the control system more unsuccessful, the methods of coercion became similarly more explicit and more desperate. (Platt, 1974: 389)

Neither the *liberal* view, with its emphasis on due process as the guarantee of equality, nor the *radical* view, with its emphasis on law as an instrument of power, is adequate, Balbus argues, for understanding how the criminal justice system actually operates or for comprehending its consequences on the society. It is necessary to ignore the current debates between liberals and radicals and return to the theories of law and society developed by Karl Marx and Max Weber.

As we will see in Chapter 10, an extensive body of research on sentencing by American criminal courts suggests that length of sentence is determined by two identifiable factors: seriousness of offense and number of prior convictions. Once these two legal variables are taken into account, none of the extralegal factors that Quinney argues "obviously" affect judicial decisions have any influence. Bear in mind that this refers only to length of sentence, not to any of the other decisions made in the criminal justice system. However, the adherence to the rule of law in sentencing does suggest that the court attempts to adhere to due process norms.

Balbus suggests, however, that following due process is only one of the goals of courts. In addition, they are committed to *maintaining order* by enforcing the law. Furthermore, as bureaucratic organizations processing large numbers of cases, the courts must face problems of what Balbus calls *organizational maintenance*. "Individual judges in the municipal court of Los Angeles typically handle case volumes ranging from 2,500 to 4,500 per month" (Balbus, 1973: 16). In these circumstances judges must not only keep their court calendars moving, but they must be aware of overloading jails and other detention centers.

The goals of due process, maintaining order and preserving organizational maintenance are "contradictory—they are all essential yet all incompatible." Only by understanding the contradictory or "dialectical" character of the court organization, Balbus suggests, can we begin to make sense out of the ways in which they reacted to persons arrested during the urban riots of the 1960s.

STRUCTURE OF CRIMINAL COURTS IN THE UNITED STATES

The three cities that Balbus has studied have a very complex set of procedures and organizations that process large numbers of cases. It will be useful to understand the outlines of this system.

The criminal justice system in the United States can be viewed as a sieve in which a large number of complaints entering the system are progressively winnowed out. To understand how and why this sieve works the way it does, it is essential to examine each of the major decision points in the system. The arrest may result either from the investigation of a citizen complaint or by the police witnessing a law violation. With the exception of such offenses as traffic and vice, most police investigations are instigated by citizen complaint. After taking the suspect into custody the police then formally register a complaint at the police station, a process called "booking." The name and address (and typically fingerprints and photograph) of the suspect are recorded. If the evidence appears insubstantial, the suspect may be released. If not released, the suspect is taken before a court for an initial hearing. This court reviews the evidence and informs the suspect of his or her rights. This court may dispose of the case if the charge is a minor misdemeanor (for example, it may impose a fine). If the charge is contested or if the charge is serious, the court will review the evidence and determine whether the suspect is to be detained. If detention is required, the court will establish bail. The amount of bail required is usually set by a standard schedule that provides specified dollar amounts depending upon seriousness, present offense, and length of previous criminal record. The purpose of the bail is to ensure that the defendant will show up for the subsequent legal proceedings. The court may choose to release trustworthy defendants "on their own recognizance" without the posting of any bond.

A preliminary court hearing is later held to determine whether the state has enough evidence to sustain a prosecution. The defendant may at this hearing attempt to have the charges dismissed as insubstantial; the hearing also provides the defendant an opportunity to view the evidence that the state has marshalled against him or her. Furthermore, this hearing may revise the amount of bail in light of the evidence. Some states have a grand jury, a panel of twelve to twenty-three citizens, who review the evidence and serve the same function of determining whether the evidence is sufficient to hold the defendant for trial.

The fifth stage involves the drawing up of a formal complaint by the prosecutor. This complaint is called an "indictment" when a grand jury is involved in its approval. In most states the prosecutor alone draws up a formal complaint, which is called an "information."

This indictment or information is then reviewed by another court hearing, sometimes called the "arraignment." At this hearing the evidence is reviewed by the court, and the defendant enters a plea (guilty or not guilty). Pretrial motions may be introduced to change venue or quash evidence. The charge may be reduced if the defendant pleads guilty. A defendant who contests the information or indictment will be tried. If a defendant pleads guilty or is found guilty, the next stage is a sentencing hearing in which the court determines the punishment to be imposed.

RESPONSES OF THE CRIMINAL JUSTICE SYSTEM TO URBAN RIOTS

Balbus's full analysis involves complex comparisons of the reactions of the criminal courts in Los Angeles, Chicago, and Detroit to criminal cases in major riots, minor riots, and nonriot situations. We will not consider these complex comparisons. It will be sufficient to get a sense of the analysis and the relevance of Weber's procedural types in interpreting the results if we confine our attention to one case: the Watts riot.

On August 11, 1965, spontaneous isolated acts of violence in response to rumors of police brutality broke out in the black ghetto of Watts in Los Angeles. By August 13, looting and burning had become widespread. The National Guard was called in to aid police, and within a week over 4000 arrests had been made. The riot constituted a severe threat to the city, with thirty-five persons killed, over 1000 persons injured, and $50 million in property loss suffered. The initial reaction of the legal system was to quell the disturbance. Mass arrests were made, mostly of people found in stores or on the streets in possession of small amounts of stolen property. Arrest reports were hastily written; suspects, arresting officers, and evidence became tangled in confusion. Since the state penal code stipulates that an arrested person must be charged within 48 hours (not counting weekends) or be released, and court officials did not want the arrested persons to return to the scene of the riot, they drew up uniform complaints of burglary (a felony) regardless of the quality of evidence. Prosecutors similarly abandoned their gatekeeper roles. While they normally throw out for lack of evidence the cases of half the suspects the police charge, they retained most cases regardless of the nature of the evidence. The result of dropping the normal operating procedures was to increase massively the number of persons detained for trial. Judges behaved in a similar fashion in setting bail. Normally, bail decisions are made on the basis of prior record. With the overwhelming number of defendants, however, it became physically impossible to obtain the conviction records within the time prescribed by law for the bail hearing.

Therefore the judges uniformly set maximum bail. Bail bondsmen and defense attorneys were, for the most part, so shocked by the riot that they did not become involved in the proceedings until after the riot had been controlled. In the meantime, thousands of suspects were crowded into existing jail facilities and whatever additional secure space officials could locate. They were forced to live for several days without adequate food, shelter, or sanitation.

Throughout the crisis the legal system adhered to statutory deadlines. The California statutes, for example, contain the following provision:

> When a defendant is not brought to trial in a superior court within 60 days after the finding of the indictment or filing of the information ... the court, unless good cause to the contrary is shown, must order the action to be dismissed. (California Code, Sec. 1382)

Felony suspects arrested during the riot were almost twice as likely to be prosecuted as during normal periods. This massive exercise in preventive detention, while within the formal detention standards, deprived suspects of freedom solely on the grounds that if they were released they *might* engage in rioting or looting. Deprivations of freedom for a crime not yet committed was not acknowledged as a policy, but here the demand for order overrode formal rational values of justice.

The massive short-term increase of arrests and detention created another kind of problem for the system. Under the best of circumstances the criminal justice system can barely keep up with the flow of cases. Now the jails became so overcrowded that jail riots loomed as a real possibility. Furthermore, the criminal justice system would have collapsed were the 4000 defendants to demand jury trials.

Given the lack of evidence in most cases and the willingness of the court to abide by the normal standards of evidence, individual suspects found themselves in a much stronger bargaining position than they would have been in had they been charged with comparable offenses during normal periods. Whereas 32 percent of persons arrested for felonies are normally convicted on that charge, only 18 percent of the riot felons were convicted. Furthermore, the sentences were generally less severe for convicted riot felons than for convicted nonriot felons. While normally 33 percent of convicted felons are placed on probation, over twice that proportion of the riot felons were placed on probation. This greater leniency holds for riot felons regardless of prior arrest or conviction records. Faced with a major crisis, the Los Angeles criminal court abandoned the informal screening procedures, which in normal circumstances release most suspects early in the process. The result was a massive arrest and incapacitation of potential riot participants. For the most part, this detention was accomplished within the formal requirements of due process; no statutory time limits were violated, bail was not totally abrogated. In conviction and sentencing decisions the court appeared to adhere to the standards of evidence followed in the nonriot period. Since the state had such inadequate evidence in most cases, the courts were more inclined to avoid felony convictions and prison sentences.

Balbus's discovery of this pattern (with some minor modifications) in Detroit and Chicago as well suggests that the criminal justice system in times of crisis does not respond with maximum coercion, abandoning the formal rational standards of justice. It suspends these standards in the short run to restore order, but returns to these standards even though the result is a lower conviction rate for riot felons than for nonriot felons. To explain this paradox, Balbus draws our attention to the functions performed by formal rationality in capitalist society.

Repression by formal rationality implies that every effort will be exercised to employ ordinary legal procedures and the ordinary sanctioning mechanisms in the course of the elite effort to repress collective violence. This strategy offers important advantages to the elite in its struggle to minimize revolutionary potential and maximize long-run legitimacy. To begin with, the successful adaptation of the ordinary criminal justice system to the threat of collective violence is likely to have a profound impact on the consciousness of the participants in the violence [for] the ideological coherence of participants in collective violence is not necessarily fixed, but rather is shaped by the nature of the elite response. Repression by formal rationality, insofar as it attempts to affix the label of "crime" on the behavior of the participants, is likely to help convince participants that their violent acts represent nothing more than massive outbreaks of common "criminality." To recall the insight of Lukacs, the legal system in the liberal state tends to "confront individual events as something permanently established and exactly defined"; the effort to apply the routine administration of justice to the problems of collective violence represents nothing less than an effort to fit the violent "events" under the rubric of previously established, general categories of proscribed behavior, i.e., to deprive the violence of its special, hence political, character by defining it as ordinary "crime." Repression by formal rationality thus serves to de-politicize collective violence and to militate

against the growth of the consciousness and solidarity of the participants. The "criminalization" process entailed in repression by formal
rationality also serves to delegitimate whatever demands emerge from
the collective violence. Demands which arise from "criminals" are
unlikely to receive a hearing and thus less likely to be voiced in the
first place. Once the process of criminalization is under way, public
debate is not likely to center over the substantive grievances of the
participants but rather over the severity of punishment which they
merit: criminals do not have just grievances; criminals deserve to be
punished. Repression by formal rationality thus makes it unlikely
that the claims and grievances of the participants in collective violence
will be addressed to, or accepted by, significantly large numbers of
the population at large. (Balbus, 1973: 12)

Legal procedure thus is crucial for maintaining legitimacy of state
power. If a threat is popularly perceived to be major, normal due
process may be suspended. Perhaps the best example of this possibility
in recent American history is the creation of the relocation centers
in the 1940s.

Following the surprise attack on Pearl Harbor in December of
1941, the American public was thrown into a state of panic over
the possible imminent invasion of the West Coast by Japanese
forces. This panic led President Franklin Roosevelt to sign an executive order removing all potential Japanese collaborators from
the West Coast. No hearings were held, nor were any investigations
conducted to determine which individuals constituted security risks.
Instead, the order included all Japanese and Americans of Japanese
ancestry. In all, over 100,000 children, men, and women were rounded
up in March of 1942 and sent to detention camps in remote areas
of the American West. By July 1943, with the prospect of invasion
reduced, the government began administering loyalty tests and releasing detainees. Most were released by December 1944, but the
last of the relocation camps remained open until March 1946. In
addition to the years of detention, the Japanese Americans lost over
$400 million in homes, businesses, and other property that they
were forced to abandon (Daniels, 1971; Adams, 1944).

This emergency suspension of due process was a response to
a combination of circumstances—the perceived treachery of the
surprise attack on Pearl Harbor reinforced by a lingering racist
sentiment against Orientals. No such overwhelming threat was
perceived from the European enemies, Italy and Germany. Following
the First World War a similar panic was caused by labor unrest.
The Russian Revolution in 1917 had shown what could be accom-

plished by a small core of disciplined activists. As a result, the federal government undertook a series of raids on radical organizations and deported en masse resident aliens who were members of radical organizations. The Red Scare of 1920 and the Japanese internment of 1942–1946 were by and large successful suspensions of due process. While the urban riots of the 1960s caused widespread anxiety, the same sense of imminent danger was not present. Moreover, a substantial segment of the public viewed the riots as understandable, if not inevitable, reactions to deprivation and discrimination (Turner, 1969). Had martial law been declared under these circumstances, it is quite likely that the state would have lost legitimacy. A clear example of this scenario has been played out in Poland.

The Polish government declared martial law on December 13, 1981, following a call for a strike by the independent labor union, Solidarity, the day before a national referendum on the continuation of Communist Party rule. Solidarity had over the past two years won increasing economic and political concessions from the government by threatening strikes to cripple an already weak economy. During this period the union had become a focus of Polish nationalism. The election of a Polish Pope had galvanized this nationalism very swiftly, and neither the government nor Solidarity's leaders were fully in control of the movement. The government was in a particularly awkward position in its close relationship with the Kremlin. Much of Poland's history has been spent as a province of Russia, and her period of full independence (1919 to 1939) was short-lived. With the appearance of an independent labor movement, the government found itself competing unsuccessfully for legitimacy. The union, in turn, accelerated its claims of power, increasing the threat of invasion by Soviet forces. In response, the Polish government declared a state of martial law in which union leaders were summarily arrested and detained indefinitely, and in which ordinary civil liberties (rights of assembly, speech, and the rights to strike, etc.) were temporarily suspended. As Balbus's line of argument suggests, the result of these measures has been to enhance the legitimacy of the union and to erode further the position of the state. Attempts by the Polish government to link Solidarity with the CIA or other Western manipulation have failed to create the level of publicly perceived external threat necessary to exercise coercion and maintain legitimacy.

Balbus's analysis of court reactions to riots and the cases of American relocation centers and Polish martial law all point to the same general conclusion: Legal procedures serve to legitimate state power by depoliticizing disorder. In the absence of a consensually accepted danger, the suspension of normal procedure renders the exercise of state coercion illegitimate. As Barton Ingraham points out,

> the political nature of the crime depends upon the kind of legal response the act evokes from those in authority. A common crime may be politically motivated or have a political object, but unless it is regarded as "political" by the authorities . . . the legal response to it will be the same as for other common crimes; there will be no special handling of the case as is customary for true political crimes. (1979: 18–19)

Michel Foucault arrives at very similar conclusions in his explanation of the persistence of the prison. He begins by observing that a critique of penology appeared very early, almost simultaneously with the emergence of the penitentiary itself. The critical literature of the 1820s to 1840s contains arguments that "are today repeated almost unchanged" (1979: 265), namely:

1. The crime rate is unaffected by imprisonment. There is no evidence of a deterrent effect on would-be offenders, and the high rate of recidivism suggests that prison has little reformative value.
2. Detention breeds recidivism. The prison, by releasing unreformed offenders, simply operates as a revolving door.
3. The conditions of imprisonment socialize inmates into more serious forms of crime.
4. By bringing offenders together in one place the prison breeds criminal socialization.
5. Ex-convicts are stigmatized by their records, making gainful employment difficult. Constantly being scrutinized by the police, they are likely to be included when the police "round up the usual suspects."
6. The prison destroys the family life as well as the occupational career of the offender, since the state provides no economic assistance to families of the imprisoned. The resulting impoverishment induces the families to break up and encourages the prisoner's offspring to engage in delinquency.

After reviewing 150 years of redundant prison reform arguments, Foucault proposes a functional explanation.

Perhaps one should reverse the problem and ask oneself what is served by the failure of the prison; what is the use of these different phenomena that are continually being criticized; the maintenance of delinquency, the encouragement of recidivism, the transformation of the occasional offender into a habitual delinquent, the organization of a closed milieu of delinquency. Perhaps one should look for what is hidden beneath the apparent cynicism of the penal institution, which after purging the convicts by means of their sentence, continues to follow them by a whole series of "brandings" ... and which thus pursues as "delinquent" someone who has acquitted himself of his punishment as an offender? Can we not see here a consequence rather than a contradiction? If so, one would be forced to suppose that the prison, and no doubt punishment in general, is not intended to delineate offences, but rather to distinguish them to distribute them, to use them. ... The "failure" of the prison may be understood on this basis. (Foucault, 1979: 272)

Foucault, Balbus, and a few other contemporary writers have thus extended the essential insights of Weber's discussion of the consequences of formal rational criminal procedure. By applying uniform standards to all offenders the system individualizes deviant conduct and systematically deprives it of political content. The potential for political alternatives is well illustrated in Balbus's discussion of the outcome of a case in which the defendants refused to be treated as a large number of individuals making small deals.

In 1964 the San Francisco court system was confronted with some 400 civil rights cases resulting from a series of sit-in demonstrations. Civil rights lawyers initiated time-consuming motions to dismiss cases, refused to plead their clients guilty and instead demanded jury cases. During this time courts which normally handle civil cases were diverted for the processing of the regular criminal calendar, and the processing of civil cases was totally disrupted. According to another Los Angeles judge, "they didn't have a civil case in San Francisco for six months!" (Balbus, 1973: 23)

Legal procedure thus has major consequences for the manner in which disorder is categorized and labeled.

To explain the reaction of a legal system to crisis, the nature of its legitimation of procedure must be taken into account. Less formal rational systems, such as Puritan Massachusetts, may with relative ease respond to such a crisis with a wave of prosecution. Formal rational systems are more likely to avoid such confrontations with deviants. Some suggestive evidence along these lines is suggested by Jack Goldstone's study of rates of success of social protest groups in the United States. He concludes that such groups

> will get serious attention only when some external shock occurs, such as a major war or economic or political crisis. Only at such times, when the need for integration and support of the established order is particularly strong, are established interests likely to feel the need to compromise and accommodate to new social protest groups ... the success of protest groups would be tied to the essentially stochastic flow of major shocks to the society. (1980: 1037–8)

The process of repressive justice delineated by Durkheim in theoretical terms and applied empirically by Erikson, thus, appears to be limited by the constraints of legal procedure.

SUMMARY

In this chapter we have examined several efforts to study the consequences of legal procedure. While it is commonly assumed that changes in legal procedure have major consequences on the level of sanctioning, as, for example, the purported effect of the due process revolution on the prosecution of felons in the United States, much of the work accomplished so far on this issue has been exploratory. The explorations raise provocative questions. They suggest that a study (e.g. Erikson, 1966) of prosecutions that fails to consider the form of legal procedure may misinterpret the role of societal factors in shaping the punishment of crime. The nature of the societal reaction to deviance and crime, it appears, is shaped in important ways by the legal procedure taken as being legitimate.

SUGGESTED READING

The study by Balbus (1977) is an important contribution to this area, but its detail of analysis makes it difficult to digest. Trubek's review (1977) is quite useful in comprehending the main line of argument. There are a number of excellent treatments of the American criminal justice process. On plea bargaining, see Rosett and Cressey (1976) and the special issue of *Law and Society Review* (Winter 1979). Kaplan and Skolnick (1982) provide a comprehensive overview of the criminal justice system. Excellent analytic treatments of contradictions within the legal system are provided in the work of Heydebrand (1977; 1979) and Heydebrand and Seron (1981). Contradictions within and between therapeutic and coercive forms of control are examined by Kittrie (1971), Feld (1977), and K. S. Miller (1980). An excellent study of the line between crime and politics is provided by Ingraham (1981). Packer's models of justice are examined in Griffiths (1970).

9

Bias in Sentencing: Sociological Analyses of Its Extent and Causes

Offenses of the same nature shall be punished by the same kind of penalties whatever the rank and status of the offender.
French Declaration of the Rights of Man, 1789

Furman v. *Georgia,* heard by the Supreme Court in 1972, was the culmination of an extended series of legal efforts on the part of the NAACP Legal Defense Fund and the ACLU to abolish the death penalty on constitutional grounds. The primary argument the abolitionists advanced was that capital punishment by the middle of the twentieth century had become a rarely used sanction; very few serious criminals were being sentenced to death, and even fewer were actually being executed. None in fact had been executed in the country in the previous five years. Capital punishment was deemed arbitrary and capricious and in violation of the Eighth Amendment's ban on "cruel and unusual punishment." Furthermore, since black defendants had in the past been executed at a much higher rate than whites convicted of comparable offenses, the death penalty was discriminatory, denying black people in the United States their rights under the Fourteenth Amendment to "equal protection of the laws."

The court did not reach a conclusive decision in Furman. While the vote of five to four reversed the death sentence of William Furman, nine separate opinions were handed down, no two justices agreeing on one line of reasoning. Most of the justices agreed with William O. Douglas's observation that Georgia's capital punishment law was vague and that such "discretionary laws are pregnant with discrimination." Only justices Brennan and Marshall argued that capital punishment is inherently a violation of human dignity, regardless of the uniform character of its application.

Despite the complexity of the Furman decision, it is clear that the question of discrimination has become a key problem in determining the constitutionality of death penalty laws. In fact, Chief Justice Warren Burger wrote that he could not go along with the majority decision precisely because the evidence of discrimination was inadequate. Most of the studies cited by the majority were, in Burger's view, dated. One major study by Wolfgang, Kelly, and Nolde (1962), for example, consisted of a sample of Pennsylvania cases ranging from 1918 to 1959. It was certainly possible to believe that judges and juries during this period discriminated against blacks, but this does not necessarily tell us anything about the current situation. Similarly, the studies cited generally failed to provide information about other relevant factors affecting sentences. That blacks are disproportionately sentenced to death does not necessarily mean that the courts were basing sentences on race; the courts may have been calibrating the sentence to the circumstances of the offense or to the past record of the defendant. If blacks were more frequently involved in violent, serious crime, a racial disparity in death sentences would arise that would have nothing to do with racial discrimination on the part of the courts. The disparity is a serious problem, but the remedy in Burger's view does not lie in the courts. Such a judicial remedy would create two laws, one with lesser penalties for black felons and one with more severe punishment for white felons.

Determining the extent of racial discrimination in sentencing decisions is an issue of major significance involving complex research and policy problems. We will survey these problems in a nontechnical review of the research on criminal sentencing and then consider these results in light of general sociological theories developed in previous chapters.

PROBLEMS OF MEASURING BIAS

One of the most salient features of the criminal justice system is the inequality in the distribution of penal sanctions. Table 9.1

TABLE 9.1

Occupational Characteristics of Prison Inmates and U.S. General Population, 1974

Occupation	State Prison Inmates (percent)	Civilian Population (percent)
Professional/managerial	10.5	24.8
Sales/clerical	6.6	23.8
Blue collar	71.1	34.6
Farm	2.7	3.5
Service	10.8	13.2

SOURCES: U.S. Department of Justice (1979); U.S. Bureau of the Census (1978: 418).

compares the occupational structure of prison inmates and the general population. Imprisonment is clearly a sanction associated with low-status occupations. Much the same is true of minority status. Black people, for example, made up 11.6 percent of the population in 1977, but 30 percent of all arrests were of blacks, and 47 percent of prison inmates at that time were black. The higher proportion of blacks in the later stages of the criminal justice process would suggest that the legal system is systematically discriminating on the basis of race (cf. Woodson, 1977).

This impression is reinforced by numerous single cases that suggest that severity of punishment is a consequence of racial or class discrimination. For example,

A year after seven electrical manufacturers were sent to jail for 30 days apiece (for stealing millions of dollars from the public via price fixing), a man in Asbury Park, New Jersey stole a $2.95 pair of sunglasses and $1 box of soap and was sent to jail for four months. A George Jackson was sent to prison for ten years to life for stealing $70 from a gas station, his third minor offense; and in Dallas a Joseph Sills received a 1000 year sentence for stealing $73.10. Many states [sent] young students who [were] marijuana first offenders to jail for five to ten year sentences. But the total amount of time spent in jail by all businessmen who have ever violated anti-trust laws is a little under two years. (Nader and Green, 1972: 20)

We recognize here an instance of what we described earlier as a case of "isolated and apt illustrations." While cases can be found to illustrate Sir Francis Bacon's thesis that "the laws are like cobwebs, where the big insects break through but the small get caught," negative cases may also be cited. Thus Patricia Hearst was found guilty of bank robbery in 1976 despite the skills of the famous (and very expensive) trial lawyer F. Lee Bailey, hired by her millionaire father. While Vice-President Spiro Agnew plea bargained his way out of a possible prison sentence in his 1973 $20,000 tax evasion case, it is also true that low-income, low-status defendants routinely avoid prison by the same procedure. For political conservatives, in fact, plea bargaining appears to favor not the rich, but the "dangerous," "hardened" criminals. One can make a plausible case for either position by the method of apt and isolated illustration.

If we are interested in determining the *general* relationship between sentencing and status, we must deal with aggregates rather than selected cases. The cliché, "You can prove anything with statistics," occasionally becomes a rationalization for avoiding aggregate data. The fact is, you can prove anything with statistics, but it is more difficult to do so than it is to prove nonsensical propositions by picking out single cases with no constraints at all. The advantage of aggregate analysis is that it does impose some constraints on overly creative imaginations. In the next section we will consider how aggregate analysis allows us to distinguish between the effects of involvement in crime and bias in law enforcement.

Sociological study of bias in law enforcement has been intimately linked to the development of measures of crime. Official statistics have generally indicated a high level of involvement in crime by members of certain social categories: the young, males, the poor, and minorities. The reliability of official statistics and their implications have been questioned, however. For example, Taylor, Walton, and Young repeat a very popular refrain in the sociology of the 1960s in pointing to "immediate and obvious contradictions" in the use of official crime statistics:

> The statistics were based on crimes known to the police which were (and are) in many instances only a tiny proportion of the total number of criminal acts committed. The total amount of criminality, as represented in the statistics, therefore, could vary considerably according to the degree of police vigilance, the deployment of police resources, the willingness of the public to report particular offenses and so on without there being any real change in the amount of lawbreaking. (1973: 11)

Kitsuse and Cicourel (1963), J. Douglas (1967), and De Fleur (1975) conclude that official statistics can be used only for studying the way in which officials perceive social reality and keep records. To use the Uniform Crime Reports (UCR) as sources of information about the frequency and distribution of crimes was viewed as misleading, given the lack of reliability. Thus

> the rates of deviant behavior are produced by the actions taken by persons in the social system which define, classify, and record certain behaviors as deviant. If a given form of behavior is not interpreted as deviant by such persons it would not appear as a unit in whatever set of rates we may attempt to explain. . . . From this point of view, deviant behavior is behavior which is organizationally defined, processed, and treated as "strange," "abnormal," "theft," "delinquent," etc. by the personnel in the social system which has produced the rule. (Kitsuse and Cicourel, 1963: 135)

Surveys of victims of crime and self-reports of involvement in delinquency and crime gave credence to such warnings about the lack of reliability in official crime statistics. Ennis (1967) reported the first systematic evidence that the number of crimes reported by survey respondents was substantially more than crimes "known to the police" in the UCR. The self-report survey, pioneered by Wallerstein and Wyle (1947) and conducted on a sustained basis since Short and Nye (1957), provided an even stronger case for the unreliability of official statistics. Taylor, Walton, and Young, for example, suggest that crime

> thus defined or quantified, is found to be well-nigh ubiquitous. It is found to occur in all sections of society—amongst the rich and the poor, the young and the old—amongst men and women—and always in greater amounts and in different proportions than was previously assumed. . . . Criminological theory, however, has largely worked on the assumption that crime is an overwhelmingly youthful, masculine, working class activity. (1973: 15)

The lack of reliability in official statistics and particularly the discovery that in self-reports criminal conduct was more equally distributed across class categories provided empirical foundation for "the new criminology," the radical overthrow of previous theories. In short order this result was turned into the new catechism in criminology. For example, according to a widely used text in criminology, "There is no theory of crime that meets the most elementary demands of scientific theory. With the exception of labeling and conflict theory, all of the theories presume the existence of a phenomenon called *crime* that does not exist and that therefore cannot be distinguished from *noncrime*. As a result, they cannot distinguish criminal from noncriminal behavior or criminals from noncriminals" (Reid, 1979: 259).

Such conclusions, however, are based upon a double standard of evaluating reliability. Official statistics are dismissed because of their imperfect reliability, while self-report and victimization data are taken without concern for possible biases. More recent assessments have recognized that (1) all three indicators suffer degrees of unreliability and (2) the use of multiple indicators is the only sensible strategy in a situation in which all three indicators suffer from imperfections. This approach has yielded an alternative interpretation of the actual relationship between class position and involvement in crime and delinquency.

Victimization surveys suggest that the UCR systematically underestimates property offenses, particularly those involving small losses. Such crimes as homicide and auto theft, however, are similarly estimated by both procedures. The UCR homicide data can further be validated by coroner reports collected by the Bureau of Vital Statistics. Such comparisons reveal considerably less of a problem with official crime statistics, particularly with regard to questions concerning the distribution of offenses among social categories (Hindelang, 1973).

The self-report studies are a particularly instructive example of how far afield writers can go in combining meaningless criteria with a double standard in their quixotic quests for evidence to confirm their theoretical presuppositions. The self-report studies have had a number of odd features. They have

1. been largely limited to in-school samples of juveniles.
2. treated all forms of "deviance" as equally serious.
3. routinely included what the police would treat as "garbage offenses" as instances of serious crime.

The conclusion that "class is uncorrelated with delinquency" is thus based on surveys showing that youths of all social classes engage in trivial offenses.

What self-report research does show is variation in the frequency and seriousness of delinquent behavior. At one end of the continua of frequency and seriousness are a good many boys and especially girls who have done little or nothing in the way of delinquency. They are almost saints. And anyone attempting to apply a delinquency "label" to them would stand a good chance of being accurately labeled a nut. As we move along our continua of frequency and seriousness of delinquent acts, the number of boys and especially girls who are still with us diminishes rapidly. The proportion having been picked up by the police also begins to increase with some rapidity, but on the whole we are not yet dealing with persons sufficiently "delinquent" that they would be considered candidates for reformation in an institution. Finally, we get to boys and very few girls who have committed a good many delinquent offenses. The chances that they have been picked up by the police on more than one occasion are very good, and there is a strong likelihood that a juvenile court judge might consider placement of some kind were they to come before him or her repeatedly in a short span of time. Finally, there is a very small group (almost all boys) not around for interviewing or filling out questionnaires. Some are already in institutions. Others are currently being sought. If located, we can safely guess that some of them would remember (and may actually have committed) fewer delinquent acts than some of their cohorts who have not had so much trouble with officials but, on the whole, their self-reported delinquent behavior will be consistent with their troubles with officials. The members of this group are, to complete the story, almost crooks. And anyone so labeling them would stand a good chance of merely stating the obvious. (Hirschi, 1979: 190)

At the present time no self-report studies have sampled a sufficient number of serious offenses to say anything worthy of serious consideration about class distribution (Hindelang, Hirschi, and Weiss, 1979). The past two decades of research on the use of statistics to determine the relationship between class position and crime involvement suggest that despite the frequent errors in official statistics, they provide a reasonably accurate indicator of the incidence of crime. Thus, the data may be critically examined without embracing the empirical nihilism that became fashionable in the 1960s.[1] In place of the fetish of reliability, it is possible to assess empirically the importance of reliability.

A more useful approach would be to treat reliability as a quantity to be estimated. Instead of a preoccupation with the unreliability of police arrest records, we might ask by how much arrest statistics overestimate or underestimate heroin addiction and what consequences such a magnitude of error would have. By the use of *multiple indicator models* for a given year or a given neighborhood we would gather not only data on police arrests for possession, but coroner reports on deaths from overdose and health statistics on the incidence of serum hepatitis. These three variables aggregated across time or geographic units would allow us to estimate the actual incidence of heroin use and to determine empirically the nature and extent of reliability problems with arrest statistics.[2]

BIAS IN SENTENCING

While some researchers have attempted to sort out involvement and discrimination effects in the administration of justice through examination of official statistics, self-reports, and victimization surveys, most of the empirical work on this question has been conducted on the sentencing of convicted criminal defendants and adjudicated delinquents. In reviewing this work, bear in mind that these studies deal with only one stage of the process and that the discovery of bias at this stage (or its absence) tells us nothing about bias at the previous stages of law creation, arrest, plea bargaining, or conviction.[3]

The problem of bias in sentencing research may be summarized by the diagram in Figure 9.1. The empirical literature, for the most part, is concerned with testing two hypotheses, involvement and discrimination. The involvement hypothesis suggests that such offender characteristics as age, gender, income level, and minority status lead (via anomie, differential association, availability of illegitimate opportunities, etc.) to differential involvement in particular types of offenses. If, for example, carrying a knife or handgun is a customary practice among young black males, but not among young white males, then, other things being equal, we should expect the homicide rate to be higher among black males than among

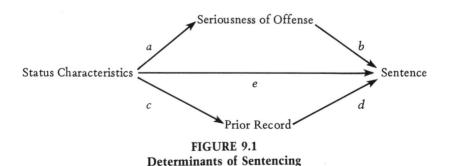

FIGURE 9.1
Determinants of Sentencing

white males. Similar factors may lead persons with particular social characteristics to engage more frequently in particular types of offense. The involvement hypothesis thus states that the differences in sentences observed among members of various social categories arise from the nature and frequency of their participation in illegal activities. The practical side of this hypothesis is that to change racial or class inequalities in the distribution of penal sanctions, the source of criminal conduct (for example, unemployment, discrimination in the job and housing markets) must be reduced.

In contrast, the discrimination hypothesis claims that criminal offenses are uniformly distributed across social categories and that resultant differences are due in part to biases on the part of judges against persons with particular social attributes. Thus

> Obviously judicial decisions are not made uniformly. Decisions are made according to a host of extra-legal factors, including the age of the offender, his race, and social class. Perhaps the most obvious example of judicial discretion occurs in the handling of cases of persons from minority groups. Negroes, in comparison to whites, are convicted with lesser evidence and sentenced to more severe punishments. (Quinney, 1970: 142)

In terms of the diagram in Figure 9.1 the difference between the involvement and discrimination hypotheses may be expressed as a difference in a single assumption. Discrimination theorists assume that e is not equal to zero, that even after consideration of the seriousness of the offense and the prior record of the offender, some relationship between offender characteristics and sentence outcome will be found, reflecting the bias of the judge. Involvement theorists, on the other hand, predict that e will be zero.

The results of the research that addresses this issue have been mixed. Quite often, prior record is simply defined as a dichotomy: no priors versus some. When racial differences are found for offenders with previous convictions, but not for first offenders, the result is ambiguous. It could mean, on one hand, that bias only becomes a factor for minority recidivists; on the other hand, it might simply reflect the fact that minority offenders had longer prior records on the average and hence received stiffer sentences for comparable convictions. Similar problems infest the assessment of seriousness of offense.[4] These measurement problems may partly explain the differences in results reported by various researchers.

In some cases the evidence of bias is unequivocal. For most types of offense, however, little can be said at the present time with much confidence about bias in sentencing. The clearest evidence of bias in sentencing is the imposition of the death penalty for rape in the South. From 1930 to 1972, 455 persons were executed for rape, of whom 405 were blacks and two were from other racial minorities. All of the executions for rape since 1930 occurred in southern or border states or in the District of Columbia (Wolfgang, 1974: 113).

In his study of 3000 convictions for rape in 250 southern counties between 1945 and 1965, Marvin Wolfgang (1974) found systematic evidence of racial discrimination. Black defendants were convicted in 823 cases, while whites were convicted in about half as many, 442 cases. Of those convicted, 13.4 percent of the blacks were sentenced to death, while 9 percent of the whites received the death sentence. This racial difference, Wolfgang claims, cannot be explained by taking into account circumstances of the offense (degree of force used; use of a weapon; amount of injury to victim; commission of trespass, robbery, or other offenses; offender's prior relation with victim) or the offender's prior record (unfortunately, Wolfgang fails to present the data supporting this conclusion).

> For most other offenses the following conclusions are typical: the data reflect the minimal contribution of rape and SES to criminal justice decision making (Wellford, 1975: 337). Review of the data from twenty studies of judicial sentencing indicates that, while there may be evidence of differential sentencing, knowledge of extra-legal offender characteristics contributes relatively little to our ability to predict judicial dispositions. Only in rare instances did knowledge of extra-legal attributes of the offender increase our accuracy in predicting judicial disposition by more than five percent. (Hagan, 1974: 379)

> Our evidence suggests that offense and prior record are the major determinants of the severity of disposition accorded in the [Denver and Memphis] juvenile courts. (L. E. Cohen and Kluegel, 1978: 174)

The studies reviewed so far do not take into account a major factor in bias, the status difference between the victim and the offender. For example,

> If caste values and attitudes mean anything at all, they mean that offenses by or against Negroes will be defined not so much in terms of their intrinsic seriousness as in terms of their importance in the eyes of the dominant group. Obviously the murder of a white person by a Negro and the murder of a Negro by a Negro are not at all the same kind of murder from the standpoint of the upper caste's scale of values, yet in crime statistics they are thrown together. (G. B. Johnson, 1941: 98)

This hypothesis is difficult to test because the relevant data are seldom gathered, the infrequency of cross-class/caste offenses demands large samples to detect any effect, and numerous plausible alternative explanations exist for the observed differences. Characteristics of victims and offenders are not routinely gathered, so such evidence as does exist has come from special investigations in isolated areas. Usually, the resources of the investigator do not permit gathering information on large numbers of cases. This is a problem because most serious crimes are committed by persons who share the economic and demographic traits of their victims. For example, a study of homicides in Cleveland between 1958 and 1974 found that

> the majority of victims are killed by male assailants of the same race (62 to 92 percent). Taking population changes into account, there has been no consistent change in this pattern over the 17 years covered by the study. (Rushforth et al., 1977: 535)

An additional difficulty is posed by Edward Green (1964) in his study of interracial crime in Philadelphia. Green found that longer sentences were received by black burglary and robbery defendants if their victims were white than if their victims were black. This empirical finding has routinely been cited as evidence that the Philadelphia courts were discriminating on the basis of race of the victim (e.g., Black, 1976: 24). However, Green cautions against this interpretation of his data. He points out that crimes differ in circumstances when the status of the victim differs. For example, combinations of black offenders and black victims typically involved crimes with lesser gravity, robberies disproportionately consisting of purse snatching and "rolling drunks." Interracial robberies, on the other hand, appeared more often to involve weapons. In addition to differences in seriousness of offense between the two categories, different types of offender engaged in the two categories of offense. Half of the black offender/black victim robberies involved offenders under 21 years of age, whereas only one-sixth of the black offender/white victim robberies involved youths. It is impossible, given the size of Green's sample, to control adequately for the effect of these complications on sentencing. The same difficulty is shared by more recent studies of interstatus crime.

Overall the evidence for racial discrimination in sentencing in interracial offenses is limited. Harold Garfinkel (1949) found more severe sentences imposed in North Carolina in (black offender, white victim) homicides. Farrell and Swigert (1978a) in a study of homicides "in a large urban jurisdiction in Northeastern

U.S." from 1955 to 1973 found no effect on sentencing of racial differences between victim and offender. LaFree (1980), however, does report such effects on sentencing for rape cases in "a large midwestern city."

The results of the systematic studies of bias in sentencing —both those that examine the direct effect of status on sentences and those that examine victim/offender dyads—generally suggest that Quinney's statement, cited earlier, that "obviously judicial decisions are not made uniformly" is anything but obvious. It is obvious that minorities are overrepresented in prisons and underrepresented in law enforcement occupations. It is readily apparent that prejudice against minorities is widely held among members of law enforcement organizations. It is, however, not apparent in any detectable fashion that decisions made in the legal system systematically discriminate against minorities. At the present time the research tends to favor the involvement hypothesis over the discrimination hypothesis.

From the standpoint of the theories we considered in Part One, however, this empirical literature on discrimination is not very informative sociologically. In essence, it takes a value standard (equal treatment by the criminal justice system) and seeks to assess whether or not the courts depart from the standard. It does not, by and large, treat discrimination as a variable to be explained by variation in social structure. If discrimination is found in some areas and not in others, this empiricist literature treats the findings as anomalies, "inconsistent findings that might well be the result of contextual and methodological peculiarities" (Thompson and Zingraff, 1981: 870).

While the relevant analyses have yet to be carried out, we can at least suggest here the outlines of an alternative approach. Wolfgang's (1974) and Garfinkel's (1949) studies showing clear patterns of racial discrimination in the South are in striking contrast to the equivocal results of studies conducted in other regions. Such regional variation may thus provide some clues about the structural basis of bias in sentencing. Recall that for Marx and Weber the hallmark of capitalist law is equality. Regional variation in discrimination may have something to do with the domination of the region's economy by the capitalist mode of production. While no systematic investigation of this hypothesis has been conducted, it should be recognized that the general theories of the sociology of law do provide alternatives to the empiricist preoccupation with the involvement versus discrimination dichotomy that has dominated the sentencing literature.

In addition to social structure determinants of variations in discrimination in sentencing, we might also consider as sociologically problematic the variable seriousness of offense (cf. Black, 1979). The empirical literature on discrimination in sentencing has generally considered seriousness of offense a variable to be held constant in order to determine whether characteristics of the offender affected the outcome of the sentencing decision. Durkheim's theory, however, suggests that seriousness of offense is not an intrinsic property of behavior, but rather a product of the community's need to engage in symbolic exclusion of outsiders. Why a particular form of behavior is considered more serious than another thus becomes in Durkheimian theory something to be explained rather than something taken as given. Again, systematic research on this problem has yet to be carried out. We can, however, illustrate the problem by considering the difference among nations or cultures in their reactions to similar forms of conduct. As we saw in Chapter 7, legal and public reaction in the United States to violation of laws governing business conduct has traditionally been quite mild. In the Soviet Union the reaction is quite the opposite. Since 1932, theft of property from collective farms has been punishable by death. In the 1960s the death penalty was extended to include other forms of offenses against state property. In addition, currency speculation, black market trading, embezzlement, and other forms of "white collar crime" in the Soviet Union receive severe punishments. In recent years a pattern of disproportion parallel to that for blacks in the United States has appeared in these executions for property crime in the Soviet Union. About 30 percent of those executed have been Jews, although Jews constitute only 1.5 percent of the population (Kline, 1965: 70). This suggests the need for examining how certain types of offenses come to be regarded as differentially serious and how the involvement of minority populations in certain types of offenses either creates or reinforces the social definition of those offenses as serious.

SUMMARY

The literature on bias in sentencing is a textbook example of a line of research that has proceeded without a clear explicit theoretical focus. The research has been guided, in large measure, by pragmatic legal considerations. In order to challenge the constitutionality of the death penalty, for example, it became necessary to discover systematic evidence of racial discrimination in sentencing in capital cases. Other studies have had the more diffuse objective of demonstrating the failure of the criminal justice system to realize its ostensible goals of equal treatment. These objectives have made the literature on sentencing disparity highly descriptive in orientation. The descriptiveness, moreover, has been localized on the single issue of the effect of individual status characteristics on legal outcomes.

The literature on bias in sentencing was subsequently adopted in a confused manner by many American Marxist criminologists (e.g., Chambliss, 1974; Jankovic, 1978), who entirely overlooked Marx's discussion of the emergence of legal equality as a consequence of and a condition for capitalism.

By returning to our discussion of Marx in Chapter 2 it should be possible to view the sentencing disparity problem in a new light. We have seen in reviewing the sentencing literature that regional differences appear to be marked. For the most part such regional differences have been ignored by empiricist researchers, who often take a single jurisdiction as a representative sample of the nation. Many studies do not even report the geographical location of the study (e.g., Chambliss, 1976). This practice is of the style of community studies conducted in the 1930s and 1940s, in which "Yankee City," "Middle Town," "Plain View," and the like were used as samples on which to base generalizations about the American stratification system. Pfautz and Duncan (1950) and others have demonstrated the fallacy involved in that approach. The lesson has still to be transferred to sentencing research.

Single-jurisdiction studies led to confusion when researchers began reporting different findings. Had an appropriate macro-level theory been guiding the research, investigators would have anticipated variations in sentencing patterns across jurisdictions. Marxian theory, for example, predicts racial bias in areas in which the mode of production requires directly coerced labor. The more the capitalist mode of production dominates the local economy, the less bias in sentencing should occur. Thus bias should be strongest in the South. Bias in sentencing should decrease in the South as precapitalist modes of labor control in agriculture give way to mechanization. It would be premature to argue that this hypothesis has more than superficial correspondence to reality; systematic research has yet to be conducted in this area. However, the hypothesis does exemplify how a coherent theoretical focus can be used to give direction to a line of research that would otherwise choose sites haphazardly, assume homogeneity in a society characterized by diversity, and find itself with a confused mass of uninterpretable conclusions.

SUGGESTED READING

Much of the literature in this area is empiricist in character, uneven in quality, and contradictory in outcome. This chapter suggests that the preponderance of evidence supports the Marx-Weber characterization of capitalist law as being characterized by formal equality. Useful reviews of the present literature will be found in Hagan (1974), Kleck (1981), and Thompson and Zingraff (1981). Basic measurement problems remain to be solved before a clear reading on discrimination can be made. The problematic character of legal variables is shown, for example, by Farrell and Swigert (1978b) and Emerson (1981). Assuming reliable estimates of the level of discrimination were available, a number of questions would still remain unanswered. First, the impact of formal equality on the preservation of inequality has not been demonstrated and is open to challenge (e.g., Trubek, 1977). Second, the literature has for the most part ignored discrimination as a *variable*, as something that depends upon such social structural variables as the mode of production. This is one area of investigation in which the insights of the founders of the field have yet to be taken seriously.

FOOTNOTES

1. As Jock Young points out,

   However dubious the positivist's acceptance of the criminal statistics at face value, the wholesale rejection of the statistics by the new deviancy theorist was equally cavalier. It would be a strange industrial sociologist, for example, who would reject the strike figures on the grounds that they were evidence only of labelling and social reaction—even though he would still be cautious in his interpretations of their significance at a particular time. (1975: 72)

2. Michael Hindus provides a good example of research that is alert to the potential of multiple indicators for estimating rates of behavior from official recordings of misconduct. In studying Puritan Massachusetts court records it is not clear whether changes in the convictions for fornication represent changes in the sexual behavior of the members of the colony. Hindus discovered, however, that "marriage and birth

records reveal the percentage of brides who were pregnant at marriage. Such premarital pregnancy ratios are indicative of changes in the relative levels of sexual offenses" (1980: 68) and thus provide a means of checking the reliability of fornication convictions as indicators of deviant sexuality. For other uses of the multiple indicator strategies see Austin (1976), Snyder and Kelley (1977), Hindelang (1978), Bridges (1978).

3. Some studies of racial discrimination by the police suggest that although white officers may be racially prejudiced, their decisions to arrest are not discriminatory and that racial inequalities in arrest rates arise from other sources (Skolnick, 1975: 83–6; Black and Riess, 1970). That there is a complex relationship between prejudiced attitudes and discriminatory behavior is well documented in the race relations literature. See, for example, the classic study by LaPiere (1934).

4. The measure of seriousness in this research is typically a category of the offense of conviction. These categories (for example, aggravated assault) are generally very broad and because of plea bargaining may only be remotely connected to the actual offense. The use of global categories of offense ignores the circumstances and situations of individual cases that may aggravate or mitigate the sentence. A homicide committed for a paltry amount of money taken from an unresisting victim is more serious than one committed by the cuckold who arrives home early to find his wife and best friend in bed. Similarly, if the death occurred in the course of a spate of armed robberies in which a dozen other victims were seriously wounded, the offense is more serious than an isolated incident. Further, if the defendant has a long history of prior offenses, the court legitimately imposes a harsher sentence.

The central issue in the research on discrimination is this: Do the poor and minorities receive differential treatment from the law on the average, or do the disparities arise because of differential involvement in serious crime by these groups?

10

Sociological Analysis of the Criminal Sanction

by James Inverarity
and Pat Lauderdale

Two features of the criminal sanction have drawn the attention of sociologists. The form of the criminal sanction and the frequency of its administration have been the subject of numerous investigations and speculations. The reason for this interest is not difficult to determine, since within the past 200 years major changes in both form and frequency of criminal sanctions have occurred in the United States and Western Europe. This chapter will elaborate on our earlier discussion of Durkheim's explanation of the relationship between sanctions and social structure as well as draw out some implications from the theories of Weber and Marx. We will focus upon three forms of the criminal sanction that have dominated Western systems of justice at various times over the past two centuries. Corporal punishment (most dramatically, execution), banishment, and fines (wergild) remained the dominant form of criminal sanction until the Industrial Revolution, when the modern penitentiary was invented. Within another hundred years, as capitalism matured into its corporate form, a variety of alternative sanctions to the penitentiary were introduced. We will outline some of the main sociological explanations of the covariation of execution, imprisonment, and probation with particular social structures.

EXECUTIONS

In the 1800s (the exact date varies among nation states) the character of legal execution underwent a dramatic change. Ritualized public executions of the sort described in Chapter 4 were part of the public life of advanced pre-industrial societies. The lynching in rural Georgia and the state execution in Paris shared the same emphasis on *supplice* (ceremonial or ritual pain) witnessed by a large public. The public dramas gave way to closed administrative procedures, in which the handful of official witnesses to the execution were forbidden by law from reporting the details of the event. The death penalty took on the character of a public health operation conducted by bureaucratic specialists. The change in the form of execution was part of a larger, profound change in the character of the criminal sanction as other forms of public corporal punishment (whipping, locking in stocks or pillories) and physical banishment simultaneously disappeared.

Not only has the death penalty undergone a transformation of its form; it has also undergone a decline in its use. Figure 10.1 illustrates the dramatic long-term decline in executions in the United States, a trend that began in the 1930s and by the 1970s

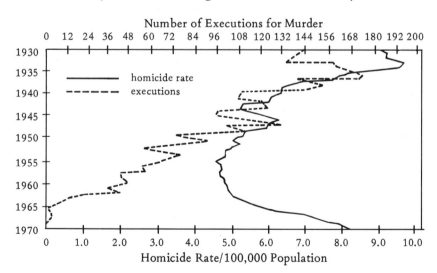

FIGURE 10.1
Trends in Executions and Homicides in the United States
1930–1970

ended in the virtual abolition of the death penalty in practice. A number of curious features make this decline in executions difficult to decipher. The decline does not reflect a corresponding reduction in serious crime; in fact, the decline in executions has been accompanied by a sharp increase in the rate of homicides. Even more puzzling is the contrast between the virtual abolition of the death penalty in practice and its continuance in law and public support. Throughout the 1970s state legislatures passed new death penalty statutes, and courts continued to condemn felons to death. Furthermore, public opinion polls suggest that sentiment for the death penalty may actually have increased since its virtual abolition. In 1960, 51 percent of the public favored and 36 percent of the public opposed capital punishment for murder, treason, rape, and skyjacking. By 1981, 66 percent of the public favored and 25 percent of the public opposed capital punishment for these offenses (Gallup, 1981).

To explain these changes in the form and incidence of execution, let us draw upon Durkheim's concept of repressive justice as a punishment in which the casting out of an offender from a community serves as a means of collective moral reaffirmation. Durkheim argues further that as the dominant form of solidarity changes, the form of penal sanction correspondingly changes. In his essay on "Two Laws of Penal Evolution" Durkheim suggests the following empirical generalization: "Punishments consisting in privation of freedom—and freedom alone—for lengths of time varying according to the gravity of the crime, tend more and more to become the normal type of punishment" (1978: 164). "One might be tempted," Durkheim argued, "to explain this process of moderation by the parallel moderation of mores" (1978: 171), that is, an increase in humanitarianism. Durkheim reasons, however, that if humanitarianism were the primary factor, capital crimes would elicit even greater condemnation, since "our sympathy must be less for the guilty party than for his victim" (1978: 171). This point is often made by contemporary proponents of the death penalty: It is all very well to be concerned with the life of the criminal, but what about the lives of the victims? The value emphasis on the sanctity of the individual, Durkheim suggests, cannot account for the abandonment of harsh sanctions.

Alternatively, the declining use of the death penalty might occur as a result of changes in ideas rather than changes in sentiments. Thus capital punishment may have become less frequent because of the diffusion of new, compelling arguments against its effectiveness as a deterrent or fairness in administration. Finn

Hornum (1967), however, has carefully analyzed two legislative debates over capital punishment, one that took place in 1791 and the other in 1956. As summarized in Table 10.1, the essential features of the debate over the death penalty have remained essentially the same over the 165-year period. It seems unlikely, given the consistency of the debate, that new intellectual creations have much to do with the decline in the use of the death penalty.

If neither humanitarian sentiment nor reasoned argument can account for variations in use of the death penalty, we might consider social structure rather than psychology as the effective source of

TABLE 10.1
Two Debates on Capital Punishment: France 1791 and England 1956

	Retentionists		Abolitionists	
Argument	1791	1956	1791	1956
1. The death penalty deters would-be criminals.	+	+	±	−
2. Society has a right to invoke the death penalty (implicit in social contract).	+	+	−	−
3. Alternative penalties would be more equitable, as effective.	−	−	+	+
4. The necessity of the death penalty is borne out by experience of other nations.	+	+	−	−
5. In violent times ("the present"), abolition is impractical.	+	+	o	o
6. The risk of error—execution of an innocent—outweighs any possible benefits of the death penalty.	o	−	+	+
7. Public opinion demands an end to the use of the death penalty.	o	o	+	+

+ = argument affirmed
− = argument disputed
± = inconsistency within group
o = argument not made

SOURCE: Summarized from Finn Hornum (1967). "Two debates: France, 1791; England, 1956." In Thorsten Sellin (ed.), *Capital Punishment*, pp. 55–76. New York: Harper & Row.

the change. Durkheim suggests one possible social structural explanation.

We may, Durkheim suggests, divide crimes into two classes, those directed against "collective things" and those that "offend only individuals." For example, a murder in New York City may only concern a limited number of persons involved, whereas a murder in a small town in upstate New York may represent a greater affront to the community. If the crime involves essentially relationships between individuals, "there is no longer the same distance between the offender and the offended; they are more nearly on an equal footing . . . the feelings of pity evoked in us by him who is struck by the punishment cannot be as easily nor as completely choked off by the sentiments which he violated and which react against him, for both are of the same nature. The first are only a variety of the second" (1978: 175). However, violations of community sentiment call forth ritual degradations of the offenders. The collective stands apart from the individual and demands periodic sacrifices of self.

> We have no inclination to fast, to humiliate ourselves, to forbid ourselves one or another meat, to sacrifice on the altar our favorite animals, to trouble ourselves out of respect for custom, and so forth. . . . such sentiments exist within us independent of ourselves and even, to some extent, despite ourselves. (Durkheim, 1978: 172–3)

The collective sentiments, then, create a wide distance between the offended community and the individual offender. This social distance makes possible the lack of humanitarian sentiments in ritual forms of punishment.

American law implicitly uses the distinction between collective and individual offenses as one dimension in defining criminal versus civil law. Crimes are those offenses in which the society undertakes prosecution on the initiative of state authorities, while civil suits are brought by individual plaintiffs. However, it is erroneous to assume because the law formally describes the difference between criminal and civil law in this fashion that in practice criminal law invariably deals with offenses against "collective things" whereas civil law deals in practice with offenses against individuals. Many civil suits involve collective interests (as, for example, class action suits). Moreover, criminal prosecution is highly dependent upon individual citizens' complaints to police, the complainant's willingness to testify, and his or her preference for outcome. The classification of an offense as having a collective or individual object is thus a complex empirical question, not a simple legal classification. For example, Martin Levin observes that

> twelve of the eighteen judges in Pittsburgh tended to view the behavior of the typical criminal court defendant as a manifestation of a dispute between two private parties rather than between an individual and "society" . . . in effect these judges acted as if they viewed the defendant's behavior less as a criminal act than as a civil act or tort. (1977: 125)

We ought therefore to resist the temptation of equating criminal prosecution with repressive justice. Repressive justice encompasses a limited range of homogeneous phenomena, in which exclusion of a deviant solidifies a community. To the extent that executions lack this characteristic, their occurrence cannot be explained by Durkheim's theory, which predicts their disappearance with the increasing predominance of organic solidarity.

We will next examine three historical instances of execution and see the extent to which these instances constitute episodes of repressive justice. The first, lynching in the American South in the 1890s, is a clear case of repressive justice involving a public ritual and collective affirmation of common values among Southern whites. As such, variations in lynchings can be explained by use of Durkheim's theory. The second historical instance of executions, in London in the 1700s, provides a case of public ritual but without the consensus displayed in southern lynchings. This case requires a different set of theoretical principles to arrive at a satisfactory explanation of variation. Finally, we will consider modern executions conducted out of the public view, explore more of the features of the deritualization of executions, and search for some clues to explain the gradual decline of capital punishment in the United States.

Lynching in the South

A lynching is "an illegal and summary execution at the hands of a mob, or a number of persons, who have in some degree the public opinion of the community behind them" (Cutler, 1905: 276). Such episodes clearly epitomize Durkheim's concept of repressive justice as ritual punishments "in which the whole society participates in rather large measure" (Durkheim, 1964: 76).

From 1889 to 1918, over 1400 lynchings took place in eight

southern states, outnumbering legal executions by about two to
one. Southern lynchings typically involved hundreds and occasionally thousands of participants engaged in open, public rituals. Although lynchings were illegal, prosecution of the participants was
rare. Law enforcement officials often gave their open approval or
spent the time directing traffic. Although photographs of the participants were frequently published in newspapers, coroner's in-
quests invariably returned a verdict of "death at the hands of parties
unknown." This local support was further reinforced by many
prominent Southerners, who viewed lynching as a necessary and
legitimate extension of the conventional legal system, which was
too often cumbersome and inefficient (e.g., Collins, 1918). In 1905,
Tom Watson of Georgia, a leader of the Populist party in the 1890s
and candidate for President in 1904, argued that "lynch law is a
good sign; it shows that a sense of justice yet lives among the
people" (Woodward, 1963: 432).

The peak of southern lynchings in the early 1890s coincided
with a boundary crisis in solidarity among southern whites. This
coincidence is explicable in terms of Durkheim's theory of ritual
punishment and solidarity in much the same manner as Erikson's
explanation of prosecutions in Puritan Massachusetts. After the
Civil War, southern whites had been united into "the Solid South."

> In the monolithic Democratic party the whites could thresh out their
> differences; but these differences would never become troublesome
> because no issue must be permitted to divide white solidarity. It was
> an admirable arrangement to head off any economic stirrings on the
> part of the masses. Indeed, it was understood that there was supposed
> to be no relationship between politics and economics. (Williams,
> 1961: 47)

This consensus on values, harmony of interests, and unity of
purpose among southern whites was generated and sustained by
two major external threats, the North and the Negro. After the
Civil War, Congress reconstituted the governments of the former
Confederate States. Through Constitutional amendment and national legislation the Negro became not only a citizen but an of-
ficeholder as well. Black legislators were a majority in South Carolina and a powerful influence on other southern states. Sixteen
black Congressmen were elected during this period. The sudden
elevation of the Negro, the incursion of northern adventurers, and
the occupation by federal troops galvanized southern whites around
the Democratic party. "The upshot [of Reconstruction] was a

suppression of class feelings . . . the like of which has probably not been seen in any other developed society of modern times" (Cash, 1941: 112).

As agricultural prices declined and credit became tighter in the 1870s and 1880s, lower-class southern whites began to join farmers throughout the country in forming such agrarian social and political movements as the Grange, the Farmer's Alliance, and the People's (Populist) Party. While most of these organizations sought to work within the framework of existing political parties, the Populists organized as a distinct political entity, which became "no less than a political and social earthquake" (Degler, 1974: 320).

The conflict between the two classes of whites was complicated by the guarantee of voting rights of blacks by the Fifteenth Amendment. After Reconstruction larger landowners supported those rights, since black males of voting age outnumbered poor whites in many areas. These landowners were able to use economic and physical coercion to deliver black votes in their districts. Lower-class whites, on the other hand, opposed the black franchise both for the threat it posed to their status and for the power it gave to the elites.

Populist leaders sought to overcome the racism of the lower-class whites and pragmatically sought to attract the black vote. Georgia's Tom Watson argued that "the accident of color can make no possible difference in the interest of the farmers, croppers, and laborers" (Woodward, 1951: 402). The Populists viewed the ideal of the Solid South as a form of false consciousness and saw that the true interest of lower-class whites was not in racial status but in economic position. As the Democratic *Tensas Gazette* editorialized, "We can no longer depend upon the solidarity of the white race" (Hair, 1969: 238).

While the Populists waged strong campaigns in the state and national elections, the Democrats controlled both the black vote and the election machinery in too many areas. The agrarian revolt died quietly after 1896. Many of the supporters of Populism withdrew from politics altogether or returned to the Democratic Party, which restored white solidarity in two ways. First, it adopted such Populist demands as inflationary monetary policy. Second, the Democrats adopted the policy of disfranchising and segregating the black population. In effect, this policy reestablished racial status rather than economic interest as the basis of political organization.

Hopes for reform and the political means employed in defiance of tradition and at great cost to emotional attachments to effect reform had likewise met with cruel disappointments and frustration. There had to be a scapegoat. And all along the line signals were going up to indicate that the Negro was an approved object of aggression. (Woodward, 1957: 64)

While de facto discrimination and disenfranchisement had been widespread previously, the systematic exclusion of blacks from social, political, and economic life followed the collapse of Populism in the latter part of the 1890s. As a result of this reaffirmation of white supremacy, the crisis precipitated by the Populist movement was resolved, and the Solid South was restored (Woodward, 1957).

This application of Durkheim's theory permits us to explain several features of lynching that are puzzling from the standpoint of alternative accounts of this phenomenon. Viewing lynching as simply one of several manifestations of white racism fails to explain why lynching increased during the intense conflict among southern whites in the early 1890s and failed to increase in the late 1890s when white racism became particularly intense and violent in other forms.[1] Durkheim's theory suggests that lynching as a collective ritual served to displace the crisis of white solidarity generated by the Populist revolt onto deviants in the local community. This interpretation also allows us to explain why lynching was infrequently practiced among South African whites, whose white supremacist ideology bears much in common with that of southern American whites; as Albie Sachs points out,

> despite the strong feelings of group identity which characterised their populations, lynching was very rarely resorted to by members of the dominant white communities. Superficially looked at, all the apparent ingredients of lynch-situations would seem to have been present: weak law enforcement agencies, a ruling group with a monopoly of power and a strong sense of racial solidarity, a frontier tradition of lawlessness and commando raids, and a mythology of smiting the forces of darkness. Private violence against African servants, including lethal thrashings, were not uncommon; nor were punitive raids by self-appointed commandos. What was almost nonexistent, however, was the banding together of groups of whites in small towns and villages to engage in frenzied attacks, involving violent and obscene rituals, upon defenceless Africans. Neither mob nor vigilante lynchings have been characteristic of the South African scene. (1973: 71)

The absence of a conflict similar to the Populist revolt among the whites of the South African republics would, according to Durkheim's thesis, reduce the likelihood of upsurges in the incidence of repressive justice.

While the case of lynching in the South illustrates how Durkheim's theory may be used to account for the exercise of repressive justice, the theory has equally important implications for the failure of ritual forms of punishment. In particular, the theory implies that as mechanical solidarity decreases in importance, the ritual forms of punishment will lose their symbolic power rather than increase solidarity within the community, serving instead to reinforce cleavages within it. The next two sections trace such a development in the evolution of capital punishment in Anglo-American justice.

Ritual Punishments in London in the 1700s

Hanging, whipping, and the pillory were three public rituals common to the period before the invention of the penitentiary in early nineteenth century England. The success of the ritual depended heavily upon the audience. In homogeneous mechanically solidary societies, such as Puritan Massachusetts of the 1600s or the white population of the rural South in the 1890s, the audience could be counted upon to join in collective condemnation of the deviant. London in the 1700s lacked that homogeneity. As class divisions grew sharper, many of the new capital crimes became little more than transparent devices to protect the property and haunts of the elite. Public sympathy often lay more with the prisoner than with the authorities.

In London the ritual of execution was highly elaborate. A three-mile procession moved through the most densely populated areas of the city from Newgate prison to the gallows at Tyburn. Thousands of spectators witnessed the procession and execution. Public execution was felt to serve two purposes. First, officials believed that a dramatic demonstration of the power of the state would have a deterrent effect on crime. Second, the public saw open executions as a guarantee that the wealthy would not buy their way out of punishment.

An optimal execution from the standpoint of officials was one in which the prisoner repented of his crime and admonished the audience to avoid the errors of his ways. On occasion, however, unrepentant prisoners used their death march to protest the injustice of their sentences and to undermine the legitimacy of the system.

All such ritual punishments depended for their effectiveness as a ceremonial of deterrence on the crowd's tacit support of the authorities' sentence. Hence, the magistrates' control of the ritual was limited. In theory, the processional to the gallows and the execution itself were supposed to be a carefully stage-managed theater of guilt in which the offender and the parson acted out a drama of exhortation, confession, and repentance before an awed and approving crowd. The parson's sermons were set pieces on social obligation, delivered at the gallows and subsequently hawked in the streets with an account of the offender's life and descent into crime.

The trouble was that if the spectators did not approve of the execution, the parson would find his worthy sentiments drowned in the abuse welling up from the crowd. Moreover, the crowd had a highly developed sense of the rights due the condemned, and if any of these rights were abridged, they were quick to vent their wrath on the authorities, especially if the condemned also happened to contest the justice of the execution itself. This double sense of outrage, at rights ignored and at offenders wrongfully sacrificed, drove the Tyburn crowd attending the execution of the silk weavers who cut looms during the Spitalfields agitation of 1769 to attack and destroy the sheriff's house after the execution. What irked them particularly, one of them told a gentleman bystander, was that the sheriff had not even had the decency to give the men time to say their prayers. This was a courtesy that the poor of London defined as one of the rights of the dying. (Ignatieff, 1978: 21–2)

The crowd occasionally rescued prisoners or attacked officials and often indulged in unconstrained revelry and riot. The crowd also saw to the efficiency of the execution, making sure that the prisoner's final privileges were granted and that the execution was properly conducted; a bungled hanging at times meant death to the executioner.

Executions in this case were public rituals, but they seldom provided a forum for ritual reaffirmation of collective values. The shared values were not there to begin with, and the chaotic nature of the executions did little to cement collective sentiments behind the law. In 1783, executions were moved behind the walls of Newgate prison in an effort to avoid the worst excesses of ritual.

Capital Punishment in the United States

Public execution ended in England in 1868 and in the United States in 1938. France permitted open executions until the 1930s, when the government became concerned with the sensationalism of press coverage. Removal of execution and punishment in general from the public view is an important, systematic change that is accompanied by a general reduction in the severity of punishment and a transformation of physical punishment into deprivation of time.

Capital punishment in modern society differs fundamentally from capital punishment in mechanically solidary societies. Trial and execution involve only a small segment of the population, and the general public is only remotely involved through mass media. The modern execution is essentially "a medical operation performed in an antiseptic environment by dispassionate experts" (Bowers, 1974: 29). The contrast between modern and preindustrial forms of execution is elaborated in Table 10.2. The roles and setting have thus completely altered as the execution has been deprived of its ceremonial function. The failure of modern capital punishment to have its former immediate public impact led Camus to recommend sardonically that

> executions be given the same promotional campaign ordinarily reserved for government loans or a brand new aperitif. Yet it is well known on the contrary that in France executions no longer take place in public—they are perpetrated in prison yards before an audience limited to specialists. (1957: 9)

Camus's statement captures the essential distinction between modern capital punishment and repressive justice. When punishment is limited to an audience of specialists and excludes the general public, it will not have the same impact as in a homogeneous society.

Thus the trends in execution, rather than reflecting the changing collective consciousness, are partly the work of "an audience of specialists." In particular, the NAACP Legal Defense and Education Fund and the American Civil Liberties Union have taken cases involving the death sentence in an attempt to obtain Supreme Court rulings that would ban legal executions. In organically solidary society, as law becomes relatively autonomous both of collective conscience and of individual interests, legal change becomes increasingly the concern of specialists whose activity may reflect only slightly societal configurations of interest or consensus (cf. Bedau, 1979; Berk et al., 1977). The changes that have led to the gradual decline in the use of the death penalty over the last eighty years may be related to the decline of other direct forms of state coercion. We will consider one such trend in the next section.

TABLE 10.2
Open and Concealed Dramaturgy of State Executions

	Open	*Concealed*
Death Wait	Long.	Short.
Death Confinement	Many, self-chosen visitors.	Few, regulated visitors.
	Diverse activities allowed.	Few activities allowed.
	Exhorted about death.	Left alone about death.
	Exposed to death preparations.	Insulated from death preparations.
Execution	Socially conspicuous day and hour.	Socially inconspicuous day and hour.
Death Trip	Long.	Short.
	Elaborate and specialized transport devices.	No transport devices.
	Large cortege.	Tiny cortege, if any.
	Dramatic events en route.	No events en route.
	Complicated, public route.	Simple, private route.
Death Place	Public, outdoors.	Private, indoors.
	Large, open, visible.	Small, enclosed, buffered.
	Multiple and dispersed locations.	Centralized location.
	Specialized decoration.	Neutral decoration.
Death Witnesses	Unlimited number.	Small, controlled number.
	Socially diverse.	Socially homogeneous.
	Perform personal and diverse activities.	Perform impersonal and restricted activities.
Executioner	Professional.	Part-time.
	Publicly known.	Publicly anonymous.
	Performance discretionary.	Performance drilled.
	Strong, colorful, deviant personal style.	Bland, conformist, quiet personal style.
	Personal contact with condemned.	Impersonal, limited contact with condemned.
Condemned	Self-chosen, diverse accouterments.	Narrowly restricted accouterments.
	Diverse acts and speech.	Narrow range of acts and speech.

TABLE 10.2 (continued)

Death Technique	Unreliable, long-acting, noisy, painful, scream-provoking, mutilating, struggle-inducing, odor-causing, highly visible.	Reliable, fast-acting, quiet, painless, non-scream-provoking, nonmutilating, non-struggle-inducing, odorless, concealed.
Corpse Disposal	Public display. Prolonged. Marked grave.	No display. Quick. Anonymous grave.
Death Announcement	Unrestricted media. Suspension of institutional activities and other symbols.	Restricted media. No suspension of institutional activities or other symbols.

SOURCE: John Lofland, "The Dramaturgy of State Executions," pp. 275–325 in Horace Bleackley and John Lofland, State Executions, Viewed Historically and Sociologically (Montclair, N.J.: Patterson Smith, 1977). Reprinted by permission.

CREATION OF THE PENITENTIARY

The elimination or reduction of traditional forms of repressive justice has been accompanied by the rise of new forms of criminal sanction. The modern prison is the form that has received the most attention by sociologists. We will outline here the major historical developments and introduce some of the lines of explanation that have been proposed following, primarily, Marx's base-superstructure model.

Before 1800, punishment of convicted criminals typically entailed fines (wergild), beatings, mutilation, or banishment rather than confinement. The punishment of confinement in the penitentiary originated in the invention of the "workhouse" in major Western European commercial centers in the sixteenth and seventeenth centuries. These institutions sought to rehabilitate vagrants and the unemployed by providing a disciplined work environment. Over a period of 200 years the workhouse evolved into a novel institutional solution to the "crime problem" that seemed to offer a rational and more humane way of responding to violations of the criminal law.

Prisons were designed to separate offenders from the community and to isolate them from each other in a structured and disciplined regime. One penal model (the Pennsylvania system) carried isolation from corruption to its logical conclusion, solitary confinement. Regardless of the details of the reform model used, however, the prisons relied on an unrelenting regime of hard work, discipline, and prompt obedience to inculcate virtue and respect for authority. Reformers also hoped to provide both a model of an orderly community and a useful form of control in a fluid society for which traditional modes of control were proving increasingly inadequate and unreasonable (Rothman, 1971: 84).

Why did this idea emerge when and where it did? The invention of the penitentiary is often viewed as a reform inspired by the eighteenth century philosophers who stressed the role of reason in examining human institutions. The use of ceremonial public torture of convicted criminals, the imposition of death for relatively minor property offenses, and other "irrational" features of the criminal justice system were rigorously attacked by enlightened intellects during the 1700s. Cesare Beccaria in 1764, for example, published a very influential essay "On Crimes and Punishments," in which he concluded that

> in order for punishment not to be, in every instance, an act of violence of one or many against a private citizen, it must be essentially public, prompt, necessary, the least possible in given circumstances, proportionate to the crime, dictated by laws. (Beccaria, 1963: 99)

Punishment thus should be administered rationally, Beccaria argued, to deter criminal conduct. Celerity (swiftness) and certainty of punishment are consequently the most crucial factors; severity of punishment might also have a deterrent effect, but in itself severity was not effective or efficient. For Beccaria and the other eighteenth century writers in "The Age of Reason," society should not respond to crime in an impulsive manner, blindly striking out to avenge a wrong committed by the criminal. Instead, society should weigh the costs of assault, burglary, rape, and homicide against the costs of arresting, convicting, and punishing offenders. Crime and punishment should be weighed by the state in the same way that demand and supply are related in the marketplace. Punishment proportional to the crime should be administered only when the actor has exercised free choice in committing the crime and thus had a reasonable chance to assess the costs and benefits of his or her action. The practical consequence of such arguments was to reduce the use of corporal punishment and the death penalty in Western legal systems. According to this idealist account, then, the novel and persuasive ideas of reformers led to the innovative use of imprisonment as a more humane and rational form of punishment.

Rusche and Kirchheimer's Labor Supply Explanation

Two German Marxist sociologists writing in the 1930s, Georg Rusche and Otto Kirchheimer, offer an alternative account of the invention of the penitentiary. Following Marx's orientation they reject the notion that ideas of reform are spontaneously generated in an intellectual climate. Instead, they argue, the legal superstructure responds to the labor needs of the economy. Thus when labor is scarce, punishments are mild; labor surplus, on the other hand, generally produces harsh penal sanctions. For example,

> until the fifteenth century the death penalty and serious mutilation were only used in extreme cases to supplement the complicated and carefully differentiated system of fines. . . . The whole system of punishment in the later Middle Ages makes it quite clear that there was no shortage of labor, at least in the towns. As the price of labor decreased, the value set on human life became smaller and smaller. (Rusche and Kirchheimer, 1968: 19, 29)

The penitentiary, Rusche and Kirchheimer argue, arose during a period of labor scarcity. Initially, the earliest prisons were used to harness labor power. The link between labor needs and rate of imprisonment is clear, for example, in the case of the galley sentence. Countries with Mediterranean fleets, for example, were unable during periods of labor scarcity to recruit oarsmen for their galleys. Throughout the sixteenth and seventeenth centuries, criminal sentences in these countries were routinely commuted to galley services. Monarchs communicated their fluctuating labor needs for oarsmen directly to the courts, which passed sentences accordingly. A more direct forebear of the modern penitentiary was the workhouse. Again the primary basis of confinement was labor shortage. Rather than damage or destroy the labor power of criminals, the workhouse was designed to instill labor discipline, to transform the inmate into a productive worker. The workhouse proved to be a profit-making enterprise, effectively exploiting the coordinated labor power of inmates in manufacturing.

Rusche and Kirchheimer thus trace the origin of imprisonment to a period that uniquely combined a labor shortage with special demands for large-scale organization of labor. They were, however, unable to give a satisfactory account of the persistence of the penitentiary when labor surpluses reappeared.

> Though [the return to late medieval methods of punishment] was demanded loud enough, it did not materialize because hard-earned humanitarian ideals hindered it and political wisdom kept the ruling class from overstraining an already revolutionary situation with such open provocation. (Rusche, 1980: 14)

While this explanation may be historically valid, it is sociologically a disaster. Rusche has interjected an ad hoc idealist explanation of the persistence of the prison through periods of labor scarcity without modifying the original theory.

Ivan Jankovic has amended the Rusche-Kirchheimer thesis so that *severity* of sanction includes not only the form of sanction, but the extent of its use. He proposes the following two hypotheses:

1. Economic conditions and severity of punishment are negatively related. "When the economy is bad, the punishments are more severe (holding crime rates constant). Unemployment is taken as an index of the state of the economy, and imprisonment as an index of severity of punishment" (Jankovic, 1977: 19).
2. Imprisonment reduces unemployment (Jankovic, 1977: 23).

He then tests these two hypotheses by examining aggregate data for the United States from 1926 to 1974 on prison population, unemployment, and arrests. Jankovic could find no support for the second proposition. This is not too surprising since the prison population constitutes less than one-half of one percent of the civilian labor force. (A better argument for a safety valve function can be made for the armed forces and higher education, although even these combined constitute only about 8 percent of the potential civilian labor force.)

The first hypothesis, however, is consistent with the data. On the average, unemployment rates in one year are positively associated with imprisonment rates in the following year. Greenberg observes that

> during the mid to late 1960s, a period of economic expansion, crime rates and arrest rates rose. Since increased crime rates were the sub-

ject of extensive public discussion and figured in national political campaigns it is likely that judges were aware of this increase. Yet admissions to prison declined during this period. With the recession of the early 1970s, crime rates continued to rise, but no more rapidly than before, and prison commitments increased dramatically. (D. Greenberg, 1977b: 650)

There is, then, some evidence that imprisonment varies with unemployment levels apart from the crime rate, which itself may be influenced by the unemployment rate.[2]

While rates of unemployment and rates of imprisonment are empirically related in recent American history, it is by no means clear that this correlation supports the labor supply thesis. The relationship is probably much more indirect today. As Greenberg suggests, high rates of unemployment probably discourage judges from granting probation to convicted felons, since the opportunities for legitimate employment are reduced. Imprisonment may have been used self-consciously by elites as a means of labor control in earlier periods, but nothing in the modern criminal justice system corresponds to the direct orders of King Louis XIV to the French courts demanding an increase in galley sentences to maintain the manpower needs of the French navy. The relationship between prison sentences and labor market requirements is far more subtle and complex, involving welfare programs, unemployment compensation, and other manpower management strategies (cf. Pivan and Cloward, 1971). Thus the Rusche and Kirchheimer thesis is best viewed as raising interesting questions about imprisonment and the labor market, rather than as providing a coherent and integrated explanation of this relationship among the diverse forms of capitalist modes of production.

Pashukanis's Commodity Form Explanation

Rusche and Kirchheimer's labor supply thesis is but one explanation of imprisonment derivable from Marx's base-superstructure model. A number of Marxists have gone beyond the relatively narrow variables of labor market demand and supply to consider the implications of other aspects of the capitalist mode of production for forms of punishment.

The Russian legal scholar Evgeny Pashukanis, for instance, developed some of Marx's ideas tracing the link between the form of economic exchange and the form of law, which we reviewed in

Chapter 2. Pashukanis argued that all law is specific to particular modes of production. The basic precondition that gives legal norms their meaning is the existence of a particular commodity and money economy. In developing his thesis Pashukanis gives us an interesting explanation of the coincidental emergence of the penitentiary and the capitalist market economy.

> Its most characteristic feature is the arithmetical expression of the severity of the sentence: so and so many days, weeks and so forth, deprivation of freedom and so and so high a fine, loss of these or those rights. Deprivation of freedom for a definite period stipulated in the court sentence, is the specific form in which modern, that is to say bourgeois-capitalist, criminal law embodies the principle of equivalent recompense. This form is unconsciously yet deeply linked with the conception of man in the abstract and abstract human labor measurable in time. It is not coincidence that this form of punishment became established precisely in the nineteenth century and was considered natural (at a time, that is, when the bourgeoisie was able to consolidate and develop to the full all its particular features . . .). For the idea to emerge that one could make recompense for an offense with a piece of abstract freedom determined in advance, it was necessary for all concrete forms of social wealth to be reduced to the most abstract and simple form, to human labor measured in time. Here we undoubtedly have a further example of the dialectical connection between various aspects of culture. Industrial capitalism, the declaration of human rights, the political economy [labor theory of value] of Ricardo, and the system of terms of imprisonment for a stipulated term are phenomena peculiar to one and the same historical epoch. (Pashukanis, 1978: 180–1)

Pashukanis thus sees a logical connection between the emphasis given to duration of confinement in capitalist penal sanctions and the emphasis given to duration of labor as a measure of value in capitalist economic production. Just as production has become increasingly rationalized, so has the distribution of penal sanctions. Perhaps the clearest example of the orientation Pashukanis describes as "bourgeois-capitalist" is to be seen in the sentencing guidelines passed by several state legislatures in the United States. While these guidelines seek to reduce the degree of arbitrariness and inequality that arise from Khadi decisions made under indeterminate sentencing statutes, they exemplify the underlying exchange of equivalents, the marks of the capitalist system of justice. Table 10.3 reproduces a draft of the sentencing guidelines for the state of Minnesota adopted in 1980. Under this law the judge is

TABLE 10.3

Outline of the Guidelines for Sentencing Felons in Minnesota, 1980

(Presumptive Sentence Lengths in Months)

Conviction Offense	Severity Levels	Criminal History Score						
		0	1	2	3	4	5	6 or more
Unauthorized Use of Motor Vehicle; Possession of Marijuana	I	12	12	12	15	18	21	24
Theft-Related Crimes ($150–$2500); Sale of Marijuana	II	12	12	14	17	20	23	27 25–29
Theft Crimes ($150–$2500)	III	12	13	16	19	22 21–23	27 25–29	32 30–34
Burglary—Felony Intent; Receiving Stolen Goods ($150–$2500)	IV	12	15	18	21	25 24–26	32 30–34	41 37–45
Simple Robbery	V	18	23	27	30 29–31	38 36–40	46 43–49	54 50–58
Assault, Second Degree	VI	21	26	30	34 33–35	44 42–46	54 50–58	65 60–70
Aggravated Robbery	VII	24 23–25	32 30–34	41 38–44	49 45–53	65 60–70	81 75–87	97 90–104
Assault, First Degree; Criminal Sexual Conduct, First Degree	VIII	43 41–45	54 50–58	65 60–70	76 71–81	95 89–101	113 106–120	132 124–140
Murder, Second Degree	IX	97 94–100	119 116–122	127 124–130	149 143–155	176 168–184	205 195–215	230 218–242
Murder, Third Degree	X	116 111–121	140 133–147	162 153–171	203 192–214	243 231–255	284 270–298	324 309–339

303

guided by a schedule that takes into account the severity of the offense and the prior record in a metric fashion. Severity of offense is rank ordered. Criminal History Scores are a composite of prior convictions and current parole/probation status. Above the diagonal, the judge is encouraged to place the offender on probation. The numbers then refer to the months in prison to be spent upon violation of probation. Thus a first offender convicted of simple robbery will be placed on probation, but will serve eighteen months in prison if the terms of probation are violated. Below the diagonal the guidelines recommend a range of months in prison. This matrix represents an effort to establish clear standards of equivalent recompense. Such guidelines still require the judge to exercise case-by-case discretion concerning aggravating and mitigating circumstances of each offense, but nothing in principle prevents the further elaboration of scales comparable to those developed so far to measure seriousness and prior record.

By providing a form of punishment that was uniform, continuous, and metric the penitentiary reflected changes that were occurring simultaneously in work relations. The Industrial Revolution transformed the way in which time was allocated to work. In the preindustrial crafts

> the work pattern was one of alternate bouts of intense labor and idleness, wherever men were in control of their working lives. (The pattern persists among some self-employed—artists, writers, small farmers, and perhaps also with students—today, and provokes the question whether it is not a "natural" human work rhythm. . . . There are few trades not described in the eighteenth century as honoring Saint Monday: shoemakers, tailors, colliers, printing workers, hosiery workers, cutlers, all Cockneys. (Thompson, 1967: 73)

Industrial manufacturing with its detailed division of labor and necessity of carefully coordinated work put an end to the casual attitude toward time. Clock towers had appeared in the towns of Western Europe in the fourteenth century, but they tended to be inaccurate and played little role in coordinating the economic life of the community. The invention of the pendulum in 1658 and the pocket watch twenty years later made possible the careful, coordinated calibration of the day into hours and minutes.

> A general diffusion of clocks and watches is occurring (as one would expect) at the exact moment when the industrial revolution demanded greater synchronization of labor. (Thompson, 1967: 69)

Following Marx's base-superstructure model, then, it is possible to account for the spread of the penitentiary idea as a consequence of the corresponding change in the way in which time was becoming the measure of value in the economic calculations of the capitalist mode of production.

As was true of the Rusche-Kirchheimer explanation of the origins of imprisonment, the Pashukanis explanation yields some predictions about current variations in the rate of imprisonment. Rather wide variations in the use of imprisonment can be found among geographical areas, and these variations pose challenging problems of interpretation. Thus prisons in the United States (federal and state) held in 1978 some 306,602 inmates, or 150 per 100,000 population. This represents one of the highest rates of imprisonment in the world. Most other industrialized nations have half the United States' rate, and several (for example, Sweden and Denmark) have about one-tenth of the imprisonment rate of the United States. Within the United States, rates of imprisonment vary substantially from a high (in South Carolina) of 243 inmates per 100,000 population to a low (in North Dakota) of 21 per 100,000 population.[3]

Unfortunately, little analysis of such variations has so far been conducted from a Marxist theoretical perspective. In large measure this is due to the failure of Marxists to recognize regional variation in dominant modes of production. The tendency has been for Marxists to use national averages to discuss the penal institutions of "monopoly capitalism" (see, for example, Spitzer, 1975b; Quinney, 1977). Therefore we can in this chapter only suggest in a broad way the applicability of Pashukanis's thesis to an explanation of variations in the use of imprisonment.

The graph in Figure 10.2 indicates one such pattern of variation in imprisonment to be explained. Imprisonment rates in the South have remained high for fifty years, while the rate of imprisonment has fallen in the North. While part of this difference is due to the higher rate of violent crime in the South, Pashukanis's account suggests that such regional variations in imprisonment may be explained by corresponding differences in dominant mode of production. We have seen in Chapter 2 that in the 1800s southern agriculture, with its high reliance on unskilled labor, provided the economic base of segregationist law. In the same fashion it is possible that a similar economic basis is responsible for the disproportionate use of imprisonment in that region. For example, since corporate capitalism has failed to dominate the economy of the

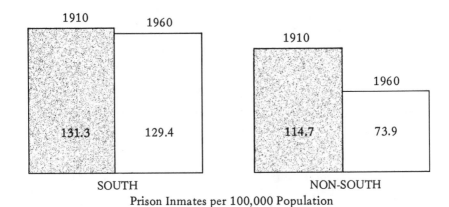

SOUTH   NON-SOUTH
Prison Inmates per 100,000 Population

FIGURE 10.2
Number of Prison Inmates (1910, 1960) Per 100,000
Population by Region

SOURCES: Computed from data in U.S. Bureau of the Census
(1918: 65; 1960: 22–36; 1978: 198)

South, the transformation of the legal system from predominant
reliance on imprisonment to reliance on probation will not have
taken place in the same fashion that it did in the rest of the country
during the Progressive Era. It is possible at this point only to suggest
this account as a researchable hypothesis.[4] Further investigation
will be required to determine the nature of the relationship between
dominant forms of economy and the use of imprisonment and to
examine the various implications of the Pashukanis thesis for variations over time in the use of imprisonment in the South (for
example, there should be a lower rate in the coal and iron regions
of Alabama, where monopoly capitalism has long played a dominant
role in the economy).

While neither the Rusche-Kirchheimer nor the Pashukanis
variants of Marxian analysis have been fully investigated or confirmed by systematic studies at the present time, they are worthy
of serious consideration. They illustrate how sociological theory
may be applied to account not only for the origins of forms of
sanctions, but for their variations across time and among regions
as well. Once such accounts have been refined and tested, our
understanding of imprisonment will go beyond the current level
of descriptive accounts of its curious beginning and unequal
distribution.

DIFFUSION OF PROBATION

While imprisonment entails incarceration in a penal institution such as a jail or prison, probation is a sanction that involves the threat of incarceration. Probation diverts the convicted offender from incarceration. The individual convicted of a crime is allowed to remain at liberty subject to conditions set down by the court. Probation usually is a substitute for incarceration after an offender has been found guilty; under this plan the offender's sentence is suspended as long as the court does not find him or her in violation of the conditions of probation.

Probation decisions are usually made on the basis of presentencing reports concerning the offender's personality and background. Candidates for probation are people whose job, family, skills, and other traits are more likely to lead to rehabilitation and whose records lack violent or multiple offenses. This information collected by probation or court services departments is in principle to be used to tailor the conditions of probation for the individual. "Rehabilitative" contingencies are often attached; the offender may have to take special training, join a treatment program, get a job, or go back to school. These conditions may be monitored more or less closely by a probation officer. To maintain probation, the offender must abide by the conditions and keep a clean record. Violations are grounds for summary imposition of the regular sentence.

The term probation has its roots in the Latin meaning of "a period of proving or trial," and as early as the thirteenth century the church used the concept to protect clergy when they were accused of criminal activity (Dressler, 1969: 17). The origins of the present institution is the work of two moral entrepreneurs in the early 1840s.

> The coincidence need not surprise us. An innovation occurs when the time is right. Then it sometimes springs to life in different places simultaneously, because the requisite groundwork has been done. As Darwin was crystallizing his theories, scientists on the Continent were arriving at similar insights on the origin of the species. The juvenile court became the reality in two states at almost the same time. Medical social work came into use in two hospitals, both in Boston, in the same year, the innovator in one institution being unaware of the development of the other.
>
> The social climate was right for the birth of probation in the nineteenth century. Thoughtful observers had become convinced that prisons were not "teaching a lesson," penitentiaries not making inmates penitent. . . . (Dressler, 1969: 21)

In England, Matthew Hill initiated experiments in which primarily young offenders were put under the supervision of guardians. In the United States, John Augustus, a Boston shoemaker, began a one-man social work experiment by bailing out juvenile and petty offenders from the city jails and providing some of them with temporary lodging. Between 1841 and 1858, Augustus handled over 2000 cases. Despite his success, court officials remained hostile to this maverick and his ideas (Hindus, 1980: 208–9). Not until 1878 did Massachusetts adopt probation. By 1900 only five other states had followed suit. During the Progressive Era, however, probation became institutionalized. The initial Progressive thrust (1900–1915) was to mold the probation officer into the role of friend. The officer was the volunteer visitor, typically a middle-class person entering the homes of the disadvantaged on behalf of private charities. The disadvantaged in the cities included an alien collection of people, for example, immigrants from outside the United States and those migrating from the rural areas within the country. It was believed that "continued intercourse must be kept up between those who have a high standard and those who have not, that the educated and happy and good are to give some of their time as a duty, year in and year out, to the ignorant, the miserable, and the vicious" (Rothman, 1980: 64). Probation officers were expected to study their "friend's" temperament, abilities, and special needs. They were told to "inspire laudable and practical ambitions, and suggest practical ways of bettering their surroundings and manner of life" (Rothman, 1980: 65).

By 1915, 33 states had probation provisions (Rothman, 1980: 44). This rapid diffusion of probation was accelerated by the juvenile court movement, since probation gave the judge

> an attractive middle course between incarceration and release, and would, at least in theory, provide the leverage to make possible a wide variety of different dispositions to match the variety of juveniles and their problems. (Schultz, 1973: 247)

In addition, the probation movement was aided by the growth of social work and state and federal agencies that controlled the specialization and professionalization of persons concerned with criminal offenders. The emergence of "scientific" casework went hand in hand with the professional supervision of offenders. Casework became "rooted in a psychiatric explanation of human behavior" and "was a key, presumably, to a knowledge base and helping technique more 'scientific' and hence more professional than 'social diagnosis or social reform'" (Lubove, 1965: 220). Probation officers changed from voluntary members of the community to paid professionals. Efficiency became a standard of control without specific reference to the common exhortations to virtue and duty. The professional groups of social workers and probation officers began to view reform along the lines of efficient management, control, and regulation (Haber, 1964: 54). Professional organizations of social workers and probation officers with bureaucratic administrations offered to meet these new problems with their supposedly more efficient procedures and specialized skills (cf. Lubove, 1965).

The appearance of probation in the Progressive Era is probably not accidental, since progressivism marked a general shift in industrial management strategies in the direction of further rationalization (cf. Weber, 1978). Frederick W. Taylor's school of Scientific Management, for example, sought to eliminate production workers' inefficient movements and restriction of output. Simultaneously, a strategy for rationally treating social problems began to emerge. Taylorism

> carried the ethics of professionalism—so appealing to the middle-class—into the heartland of commercialism. It opened the possibility of bringing the college-bred into important positions. It entailed a trend away from old-fashioned reform that relied upon appeal to conscience. It influenced a trend toward a newer style of reform—looking to social control and manipulation. Social control had found corroboration in scientific management. Taylorism crystallized the sentiment for social control into a concept of planning. (Haber, 1964: 167)

Thus scientific management forwarded the idea that social control should be a program of planning with the professional expert near the top. Science was presented as having risen above class interests, and probation officers were seen as part of the scientific management of social problems.

In addition to the diffusion of scientific management strategies from the workplace to the criminal justice system, an additional source of the increased use of probation derives from the character of corporate capital. Competitive capitalism had supported the conception of free-willed independent actors responsible for their actions and for the consequences of their actions. This conception of autonomous actors served the function of maintaining a free market in labor power, which was necessary for rapidly changing flows of capital. We see this philosophy plainly manifested in the tort law of the early industrial revolution. This period brought about a

> change from emphasis on liability for harmful acts regardless of fault to liability for fault only, a change which reflects the philosophy of free will, symbol of the self-reliant individual who makes and un-makes his legal engagements freely and who bears responsibility for his behavior in society because he has a choice between good and evil. (Friedmann, 1972: 163)

Corporate capital, however, supports an entirely different philosophy which appears in tort law as an emphasis on "the responsibility of the community for accidents that befall the individual" (Friedmann, 1972: 163). For example, corporate capitalism tended to foster workman's compensation laws, which provided a schedule of compensation for injuries at the workplace in lieu of court suits in which fault had to be proven. In a similar fashion, corporate capitalism fostered a "liberal" view of the "crime problem," which viewed the community as the breeding ground of crime. Rather than seeking out culpable individuals, this liberal orientation seeks through "scientific" analysis to attack the "root causes" of the crime problem (cf. Matza, 1969). Such analyses would provide the base of knowledge for supervision by professional probation officers.

In the 1920s and 1930s the probation officer became increasingly professional. The social psychological approach of this movement helped maintain "the confidence in the soundness of the American system: if mental conflict was the problem of crime, then social conflict was not" (Rothman, 1980: 56). The probation officer as "social worker" was to observe the causes and effect of human conduct and record the manner in which the probationer responded to methods of treatment (Rothman, 1980: 67). Probationers received a complete battery of psychological tests as well as psychological counseling. Social work moved from being an essentially religious avocation to being a state-financed profession employing the techniques of psychoanalysis and the other social sciences (including behaviorism, reality therapy, and group dynamics) (Dressler, 1969: 225–33).

By expanding the scope of state action and supervision, probation satisfied the demand for crime control. Since one criterion for gaining a probationary sentence was a guilty plea to a lesser offense,

> in view of the burgeoning number of criminal cases, plea bargaining arrangements were not merely convenient, but necessary. Probation clearly facilitated the process, and thus seemed made to order for an overburdened system. (Rothman, 1980: 101)

Similarly, the definition of appropriate court information was enlarged, as were relevant probation conditions and the investigative power of the probation officer.

> In the end, all of the arguments in favor of probation made good sense to reformers because of their underlying progressive belief in a harmony of interests within American society. An effort to do good for the offender and simultaneously to protect the social order, to serve the individual and the community, would ultimately succeed, or at least, could not produce harmful results. How much better for the offender not to be the object of vengeance, but benevolence; how much better for the society to rehabilitate criminals than to punish them. Unable to imagine that the effort to do good might subject the offender to arbitrary or excessive state action, or conversely, that an open-ended criminal justice system might not be protective of a society's safety, reformers saw no reason to lessen their support of probation. (Rothman, 1980: 115)

The role of probation has expanded greatly. In 1976 of the 710,547 convicted felons under state supervision, some 64 percent were on probation. "In some jurisdictions only 20 percent of those convicted on felony charges are sentenced to a period of incarceration" (J. Hylton, quoted in Kaplan and Skolnick, 1982: 527). The increased reliance on probation is not only consistent with the liberal orientation of corporate capitalism, but it has been justified as well by fiscal considerations. By the late 1970s the annual cost of maintaining an inmate under maximum security was in the range of $30–$80,000 (Sherman and Hawkins, 1981: 2). The rising costs of incarceration combined with the fiscal crises of the state, have produced a strong financial undertow to the demands to "get tough on criminals" by increasing the risk of incarceration (cf. Scull, 1977). The scientific management approach to crime control and the cost-benefit calculations that enter into correctional decisions set the legal system of corporate capital apart from that era in the not too distant past in which the criminal sanction played a major ritual role in society.

SUMMARY

This chapter has sketched several of the major features and trends in the imposition of the three major forms of criminal sanction in the American legal system: imprisonment, probation, and executions. The theoretical issues in Part One have been shown to illuminate several features of both the origins of these sanctions and the variations in their applications. Of particular significance for any attempt to reach a general understanding of the relationship between social structure and punishment is the recognition of the recency of the invention of both the penitentiary and probation. We have suggested how the emergence of these legal institutions can be understood in terms of the emergence of novel forms of economic organization and labor control. The same ideas may be applied, as we have seen, to understanding regional and time series variations in the deployment of sanctions. It should be recognized, however, that this area remains an underdeveloped region for research and that the conclusions we have drawn above must at present be taken as suggestive.

In considering these changes in form and trend we need to beware of overly simplified assessments. Much of the discussion about criminal sanction is normative in character and concerns at its base political questions concerning the ultimate relationship between the state and the individual. For these concerns, the empirical work we have reviewed has mixed implications. While the direct forms of state coercion have tended to disappear with the advent of capitalism, more subtle, and in many ways stronger, webs of power have taken their place. In 1767 Joseph Servan summed up the situation in the following terms:

> When you have thus formed the chain of ideas in the heads of your citizens, you will then be able to pride yourselves on guiding them and being their masters. A stupid despot may constrain his slaves with iron chains; but a true politician binds them even more strongly by the chain of their own ideas; it is at the stable point of reason that he secures the end of the chain; this link is all the stronger in that we do not know of what it is made and we believe it to be our own work; despair and time eat away the bonds of iron and steel,

but they are powerless against the habitual union of ideas, they can only tighten it still more; and on the soft fibres of the brain is founded the unshakable base of the soundest of Empires. (quoted in Foucault, 1979: 102–3)

SUGGESTED READING

Foucault (1979) provides a provocative interpretation of the changes in the mode of social control in Western society over the past two centuries; his account, however, is complex and idiosyncratic. Most studies of criminal sanction are far less ambitious. Scull (1977) gives a succinct history of incarceration and an interesting interpretation of its trends. On the origins of the penitentiary and related institutions in the United States, Rothman (1971) remains one of the best accounts. Ignatieff's (1978) survey of the recent historical literature dealing with the origin of imprisonment is useful, as are Melossi and Pavarini (1981) and the collection of articles by Platt and Takagi (1980). On capital punishment, Bowers (1974) gives a comprehensive review of the empirical literature and a useful bibliography. On the penal reforms of the Progressive Era, Hagan's (1979) discussion of probation is useful, while Rothman (1980) provides a detailed description of the rationalization of the criminal sanction. Cavander (1982) explores recent developments in probation. Waller and Chan (1974) provide a good introductory survey of comparative data on imprisonment.

FOOTNOTES

1. During this period, C. Vann Woodward notes,

   lynch law still took a savage toll of Negro life, though the number of lynchings in the country declined markedly from the peak reached in the [early] nineties, a tendency happily not in conformity with the deterioration in race relations already noted. (1951: 351)

2. Blumstein and Cohen (1973) offer an alternative explanation of trends in imprisonment. Their analysis reveals that from 1930 to 1970 the rate of imprisonment has been constant in the United States at 110 prisoners per 100,000, with annual variations accountable as random variations about this mean. They suggest that this long-term constancy indicates that when large numbers of people begin to violate the law, the central tendency of the legal system is not to increase the overall size of social control facilities to deal with the new wave of deviance, but to decriminalize some forms of behavior or to shorten sentences. In some instances the decriminalization will involve displacement by

one form of deviance. Erikson discovered this pattern in examining conviction statistics of the Puritan Massachusetts court during the Quaker crisis. While convictions of Quakers rose sharply, the convictions of other offenses fell, making room, as it were, for the new, threatening deviants to be processed by the courts. In Balbus's study the legal system faced with an overwhelming number of criminal cases chose to reduce the level of prosecution. The recent decline in marijuana prosecutions reveals a similar tendency to reduce law enforcement in the face of massive violation. At the present time there is no clear resolution of the two interpretations (see, for example, D. Greenberg, 1977b). Further aspects of Blumstein and Cohen's constancy argument were considered in Chapter 8.

3. Part of these variations, of course, reflects differences among states in crime rates. Variation persists, however, after controlling for this factor. A simple way to see this is to compare the risk of imprisonment for the same offense among states. For instance, the risk of imprisonment (that is, the number of prison inmates/reported crimes) for assault is .03 in South Carolina, .12 in North Dakota, .25 in Indiana, and .64 in North Carolina in 1960. Another clue to the dependence of imprisonment rates on factors other than the crime rate is the failure of the two to covary over time.

4. Only recently have regional variations become a focus of concern for Marxist analysis (e.g., Hechter and Brustein, 1980). Meanwhile empirical studies of regional variations in the United States have been conducted primarily by persons interested in "subcultures" (e.g., Gastil, 1975). The task for future research clearly is to explore regional variations in dominant modes of production within the United States to see whether the considerable variations in penal policy can be explained in terms of their corresponding social structure.

Although some writers have attempted to perceive meaningful short-term trends (e.g., Scull, 1977), Blumstein, Cohen, and Nagin (1976) suggest that the constant rate of imprisonment (which they also find for Canada and Norway) is consistent with Durkheim's model of repressive justice: random "crime waves" that are balanced out in the long run by a constant propensity of the societies to imprison offenders. While the data are consistent with this rendition of Durkheim, recall that repressive justice is related to solidarity only under circumstances in which mechanical solidarity is dominant. It therefore seems more likely that the long-term constancy is a product of factors other than the restoration of mechanical solidarity by episodes of repressive justice.

11

Conclusion

This chapter returns to the general perspective on the sociology of law outlined in the first section of the book. Drawing on the substantive issues covered in the last nine chapters, it will first provide an overview of the levels of abstraction that have been involved in the various analyses. It is useful and important to recognize in a clear and systematic way that sociological analysis works at several levels of abstraction simultaneously. This chapter will suggest a way of visualizing levels and their relations and will suggest how to avoid some of the common confusions that arise in reasoning between levels of analysis. Second, the chapter considers the relationships among the three major theorists whose ideas have been the focal points for our discussion. Having reviewed some of their basic contributions, we are now in a better position to arrive at some overall assessments of their relative merit. Finally, this discussion will draw from the earlier chapters' general guidelines for thinking about law and society from a sociological point of view. These guidelines will not provide cookbook formulae for conducting research but may serve the reader as a convenient, preliminary checklist for evaluating further work.

LEVELS OF ABSTRACTION

The American sociologist C. Wright Mills once observed that

every self-conscious thinker must at all times be aware—and hence be able to control—the levels of abstraction on which he is working.

The capacity to shuttle between levels of abstraction, with ease and with clarity, is a signal mark of the imaginative and systematic thinker. (Mills, 1959: 34)

Sociological work on any given problem typically involves negotiating among several such levels of abstraction.

To simplify this discussion, we will distinguish among five levels of abstraction to be found in our discussion of civil rights laws in Chapter 2. Table 11.1 presents five types of concepts ranging from the specific, singular historical event to the abstract, theoretical concept. Each level represents a progressively higher level of abstraction in thinking about civil rights law. Level I represents description of some particular event such as the Civil Rights Act of 1964 or the Supreme Court's decision in *Brown* v. *the Board of Education of Topeka* (1954). A casual observer takes these "events" as naturally occurring, requiring no special effort on the part of the observer to classify them. We know, however, that a description of a particular "event" such as the passage of the 1964 Civil Rights Act must somehow select details and order facts.

It would be physically impossible to record all the events that transpired in Congress, in the mass media, in the White House, and so on that influenced in some way the passage of this act. The act of describing this episode necessarily involves some active choice on the part of the observer in deciding what facts are important and what facts are secondary. Somewhere in the description lurks some theoretical assumptions that provide the basis for selecting and organizing pieces of information.

Level II in this scheme combines a number of distinct events, which share a common location in time and space and which are interrelated by some criterion. "The Civil Rights Revolution of the 1960s" or "The Civil Rights Revolution of the 1870s" designates legislative, judicial, and public acts that, in retrospect, are manifestations of some larger movement. Generally, the application of Level II concepts such as "the civil rights revolution" involves more than the cataloging of events. When we use such concepts we generally assert (or at least assume) that a general process exists beyond the individual events. If the 1964 Civil Rights Act had failed to pass Congress, we would anticipate that the civil rights revolution would have generated other attempts to enact similar bills. Thus the focus of concern at Level II typically is away from efforts to explain a particular piece of legislation; instead, the individual act is looked upon as a symptom or manifestation of a more general

TABLE 11.1

Levels of Abstraction: The Case of Civil Rights Revolutions

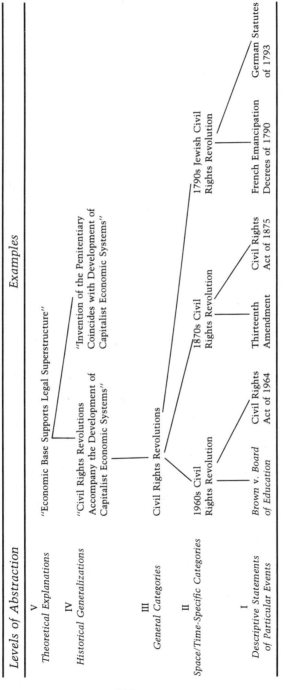

Levels of Abstraction	Examples
V Theoretical Explanations	"Economic Base Supports Legal Superstructure"
IV Historical Generalizations	"Civil Rights Revolutions Accompany the Development of Capitalist Economic Systems" / "Invention of the Penitentiary Coincides with Development of Capitalist Economic Systems"
III General Categories	Civil Rights Revolutions
II Space/Time-Specific Categories	1960s Civil Rights Revolution / 1870s Civil Rights Revolution / 1790s Jewish Civil Rights Revolution
I Descriptive Statements of Particular Events	Brown v. Board of Education / Civil Rights Act of 1964 / Thirteenth Amendment / Civil Rights Act of 1875 / French Emancipation Decrees of 1790 / German Statutes of 1793

317

process. Eliminating one symptom may simply mean that another manifestation of the general process will occur. Level II generalizations thus entail some fairly strong theoretical assumptions.

Level III moves us to an even higher degree of abstraction that includes "The Civil Rights Revolution of the 1960s" (a proper noun) in a general category of similar events. Proper nouns thus give way at this level to ideal types or variables that are not limited to particular locations and times. The category *civil rights revolutions*, for example, includes those in the United States in the 1960s and the 1870s as well as similar episodes in Europe in the 1700s. At this level of abstraction the most commonly used method of analysis is the *analogy*, the assumption that if two or more phenomena are alike in one respect, they will share a number of similar characteristics.

While analogies are often useful in discovering more general connections, taken by themselves they are frequently limiting and misleading. This is because, in the absence of a more general theory that tells us what is most important about the two phenomena, we have little protection against superficial analogies. Equally important, we have no good way of resolving the charge that the analogy is superficial. From the standpoint of Marxian theory the Jewish emancipation is, as we saw in Chapter 2, an interesting analogy to the civil rights revolutions of American blacks. Without the theory, we can readily see a vast number of differences in the details of the two cases. Good analogies, however, are not those that correspond in one-to-one fashion in every detail, but rather those parallel cases that allow us to construct or to comprehend general concepts and principles.

A close cousin of the analogy is the extrapolation, an effort to use existing observation to derive a general trend or theme by applying some simple, standard rule of thumb. Like analogy, extrapolation does not give us a more abstract explanation about why the extrapolation works. The difficulties this practice creates have been exposed best by Mark Twain, in his observations about the declining length of the Mississippi River:

> The Mississippi between Cairo and New Orleans was 1,215 miles long 176 years ago. It was 1,180 after the cut-off of 1722. It was 1,040 after the American Bend cut off. It has lost 67 miles since. Consequently, its length is only 976 miles at present ... any calm person, who is not blind or idiotic, can see that ... 742 years from now the Lower Mississippi will be only a mile and 3/4 long and Cairo and New Orleans will have joined their streets together and be plodding

comfortably along under a single mayor and mutual board of alder-
men. There is something fascinating about science. One gets such
wholesale returns of conjecture out of such a trifling investment of
fact. (1911: 41–2)

Level IV involves concepts that go beyond empirical generalizations or analogies to specify the underlying (often hidden) structure of the events. Many historians and some sociologists question
the possibility of making nontrivial statements about social phenomena at this level of abstraction. Chapter 2 showed how Karl
Marx explained the civil rights revolution of the 1700s in terms
of the economic changes involved in the development of capitalism
and how the same economic factors may account for the civil rights
developments in the United States in the 1870s and 1960s.

At Level V we find Level IV statements such as "civil rights
movements are caused by the development of a capitalist economic
order" being explained by even more general principles. For Marx
the general principle that underlies the revolution in capitalist law
is the base-superstructure model of society, which pictures social
structure as having two components, a set of activities involved
in the production and distribution of economic goods (the base) and
a set of noneconomic institutions, including law, politics, and religion (the superstructure). In Marx's model the superstructure rests
on the base in such a way that major changes in the economic
organization result in corresponding alterations of the superstructure. This model, then, as we saw in detail in Chapter 2, may be
used to explain the nature of legal changes accompanying the rise
of a new form of economic organization, such as capitalism.

Sociologists typically deal with multiple levels of abstraction
in examining the relationships between law and society. Marx,
Weber, and Durkheim successfully developed general theories of
such relationships, as well as provided adequate lower-level descriptions of social phenomena. Such ability to negotiate among
levels of abstraction is seldom found. Much confusion arises from
failure to recognize some basic features of levels of abstraction and
the relations between them.

Misplaced Concreteness

A difficulty we frequently encounter in moving between levels
of abstraction is the error Alfred North Whitehead (1925) has labeled
"the fallacy of misplaced concreteness," the confusion of one level

with another. This confusion is tantamount, as Marx once pointed out, to asking the color of logarithms. In sociology the fallacy of misplaced concreteness frequently appears as a confusion of a Level IV analytic concept, such as "class," with a Level I descriptive category, such as "class divisions in the United States in the 1980s."

> For Marx the concept of "class" was inseparably linked to a dialectical theory of social change; "class" was not primarily a category for describing how a particular capitalist society looked at any given point in time, but rather above all an analytic tool for elucidating the sources of structural change within the capitalist system, a theory of the direction in which capitalist societies were developing. This is why the Marxist model of capitalist society is normally a two-class model: the two classes represent the two sides of a fundamental contradiction which is assumed to be the source of conflicts sufficiently important to produce significant structural change. (Balbus, 1971a: 37–8)

Frequently, however, the dichotomous class model has been utilized as a description of class structure in a particular society and as a basis for analyzing the class basis of the legal system. For example, Richard Quinney writes that

> the existence of this ruling class in America, rooted mainly in corporations and financial institutions of monopoly capitalism, is well documented. This is the class that makes the decisions that affect the lives of those who are subordinated to it. It is according to the interests of the ruling class that American society is governed. . . . Superficially, groups within the ruling class may differ on some issues. But in general they have common interests, and they can exclude members of the other classes from the political process entirely. (1974: 20)

American conflict theorists characteristically attempt to analyze law and politics in the United States in terms of this dichotomous class structure. This effort entails the fallacy of misplaced concreteness because it seeks to find literal empirical counterparts to concepts that are analytic. As a result, for instance, Quinney is led to argue that

> the ruling class . . . is composed of (1) members of the upper economic class (those who own or control the means of production) and (2) *those who benefit in some way* from the present capitalist economic system. (Quinney, 1974: 55, emphasis added)

Since everyone "benefits in some way" from the system, membership in the ruling class is unrestricted. Quinney's thesis that law reflects the interests of the powerful is true by definition. This unfortunate result is the consequence of attempting to superimpose a theoretical concept directly upon observable data. It is instructive to consider how Marx avoided this fallacy. In the *Communist Manifesto* he presents a dichotomous class structure as part of his theory of social change. However, in examining the politics in a specific nation at a particular time—for example, in his essay on "The 18th Brumaire of Louis Napoleon Bonaparte"—the dichotomous class structure gives way to a "pluralistic" picture of the class structure of France, consisting of "class fractions" or divisions within both the ruling class and the working class. This is not an inconsistency on Marx's part, but a recognition of the different levels of analysis involved in examining (1) major transformations of society from feudalism to capitalism or capitalism to socialism and (2) the political life of a relatively stable society.

Failure to recognize the distinction between these levels leads to committing the fallacy of misplaced concreteness. Avoiding this fallacy requires understanding that all levels entail some degree of abstraction. Common language terms such as "individual," "group" and "nation state" are more familiar because of their daily usage, but this does not mean that they are more real than less familiar abstractions.

ASSESSING THE CORE TRADITIONS

Within the segment of thought and investigation in the sociology of law that has been the focus of this volume, we have seen how the lines of investigation established by Marx, Weber, and Durkheim provide the foundations both of the questions posed and of the methods used for their resolution. Workers following one of these traditions tend to develop partisan attachments that lead to the rejection of the alternative lines of investigation. This tendency is perhaps most pronounced among some Marxists, who draw a sharp boundary between Marx and the "bourgeois" sociologists. However, it appears to us somewhat premature at this stage to subject the three lines of analysis we have been following to invidious comparison. While much work has been accomplished, the full range of implications has yet to be drawn from any of the traditions. This is not to say that no significant differences separate the Weberian, Marxian, and Durkheimian sociologies of law; still less is it to argue for a convergence or fusion of these approaches.

We may put the problem in simple terms without doing great violence to its actual complexity. We may conveniently regard Marx, Weber, and Durkheim as differing in the features of social structure and law that they take as being primary. For Marx the critical variable for understanding law and society is *exploitation* and its consequences for class formation. For Weber the economic system is central, but its most critical feature is *rationalization;* the rationalization of law and economy are intertwined in complex ways that constitute the basic problem for analysis. For Durkheim, economic relations are of significance only insofar as they affect the type and intensity of *social solidarity.* These three theories, then, may be viewed as efforts to spell out the implications of taking exploitation, rationalization, or solidarity as the key social structural variable in explaining law. Viewing them in this way, we see that the theories are like alternative maps of a common terrain. As physicist John Ziman suggests,

> A map . . . has to be drawn to fit the data in the surveyor's notebooks —information that is always incomplete and subject to error. In many of its details, therefore, the map may be no more reliable than a shrewd guess or a rough interpolation. In the same way, a scientific theory is an attempt to fit incomplete and imperfect experimental evidence and necessarily contains many uncertain or conjectural elements. (1979: 82)

GUIDELINES FOR EVALUATION

In 1895, Emile Durkheim published a short work on *The Rules of Sociological Method.* His rules are not so much precise prescriptions of the sort one encounters in a statistics text as they are succinctly stated general conclusions drawn from his substantive studies. Any effort to codify the sociological perspective must anticipate a limited success. Despite the limits of the format, it may be worthwhile to draw such a list from the material we have covered in this volume. The following guidelines are thus to be taken primarily as distillations rather than as commandments.

1. *Make as explicit as possible the theory underlying the description or explanation, in particular the link between legal phenomenon and social structure.*

Even card-carrying professional social scientists are often lax in making explicit the theory that informs what they choose to see and how they choose to understand it. Several costs are associated with this practice. First, it is not uncommon to discover that we in fact entertain two incompatible theories simultaneously. This, of course, makes it possible to explain virtually any event, since we freely invoke Theory A or its opposite to suit the occasion. This practice, however, does not do anything to increase our understanding of the phenomenon nor to gain control over it. Second, failure to be clear about the theories we employ to describe or explain events prevents us from identifying other formulations of the same problem; the time spent "reinventing" Marxian or Weberian analyses of, say, the distinction between formal and substantive inequality would be better spent in less redundant ways.

2. *Gain control over the connotations of key concepts.*
Much fruitless discussion is devoted to the secondary or connotative meaning of key concepts. We have seen, for example, that *exploitation* and *repressive justice* are terms used in a very narrow, "technical" fashion. Their meaning can only be understood properly in the context of a specific theoretical argument. If we indulge in the urge to mix into the analysis moral connotations of such concepts or refuse to excise the vernacular from the sociological meaning of the terms, we will remain incapable of advancing our understanding of the phenomenon through a sociological perspective.

3. *Recognize the equivalence of forms of explanation.*
The field has long suffered from superstitious reverence toward or rejection of modes of explanation (causal, functional, dialectical). We have seen that most theorists use some combination of various forms of explanation. Furthermore, we have seen that all modes of explanation share common properties and deficiencies.

4. *In constructing explanations, seek out variation.*
Explanation can only be accomplished by constructing generalizations, which in turn depend for their formulation and evaluation on variation in the phenomenon. This is the central reason for the emphasis on historical and cross-cultural evidence in the sociology of law. Our attention has repeatedly been drawn, for example, to critical historical periods such as the Progressive Era in which we can observe major changes in social structure and law taking place. Similarly, the contrast between English and Continental legal developments has continually provided

sociologists with a strategic research site for developing and testing generalizations.

5. *Remain ambivalent about "outliers," extreme cases and anomalies.*
While the temptation to build upon isolated observations is dangerous, the deviant case or crisis situation may provide a wedge for opening up new perspectives on the phenomenon. Thus, for example, Balbus's study of the reaction of American criminal courts to urban riots and Erikson's study of the reaction of Puritan courts to boundary crises both represent studies that effectively use unusual circumstances to discover the nature of those legal systems that in normal periods would remain obscure.

6. *Recognize the tentative nature of all sociological investigation.*
While the sociological perspective offers to illuminate law and society in a unique fashion, it does not offer certainty. Max Weber put this best when he pointed out that all such work

will be antiquated in ten, twenty, fifty years. That is the fate to which science is subjected; it is the very meaning of scientific work. ... Every scientific "fulfillment" raises new "questions"; it asks to be "surpassed" and outdated. Whoever wishes to serve science has to resign himself to this fact ... for it is our common fate and, or, our common goal. ... We cannot work without hoping that others will advance further than we have. (1958: 138)

SUMMARY

This volume has presented exemplars of sociological analyses of law and society rather than strictly representative samples of work in the field. These exemplars of accomplishment and error reveal the central features of the peculiar craft of sociology, which searches for general explanations of the intersections of law and society. We have tried in this outline to make clear both its special myopias as well as its unique perspective on the law.

Bibliography

Adams, Ansel
1944   *Born Free and Equal.* New York: U.S. Camera.
Allen, Francis A.
1964   *The Borderland of Criminal Justice.* Chicago: University of Chicago Press.
1974   *The Crimes of Politics: Political Dimensions of Criminal Justice.* Cambridge: Harvard University Press.
1978   The decline of the rehabilitative ideal in American criminal justice. *Cleveland State Law Review* 27: 147–156.
Althusser, Louis
1969   *For Marx.* New York: Random House.
Anslinger, Harry J., and W. S. Thompkins
1953   *The Traffic in Narcotics.* New York: Funk and Wagnalls.
Applebaum, Richard P.
1978   Marx's theory of the falling rate of profit. *American Sociological Review* 43: 67–80.
Aries, Philippe
1962   *Centuries of Childhood: A Social History of Family Life.* New York: Vintage Books.
Aristotle
1921   *The Works of Aristotle:* Volume 10, *Politica.* Translated by Benjamin Jowett. Oxford: Oxford University Press.
Asimov, Isaac
1965   *Of Time, Space, and Other Things.* New York: Avon.
Aubert, Vilhelm
1965   *The Hidden Society.* Totowa, N.J.: Bedminster Press.
Austin, Roy L.
1976   Comment on DeFleur, On bias in drug arrest records. *American Sociological Review* 41: 893–6.

Bailyn, Bernard
1964   *The New England Merchants in the Seventeenth Century.* New
       York: Harper & Row. (First published in 1955).
Baker, J. H.
1977   Criminal courts and procedure at common law, 1550–1800. In
       J. S. Cockburn (ed.), *Crime in England 1550–1800.* Princeton, N.J.:
       Princeton University Press.
Balbus, Isaac D.
1971a Ruling elite theory vs. Marxist class analysis. *Monthly Review*
       23: 36–46.
1971b The concept of interest in pluralist and Marxian analysis. *Politics
       and Society* 1: 151–77.
1973   *The Dialectics of Legal Repression: Black Rebels before the
       American Criminal Courts.* New York: Russell Sage.
1977   Commodity form and legal form: An essay on the "relative au-
       tonomy" of the law. *Law and Society Review* 11: 571–88.
Baldwin, James
1962   *Nobody Knows My Name.* New York: Dell.
Baron, Harold
1975   Racial domination in advanced capitalism: A theory of nationalism
       and divisions in the labor market. In Richard C. Edwards, Michael
       Reich, and David M. Gordon (eds.), *Labor Market Segmentation.*
       Pp. 173–216. Lexington, Mass.: D. C. Heath.
Barron, Milton L.
1954   *The Juvenile Delinquent in Society.* New York: Knopf.
Barry, Brian
1965   On analogy. *Political Studies* 23: 208–24.
Baxi, Upendra
1974   Durkheim and legal evolution: Some problems of disproof. *Law
       and Society Review* 8: 645–51.
Beccaria, Cesare
1963   *On Crimes and Punishments.* Translated by Henry Paolucci. In-
       dianapolis, Ind.: Bobbs-Merrill. (First published in 1764.)
Becker, Howard S.
1973   *Outsiders: Studies in the Sociology of Deviance.* Second Edition.
       New York: Free Press. (First published in 1963.)
Becker, Howard S., and Irving L. Horowitz
1972   Radical politics and sociological research: Observations on meth-
       odology and ideology. *American Journal of Sociology* 78: 48–66.
Bedau, Hugo Adam
1979   The death penalty in the United States: Imposed law and the role
       of moral elites. In Sandra B. Burman and Barbara E. Harrel-Bond
       (eds.), *The Imposition of Law.* Pp. 45–68. New York: Academic
       Press.
1982   *The Death Penalty in America.* Third edition. New York: Oxford
       University Press.

Beirne, Piers
1979 Empiricism and the critique of Marxism on law and crime. *Social Problems* 26: 373–85.
Beirne, Piers, and Richard Quinney (eds.)
1982 *Marxism and Law.* New York: Wiley.
Bell, Derrick A.
1980 *Race, Racism and American Law.* Second edition. Boston: Little, Brown.
Bendix, Reinhard
1977 *Max Weber: An Intellectual Portrait.* Second edition. Berkeley, Calif.: University of California Press. (First published in 1960.)
Benedict, Ruth
1938 Continuities and discontinuities in cultural conditioning. *Psychiatry* 1: 161–167.
Bequai, August
1978 *White Collar Crime: A Twentieth Century Crisis.* Lexington, Mass.: Lexington Books.
Berger, Morroe
1967 *Equality by Statute.* Revised edition. Garden City, N.Y.: Doubleday and Company, Inc. (First Published in 1950.)

1977 *Real and Imagined Worlds: The Novel and Social Science.* Cambridge, Mass.: Harvard University Press.
Berk, Richard A., David Rauma, Sheldon L. Messinger, and Thomas F. Cooley
1981 A test of the stability of punishment hypothesis: The case of California, 1851–1970. *American Sociological Review* 46: 805–29.
Berkowitz, Edward D., and Kim McQuaid
1980 *Creating the Welfare State: The Political Economy of Twentieth Century Reform.* New York: Praeger.
Bernstein, I., W. Kelly, and P. Doyle
1977 Societal reaction to deviants: The case of criminal defendants *American Sociological Review* 42: 743–56.
Bernstein, Marc A.
1975 *Legal Systems and Rates of Deviance.* Ph.D. dissertation, Stanford University.
Bettelheim, Charles
1972 Theoretical comments. In Arghiri Emmanuel (ed.), *Unequal Exchange: A Study of the Imperialism of Trade.* Pp. 271–322. New York: Monthly Review Press.
Bierstedt, Robert
1949 A critique of empiricism in sociology. *American Sociological Review* 14: 584–92.
Birnbaum, Norman
1955 Monarchs and sociologists: A reply to Shils and Young. *Sociological Review* 3: 5–23.

Black, Donald
1973 The boundaries of legal sociology. In Donald Black and Maureen Mileski (eds.), *The Social Organization of Law*. New York: Seminar Press.
1976 *The Behavior of Law*. New York: Academic Press.
1979 Comment: Common sense in the sociology of law. *American Sociological Review* 44: 18–27.

Black, Donald J., and Albert J. Reiss
1970 Police control of juveniles. *American Sociological Review* 35: 63–77.

Blaug, Mark
1980 *The Methodology of Economics, or How Economists Explain*. Cambridge: Cambridge University Press.

Bloch, Sidney and Peter Reddaway
1977 Psychiatric Terror: How Soviet Psychiatry is Used to Suppress Dissent. New York: Basic Books.

Block, Fred
1977 The ruling class does not rule: Notes on the Marxist theory of the state. *Socialist Revolution* 7: 6–28.

Blumstein, Alfred, and Jacqueline Cohen
1973 A theory of the stability of punishment. *Journal of Criminal Law and Criminology* 64: 198–207.

Blumstein, Alfred, Jacqueline Cohen, and Daniel Nagin
1976 The dynamics of a homeostatic punishment process. *Journal of Criminal Law and Criminology* 68: 317–34.

Blumstein, Alfred, Jacqueline Cohen, and Daniel Nagin (eds.)
1978 *Deterrence and Incapacitation: Estimating the Effects of Criminal Sanctions on Criminal Rates*. Washington, D.C.: National Academy of Sciences.

Bonacich, Edna
1972 A theory of ethnic antagonism: The split labor market. *American Sociological Review* 37: 547–59.

Bond, Horace Mann
1939 *Negro Education in Alabama: A Study in Cotton and Steel*. Washington, D.C.: Associated Publishers.

Bowers, William J.
1974 *Executions in America*. Lexington, Mass.: D. C. Heath.

Boyer, Paul, and Stephen Nissenbaum
1974 *Salem Possessed: The Social Origins of Witchcraft*. Cambridge, Mass.: Harvard University Press.

Brecher, Edward M.
1972 *Licit and Illicit Drugs*. Boston: Little, Brown.

Breen, T. H.
1980 *Puritans and Adventurers: Change and Persistence in Early America.* New York: Oxford University Press.
Bremner, Robert
1970 *Children and Youth in America.* Cambridge, Mass.: Harvard University Press.
Bridges, George
1978 Errors in the measurement of crime: An application of Joereskog's method for the analysis of general covariance structures. In Charles Wellford (ed.), *Quantitative Studies in Criminology.* Pp. 9–29. Beverly Hills, Calif.: Sage.
Brown, B. W.
1978 Statistics, scientific method, and smoking. In Judith Tanur et al. (eds.), *Statistics: A Guide to the Unknown.* Second edition. Pp. 59–70. San Francisco: Holden-Day.
Burgess, Ernest W.
1950 Rejoinder. *American Journal of Sociology* 56: 35–7.
Cain, Maureen, and Alan Hunt (eds.)
1979 *Marx and Engels on Law.* New York: Academic Press.
Caldwell, Robert G.
1958 A re-examination of the concept of white-collar crime. *Federal Probation* 22: 30–6.
Campbell, Donald T.
1969 Reforms as experiments. *American Psychologist* 24: 409–29.
Camus, Albert
1957 Reflections on the guillotine. *Evergreen Review* 1: 5–55.
Carlebach, Julius
1978 *Karl Marx and the Radical Critique of Judaism.* London: Routledge and Kegan Paul.
Carroll, Lewis
1960 *The Annotated Alice: Alice's Adventures in Wonderland and Through the Looking Glass.* New York: Bramhall. (First published 1865–1871.)
Cartwright, Bliss, and Richard Schwartz
1973 The invocation of legal norms: An empirical investigation of Durkheim and Weber. *American Sociological Review* 38: 340–354.
Cash, W. J.
1941 *The Mind of the South.* New York: Knopf.
Cavender, Gray
1982 *Parole: A Critical Analysis.* Port Washington, N.Y.: Kennikat Press.
Chambliss, William J.
1964 A sociological analysis of the law of vagrancy. *Social Problems* 12: 66–67.

1973 The saints and the roughnecks. *Society* 11: 24–31.

1974 The state, the law and the definition of behavior as criminal or delinquent. In Daniel Glaser (ed.), *Handbook of Criminology*. Pp. 8–43. Chicago: Rand McNally.

1975 The political economy of crime: A study of Nigeria and the U.S. In Ian Taylor et al. (eds.), *Critical Criminology*. Pp. 167–79. London: Routledge and Kegan Paul.

1976 Functional and conflict theories of crime: The heritage of Emile Durkheim and Karl Marx. In William J. Chambliss and Milton Mankoff (eds.), *Whose Law; What Order: A Conflict Approach to Criminology*. Pp. 1–28. New York: Wiley.

1979 Contradictions and conflicts in law creation. *Research in Law and Sociology* 2: 3–27.

Chambliss, William, and Robert B. Seidman

1982 *Law, Order and Power*. Second edition. Reading, Mass.: Addison-Wesley.

Clarke, Dean

1978 Marxism, justice and the justice model. *Contemporary Crises* 2: 27–67

Clinard, Marshall B.

1946 Criminological theories of violations of wartime regulations. *American Sociological Review* 11: 258.

1979 *Illegal Corporate Behavior*. Washington, D.C.: U.S. Department of Justice, Law Enforcement Assistance Administration.

Cochran, Thomas C.

1972 *Business in American Life*. New York: McGraw-Hill.

Cohen, Gerald A.

1978 *Karl Marx's Theory of History: A Defense*. Princeton, N.J.: Princeton University Press.

Cohen, Lawrence E. and James R. Kluegel

1978 Determinants of juvenile court dispositions: Ascriptive and achieved factors in two metropolitan courts. *American Sociological Review* 43: 177–98.

Cohen, Percy

1968 *Modern Social Theory*. New York: Basic Books.

Cohn, Norman

1961 *The Pursuit of the Millennium*. New York: Harper.

Collins, Winfred H.

1918 *The Truth About Lynching and the Negro in the South*. New York: Neale.

Connor, Walter D.

1972 The manufacture of deviance: The case of the Soviet purge 1936–1938. *American Sociological Review* 37: 403–13.

Conrad, Peter, and Joseph W. Schneider

1980 *Deviance and Medicalization: From Badness to Sickness*. St. Louis, Mo.: Mosby.

Currie, Elliot P.
1968   Crimes without criminals: Witchcraft and its control in Renaissance Europe. *Law and Society Review* 3: 7–32.
Cutler, James E.
1905   *Lynch Law: An Investigation into the History of Lynching in the United States.* New York: Longmans, Greene.
Dahrendorf, Ralf
1957   *Class and Class Conflict in Industrial Society.* Stanford, Calif.: Stanford University Press.
1968   *Essays in Social Theory.* Stanford, Calif.: Stanford University Press.
Damaska, Mirjan
1973   Evidentiary barriers to conviction and two models of criminal procedure. *University of Pennsylvania Law Review* 121: 506–89.
D'Andrade, Roy G.
1965   Trait psychology and componential analysis. *American Anthropologist* 67: 215–28.
Daniels, Roger
1971   *Concentration Camp U.S.A.* New York: Holt, Rinehart & Winston.
Davies, John
1955   *Phrenology: Fad and Science: A 19th Century American Crusade.* New Haven, Conn.: Yale University Press.
Davis, Kenneth C.
1969   *Discretionary Justice.* Baton Rouge, La.: University of Louisiana Press.
Day, Richard H.
1967   The economies of technological change and the demise of the sharecropper. *American Economic Review* 57: 427–49.
DeFleur, Lois
1975   Biasing influences on drug arrest records: Implications for research. *American Sociological Review* 40: 88–103.
Degler, Carl N.
1974   *The Other South: Southern Dissenters in the Nineteenth Century.* New York: Harper & Row.
DeLone, Richard
1979   *Children, Inequality, and the Limits of Liberal Reform.* New York: Harcourt Brace Jovanovich.
DeMause, Lloyd
1974   *The History of Childhood.* New York: Harper & Row.
Diamond, Sigmund
1958   From organization to society: Virginia in the seventeenth century. *American Journal of Sociology* 6: 457–75.
Dibble, Vernon
1973   What is and what ought to be: A comparison of certain characteristics of legal and ideological styles of thought. *American Journal of Sociology* 79: 511–49.

Dillingham, Harry C., and David. F. Sly
1966   The mechanical cotton-picker, Negro migration and the integration movement. *Human Organization* 25: 344–511.

Douglas, Jack D.
1967   *The Social Meaning of Suicide.* Princeton, N.J.: Princeton University Press.

Douglas, Mary
1970   *Purity and Danger: An Analysis of Concepts of Pollution and Taboo.* Harmondsworth, England: Penguin. (First published in 1966.)

Dressler, David
1969   *Practice and Theory of Probation and Parole.* New York: Columbia University Press.

Dumont, Louis
1965   The modern conception of the individual: Notes on its genesis and that of concomitant institutions. *Contributions to Indian Sociology* 8: 13–61.

Durkheim, Emile
1948   *The Elementary Forms of the Religious Life.* Glencoe, Ill.: Free Press. (First published in 1912.)
1950   *The Rules of Sociological Method.* Glencoe, Ill.: Free Press. (First published in 1893.)
1964   *The Division of Labor in Society.* New York: Free Press. (First published in 1893.)
1978   *On Institutional Analysis.* Edited by Mark Traugott. Chicago: University of Chicago Press.

Duster, Troy
1970   *The Legislation of Morality.* New York: Free Press.

Eddington, Arthur S.
1929   *The Nature of the Physical World.* New York: Cambridge University Press.

Ehrlich, Isaac
1975a   The deterrent effect of capital punishment: A question of life or death. *American Economic Review* 65: 397–417.
1975b   Deterrence: Evidence and inference. *Yale Law Journal* 86: 209–27.
1977a   Fear of deterrence. *Journal of Legal Studies* 6: 293–316.
1977b   Capital punishment and deterrence: Some further thoughts and additional evidence. *Journal of Political Economy* 85: 741–788.

Ehrlich, Isaac, and Randall Mark Redlich
1979   Deterrence and economics: A perspective on theory and evidence. In J. Milton Yeager and Stephen Cutler (eds.), *Major Social Problems: A Multidisciplinary View.* Pp. 172–86. New York: Free Press.

Elster, Jon
1978   *Logic and Society: Contradictions and Possible Worlds.* New York: Wiley.

Elton, George
1967   *The Practice of History.* New York: Crowell.

Emerson, Robert
1981   On last resorts. *American Journal of Sociology* 87: 1–22.
Empey, LaMar T.
1980   The social construction of childhood and juvenile justice. In Empey
(ed.), *The Future of Childhood and Juvenile Justice.* Pp. 1–34.
Charlottesville, Va.: University of Virginia Press.
1979   *Juvenile Justice: The Progressive Legacy and Current Reforms.*
Charlottesville, Va.: University of Virginia Press.
Engels, Friedrich
1976   *Anti-Duehring.* New York: International. (First published in 1878.)
Ennis, Bruce J., and Thomas R. Litwack
1974   Psychology and the presumption of expertise: Flipping coins in
the courtroom. *California Law Review* 62: 671–93.
Ennis, Philip H.
1967   *Criminal Victimization in the United States: A Report of a National
Survey.* Field Surveys II, President's Commission on Law Enforce-
ment and the Administration of Justice. Washington, D.C.: U.S.
Government Printing Office.
Epstein, Edward J.
1977   *Agency of Fear: Opiates and Political Power in America.* New
York: G. P. Putnam.
Erikson, Kai T.
1966   *Wayward Puritans: A Study in the Sociology of Deviance.* New
York: Wiley.
Evans, Edward P.
1906   *The Criminal Prosecution and Capital Punishment of Animals.*
London: W. Hineman.
Evans-Pritchard, Edward E.
1937   *Witchcraft, Oracles and Magic Among the Azande.* Oxford: Oxford
University Press.
Farley, Reynolds
1977   Trends in racial inequalities: Have the gains of the 1960's disappeared in the 1970's? *American Sociological Review* 42: 189–
208.
Farley, Reynolds, and Albert Hermalin
1972   The 1960s: A decade of progress for blacks? *Demography* 9: 353–
70.
Farrell, Ronald A., and Victoria Swigert
1978a Legal disposition of inter-group and intra-group homicides. *Sociological Quarterly* 19: 565–76.
1978b Prior offense as a self-fulfilling prophecy. *Law and Society Review*
12: 437–55.
Feld, Barry C.
1977   *Neutralizing Inmate Violence: Juvenile Offenders in Institutions.*
Cambridge, Mass.: Ballinger.

1978   Reference of juvenile offenders for adult prosecution: The legislative alternative to asking unanswerable questions. *Minnesota Law Review* 62: 515–618.

1981   Juvenile court legislative reform and the serious young offender: Dismantling the "rehabilitative ideal." *Minnesota Law Review* 65: 167–242.

Femia, Joseph

1975   Hegemony and consciousness in the thought of Antonio Gramsci. *Political Studies* 23: 29–48.

Finestone, Harold

1976   *Victims of Change: Juvenile Delinquency in American Society.* Westport, Conn.: Greenwood.

Fligstein, Neil

1981   *Going North: Migration of Blacks and Whites from the South, 1900–1950.* New York: Academic Press.

Foucault, Michel

1965   *Madness and Civilization.* Translated by Richard Howard. New York: Pantheon Books.

1979   *Discipline and Punish: The Birth of the Prison.* New York: Vintage.

France, Anatole

1925   *The Red Lily.* Translated by Winifred Stephens. New York: Dodd, Mead, and Co.

Freeman, Alan D.

1978   Legitimizing racial discrimination through antidiscrimination law: A critical review of Supreme Court doctrine. *Minnesota Law Review* 62: 1049–1119.

Friedman, Lawrence M., and Jack Ladinsky

1967   Social change and the law of industrial accidents. *Columbia Law Review* 7: 50–82.

Friedmann, Wolfgang

1972   *Law in Changing Society.* Second edition. Middlesex, England: Penguin. (First published in 1959.)

Fusfeld, Daniel R.

1972   The rise of the corporate state in America. *Journal of Economic Issues* 6: 1–22.

Galanter, Marc

1974   Why the "haves" come out ahead: Speculations on the limits of legal change. *Law and Society Review* 9: 95–160.

Galbraith, John Kenneth

1967   *The New Industrial State.* Boston: Houghton Mifflin.

Galliher, John F., and Allynn Walker

1977   The puzzle of the social origins of the marijuana tax act of 1937. *Social Problems* 24: 367–76.

Gallup, George

1981   Support for death penalty increases. *Minneapolis Tribune* March 1: 14A.

Garfinkel, Harold
1949 Research note on inter- and intra-racial homicides. *Social Forces* 27: 369–81.
1956 Conditions of successful status degradation ceremonies. *American Journal of Sociology* 61: 420–24.

Gastil, Raymond D.
1975 *Cultural Regions of the United States*. Seattle, Wash.: University of Washington Press.

Geis, Gilbert, and Robert F. Meier (eds.)
1977 *White Collar Crime: Offenses in Business, Politics, and the Professions*. New York: Free Press.

Geis, Gilbert, and Ezra Stotland (eds.)
1980 *White Collar Crime: Theory and Research*. Beverly Hills, Calif.: Sage Publications.

Genovese, Eugene D.
1972 *In Red and Black: Marxian Explorations in Southern and Afro-American History*. New York: Vintage Books. (First published in 1968.)

Giddens, Anthony
1971 Durkheim's political sociology. *Sociological Review* 19: 477–519.
1976 Classical social theory and the origins of modern sociology. *American Journal of Sociology* 81: 703–29.

Ginzberg, Ralph
1962 *100 Years of Lynching*. New York: Lancer Books.

Girard, Rene
1977 *Violence and the Sacred*. Baltimore, Md.: Johns Hopkins Press.

Glantz, Oscar
1960 The Negro voter in northern industrial cities. *Western Political Quarterly* 13: 999–1010.

Gluckman, Max
1965 *Politics, Law, and Ritual in Tribal Society*. New York: New American Library.

Goffman, Erving
1961 *Asylums*. New York: Doubleday.

Gold, David, Clarence Lo, and Erik Wright
1975 Recent developments in Marxist theories of the capitalist state. *Monthly Review* 5: 29–43 and 6: 36–41.

Goldstone, Jack A.
1980 The weakness of organizations: A new look at Gamson's *The Strategy of Social Protest. American Journal of Sociology* 85: 1017–1042.

Goode, Eric
1975 On behalf of labeling theory. *Social Problems* 22: 570–83.

Goodhart, Arthur L.
1930 Determining the *ratio decidendi* of a case. *Yale Law Journal* 40: 161.

Gouldner, Alvin
1973   *For Sociology: Renewal and Critique in Sociology Today.* New York: Basic Books.
Gove, Walter R. (ed.)
1980   *The Labelling of Deviance: Evaluating a Perspective.* Second edition. Beverly Hills, Calif.: Sage. (First published in 1975.)
Graham-Mulhall, Sara
1926   *Opium the Demon Flower.* New York: Montrose.
Granovetter, Mark S.
1973   The strength of weak ties. *American Journal of Sociology* 78: 1360–1380.
Grant, Donald
1975   *The Anti-Lynching Movement.* San Francisco: R and E Research Associates.
Green, Edward
1964   Inter- and intra-racial crime relative to sentencing. *Journal of Criminal Law, Criminology and Police Science* 55: 348–58.
Greenberg, David
1976   On one dimensional Marxist criminology. *Theory and Society* 3: 611–21.
1977a   Delinquency and the age structure of society. Contemporary Crises 1: 189–223.
1977b   The dynamics of oscillatory punishment processes. *Journal of Criminal Law and Criminology* 68: 643–51.
Greenberg, David (ed.)
1981   *Crime and Capitalism: Readings in Marxist Criminology.* Palo Alto, Calif.: Mayfield.
Greenberg, David F., and Drew Humphries
1980   The co-optation of fixed sentencing reform. *Crime and Delinquency* 26: 206–25.
Griffiths, John
1970   Ideology in criminal procedure of a third "model" of the criminal process. *Yale Law Journal* 79: 359–417.
Gusfield, Joseph R.
1963   *Symbolic Crusade: Status Politics and the American Temperance Movement.* Urbana, Ill.: University of Illinois Press.
1967   Moral passage: The symbolic process in public designations of deviance. *Social Problems* 15: 175–188.
Haber, Samuel
1964   *Efficiency and Uplift: Scientific Management in the Progressive Era.* Chicago: University of Chicago Press.
Hackney, Sheldon
1969   Southern violence. In Hugh D. Graham and Ted R. Gurr (eds.), *Violence in America: Historical and Comparative Perspectives.* Pp. 505–27. New York: Ballantine.

Hagan, John
  1974 Extra-legal attributes and criminal sentencing: An assessment of a sociological viewpoint. *Law and Society Review* 8: 357–83.
  1979 Symbolic justice: The status politics of the American probation movement. *Sociological Focus* 12: 295–309.
  1980 The legislation of crime and delinquency: A review of theory, method, and research. *Law and Society Review* 14: 603–28.
Hair, William T.
  1969 *Bourbonism and Agrarian Protest: Louisiana Politics, 1877–1900.* Baton Rouge, La.: Louisiana University Press.
Hall, Jerome
  1952 *General Principles of Criminal Law.* Indianapolis, Ind.: Bobbs-Merrill. (First published in 1935.)
Hartung, Frank E.
  1950 White collar offenses in the wholesale meat industry in Detroit. *American Journal of Sociology* 56: 25–34.
Hechter, Michael, and William Brustein
  1980 Regional modes of production and patterns of state formation in Western Europe. *American Journal of Sociology* 85: 1061–94.
Hempel, Carl
  1965 The logic of functional explanation. In *Aspects of Scientific Explanation.* Pp. 297–330. New York: Free Press.
Hertzberg, Arthur
  1968 *The French Enlightenment and the Jews.* New York: Columbia University Press.
Heydebrand, Wolf
  1977 Organizational contradictions in public bureaucracies. *Sociological Quarterly* 18: 83–107.
  1979 The technocratic administration of justice. *Research in Law and Sociology* 2: 29–64.
Heydebrand, Wolf, and Carroll Seron
  1981 The double bind of the capitalist judicial system. *International Journal of the Sociology of Law* 9: 407–37.
Hindelang, Michael
  1973 The Uniform Crime Rates revisited. *Journal of Criminal Justice* 2: 1–17.
  1974 Public opinion regarding crime, criminal justice, and related topics. *Crime and Delinquency Literature* 5: 101–16.
  1978 Race and involvement in common law personal crimes. *American Sociological Review* 43: 93–100.
Hindelang, Michael, Travis Hirschi, and Joseph G. Weis
  1979 Correlates of delinquency: The illusion of discrepancy between self-report and official measures. *American Sociological Review* 44: 995–1014.

Hindus, Michael Stephen
1980 *Prison and Plantation: Crime, Justice and Authority in Massa-chusetts and South Carolina, 1767–1878.* Chapel Hill, N. C.: University of North Carolina Press.
Hirschi, Travis
1979 Reconstructing delinquency: Evolution and implications of twen-tieth century theory. In Lamar T. Empey (ed.), *Juvenile Justice: The Progressive Legacy and Current Reform.* Pp. 183–212. Char-lottesville, Va.: University of Virginia Press.
Hirschi, Travis, and Michael Hindelang
1978 Reply to Ronald L. Simons. *American Sociological Review* 43: 610–13.
Hirschi, Travis, and Hanan C. Selvin
1966 False criteria of causality in delinquency research. *Social Problems* 13: 254–68.
Hobsbawm, Eric J.
1962 *The Age of Revolution, 1789–1848.* New York: New American Library.
Hodnett, Grey
1974 Technology and social change in Soviet Central Asia: The politics of cotton growing. In Henry W. Norton and Rudolf L. Tokes (eds.), *Soviet Politics and Society in the 1970's.* Pp. 60–117. New York: Free Press.
Hodson, Randy
1978 Labor in monopoly, competitive and state sectors of production. *Politics and Society* 8: 429–80.
Hofstadter, Richard
1955 *Age of Reform.* New York: Vintage Books.
Hopkins, Andrew
1975 On the sociology of criminal law. *Social Problems* 22: 608–19.
Hornum, Finn
1967 Two debates: France, 1791; England, 1956. In Thorsten Sellin (ed.), *Capital Punishment.* Pp. 55–76. New York: Harper & Row.
Horowitz, Irving L., and Martin Liebowitz
1968 Social deviance and political marginality: Toward a redefinition of the relation between sociology and politics. *Social Problems* 15: 280–96.
Horton, John
1966 Order and conflict theories of social problems as competing ideo-logies. *American Journal of Sociology* 71: 701–13.
Horwitz, Morton
1977 *The Transformation of American Law, 1700–1860.* Cambridge, Mass.: Harvard University Press.
Hunt, Alan
1978 *The Sociological Movement in Law.* Philadelphia: Temple Uni-versity Press.

Husami, Ziyad I.
1980   Marx on distributive justice. In Marshall Cohen, Thomas Nagel
        and Thomas Scanlon (eds.), *Marx, Justice, and History.* Pp. 42–
        79. Princeton, N.J.: Princeton University Press.
Huxley, Aldous
1953   *The Devils of Loudun.* New York: Harper & Row.
Ignatieff, Michael
1978   *A Just Measure of Pain: The Penitentiary in the Industrial Rev-
        olution, 1750–1850.* New York: Columbia University Press.
1981   State, civil society and total institutions: A critique of recent
        social histories of punishment. *Crime and Justice: An Annual
        Review of Research* 3: 153–92.
Inbau, Fred E.
1962   Public safety v. individual civil liberties: The prosecutor's stand.
        Journal of Criminal Law, Criminology, and Police Science 53:
        85–89.
Ingraham, Barton L.
1979   *Political Crime in Europe: A Comparative Study of France, Ger-
        many and England.* Berkeley, Calif.: University of California Press.
Inverarity, James M.
1976   Populism and lynching in the South: A test of Erikson's theory
        of the relationship between boundary crisis and repressive justice.
        American Sociological Review 41: 262–80.
1980   Theories of the political creation of deviance: Legacies of conflict
        theory, Marx, and Durkheim. In Pat Lauderdale (ed.), *A Political
        Analysis of Deviance.* Pp. 175–217. Minneapolis, Minn.: University
        of Minnesota Press.
Jackson, George
1970   *Soledad Brother: The Prison Letters of George Jackson.* New York:
        Coward-McCann.
Jaffe, Adrian
1967   *The Process of Kafka's* Trial. East Lansing, Mich.: Michigan State
        University Press.
Jankovic, Ivan
1977   Labor market and imprisonment. *Crime and Social Justice* 8: 17–
        31.
1978   Social class and criminal sentencing. *Crime and Social Justice*
        5: 9–16.
Janowitz, Morris
1964   *The Professional Soldier: A Social and Political Portrait.* New
        York: Free Press.
Johnson, Guy B.
1941   The negro and crime. *Annals of the American Academy of Political
        and Social Science* 217: 93–104.
Johnson, John, and Jack Douglas
1978   *Crime at the Top: Deviance in Business and the Professions.*
        Philadelphia: J. B. Lippincott Co.

BIBLIOGRAPHY

Kafka, Franz
1964   *The Trial.* New York: Vintage. (First published in 1937.)
Kanter, Rosabeth M.
1972   *Commitment and Community: Communes and Utopias in So-
       ciological Perspective.* Cambridge, Mass.: Harvard University Press.
Kaplan, John, and Jerome Skolnick
1982   *Criminal Justice.* Third edition. Mineola, N. Y.: Foundation Press.
Kastenmeir, Robert K., and Howard C. Eglit
1973   Parole release decision-making: Rehabilitation, expertise, and the
       demise of mythology. *American University Law Review* 22: 477–
       525.
Keat, Russell, and John Urry
1975   *Social Theory as Science.* London: Routledge and Kegan Paul.
Kern, Fritz
1939   *Kingship and Law in the Middle Ages.* Oxford: Blackwell.
Kett, Joseph F.
1977   *Rites of Passage: Adolescence in America 1790 to the Present.*
       New York: Basic Books.
Kitsuse, John I., and Aaron V. Cicourel
1963   A note on the uses of official statistics. *Social Problems* 11: 131–
       139.
Kittrie, Nicholas N.
1971   *The Right to Be Different: Deviance and Enforced Therapy.* Bal-
       timore, Md.: Johns Hopkins Press.
Kleck, Gary
1979   Capital punishment, gun ownership and homicide. *American
       Journal of Sociology* 84: 882–910.
1981   Racial discrimination in criminal sentencing: A critical evaluation
       of the evidence with additional evidence on the death penalty.
       American Sociological Review 46: 783–805.
Kline, George
1965   Economic crime and punishment. *Survey* 57: 67–72.
Knowles, Louis L., and Kenneth Prewitt (eds.)
1969   *Institutional Racism in America.* Englewood Cliffs, N.J.: Prentice-
       Hall.
Kolko, Gabriel
1963   *The Triumph of Conservatism.* New York: Free Press of Glencoe.
1965   *Railroads and Regulations.* Princeton, N.J.: Princeton University
       Press.
Krisberg, Barry
1975   *Crime and Privilege: Toward a New Criminology.* Englewood
       Cliffs, N.J.: Prentice-Hall.
Kuhn, Thomas S.
1962   *The Structure of Scientific Revolutions.* Chicago: University of
       Chicago Press.

Ladinsky, Jack, and Allan Silver
1967   Popular democracy and judicial independence: Electorate and elite reactions to two Wisconsin Supreme Court Decisions. *Wisconsin Law Review.* 1967: 128–69.

LaFree, Gary D.
1980   The effect of sexual stratification by race on official reactions to rape. *American Sociological Review* 45: 842–54.

Lakatos, Imre
1978   *The Methodology of Scientific Research Programmes; Philosophical Papers.* Volume 1. New York: Cambridge University Press.

Langbein, John H.
1977   *Torture and the Law of Proof: Europe and England in the Ancient Regime.* Chicago: University of Chicago Press.

Lanzillotti, Robert F.
1971   The automobile industry. In Walter Adams (ed.), *The Structure of American Industry.* Fourth edition. Pp. 256–301. New York: Macmillan.

LaPiere, Richard
1934   Attitudes and actions. *Social Forces* 13: 230–7.

Larson, Magali S.
1977   *The Rise of Professionalism: A Sociological Analysis.* Berkeley, Calif.: University of California Press.

Lasch, Christopher
1977   *Haven in a Heartless World: The Family Besieged.* New York: Basic Books.

Lauderdale, Pat
1976   Deviance and moral boundaries. *American Sociological Review* 41: 660–76.

Lauderdale, Pat (ed.)
1980   *A Political Analysis of Deviance.* Minneapolis, Minn.: University of Minnesota Press.

Lauderdale, Pat, Harold Grasmick, and John P. Clark
1978   Corporate environments, corporate crime, and deterrence. In Marvin Krohn and Ron Akers (eds.), *Crime, Law, and Sanctions.* Pp. 137–158. Beverly Hills, Calif.: Sage.

Lauderdale, Pat, and James Inverarity
1980   From apolitical to political analyses of deviance. In Pat Lauderdale (ed.), *A Political Analysis of Deviance.* Pp. 15–46. Minneapolis, Minn.: University of Minnesota Press.

Lauderdale, Pat, and Rhoda E. Estep
1980   An examination of hegemony in the definition of deviant political activity. In Pat Lauderdale (ed.), *A Political Analysis of Deviance.* Pp. 72–94. Minneapolis, Minn.: University of Minnesota Press.

Lemert, Edwin
1962   Paranoia and the dynamics of exclusion. *Sociometry* 25: 2–25.
1967   *Human Deviance, Social Problems, and Social Control.* Englewood Cliffs, N.J.: Prentice-Hall.

1974   Beyond Mead: The societal reaction to deviance. *Social Problems*
       21: 457–68.
Leon, Abram
1950   *The Jewish Question: A Marxist Interpretation.* Mexico City:
       Ediciones Pioneras.
Levin, Martin A.
1977   *Urban Politics and the Criminal Courts.* Chicago: University of
       Chicago Press.
Liazos, Alexander
1972   The poverty of the sociology of deviance: Nuts, sluts, and perverts.
       Social Problems 20: 12–20.
Lindesmith, Alfred R.
1965   *The Addict and the Law.* Bloomington, Ind.: University Press.
1968   *Addiction and Opiates.* Chicago: Aldine.
Lipschutz, Mark
1977   Runaways in history. *Crime and Delinquency* 23: 321–32.
Lipset, Seymour, and Reinhard Bendix
1959   *Social Mobility in Industrial Society.* Berkeley, Calif.: University
       of California Press.
Lipsitz, Lewis
1968   If, as Verba says, the state functions as religion, what are we to
       do to save our souls? *American Political Science Review* 62: 527–
       535.
Lofland, John
1977   The dramaturgy of state executions. In Horace Breackley and John
       Lofland (eds.), *State Executions Viewed Historically and Socio-
       logically.* Pp. 275–325. Montclair, N.J.: Patterson Smith.
Lubove, Roy
1965   *The Professional Altruist.* Cambridge, Mass.: Harvard University
       Press.
Lukes, Steve
1977   Political ritual and social integration. In his *Essays in Social Theory.*
       Pp. 52–73. New York: Columbia University Press.
Lynd, Staughton
1968   Slavery and the founding fathers. In Melvin Drimmer (ed.), *Black
       History: A Reappraisal.* Pp. 115–131. Garden City, N.Y.: Doubleday.
Malinowski, Bronislaw
1962   *Crime and Custom in Savage Society.* Paterson, N.J.: Littlefield,
       Adams. (First published in 1926.)
Mandle, Jay R.
1978   *The Roots of Black Poverty: The Southern Plantation Economy
       after the Civil War.* Durham, N.C.: Duke University Press.
Mann, Michael
1970   The social cohesion of liberal democracy. *American Sociological
       Review* 35: 423–39.

Marcuse, Herbert
1965   Repressive tolerance. In Robert P. Wolff, Barrington Moore, and Herbert Marcuse, *A Critique of Pure Tolerance.* Pp. 81–123. Boston: Beacon Press.
1968   Industrialization and capitalism in the work of Max Weber. In Herbert Marcuse (ed.), *Negations: Essays in Critical Theory.* Pp. 201–26. Boston: Beacon Press.

Mark, Gregory Yee
1975   Racial, economic, and political factors in the development of America's first drug laws. *Issues in Criminology* 10: 49–72.

Marks, F. Raymond
1975   Detours on the road to maturity: A view of the legal conception of growing up and letting go. *Law and Contemporary Problems* 39: 78.

Marshall, T. H.
1965   Citizenship and social class. In his *Class, Citizenship and Social Development.* Pp. 71–134. New York: Anchor. (First published in 1949.)

Marx, Karl
1963   *The Poverty of Philosophy.* New York: International. (First published in 1847.)
1967   *Capital.* Volume 1. New York: International. (First published in 1867.)
1973   *Grundrisse: Foundations of the Critique of Political Economy.* New York: Vintage Books. (Written 1857–8.)
1981   *Capital.* Volume 3. Translated by David Fernbach. New York: Vintage Books.

Matza, David
1964   *Delinquency and Drift.* New York: John Wiley.
1969   *Becoming Deviant.* Englewood Cliffs, N.J.: Prentice-Hall.

McCormick, Albert E.
1977   Rule enforcement and moral indignation: Some observations on the effects of criminal antitrust convictions upon societal reaction processes. *Social Problems* 25: 30.

McGahey, Richard M.
1980   Dr. Ehrlich's magic bullet: Econometric theory, econometrics, and the death penalty. *Crime and Delinquency* 26: 485–502.

Means, Gardiner
1970   Economic concentration. In Maurice Zeitlin (ed.), *American Society, Inc.:* Pp. 3–16. Chicago: Markham.

Medvedev, Zhores
1969   The Rise and Fall of T. D. Lysenko. New York: Columbia University Press.

Medvedev, Zhores, and Roy Medvedev
1971   *A Question of Madness: Repression by Psychiatry in the Soviet Union.* Translated by Ellen de Kadt. New York: Vintage Books.

Meehl, Paul
  1967 Theory testing in psychology and physics: A methodological paradox. *Philosophy of Science* 34: 103–15.
  1970a Psychology and the criminal law. *University of Richmond Law Review* 5: 1–30.
  1970b Nuisance variables and the ex post facto design. In M. Radner and S. Winokur (eds.), *Minnesota Studies in the Philosophy of Science*. Volume 4. Pp. 373–402. Minneapolis, Minn.: University of Minnesota Press.
Melossi, Dario
  1980 Strategies of social control in capitalism: A comment on recent work. *Contemporary Crises* 4: 381–402.
Melossi, Dario and Massimo Pavarini
  1981 *The Prison and the Factory: The Origins of the Penitentiary System.* Giynis Cousin (tr.) Totowa, N.J.: Barnes & Noble.
Mennel, Robert M.
  1973 *Thorns and Thistles: Juvenile Delinquency in the United States, 1825–1940.* Hanover, N.H.: University Press of New England.
Merton, Robert
  1965 *On the Shoulders of Giants: A Shandean Postscript.* New York: Free Press.
  1968 *Social Theory and Social Structure.* Third edition. New York: Free Press.
  1972 Insiders and outsiders: A chapter in the sociology of knowledge. *American Journal of Sociology* 78: 9–47.
Mill, John Stuart
  1962 *Utilitarianism and On Liberty.* Edited by Mary Warnock. Cleveland, Ohio: Meridian Books. (*On Liberty* was first published in 1859.)
Miller, Arthur S.
  1968 *The Supreme Court and American Capitalism.* New York: The Free Press.
  1976 *The Modern Corporate State? Private Governments and the American Constitution.* Westport, Conn.: Greenwood Press.
Miller, Kent S.
  1980 *The Criminal Justice and Mental Health Systems: Conflict and Collusion.* Cambridge, Mass.: Oeleschlager, Gunn and Hain.
Mills, C. Wright
  1942 The professional ideology of social pathologists. *American Journal of Sociology* 49: 165–80.
  1959 *The Sociological Imagination.* New York: Oxford University Press.
Moore, Barrington
  1966 *Social Origins of Dictatorship and Democracy: Lord and Peasant in the Making of the Modern World.* Boston: Beacon Press.
  1973 *Reflections on the Causes of Human Misery and Upon Certain Proposals to Eliminate Them.* Boston: Beacon Press.
Morris, Norval, and Gordon Hawkins

1977 *Letter to the President on Crime Control.* Chicago: University of Chicago Press.

1980 Strategies of social control in capitalism: A comment on recent work. *Contemporary Crises* 4: 381–402.

Mueller, Claus

1973 *The Politics of Communication.* Oxford: Oxford University Press.

Musto, David F.

1973 *The American Disease: Origins of Narcotics Control.* New Haven, Conn.: Yale University Press.

Nader, Ralph, and Mark Green

1972 Crime in the suites. *New Republic* April 28: 20–1.

Nagel, Ernest

1961 *The Structure of Science.* New York: Harcourt, Brace and World.

Newman, Donald J.

1958 White collar crime: An overview and analysis. *Law and Contemporary Problems* 23: 735–53.

Noble, David F.

1977 *America by Design: Science, Technology and the Rise of Corporate Capitalism.* New York: Knopf.

Packer, Herbert L.

1968 *The Limits of the Criminal Sanction.* Stanford, Calif.: Stanford University Press.

1969 The police and the community. *Stanford Law Review* 22: 1314–1317.

Paige, Jeffrey M.

1975 *Agrarian Revolution: Social Movements and Export Agriculture in the Underdeveloped World.* New York: Free Press.

Pashukanis, Evgeny Bronislavovich

1978 *The General Theory of Law and Marxism.* Translated by Barbara Einhorn. London: Ink Links.

Pearson, Geoffrey

1975 *The Deviant Imagination.* New York: Holmes and Meier.

Pepinsky, Harold

1974 From white collar crime to exploitation: Redefinition of a field. *Journal of Criminal Law and Criminology* 65: 225–233.

1978 Communist anarchism as an alternative to the rule of criminal law. *Contemporary Crises* 2: 315–34.

Pfautz, Harold W., and Otis D. Duncan

1950 A critical evaluation of Warner's work in community stratification. *American Sociological Review* 15: 205–215.

Pickett, Robert S.

1969 *House of Refuge: Origins of Juvenile Reform in New York State, 1815–1852.* Syracuse, N.Y.: Syracuse University Press.

Piliavin, Irving, and Scott Briar

1964 Police encounters with juveniles. *American Journal of Sociology* 70: 206–14.

Piven, Frances F., and Richard A. Cloward
  1971 *Regulating the Poor: The Functions of Public Welfare.* New York: Random House.
  1979 *Poor People's Movements.* New York: Vintage. (First published in 1977.)
Platt, Anthony
  1969 *The Childsavers: The Invention of Delinquency.* Chicago: University of Chicago Press.
  1974 The triumph of benevolence: The origins of the juvenile justice system in the United States. In Richard Quinney (ed.), *Criminal Justice in America.* Pp. 356–89. Boston: Little, Brown.
Platt, Tony, and Paul Takagi (eds.)
  1980 *Punishment and Penal Discipline: Essays on the Prison and the Prisoner's Movement.* Berkeley, Calif.: Crime and Justice Associates.
Pollock, Frederick, and Frederick W. Maitland
  1923 *The History of English Law.* Cambridge: Cambridge University Press. (First published in 1895.)
Pratten, Clifford
  1980 The manufacture of pins. *Journal of Economic Literature* 43: 93–96.
Przeworski, Adam, and Henry Teune
  1970 *The Logic of Comparative Social Inquiry.* New York: Wiley.
Quinney, Richard
  1970 *The Social Reality of Crime.* Boston: Little, Brown.
  1973 *Critique of Legal Order: Crime Control in Capitalist Society.* Boston: Little, Brown.
  1974 *Critique of Legal Order: Crime Control in Capitalist Society.* Boston: Little, Brown.
  1975 *Criminology.* Boston: Little, Brown.
  1977 *Class, State and Crime: On the Theory and Practice of Criminal Justice.* New York: McKay.
Rader, Melvin
  1979 *Marx's Interpretation of History.* New York: Oxford University Press.
Ralph, John H., and Richard Rubinson
  1980 Immigration and expansion of schooling, 1890–1970. *American Sociological Review* 45: 943.
Randall, John H.
  1976 *The Making of the Modern Mind.* New York: Columbia University Press. (First published in 1926.)
Ransom, Roger, and Richard Sutch
  1977 *One Kind of Freedom: The Economic Consequences of Emancipation.* Cambridge: Cambridge University Press.
Ray, Oakley
  1974 *Drugs, Society and Human Behavior.* St. Louis, Mo.: C. V. Mosby.

Reich, Michael
  1981 *Racial Inequality: A Political-Economic Analysis.* Princeton,
         N.J.: Princeton University Press.
Reichenbach, Hans
  1951 *The Rise of Scientific Philosophy.* Berkeley, Calif.: University of
         California Press.
Reid, Sue Titus
  1979 *Crime and Criminology.* Second edition. New York: Holt, Rine-
         hart and Winston.
Rheinstein, Max
  1954 Introduction. In Max Rheinstein (ed.), *Max Weber on Law in
         Economy and Society.* Pp. xvii-lxiv. Cambridge, Mass.: Harvard
         University Press.
Robert, Joseph Clarke
  1949 *The Story of Tobacco in America.* New York: Knopf.
Roberts, John M.
  1965 Oaths, autonomic ordeals and power. *American Anthropologist*
         67 Supplement, part 2: 186–212.
Rodgers, Harrell R., and Charles S. Bullock
  1972 *Law and Social Change: Civil Rights Laws and Their Conse-
         quences.* New York: McGraw-Hill.
Rosen, George
  1972 *Madness in Society: Chapters in the Historical Sociology of
         Mental Illness.* Chicago: University of Illinois Press.
Rosenthal, Robert, and Lenore Jacobson
  1968 *Pygmalion in the Classroom: Teacher Expectations and Pupils'
         Intellectual Development.* New York: Holt, Rinehart & Winston.
Rosett, Arthur and Donald Cressey
  1976 *Justice by Consent: Plea Bargains in the American Courthouse.*
         New York: J. B. Lippincott.
Roshier, Bob
  1977 The function of crime myth. *Sociological Research* 25: 309–23.
Ross, H. Lawrence
  1970 *Settled Out of Court: The Social Process of Insurance Claims
         Adjustment.* Chicago: Aldine.
Rossi, Peter, et al.
  1974 The seriousness of crimes: Normative structure and individual
         differences. *American Sociological Review* 39: 224–37.
Rothman, David J.
  1971 *The Discovery of the Asylum: Social Order and Disorder in the
         New Republic.* Boston: Little, Brown.
  1978 The State as parent: Social policy in the Progressive Era. In Willard
         Gaylin, Ira Glasser, Steven Marcos, and David J. Rothman (eds.),
         Doing Good. Pp. 67–96. New York: Pantheon Books.
  1980 *Conscience and Convenience: The Asylum and its Alternatives
         in Progressive America.* Boston: Little, Brown.
Rule, James, and Charles Tilly

1972   1830 and the unnatural history of revolution. *Journal of Social Issues* 28: 49–76.

Rusche, Georg
1980   Labor market and penal sanction: Thoughts on the sociology of criminal justice. In Tony Platt and Paul Takagi (eds.), *Punishment and Penal Discipline: Essays on the Prison and the Prisoner's Movement.* Pp. 10–16. Berkeley, Calif.: Crime and Social Justice Associates.

Rusche, Georg, and Otto Kirchheimer
1968   *Punishment and Social Structure.* New York: Russell and Russell. (First published in 1939.)

Rushforth, Norman B., et al.
1977   Violent death in a metropolitan county: Changing patterns in homicide (1958–74). *New England Journal of Medicine* 207: 531–538.

Ryerson, Ellen
1978   *The Best-Laid Plans: America's Juvenile Court Experiment.* New York: Hill and Wang.

Sachs, Albie
1973   *Justice in South Africa.* Berkeley, Calif.: University of California Press.

Sagarin, Edward
1981   *Raskolnikov and Others: Literary Images of Crime, Punishment and Atonement.* New York: St. Martins Press.

Scheff, Thomas J.
1966   *Being Mentally Ill: A Sociological Theory.* Chicago: Aldine.

Schultz, J. Lawrence
1973   The cycle of juvenile court history. *Crime and Delinquency* 19: 457–76.

Schumpeter, Joseph A.
1975   *Capitalism, Socialism and Democracy.* Third edition. New York: Harper. (First published in 1942.)

Schwendinger, Herman, and Julia R. Schwendinger
1970   Defenders of order or guardians of human rights? *Issues in Criminology* 7: 71–81.

Scott, James M.
1969   *The White Poppy: A History of Opium.* London: Heinemann.

Scull, Andrew
1977   *Decarceration — Community Treatment and the Deviant: A Radical View.* Englewood Cliffs, N.J.: Prentice-Hall.

Sherman, Michael, and Gordon Hawkins
1981   *Imprisonment in America: Choosing the Future.* Chicago: University of Chicago Press.

Shils, Edward, and Michael Young
1953   The meaning of the coronation. *Sociological Review* 1: 638–80.

Short, James F. and F. Ivan Nye

1957   Reported behavior as a criterion of deviant behavior. *Social Problems* 5: 207–13.
Singer, Max
1971   The vitality of mythical numbers. *Public Interest* 23: 3–9.
Skocpol, Theda
1977   Wallerstein's world capitalist system: A theoretical and historical critique. *American Journal of Sociology* 82: 1075–90.
Skolnick, Jerome
1967   Social control in an adversary system. *Journal of Conflict Resolution* 11: 53–70.
1975   *Justice Without Trial: Law Enforcement in Democratic Society.* Second edition. New York: Wiley. (First published in 1966.)
Smelser, Neil
1976   *Comparative Methods in the Social Sciences.* Englewood Cliffs, N.J.: Prentice-Hall.
Smigel, Erwin, and H. Lawrence Ross
1970   *Crimes Against Bureaucracy.* New York: Van Nostrand Reinhold.
Smith, Adam
1950   *An Inquiry into the Nature and Causes of the Wealth of Nations.* London: Methuen. (First published in 1776.)
Smith, Preserved
1930   *A History of Modern Culture.* Volume 1. New York: Holt.
Snyder, David, and William Kelly
1977   Conflict intensity, media sensitivity and the validity of newspaper data. *American Sociological Review* 42: 105–23.
Snyder, Frances G.
1980   Law and development in light of dependency theory. *Law and Society Review* 14: 723–804.
Sorokin, Pitirim
1937   Fluctuations of ethicojuridical mentality in criminal law. In *Social and Cultural Dynamics.* Volume 2. Pp. 523–632. New York: American Book Company.
Southwood, Kenneth E.
1978   Substantive theory and statistical interaction: Five models. *American Journal of Sociology* 83: 1154–1203.
Spitzer, Stephen
1975a Punishment and social organization: A study of Durkheim's theory of penal evolution. *Law and Society Review* 9: 613–35.
1975b Toward a Marxian theory of deviance. *Social Problems* 22: 638–651.
Stannard, David E.
1974   *The Puritan Way of Death.* New York: Oxford University Press.
Starosolskyj, Jurij
1954   *The Principle of Analogy in Criminal Law: An Aspect of Soviet Legal Thinking.* Monograph no. 55. New York: Research Program on the USSR.

Stars, James
  1961   The regulatory offense in historical perspective. In Gerhard D.
         Mueller (ed.), *Essays in Criminal Science.* Pp. 235–67. South
         Hackensack, N.J.: F. B. Rothman.
Steinert, Heinz
  1978   Can socialism be advanced by radical rhetoric and sloppy data?
         Some remarks on Richard Quinney's latest output. *Contemporary
         Crises* 2: 305–13.
Stern, David, Sandra Smith, and Fred Doolittle
  1975   How children used to work. *Law and Contemporary Problems*
         39: 93–117.
Stinchcombe, Arthur
  1959   Bureaucratic and craft administration of production: A comparative
         study. *Administration Science Quarterly* 4: 168–87.
  1961   Agricultural enterprise and rural class relations. *American Journal
         of Sociology* 67: 165–76.
  1968   *Constructing Social Theories.* New York: Harcourt, Brace and
         World.
  1978   *Theoretical Methods in Social History.* New York: Academic Press.
Stone, Christopher D.
  1975   *Where the Law Ends: The Social Control of Corporate Behavior.*
         New York: Harper & Row.
Stone, Julius
  1966   *Social Dimensions of Law and Justice.* Stanford, Calif.: Stanford
         University Press.
Strauss, Maurice B. (ed.)
  1968   *Familiar Medical Quotations.* Boston: Little, Brown.
Sutherland, Edwin
  1940   White collar crime. *American Sociological Review* 5: 1–12.
  1945   Is "white collar crime" crime? *American Sociological Review*
         10:132–9.
  1949   *White Collar Crime.* New York: Holt, Rinehart, and Winston.
Sutherland, Edwin, and Donald R. Cressey
  1970   *Criminology.* Eighth edition. Philadelphia: J. B. Lippincott.
Sweezy, Paul
  1942   *The Theory of Capitalist Development: Principles of Marxian
         Political Economy.* New York: Monthly Review Press.
Sykes, Gresham M.
  1978   *Criminology.* New York: Harcourt, Brace, Jovanovich.
Szasz, Thomas
  1970   *The Manufacture of Madness: A Comparative Study of the In-
         quisition and the Mental Health Movement.* New York: Harper
         & Row.
Takagi, Paul, and Tony Platt
  1978   Behind the gilded ghetto: An analysis of race, class, and crime in
         Chinatown. *Crime and Social Justice* 9: 2–25.

Talarico, Susan
 1980 The dilemma of parole decision making. In George F. Cole (ed.), *Criminal Justice: Law and Politics.* Third edition. Pp. 418–26. North Scituate, Mass.: Duxbury.
Tannenbaum, Frank
 1938 *Crime and Community.* Boston: Ginn.
Tappan, Paul W.
 1947 Who is the criminal? *American Sociological Review* 12: 96–102.
Taylor, Ian, Paul Walton, and Jock Young
 1973 *The New Criminology: For a Social Theory of Deviance.* New York: Harper & Row.
Terry, Charles E., and Mildred Pellens
 1970 *The Opium Problem.* Montclair, N.J.: Patterson Smith. (First published in 1928.)
Thernstrom, Stephen
 1964 *Poverty and Progress: Social Mobility in a Nineteenth Century City.* Cambridge, Mass.: Harvard University Press.
Thompson, E. P.
 1967 Time, work-discipline, and industrial capitalism. *Past and Present* 38: 56–97.
 1975 *Whigs and Hunters: The Origins of the Black Act.* New York: Pantheon.
Thompson, Edgar T.
 1975 *Plantation Societies, Race Relations, and the South: The Regimentation of Populations.* Durham, N.C.: Duke University Press.
Thompson, Randall J., and Matthew T. Zingraff
 1981 Detecting sentencing disparity: Some problems and evidence. *American Journal of Sociology* 86: 869–80.
Thorelli, Hans B.
 1954 *The Federal Anti-Trust Policy.* Baltimore, Md.: Johns Hopkins Press.
Tigar, Michael E., and Madeline R. Levy
 1977 *Law and the Rise of Capitalism.* New York: Monthly Review Press.
Timberlake, James H.
 1963 Prohibition and the Progressive Movement, 1900–1920. Cambridge, Mass.: Harvard University Press.
Tiruchelvam, Neelan
 1978 The ideology of popular justice. In Charles E. Reasons and Robert M. Rich (eds.), *The Sociology of Law: A Conflict Perspective.* Pp. 263–80. Toronto: Butterworth.
Trachtenberg, Joshua
 1943 *The Devil and the Jews: The Medieval Conception of the Jew and Its Relation to Modern Anti-Semitism.* New Haven, Conn.: Yale University Press.
Trocchi, Alexander
 1960 *Cain's Book.* New York: Grove.

Trubek, David
1972a Max Weber on law and the rise of capitalism. *Wisconsin Law Review* 1972: 720–53.
1972b Toward a social theory of law. *Yale Law Journal* 82: 1–50.
1977 Complexity and contradiction in the legal order: Balbus and the challenge of critical social thought about the law. *Law and Society Review* 11: 529–69.

Tucker, Robert C. (ed.)
1978 *The Marx-Engels Reader.* Second edition. New York: Norton.

Turk, Austin
1976a Law as a weapon in social conflict. *Social Problems* 23: 270–91.
1976b Law, conflict and order: From theorizing toward theories. *Canadian Review of Sociology and Anthropology* 13: 282–92.

Turkel, Gerald
1979 Testing Durkheim: Some theoretical considerations. *Law and Society Review* 13: 720–38.

Turner, Ralph
1967 Types of solidarity in the reconstruction of groups. *Pacific Sociological Review* 10: 60–8.
1969 The public perception of protest. *American Sociological Review* 34: 815–31.

Tushnet, Mark
1975 The American law of slavery, 1810–1860: A study in the persistence of legal autonomy. *Law and Society Review* 10: 119–84.

Twain, Mark
1911 *Life on the Mississippi.* New York: Harper. (First published in 1874.)

Unger, Roberto M.
1976 *Law in Modern Society: Toward a Criticism of Social Theory.* New York: Free Press.

U. S. Bureau of the Census
1918 *Statistical Abstract of the U. S.* Washington, D.C.: U. S. Government Printing Office.
1960 *Historical Statistics of the U.S. from Colonial Times to 1957.* Washington, D.C.: U.S. Government Printing Office.
1978 *Statistical Abstract of the U.S.* Washington, D.C.: U.S. Government Printing Office.

U.S. Department of Justice. Bureau of Prisons.
1979 *Profile of State Prison Inmates, 1974.* Washington, D.C.: U.S. Government Printing Office.
1980 *National Prisoner Statistics: Prisoners in State and Federal Institutions, 1978.* Washington, D.C.: U.S. Government Printing Office.

Vago, Steven
1981 *Law and Society.* Englewood Cliffs, N.J.: Prentice-Hall.

Verba, Sidney
1965 The Kennedy assassination and the nature of political commitment. In B. S. Greenberg and E. B. Parker (eds.), *The Kennedy Assassination and the American Public: Social Communication in Crisis.* Pp. 348–60. Stanford, Calif.: Stanford University Press.

Vogel, Ezra F., and Norman Bell
1968 The emotionally disturbed child as the family scapegoat. In Norman Bell and Ezra Vogel (eds.), *A Modern Introduction to the Family.* Pp. 417–27. New York: Free Press.

Wald, Patricia M.
1974 Making sense out of the rights of youth. *Human Rights* 4: 13–29.

Waller, Irvin, and Janet Chan
1974 Prison use: A Canadian and international comparison. *Criminal Law Quarterly* 17: 47–71.

Wallerstein, Immanuel
1974 *The Modern World System.* New York: Academic Press.

Wallerstein, James S., and Clement J. Wyle
1947 Our law-abiding law breakers. *Probation* 25: 107–12.

Walton, Paul
1973 Social reaction and radical commitment: The case of the Weathermen. In Laurie Taylor and Ian Taylor (eds.), *Politics and Deviance.* Pp. 157–81. Harmondsworth, England: Penguin.

Weber, Max
1946 The social psychology of the world religions. In Hans H. Gerth and C. Wright Mills (eds.), *From Max Weber: Essay in Sociology.* Pp. 267–301. New York: Oxford University Press.

1951 *The Religion of China.* Glencoe, Ill.: Free Press.

1954 *On Law in Economy and Society.* Edited by Max Rheinstein. Cambridge, Mass.: Harvard University Press.

1958 *The Protestant Ethic and the Spirit of Capitalism.* Translated by Talcott Parsons. New York: Scribners. (First published in 1904.)

1978 *Economy and Society: An Outline of Interpretative Sociology.* Edited by Guenther Roth and Claus Wittich. Berkeley, Calif.: University of California Press.

Weinstein, James
1968 *The Corporate Ideal in the Liberal State 1900–1918.* Boston: Beacon Press.

Wellford, Charles
1975 Labeling theory and criminology: An assessment. *Social Problems* 22: 332–45.

Whitehead, Alfred North
1925 *Science and the Modern World.* New York: Macmillan.

Wiebe, Robert H.
1967 *The Search for Order 1877–1920.* New York: Hill and Wang.

Wiener, Jonathan
  1980 Planters, merchants, and political power in Reconstruction Alabama.
        In Maurice Zeitlin (ed.), *Classes, Class Conflict and the State:
        Empirical Studies in Class Analysis.* Pp. 42–61. Cambridge, Mass.:
        Winthrop.
Willhelm, Stanley
  1971 *Who Needs the Negro?* Garden City, N.Y.: Doubleday.
Williams, T. Harry
  1961 *Romance and Realism in Southern Politics.* Athens, Ga.: University
        of Georgia Press.
Wilson, James Q.
  1968a The police and the delinquent in two cities. In Stanton Wheeler
        (ed.), *Controlling Delinquents.* Pp. 9–30. New York: Wiley.
  1968b *Varieties of Police Behavior.* Cambridge, Mass.: Harvard University
        Press.
Wilson, William J.
  1980 *The Declining Significance of Race: Blacks and Changing American
        Institutions.* Second edition. Chicago: University of Chicago Press.
        (First published in 1978.)
Wolfgang, Marvin E.
  1974 Racial discrimination in the death sentence for rape. In William
        Bowers (ed.), *Executions in America.* Pp. 109–120. Lexington, Mass.:
        D. C. Heath.
Wolfgang, Marvin, A. Kelly, and H. C. Nolde
  1962 Comparison of executed and commuted. *Journal of Criminal Law
        and Criminology* 53: 301–11.
Wolfgang, Marvin, and M. Riedel
  1973 Race, judicial discrimination and death penalty. *Annals* 407: 119–
        37.
Woodson, Robert L. (ed.)
  1977 *Black Perspectives on Crime and the Criminal Justice System:
        A Symposium.* Boston: G. K. Hall.
Woodward, C. Vann
  1951 *Origins of the New South, 1877–1913.* Baton Rouge, La.: Louisiana
        State University Press.
  1957 *The Strange Career of Jim Crow.* New York: Oxford University
        Press.
  1963 *Tom Watson: Agrarian Rebel.* New York: Oxford University Press.
  1971 The strange career of an historical controversy. In his *American
        Counter-Point: Slavery and Racism in the North-South Dialog.*
        Pp. 234–60. Boston: Little, Brown.
Wright, Erik O.
  1979 *Class Structure and Income Determination.* New York: Academic
        Press.

Wrong, Dennis
1970   Introduction. In Dennis Wrong (ed.), *Max Weber*. Pp. 1–76. Englewood Cliffs, N.J.: Prentice-Hall.
Yale Law Journal
1967   Interrogations in New Haven: The impact of Miranda. *Yale Law Journal* 76: 1519–1648.
Young, Gary
1976   The fundamental contradictions of capitalist production. *Philosophy and Public Affairs* 5: 196–234.
Young, Jock
1975   Working class criminology. In Ian Taylor et al. (eds.), *Critical Criminology*. Pp. 63–94. London: Routledge & Kegan Paul.
Zangrando, Robert L.
1980   *The NAACP Crusade Against Lynching, 1909–50*. Philadelphia: Temple University Press.
Zeitlin, Maurice
1980   On classes, class conflict and the state. In Maurice Zeitlin (ed.), *Classes, Class Conflict and the State: Empirical Studies in Class Analysis*. Pp. 1–37. Cambridge, Mass.: Winthrop.
Ziman, John
1979   *Reliable Knowledge: An Exploration of the Grounds of Belief in Science*. Cambridge: Cambridge University Press.

Index